THE HISTORY & DESCRIPTION OF THE T IPSWICH • G. R. CLARKE (OF IPSWICH ⁄

⫷ ⫷ ⫷ ⫷ ⫷ ⫷ ⫷ ⫷

/ THE HISTORY AND TOPOGRAPHY Of IPSWICH.

History may be supposed to be a reverend gentleman with a flowing beard and a grave face. Now I assure you, gentle reader, that I have neither one or the other; I shall therefore endeavour to render my antiquarian and topographical researches as entertaining as the subject will admit; for it may safely be asserted, that gravity is not always wisdom. In the character of historian, after being half blinded by poring over the dusty records of antiquity, I may have been seen searching among the repositories of the dead, peeping through the chasms of dilapidated edifices, scrambling over stone dykes, or leaping brick walls; and in the same manner as Old Mortality with his chisel renovated the memorials of the departed which Time had nearly erased, so have I with my pen brought into notice events and personages that would have been probably forgotten, giving them of course a greater chance of immortality than they otherwise would have enjoyed. It is extremely difficult to define the boundaries between positive truth and legendary fiction, and almost impossible to find printed or written documents for every assertion; and as it does not follow of necessity that every thing must be true because it appears

B in black and white, I have not altogether rejected the assistance of tradition; I have however never falsified facts merely from fancy, but have in all cases drawn my conclusions from the best possible authenticated sources of information—I have not, certainly, taken my oath before the bailiffs of the verity of these pages, but I positively affirm, that my readers in no instance run the hazard of being wantonly deceived.

As in the narration of a story it is desirable to begin at the beginning, I shall commence with the name. The town of

⹂n its
⹂ the fresh water river ⹂pping connects itself with the Orwell, and loses its own name by its being joined to another river, thence owning the Orwell for its lord and master. "What's in a name?" a great deal! and formerly a great deal more than was necessary, for in Doomsday it is spelt Gyppeswid, Gippeswiz, Gippeswic, and afterwards Yppyswyche, but divested of all superfluities it now stands before us plainly and simply Ipswich. The Orwell was called, in the Saxon annals, Anvan; probably it was originally Arwell, as we have Arwerton on one side of it, and Arwich (Harwich) on the other, at which place it empties itself into the German Ocean. Towns, as well as families, pride themselves in tracing back their origin to the earliest periods; and if any person could discover that one of his ancestors had been hanged for his misdemeanours in the time of William the Conqueror, he would not think himself disgraced by the relationship; so if we can discover any thing like the remnants of a Roman wall, or an elevated space of earth in which are found a few bones denoting it as a place of human sepulture during our "Saxon slavery, we deem it as an evidence of the spot having formerly been a place of some notoriety; and luckily for the honour of Ipswich, on the heath which extends from Rushmere to Nacton, at a place called Seven Hills, near this town, there are seven mounds of earth, call them tumuli, barrows, or what you please, in which bones of human bodies have been met with; therefore it is determined that near this spot our forefathers, under the the command of earl Ulfketel, bravely defended themselves against the Danes, in the year 1010, and that these mounds are the burial-places of the slain. The conduct of the Danes affords a convincing proof of the importance of Ipswich at that period, for they levied the enormous fine of £10,000 upon the inhabitants. It is

likewise recorded that about the year 880, a most important engagement took place near the mouth of the Orwell, between our countrymen under the command of Alfred, and the Danes; in which sixteen of the enemy's ships were taken and destroyed, with a great number of soldiers, who were all put to the sword. The ramparts of the town had twice before been broken down by these invaders, about 991 and 1000. They also sailed up the Orwell, and made an irruption into the kingdom of Mercia, in 1016; from which we infer, that it must have been a place of note long before the Norman conquest: indeed, Ruding places this matter beyond a doubt, for he has the following account of the coins at Ipswich.

There was also a mint in the time of king John; and likewise there were pennies coined at Ipswich in the reigns of king-Stephen, and Henry II. We find in Doomsday Book, that there were then nine churches standing; viz. the Holy Trinity, St. Austin, St. Michael, St. Mary, St. Botolph, (i. e. Whitton) St. Laurence, St. Peter, St. Stephen, and Thurleston, the three former of which are now no more, and have never been rebuilt; and we are told by Stow, in his annals, that in the fifteenth year of Edward I. 1287, on new year's day, at night, as well through vehemency of the wind as violence of the sea, many churches were overthrown and destroyed, not only at Yarmouth, Dunwich, and Ipswich, but also in divers other places in England. Thus the remorseless waves, and the unruly winds, topple down high towers and moss-grown steeples, and towns and churches tumble and decay. *Sic transit gloria mundi.*

Having thus, I trust, very properly moralised upon the frailty of all terrestrial things, let us proceed to inquire into the civil institutions of the times. At, and some time previous to the Conquest, Ipswich, like the other boroughs that were in the demesne of the crown, was held by the sovereign himself, or perhaps one third of the revenue was granted to some earl, and the other two thirds remained in the possession of the crown. It was not uncommon for the earl to let the revenues of the borough to some other persons for a certain annual rent, but still he never neglected his third. There were some of the inhabitants who had possessions without the town, held by military service, and these were the only *lawful* men of the realm, and/ree *men,* properly so called. The rest had, strictly speaking, no property at all; they held what they had at the will of their superior, and consequently had no will of their own, being thus happily saved the trouble of thinking for themselves, for they could not devise their possessions to their children without permission of their lord, who had a property in their very persons, and they were denominated *his* villains, and *his* men. Alas! how are we degenerated, for who would not wish to have lived in what we have often heard so pathetically called the " good old times!" An extract from Doomsday, which was finished in the twentieth year of William, 1086, will shew that the inhabitants of Ipswich enjoyed these privileges in their fullest extent:—" Half hundred of Gippeswid. This Roger Bigod keepeth in the king's hand. In the time of king Edward the Confessor, queen Edith, who was the daughter of earl Goodwin, had two parts of the borough, and earl Guert, her brother, had the third part; and the queen had a grange in demense, to which belonged four carucates or hides of land." When this house was rebuilt it was probably called New Palace, or New Place; and the farm-house now standing retains the name of New Place to the present day. It goes on to state further, that, "In the time of king Edward, there were 538 burgesses who paid custom to the king, and they bad forty acres of land. But now there are only 110 burgesses who pay custom, and 100 poor burgesses who can pay no more than one penny a head to the king's geld. So upon the 'whole they have forty acres of land, and 328 houses now empty; and which, in the time of king Edward, scotted to the king's geld. Roger, the vice-earl, let the whole for £40, to be paid at the feast of St. Michael; afterwards he could not have their rent, and he abated sixty shillings of it, now it pays £37. And the earl always has the third part." It is not said whether the revenues were let to one or more persons, but probably to some of the principal burgesses of the town. Sometimes the king held certain boroughs himself, and appointed one or more officers, who were called *propositi,* or provosts; and under the Norman *kings* these officers were called *ballivi,* or bailives. The policy of these latter princes led them to raise the condition of the lower people, that by their means they might the better be enabled to check the inordinate power of the barons; this was done gradually, by altering the tenures of private persons, and then by enfranchising whole communities, especially the boroughs in the royal demesne, as being more immediately dependant upon the crown.

There are, doubtless, many of my readers whose pens can glide over the surface of their paper with as much rapidity as their thoughts arise in their own fertile imaginations; and these can, I fear, but imperfectly judge of the labours of the creeping man of dullness, w ho is compelled to keep strictly to matter of fact. It is, however, the duty of a writer of local history to obtain all the information he can get at, even at the risk of being sometimes considered as an impertinent or troublesome fellow; for, like the little crooked mark of interrogation, he never appears without asking questions; and if the replies he receives be sometimes incorrect, he may be led into unintentional error, without any desire to deviate from the truth; but he must exercise his own judgment, and fearlessly pursue the even tenor of his way, determining "To nothing extenuate, or set down aught in malice."

After deciphering charters, grants, records, and old MSS., referring to works of antiquities, topography, local histories, and indexes, it is necessary to go back to Kirby's Suffolk Traveller for much of the information worthy of record in the History of Ipswich. From the dry style of this volume, and the uncouth manner in which it has always been brought before the public, its merits have never been justly allowed, but it is certainly a work of labour and research; and the edition corrected by the late Rev. Richard Canning, of this town, notwithstanding some errors and deficiencies, is unquestionably a valuable county history. The editor of Kirby has drawn a great portion of his intelligence relative to Ipswich, from Mr. Bacon's MS., which I have carefully gone through, and find that he has extracted largely from it in the Suffolk Traveller; therefore it of necessity follows, that there must be in this volume a repetition of similar facts. For though you may represent either a fact or a man in a marked or particular dress, it would be folly in the author or artist to alter the features so that they could not be known. Bacon's work is a treasure of its kind, and worthy of description. It came into the possession of William Batley, esq. of this town, in his capacity of town clerk, for he many years filled that situation with honour to himself and to the universal satisfaction of the borough. As he holds this book in custody, for the corporation, it could not be in better hands; he can justly appreciate its value, and obligingly allows a reference to be made to it upon all proper occasions. It is a large thick volume, in excellent preservation, consisting of 800 folio pages, entirely written in the author's own hand; it has, besides an appendix containing some ancient records, together with a copious index. There are occasionally interspersed some judicious notes, in the hand-writing of the Rev. Richard Canning; and it is altogether a valuable record, such as few other corporations possess. It is entitled THE ANNALS OF IPSWICHE; THE LAWS, CCSTOMES, AND GOVERNMENT OF THE SAME; COLLECTED OCT OF THE RECORDS, BOOKS, AND WRITINGS OF THAT TOWNE.

BY NATHANIEL BACON,

SERVING AS RECORDER AND TOWNE CLERK IN THAT TOWNE.

ANN. DOM. 1654.

It is dedicated " *To the Bailiffs, Burgessess, and Commonalty of the Towne of Ipswiche.*" It is prefaced with an add less to the reader, in which there is given a summary of the history of Ipswich from the earliest period of antiquity to the time when he commences his extracts from the court books, memorandums, transcripts, and other public documents. But in the prefatory introduction the author has deviated into fanciful speculations respecting the truth of representations, which are palpable legendary fictions, and of course it cannot be altogether relied on as matter of veritable history. The remainder of the volume is filled up with the official proceedings of the Great Courts, and of the matters which were brought under their consideration; with the names of all persons who held the different offices in the corporation, and the date of all their appointments, changes, and re-elections; furnishing a faithful relation of the transactions of the Corporate Body for several centuries, and eliciting many curious particulars of the manners, customs, and opinions of our forefathers that cannot be mistaken. He commences his official extracts at a very early date, and finishes them at the death of Charles II., the 30th of January, 1649; and he thus concludes the volume:— "The last day of Jan. puUs a sad period to my pen. Thus, by the goodness of Almighty God, I have summed up the affairs of the government of this town of Ipswich, under bailiffs who are happy in this, that God hath established their seat more sure than the throne of kings!" Had he lived in these changeable times, he would have known that they were liable to be *ousted* by a writ of mandamus every two or three months.—As this work has never been printed, and cannot have been seen but by few of my readers, 1 shall make no apology for having said so much upon this singular production, which must have been a compilation of vast labour to the author, and will every day become of encreased value to posterity.

The next circumstance we have to relate, certainly does not reflect much honour upon our forefathers, but the truth must be told. We find that in the reign of Richard I. the town of Ipswich was fined 200 marks for supplying the enemy with corn. However, the first glimpse of freedom that dawned upon the town may be noticed in this reign, when it is observed, that " The men of Ipswich owe forty marcs for having their liberties. The men of Ipswich have accounted for sixty marcs for having their town in their own hands, by encreasing the farm one hundred shillings per annum; and for the confirmation of our Lord the King concerning their liberties, they have paid it into the treasury and are acquitted." On the back of the great rent roll of the tenth year of Richard I. are several items of rents, for which the men of Ipswich were accountable. These transactions with Richard will account for the early grant of king John's charter, which bears date the 25th of May, 1199, only one month after he came to the crown. By this charter John granted to the burgesses—1st. The borough, with all its appurtenances, liberties, &c. to be holden of him and his heirs hereditarily, by the payment of the right and usual farm rent, and one hundred shillings more at the exchecquer, by the hands of the provosts of Ipswich; which made the annual payment sixty marcs, or £40. 2nd. He exempted them from all taxes under the several names of *tholl, lastage, stallage,* and *pontage,* and all other customs throughout his lands and sea ports; which benefit is enjoyed by burgesses, masters of vessels, to the present day, not even excepting the port of London. But as they are only exempted from such tolls or dues as existed at the time of granting the charter, it is at the present day of but little advantage. 3rd. That they should have a merchants' gild and house of their own. 4th. That no person should be quartered upon them without their consent, or take any thing from them by force; which proved plainly that they were before liable to such oppression. 5th. That they might hold their lands, and recover their just dues from whomever they were owing. This was making them *lawful men,* which before they were not. 6th. That they should hold their lands and tenures within the borough, according to the custom of the borough of Ipswich. 7th. That none of them shall be fined or amerced but according to the laws of the free boroughs. 8th. And that they might chose bailives and four coroners out of the more lawful men of the said town, of which there must have then been a notable scarcity, for upwards of 200 years after this date there were no more than 1085 lawful men in all this good town. The burgesses now began to feel their own importance, and were duly sensible of the privileges granted to them by this charter, but they did not act upon it till thirteen months after its date, which probably arose from their not being able to raise the money for it, as the provident officers of the crown took especial care that these grants were not confirmed till all fines and fees were duly discharged. On the Thursday next after June 24th, in the second year of king John's reign, the lawful men assembled in the churchyard of St. Mary at Tower, and held their *first great court,* which was continued for three sessions by adjournment. At this court the burgesses elected the *first bailives.* And they resolved that there should be twelve capital portmen, as were in the other free boroughs of England. At the second session they elected four men out of each parish, to act as a committee for the whole township, which committee chose the *first twelve portmen.* At the third session, they ordered a common seal to be made; and chose an alderman of the merchants' guild, with four associates to assist him. How must our worthy ancestors have exulted when they thus found themselves emancipated from slavery, and the borough erected into a corporation! Here let us pause to reflect upon the wonderful ways of Providence, which so frequently produces good out of evil! For in the reign of king John, who was one of the most tyrannical bigots that ever sat upon a throne, two of the greatest events in English history occurred; the blessing of Magna Charta was granted to the nation, and *a charter was granted to Ipswich!*

But now let us go along with our burgesses assembled, and seriously proceed to business. The second great court was held on the Sunday next after September 8th, in the same church-

yard; and we may naturally conclude that matters were then conducted more temperately and coolly in the open air, than they sometimes are at present in the heated atmosphere of the town hall. On this occasion they re-elected the same two persons to be bailives for the ensuing year. The second session of this court was held by adjournment within the church of St. Mary at Tower, when the common seal was produced, and three persons appointed to keep that and the charter, who were the *first clavigers.* Soon after, the priors of Trinity and St. Peter were admitted as free burgesses; the one on paying twenty shillings, and the latter one mark, towards the expences of the charter. Roger Bigod, earl of Norfolk, was likewise admitted, on account of his having assisted in the procuring the charter from the king. In the fifth year of this reign, the ramparts which had been broken down by the Danes were rebuilt, and the fortifications repaired.

What few events have occurred in Ipswich, connected with English history, we shall endeavour to collect in chronological order. When Henry, son of Henry II., conspired against his father, he landed with his followers at this port, and from thence marched to Norwich. And during this unnatural contest, in which Henry II. was involved with his sons, Robert de Beaumont, earl of Leicester, landed with a large body of Flemings, near this town, when he marched to Framlingham; and being joined by Hugh Bigod, earl of Norfolk, with a strong reinforcement, they were met by the royal army, at Fornham St. Genoveve, and totally defeated on the 27th of October, 1173..

King Edward I., in the thirteenth year of his reign, for certain offences alledged against the burgesses of Ipswich, seized the borough into his own hands, and kept it till his nineteenth year; when, being pleased with the service performed by some ships from Ipswich, in his expedition to Scotland, he regranted the borough to the burgesses, and confirmed the former charters, by deed, dated at Berwick, 23rd of June, 1291. But he punished the town suf-

ficiently by raising the rent to £60; at which it ever after continued. As soon as their charter was restored, the burgesses elected twenty-four men to act as a committee, and to collect the ancient usages and customs of the borough, and to enroll them, that they might be better ascertained than they had been since the elopement of one John Blake, who was the town clerk, and in the last year of Henry III. had fled from the town, carrying away some of the records. Thus we have the origin of the present *common council,* or *twenty-four men.* Henry confirmed and improved the first charter, in the fortieth year of his reign, 1251.

In the charter granted in the tenth of Edward II., 1317, "It is ordered that there be two coroners instead of four; and that the burgesses of Ipswich may be for ever quit of murage, piccage, anchorage, standage, and segeage of all their goods and merchandise, throughout our kingdom, dominions, and sea ports." In the time of Edward II. queen Isabel landed here, from France, when she drove her husband into Wales. And in the twentieth year of the same reign, Sir John Howard was commissioned to raise 500 men in Norfolk and Suffolk, and embark them at the port of Orwell, from thence to proceed to sea against the French.

Edward III., in the month of July, 1328, collected a fleet of between 400 and 500 vessels on the coast of Suffolk, from whence he proceeded to sea, and disembarked at Antwerp, where he was received with the greatest cordiality, and, by the advice of his allies assumed the title of king of France. In 1338, Edward III. landed on the shores of the Orwell, where a large fleet was assembled, and where his army was so numerous that he was obliged to order some of those who had last joined him to return to their homes. The English, on approaching the town of Sluys, perceiving that the French ships were linked together with chains, feigned to retreat, and stood back to sea. The French, deceived by this manoeuvre, put to sea in loose order. Edward having the advantage of the weather-gage, immediately tacked, and assailed the enemy with such invincible fury, that he completely discomfited them, with the loss, it is said, of thirty thousand men; many of them leaping into the sea, rather than fall under the swords of the English. The engagement lasted, without intermission, from eight o'clock in the morning until seven at night, when the French fleet was utterly annihilated. The loss of the English amounted to about 4000 men. The king, as it were in triumph, kept the sea for three days, when he repaired to his intended place of debarkation, and soon after gained the memorable victory of Cressy, over the French king. Previous to his sailing from England he remained some time at his manor of Walton, where he transacted many considerable affairs, and confirmed the charters previously granted to Ipswich, by an inspeximus dated at Walton, in his twelfth year, 1339. The woollen manufactory was first introduced into England by Edward III., who brought over seventy families of Walloons; and it is probable that some of them were sent to settle at Ipswich about the year 1331. In the eighteenth year of the same reign, William Sharford sat as judge of assize, at Ipswich, when some sailors thought the judge stayed too long to dinner, and one of them got upon the bench and caused another to make proclamation, requiring William Sharford to come into court, and save his fine; who not appearing, the nautical magistrate, with the characteristic blunt humour of an English sailor, fined the municipal judge; which so offended the morose Sharford that he caused the king to take away the assizes from the town, to seize the liberties of the corporation, and take the management of it into his own hands; and the government of the town was committed to the sheriff of Norfolk and Suffolk, and Edward Noon was deputed by him as keeper of the town. But this did not last above a year; for, though a court was held on September 21st, before this Edward Noon, as deputy keeper, we find, on the 13th of August following, a court was holden before John de Preston and William Ringold,

bailives, as usual.

In the charter granted by Richard II. it is ordained that the bailiffs may have and take cognizance of all manner of pleas concerning lands, tenements, and rents, as well by writs of assize as the other writs of us and our heirs and successors; and also cognizance of pleas concerning' trespasses, debts, contracts, covenants of assize, *fresh* force, that is, any force newly committed and aH other pleas whatever arising within the said town.

In 1445, in the twenty-fourth year of Henry VI., he granted a charter most beneficial to the borough. By this he incorporated the town by the name of "The Burgesses of Ipswich." He authorised them, in every year to elect two burgesses to be bailives, at the accustomed time and place to exercise that office for one whole year. He granted to the bailives, four such other burgesses as the said bailives shall be pleased to take to them out of the twelve portmen, to serve the office of justice of the peace, within the said town. Here we have the first four *assistant justices;* and this is the first mention that is made of the portmen in any charter. He granted all fines, forfeitures, and amercements arising from the office of justice of the peace, &c. and the assize of bread, wine, and ale; appointed such one of the bailives as, at the time of their election, the burgesses shall chose to be their escheator; and expressly granted the admiralty, and clerkship of the market. And in the following year, John Smith and William Ridout, residents in the town, were elected burgesses of the next parliament; and an order was issued by the great court, to the treasurer, to defray their expences from the funds of the corporation. And these were the *first representatives in parliament* for the borough of Ipswich; and it is scarcely necessary to observe, that this borough has sent two members to parliament ever since. Their duty, in those days, was considered as an irksome and troublesome task; and though they were paid for their attendance, as much pains were taken to avoid being chosen, as are now exerted to obtain the honour of

election, combined with the risk of an enormous expence. In 1447, in the reign of Henry VI. it was ordered, that all the free burgesses do arm themselves with a good and substantial staff, for the mutual defence of each other; and if any one should suffer his neighbour to be molested without rendering him his assistance, he shall be disfranchised. In 1450, is an order for the payment of seven marks, for one tun of wine, given by the town to the duke of Suffolk.

In 1446, the good duke Humphry of Gloucester was, as it was said, murdered at Bury St. Edmund's, in his bed, by William de la Pole, earl of Suffolk; and after his death the general feeling became so strong against the earl, that he was banished by the king, for five years, in order to screen him from popular resentment. On this occasion he embarked from Ipswich, with the intention of sailing to France; but he was intercepted in his passage, near Dover, by some persons who watched his motions - and his death affords an awful instance of retributive justice, for his head was struck off on the gunwale of a boat, and his body thrown into the sea; but it was cast on shore, and brought and interred in the church at Wingfield, in this county, in 1450.

In the fourteenth year of Edward IV. the earl of Lancaster had an assignment of ten ships, to transport a body of horse from this port to Flanders. In 1464, in the twenty-eighth year of this reign, Edward IV. guaranteed all the privileges of former charters, with some alterations and additions: but his predecessor, Henry VI., being of the House of Lancaster, Edward does not condescend to notice the charter granted by him; and, though of the utmost importance, it is never afterwards mentioned, notwithstanding all the privileges granted by it were fully confirmed by himself, as well as future monarchs. He incorporated the town by the name of "The Bailives, Burgesses, and Commonalty, of the Town of Ipswich;" by which terms it has been designated ever since. He confined the election of bailives expressly to the 8th of September, and in the guild-hall, and they were to serve from one year thence to the next following; but by constant usage, the bailives have always been sworn in on the 29th of September, and have constantly served their office until the Michaelmas-day following. Edward likewise expressly exempted the burgesses from service on juries. This had been generally construed as exmpting the burgesses from this duty, wheresoever residing; but in this year, 1828, a free burgess of Ipswich claimed the privilege of the borough at London, in the Court of King's Bench; when the judges, on referring to the charter, declared that it only applied to the *resident* burgesses of Ipswich; and he was accordingly sworn in to serve upon the London jury. In the tenth year of this reign it was determined at a great court, for the greater convenience of the burgesses, and better furtherance of the business of the corporation, that for the future, the bailives, seven of the twelve portmen, and fourteen of the twenty-four men, should be sufficient and competent to ordain, annul, and make all laws, statutes, and ordinances, as shall be thought meet for the government of the town.

In the first of Richard III. twenty soldiers were granted to serve the king in his army, for three weeks; and the treasurer was authorized to pay five shillings for the charges of these soldiers. In our preceding summary we have only mentioned those charters which are most important and particular, but on the 16th of.March, in the second year of Richard III., this sovereign confirmed the charters of Edward IV., Richard II., Edward III., Edward II., Edward I., John, and Henry II., without any alteration: and in the same year it was resolved that the twelve capital burgesses, called head boroughs, of this town, should be constables for ever. Henry VII., by an inspeximus dated at Westminster, 20th of January, in the third year of his reign, confirmed all the former charters. In the seventh year of the same reign, the prior of Ely was made a free burgess, and of the confraternity of the guild of Corpus Christi; and in the eighteenth year of this reign several sums were ordered to be paid by the

treasurer of the corporation, towards the expenses of the pageant of this guild. And in the eleventh of Henry VIII. the great court has this order:—" Every person absent from Corp. Chri. mass shall forfeit a pound of wax. And the play and the dinner shall hold this year. The guild wardens are elected, and the pageant ordered to be ready. A priest is elected to say mass, yearly; and an order is made for the master of the grammar-school to officiate for the year coming." These guilds, or confraternities, were societies or associations of persons in the same town, profession, or class, confederated together for the common cause of trade, charity, or religion. They were bodies corporate, licensed by the crown; had power to purchase lands, to build chapels, to erect altars, to maintain chaplains or priests, to hold frequent and private meetings, to make annual processions, and to administer oaths upon the admission of their members, and occasionally they amused the public with pageants and with plays taken from the Old and New Testaments, and were, formerly, numerous and important in Ipswich. The greatest part of these guilds were founded in the fifteenth and sixteenth centuries; but this guild of Corpus Christi, with many others in the kingdom, was formed long before that period; for the office of guild-holder is mentioned among the officers of the corporation many years previously, afterwards it was dropped, and four guild-wardens chosen in his stead.

We shall here speak of the volume called Ipswich Doomsday, which we shall introduce to our readers in the author's own words. "In consequence of John Blake, town clerk of Ipswich in the reign of Henry III., having absconded, and feloniously taken and carried away with him a certain roll of laws, grants, ordinances, and other constitutions, called Doomsday, to the great detriment of the corporation. These laws, &c. having, since that time, been kept in a loose irregular manner, the present compilation, called Ipswich Doomsday, was formed, collected, and completed by Richard Peyvale, one of the portmen, and burgess of the town of

Ipswich, the eighteenth day of September, 1521, in the twelfth year of the reign of Henry VIII.;" and, as the author says in his prologue, he has "compiled and set together in this present book, called Doomsday, which is divided into six parts, as many of the old grants, liberties, ordinances, laws, and good constitutions as I could find prescription or good matter of record for, with divers and sundry other matters right necessary to be had and known in the town and borough of Ipswich, and, as near as I could, I have followed mine ancient copies; the which copies 1 have diligently sought and found out of divers and sundry other books and rolls, with the good aid and diligent labour of one Robert Bray, then being the common town clerk, of the said town; which book I humbly present to the bailiffs, burgesses, and commonalty of the same town, to the intent that it may remain in their town-house, otherwise called the moot-hall, or guild-hall, for a perpetual memory. And also to the intent that the bailiffs and governors of the same town being, or hereafter shall be, may have the better knowledge to use, maintain, and keep the same old grants, liberties, laws, and constitutions, like as they be sworn upon their solemn oaths." The first part contains the first charter of king John, with all the grants, &c. to the nineteenth year of Edward I. The second book contains the laws, bye laws, and regulations of the town, collected; and these laws, &c. were redressed, and their faults amended and revised, in the nineteenth year of Edward I. by the bailiffs, and a committee of the burgesses, and they were entered in a book, and the common seal of the corporation affixed. The third and fourth books continue the charters, rights, privileges, immunities, and gifts, down to the forty-first of Elizabeth; some of which have since been added in different hand-writing. The fifth book contains the oaths that are taken by the bailiffs, portmen, burgesses, and all officers of the borough, on coming into office. The following is the free burgesses's oath on taking up his freedom before a great court:—" Master bailiffs, portmen, coroners, and all others that be present, I desire you to hear how that I shall, from this day forward, true burgess be, and the counsel and privities of this town and burgh of Ipswich, and of the great courts of the same shall truly keep, and not disown, disuse, nor disclose; I shall colour no man's goods, nor in my name, wherethrough the town shall lose any manner of right, that is to say, custom, toll, or any profit which the town ought to have of right. And, also, I shall be aidant and obedient to my bailiffs and portmen that now be, or in time coming shall be; and the precepts of the said bailiffs at all times I shall keep and obey to my power. And I shall be *lottaunt* and *scot taunt,* as a burgess ought to be, to all manner of charge that belongeth to the said town, liberties and franchise of the same, as often as any such charge shall happen; and I shall maintain and sustain, to the best of my power, the aforesaid town, franchise, and liberties of the same, against all manner of men, except our sovereign Lord, the King, and his royal power, so help me God." This part concludes with an account of the perambulation of the liberties of the borough. Sixth part:—" Here endeth the sixth part of this present book, wherein is contained the charter for the corporation and liberties of this town of Ipswich, confirmed in the third year of the reign of our sovereign lord, king Henry VIII.; with another charter granted in the tenth year of our said sovereign lord, declaring the jurisdiction admiral and other certain articles, in more ample and larger manner than they were declared in the old charter before written; and with a copy of a confirmation made by lord Thomas, earl of Surrey, great admiral of England, confirmant of the aforesaid jurisdiction admiral."

This is a very large and thick folio volume, beautifully written on vellum, in the old black letter or German text, is usually kept in the town-hall, and is considered the official corporation book. It is the volume from which they annually proclaim the market. It includes the substance of all the charters, as well as the ordinances and regulations of the corporate body. It is the book from which the oaths of all the officers of the corporation are administered. It is their ritual, their creed, their book of faith. It is their register, their guide, their code of laws, to which, on all doubtful occasions, reference is made, and by these written laws and regulations all must abide.

The following poetical chronology of the kings of England, from William the Conqueror to Henry VI., is extracted from Ipswich Doomsday. Whether it was written by the then poet laureate of the corporation, or who is the author history is silent; and it is certainly not inserted for its poetical merit, but as a curious specimen of our forefathers' taste.

WILLIAM THE CONQUEROR.
"This mighty William of Normandy,
As books old maketh mention,
By just title and by his chivalry,
Made king by conquest of Brute's Albion,
Put out Harold and took possession,
Bare his crown full twenty-one year,
Buried at Caen, thus saith the chronicler.

WILLIAM RUFUS.
"Next in order, by succession,
William Rufus, his son, crowned king,
Which to God-ward had none devotion,
Destroyed churches of new and old building,
To make a forest pleasant for hunting,
Seventeen year bare his crown indeed,
Buried at Winchester you may read.

HENRY PRIMUS.
"His brother next, called Henry the First,
Was at London crowned, as I find;
Whose brother Robert, duke of Normandy,
'Gan war, the chronicle maketh mind,
Reconciled all parties set behind;
Full thirty-one years, by record of writing,
He reigned, and buried at Reading.

STEPHANUS.
His brother Stephen, when Henry the First was dead,
Toward England 'gan cross his sail;
The archbishop did set upon his head
A rich crowu, being of couuceil;
Nineteen years, with sorrow and great travail,
Bare the crown, and never had rest;
And, at Fulham, lieth buried in a chest.

HENRICCS II.
"Henry the Second, son of the empress,
Was crowned next, a full manly knight,
As books of old plainly doth express.
This lord Henry, by froward force and might,
Years thirty-five reigned, as it is made of mind;
At fount Everard lieth buried, as I find.

RICARDUS PRIMUS.
"Richard, his son, by succession,
First of that name, strong,, hearty, and notable,
"Was crowned king, called Coeur de Lion,
With Saracen's heads served at his table,
Slain at Calais by death lamentable,
The space reigned fully nineteen year,
His heart buried at Rouen, under the high alter.

JOHANNES.
"Next king Richard reigned his brother John,
After soon entered into France,
Lost all Anjou and Normandy, anon
This land interdicted by his governance;
And, as it is put in remembrance,
Eighteen years king of region;
Lyeth at Worcester dead of poison.

HENRICUS III.
"Henry the Third, his son, fifteen year age,
Was at Gloucester crowned, as I read;
Long war he had with his baronage;
Greatly delighted in almes deed;
Fifty-six year he reigned here indeed;
Buried at Westminster, by record of writing,
The day of St. Edmund, martyr and king.

EDWARDUS PRIMUS.
"Edward the First, with shanks long,
Was after crowned, that was a good knight,
Won Scotland maugre the Scot strong,
And all Wales, in the despight of their might,
During his life maintained true and right;

Thirty-five years he was here king,
Lyeth at Westminster, this is no leasing.

EDWARDUS II.

"Edward, his son, called Carnarvon,
Guarding after to make his asseiance,
As the chronicle well rehearseth can,
Wedded the daughter of the king of France,
Unto Thomas of Lancaster he took benisance;
Nineteen years held he regally;
Buried at Gloucester, books specify.

EDWARDUS III.

"Edward the Third, born at Windsor,
Which in knighthood had so great price,
Inheritant of France, withouten more
Bare in his arms quarter a fleur de lis,
And gate Calais high his prudent device;
Reigned in England fifty-one year,
Lyeth at Westminster, thus saith the compiler.

RICHARD II.

"The son of prince Edward, Richard the Second,
In which time was peace and great plenty,
Wedded queen Anne of *Bowau,* as it is found,
Isabel, after, of France, who lived to see,
Twenty-two years he reigned here;
At Langley buried first, so found the case.
After, to Westminster the body carried was.

HENEICUS IV.

"Henry the Fourth, next crowned in certain,
A famous knight of great comeliness;
From his exile when he came home again,
Was well travelled, and with great giftiness;
Fourteen years he reigned in godliness:
Lyeth at Canterbury, in that holy place,
God of his mercy do his soul grace.

HENRICUS QUINTUS.

"The Fifth Henry, of knighthood loadstone,
Wise, manly, plainly to determine,
Fortunate proved in peace and in war,
Greatly expert in manful discipline,
Able to stand among the worthiest: he

Reigned ten years, who that list to regard,
Lyeth at Westminster by St. Edward.

HENRICUS SEXTOS.

"Henry the Sixth, brought forth iu virtue,
By just title and by inheritance,
Provided he force, by the grace of God,
To be crowned in England and in France,
Reigned thirty-nine years, and God gave him sufferance
Of virtuous life, and chose him for his knight;
At Windsor buried, and miracles doth by God's might.

In the thirteenth year of Henry VIII. the escheator for the crown seized some goods which a felon fugitive left behind him, in a house in Whitton street, which the escheator pretended was not in the liberties of Ipswich; the bailiffs complained of this violence, and, in consequence, a commission was directed to the Abbot of St. Edmundsbury, Robert Curzon, knt., Lord Curzon, Sir Robert Drury, Sir Richard Wentworth, Sir Philip Tilney,

E

Lionel Talmage, esq., and John Sulyard, esq., to enquire how far the bounds of the liberties of Ipswich extended: a jury was empannelled, and their return filed in Chancery. The whole precincts of the borough, including the four hamlets of Stoke Hall, Brooks Hall, Wikes Uford, and Wikes Bishop, together with Thurleston, Whitton, and Westerfield, are of considerable extent. It reaches, from east to west, from Rushmere heath, near the hall gate, and along the lane which crosses the Woodbridge road, near the Gallows, to Whitton street, at a lane leading from Bramford, across the Norwich road; the distance being upwards of four miles. From north to south, from a place in the Witnesham road, beyond Westerfield Green, to Bourn Bridge, it is nearly the same distance; but through St. Clement's street, on the east side of the river, to Downham Reach, by John's Ness, the distance is five miles. I/lb circuit is upwards of nineteen miles, and

its superficial contents 8450 acres. The corporation also holds precinct and jurisdiction by water on the Orwell, to a place called Polleshead, in the high sea, beyond Walton and Felixstow cliffs.— The jury, upon their oaths, declared that the said liberties did extend according to the bounds in the said return, as above mentioned; and the said bailiffs, burgesses, and commonalty of Ipswich, have used to enjoy the said liberties and franchise, *without tnynde of man.*—The words of the charter, dated March the 12th, 1518, in the third year of Henry VIII. are very important:—" We do give wrecks of the sea, and all goods and chattels that are called wrecks; *flelson,* that is, goods that float out of a ship that has foundered at sea; *jetson,* that is, goods that are thrown out of a ship in distress, by the sailors, to lighten her; and all goods and merchandise lost in the sea, and thrown out of the sea; and all the goods and chattels that belong, or can, or ought to belong to the admiral, or his officer, within the said port and water; *and land and soil by the tide flooded or covered with water,* in any manner happening, or then in the sea, or upon the coast of the sea found, or to be found, from the aforesaid port and water running by the flowing of the sea from the said port, towards the southeast, unto the place called Polleshead." And it also grants a deodand upon the ship or vessel in which any life is lost by accident or design, within the aforesaid jurisdiction. In March/ 181,4, the corporation brought an action of ejectment against a Mr. Staton, for the recovery of the possession of a piece of land on the banks of the Orwell which had been formerly flooded by the water, but in consequence of his having had uninterrupted possession of this soil for upwards of twenty years, it was ordered by the court that his possession should not be disturbed. By this it will be seen that vigilance is necessary to preserve the rights of the corporation given by this charter. According to an order of the great court, to be acted upon once in seven years, an admiralty court was holden in due form upon the sands, at low water, near Polleshead, the corporate body attending, in the year 1826; when the corporation of Harwich, who were always, of course, exceedingly jealous of the power the borough of Ipswich formerly had of holding their admiralty court eveB.in the town and port of Harwich, would not allow these Ipswich Lords of the Admiralty to land in their judicial capacity, and this obnoxious privilege is given up as it regards the port of Harwich.

In the year 1528, in the twentieth of Henry VIII., on the fifteenth of June, the first stone of Cardinal Wolsey's college, dedicated to the blessed Virgin, was laid by John Longland, bishop of Lincoln; and, in the same year, the corporation gave to the dean and canons of the cardinal's college of St. Mary, all the interest of the town in the lands in Whitton and Ipswich bequeathed by the last will and testament of Richard Felaw or otherwise. An original deed, in the possession of Mr. Richard Taylor, of Norwich, and inserted, in his Index Monasticus, shews what little regard this ambitious prelate had for the rights of individuals, or even communities, when they stood in the way of his designs: it states " that the cardinal, with the permission of Pope Clement VII. and the concurrence of king Henry VIII. had built and founded the college of Ipswich; the monastery of St. Peter, in Ipswich, of the order of St. Augustine, with all its dependencies, having been suppressed. In consequence of this suppression, several parish churches, with their rights and emoluments attached to the said monastery were also abolished, the church of St. Peter being of that number. Since therefore the inhabitants of that parish had no place for their attendance on divine service, the cardinal determines to place them under the pastoral care of the clergy presiding over those churches which are nearest, and accordingly he appoints William Capon, &c. to go to the aforesaid college where the church of St. Peter formerly was, and to assemble the parishioners in a convenient place, in order to consider the matter, and to allot them to the churches of St. Nicholas, and of the Virgin Mary, at Keye, in Ipswich,

as the nearest churches. Dated Hampton Court, 7th August, 1528." The following letter, from William Capon, the dean of Cardinal College, Ipswich, exhibits a lively description of this institution, and we give it in the writer's own words and orthography, from the Cotton MSS.

"Pleasith it your Grace to be advertysed, the Sonday the vjte day of September, maister Stephyns, Doctor Lee, with Mr. Crumwell, repayred to Gipswiche and came to your Graces College there, and brought with theym coopes, vestements, aulter clothes, plate, and other things, the pertiuullers wherof byn comprised in a payer of Indenturs made bitwene me and the said Mr. Crumwell; the oon indenture the said Mr. Crumwell hath with hym and thoder part remeyneth with me. Also all the said parcells be ingroced and incerted into yonr Graces boke indented, emongst other of your graces stuff, which boke remeyneth in my custodye. Also the said Mr. Stephyns, Mr. Lee, and Mr. Crumwell taryed in your graces College the space of iiij dayes, in whiche tyme Mr. Crumwell dyd take moche payne and labour not only in surveying your graces stuff hether caryed sawfely, but also in prepay ring and ordering off hangings, benchis, with all other necessaries to the furniture of our hall whiche ys now well trymmed and ordered thrugh his good diligence and helpe. And upon our Ladyes evyn I, with all the company of your Grace's college, as the subdeane, Mr. Ellis, vj. prests, viij. clerks, and ix. choresters with all our servants, when we had fynished our evynsong in our college chirche, then immedyatly after we repayred to gether to our Ladyes Chapell and there song evynsong as solemply and devoutely as we cowde. And there accompanyed with Mr. Stephyns, Doctor Lee, and Mr. Crumwell, with Mr. Humfrey Wyngfylde, (to whom all we of your Grace's college byn moche boundyn unto for his loving and kynde maner shewed unto us,) the bayliffs of the towne, with the port-men and the Priour of Christs Chirche, all the whiche accompanyed us that same nyght home

agayne to your Graces college with as lovyng and kynde maner as I have sene; and at theyr commyng theder they dranke with me bothe wyne and biere, and so that nyght departed. On the next Day whiche was our Ladyes day, the viij. day of September; a day of very fowle wedder and rayned sore contynewally; so that we cowde not go lift procession thrugh the towne to our Lady's Chapell accordyng to our statute by your grace made; but we made as solempne a procession in your grace's College Chirche as cowde be devysed. In somoche there were xl. of your coopes worne there, and asmoche people as cowde stande in the Chirche and in the chirche yards. Also all the honorable gentilmen of the shyre were there; as Mr. Wenteford, Sir John Willowghbye, Sir Phelip Tylney, Mr. Bowth, Sir Thomas Tey, with Mr. Benefylde, Mr. Pyrton, Mr. Jermeyn, Mr. Humfrey Wyngfylde, with many other to the number of xxiiij. gentilmen of the contrey, bcsids the bayliffs, portemen of the towne, the Priour of Christs Chirche, the Priour of Butley, Doctor Greoe vicar of Alborowgh, as commyssaries bothe to your Grace and to the Bishop of Norwiche, and the Duke of Norfolk's almoner Mr. Hcge, all the whiche were there, with as good wille and diligence as they cowde to do your Grace honnor that day: and they all toke repast at dynner in your Grace's College, and as I trust wele enterteyned with good fare, and suche fassyon as we cowde devise, where with they were right well contented as I supposed. Pardermore as for your syngyng men byn well chosen, very well brested with sufficient cunnyng for theyr rowmes, and som of theym very excellent, whiche will not serve here with theyr good wills for that wagis, alleging for theyr selff how they had moche better wages there from whense they came fro. Moreover they will have brekefasts every day in as ample and large maner as they have had in other places. I feare that theyr commons allowed by your Grace will not suffice theym as yet: for we can make no provysions neyther for bee Si ne for muttons for want of pasture nere unto us. As for Bornebrige ys very bareyne. The subdeane and I, with Mr. Rushe, have vewed every part and percell therof, and they saye it is not mete nor convenyent for fatte ware, neyther for beeffs nor muttons. I have enterteyned theym according to your Graces commandment with good wordis and plenty of mete and drinke, promisyng to som of theym that be excellent more wagis, for they gruge sore at theyr wagis, as Mr. Doctor Stephyns and Mr. Crumwell can shew to your Grace more at lengthe. Fardermore as for your Graces College Churche, oon man ys not able bothe to attende and kepe the revestry and do all things in the Churche, as to ryng the bells, kepe the Churche clene, prepayre the aulter's lights, and other necessaries, and to see all the Ornaments wele and sufficiently repay red, and kepte withoute eny enpayringj and to set forth every day all suche things as is to be occupied abowte Godd'f service. Therfore by the advyce of Mr. Stephyns, Mr. Lee, and Mr. Crumwell I have putt in to the churche an other man to helpe the yoman off the Revestry, and named him Sexten, unto the tyme I knowe farder of your Grace's pleasure in that behalf. Also here byn but fyve prestis besids your Subdeaue, which is to litle a nomber to kepe iij. massys every day according to your Graces statuts, and the subdeane cannot attende upon his charge for surveyeng of the works and bieldyngs of yojir Grace's College, wherfor we moost humbly desyer and pray your Grace to have moo priests to performe your Grace's ordynaunce in your sayd College, or els to dyspense with us for oon of your masses, eyther the Requiem Masse or ells our Ladyes masse, unto the tyme we be better furnished with priests to accomplishe and performe your Graces ordynaunces and statutes therin. And but for Mr. Lentall we cowde in a maner do nothing in oure quere. He taketh very great paynes and is alwaye present at Mattens and all Masses with evyn song, and settith the quere in good ordre fro tyme to tyme, and fayleth not at eny time. He is very sober and discrete, and bringeth up your Choresters very wele:

assuring your Grace there shall be no better childern in no place of England then we shall have here, and that in short tyme. I have also made xv. albis of the new cloth whiche I had of your Grace, delyvered by thandis of Mr. Alvarde your graces servaunt: and yet there is xiiij. albis more to be made to the sutes now lately sent by your Grace to us by Mr. Crumwell; besids albis for xiiij. tunycles, and xij. payer of odde parrers for childern. Fardermore there hath byn sent unto your Graces College, agaynste the day of the Nativitie of our Lad ye, ix. bukks: that is to wete ij. from the Duke of Norfolke, ij. from the Duke of Suffolke, oon from my Lady of Oxford the yonger, oon from Sir Phelip Bowth, oon from Mr. Pyrton, oon from Mr. Sentcler your graces servaunt, and oon from Richard Cavendish your grace's servaunt; whiche bukks were spent on our sayd Ladyes day in your Graces College and in the towne of Gipswiche, whereof oon buk was delyv'ed to the Chamberleynsof the towne for the xxiiij. hedmen of the same towne, and in money x. to make mery with all, by the advyce of Mr. Stephins, Mr. Lee, and Mr. Crumwell: and in lyke wise to the bayliffs wyves and the portemennes wives to make mery with a buk and x? And to the Curatts of the same towne a buk with vj'. viij4 in mbifey, for theyr paynes and Iabowrs takyn in our procession. Also Mr. Rushe to whom all your Graces College is moche bedoldyn unto, ever redy to do pleasurs and also to take paynes for us in all our causes, and at the sayd day he gave to us vj. cowple of conyes, ij. fesaunts, and oon dosseyn of quayles. Also the Priour of Butley he gave to us ii. fesaunts and a futte Crane.

"Also we have receyved of Mr. Dawndy clxxj. tonnes of Cane stone, and within a fortenyght next after Mighelmes now next commyng we shall have oon c. tonnes more. So that your workemen shall not be un occupyed for wante of stone. And the sayd Mr. Dawndy hath promised to me that bifore Easter next commyng we shall have here redy M'. tonnes more of the sayd Cane stone. And thus the Holy Trinitie preserve your Grace. From your

Grace's College in Gipswiche the xxvj. day of September, by your moost boundyn servaunt and humble Chapleyn.

"WILLYAM CAPON.

"To My Lord Legato his good Grace."
We find but little other matter of note occurring in Ipswich till the disgrace of the cardinal, three years afterwards, when this college was suppressed. About this period we observe, in the minutes of the great court, that the King's Head was then the principal Inn in the town, and was adjudged to pay one shilling, as standing on the town grounds; whilst the White Horse, and the Griffin, with other houses specified, only paid sixpence. In 1530, Corpus Christi Play was taken away for ever. And in 1540, it was ordered that Mr. Bailiff' Sparrow and the town clerk shall ride to London and put to the Court of Augmentation for the half market of Woodbridge. This market was, originally, granted by the prior and canons of Woodbridge priory, upon condition that the corporation of Ipswich should have half the tolls and dues for stallage, &c. at the market and fair at Woodbridge; and that a piece of ground should be allotted to them for building a house, for the purpose of accommodating the officers and servants of the aforesaid corporation, whom they might please to send to collect these dues, and look after their rights. Constant references are made in the old court books to this half market of Woodbridge, and continual disputes arose between that town and the corporation upon the subject. The town of Woodbridge at length purchased this right of the corporation, and all claim upon the market is given up; but, to this day, any freeman of Ipswich attending Woodbridge fair, claims the right of stallage, without paying any fee.

At this period the persecutions against heretics were carried on with unrelenting severity. In the year 1546, Roger Clark, of Mendlesham, and one Kerby, were apprehended at Ipswich——where sentence was given upon them both—— Kerby to be burned in the said town the next Saturday, and Roger to be burned at Bury the Monday after. Hereby, when his judgment was given by the Lord Wentworth, with most humble reverence, holding up his hands and bowing himself, devoutly said, "Praised bo God," and so stood still without any more words. Then did the Lord Wentworth talk secretly, putting his head behind another j ustice that sate between them. The said Roger perceiving that, said with a loud voice, " Speak out, my lord, and if you have done any thing contrary to your conscience, ask God mercy, and we, for our parts, do forgive you, and speak not in secret, for ye shall come before a judge, and then make answer openly before him that shall judge all men." The Lord Wentworth, somewhat blushing, and changing his countenance, through remorse, as it was thought, said," I did speak nothing of you, nor I have done nothing unto you but as the law is." Then was Kerby and Roger sent forth—Kerby to prison, and Roger to Edmund's Bury, where he suffered on the following Monday, amidst shocking tortures, but with great firmness and resolution, exclaiming against the mediation of saints, and declaring from the midst of the flames, that " no one but the Son of God could take away the sins of the world." The day after their condemnation, Saturday, about ten of the clock, Kerby was brought to the market-place, at Ipswich; whereas a stake was ready with wood, broom, and straw, and did off his clothes unto his shirt, having a night-cap upon his head, and so was fastened to the stake with irons; there being in the gallery the Lord Wentworth, with the most part of all the justices of these quarters, that they might see his execution, how every thing should be done, and also might hear what Kerby did say; and a great number of people, about two thousand by estimation. Much persuasion was used by Mr. Wingfield, Justice Foster, and one Dr. Rugham, to induce him to recant; but he argued stoutly with them, and so silenced and confuted the latter, that "then was the doctor in the dumps, and spake not one word to Kerby after." He prayed fervently, and said and sung the Te Deum and the Belief, in the English tongue. The Lord Wentworth, while

Kerby was thus doing, did shroud himself behind a post in the gallery, and wept; and so did many others. Whilst the fire was burning around him, he called unto God with a loud voice—the people shouting and praising God with great admiration of his constancy, being so simple and unlettered.

In the beginning of the story of Kerby, and Roger Clark, mention was made of a certain bill put upon the town-house door, and brought, the next day, to the Lord Wentworth—the words of which bill are these.

"THE BILL SET UPON THE TOWNE HOUSE DOORE IN IPSWICH.

" *Jul e judicale Jili hominutn:*' yet when ye shall judge, minister your justice with mercy.

"A fearful thing it i to fall into the hands of the thong God; he ye learned therefore in true knowledge, ye that judge the earth, lest the
Lord he angry with you.

"The hlood of the righteous shall he required at your hands.

"What though the veil hanged hefore Moses' face; yet at Christ's death it fell down.

"The stones shall speak, if these should hold their peace; therefore harden not your hearts against the verity.

"For fearfully shall the Lord appear in the day of vengeance to the trouhled in conscience. No excuse shall there he of ignorance, hut every fatshall stand on his own hottom. Therefore have remorse in your conscience:
fear him that may kilt hoth hody and soul.

"Beware of innocent hlood shedding: take heed of justice ignorantly administered: work discreetly, as the Scripture doth command. Look to it, that ye make not the truth to he forsaken.

We heseech God to save our King, Henry the Eighth, that he he not led into temptation. So he it."

Literature began to rear its head in Ipswich, under the patronage of Cardinal Wolsey, and continued to flourish after the demolition of the college; for we have account of no less than three printers in the town who printed several works about the same period. Several

different publications issued from the press of Anthony Skolloker, St. Nicholas' parish, Ipswich, 1548; one of which is entitled " *Six Sermons of Master Bernardine Ockine."* The names of the rest we are unacquainted with. The title of another work was "*Catalogus Scriptorum Illustrium Brittannice, Bale, Ipswich,* 1548," by Overton. The following is a transcript of the title-page of another little book we have seen.
A NEWE BOKE CONTEVNINGE
Q AN EXHORTATIO TO THE SVCKE,
THE SYCKE MAN'S PRAYER,
A PRAYER WITH THANKES AT THE PURIFICACIO OF WOMB,
  A CONSOLATIO AT BURIALL.
COLOSS. 3.
Whatsoever ye do in word or dede, do all in the name of the Lord Jesu, and give thanks unto God the father hy hym.
  M.D.XLVUI.
IMPRITNTED AT IPPESW1CHE,
BY ME, JOHN OIWEN.
Cum privilegio ad imprimendtun solum.

This is a perfect and unique copy, beautifully printed in black letter, in the possession of Mr. W. S. Fitch—whose collection of books, prints, MSS. and autographs, relative to Ipswich and the county of Suffolk, is of the most curious and valuable description he is ever ready to give information, and his liberality is equal to his judgment and his taste.

In 1548, Edward VI. confirmed all former charters, by an inspeximus dated at Westminster, 8th of July, in the first year of his reign.

Robert Samuel, who was minister of East Bergholt, was removed from his benefice for being married. He sent away his wife to Ipswich, and continued in and about his parish, preaching to his people, privately, and confirming them in the sound doctrine; yet now and then visiting his wife, as a husband ought to do. This was not unknown to Justice Foster, of Copdock, near Ipswich, a furious zealot for the Popish superstitions, and one who sought all ways to entrap the professors of the Reformed Church. He set some persons at Ipswich to find out when Samuel was with his wife; and it was not long before Samuel was discovered, and taken and carried to Ipswich gaol; but was afterwards removed to Norwich prison, where he was loaded with chains, and almost starved, at the instigation of the bishop and his chancellor, Dunnings; but this had no effect upon his constancy, and he was burnt at Ipswich, August 31st, 1555.

Nicholas Peke, of Earl Stonham—who suffered with great firmness—was burnt at Ipswich about the same time. Also two women, viz. Anne Potter, a brewer's wife, and Joan Trunchfield, a shoemaker's wife, were apprehended and imprisoned, and were both burnt at Ipswich, February 19th, 1556.

The next reign was still further distinguished for cruelty and persecution, and no parts of the kingdom were exempt from the horrors of the prevailing bigotry of the times. On the 4th of November, 1558, Alexander Gouch and Alice Driver were brought from Melton jail to Ipswich, at seven o'clock in the morning — Sir Henry Dodwell being high sheriff: this woman had suffered great persecution, having had her ears cut off at Bury for comparing the queen to Jezabel. They now rejected the mass, and denied the supremacy of the Pope. When they came to the stake, they sung psalms together, and then prayed; at which the sheriff was much displeased, and bid the bailiffs of Ipswich speak to them to make an end. Gouch then rose from his knees, and said,' Pray Mr. Sheriff let us pray a little while, for we have but a little time to live here.' But the bailiffs were bidden to have them to the fire without further delay. They were fastened to the stake; many shook them by the hands, notwithstanding the sheriff's threatnings; and they joyfully resigned their souls to God, in the middle of the flames.

On the accession of Elizabeth we find the town determined to petition for a renewal of the charter, and in the second year of her reign she confirmed all the charters by an inspeximus dated at Westminster, Sept. 23rd, 1560. She visited Ipswich more than once. On the tenth of June, in the third year of her reign, 1561, it is ordered that all the inhabitants of Ipswich shall be assessed

to the costs and entertainments of the queen, at her next coming to the town. And the assessors are named; and such as shall not pay their assessment, shall be disfranchised. And on Tuesday, July 17th, is the following entry: — "Perambulation liberty by water with the queen.—There shall be two vessels or *botes,* decently furnished, to attend on the queen's majestie, so far as the liberty do extend." And in *"Q. Elizabeth's Progresses,"* published by Nichols, we have the followin statement of her household expenses, during her visit to Ipswich; where it may be noticed that the *largest* item is for cookery, and the *smallest* for benevolence.

IPPESWICHE.

Die Mercurii, sexto die Augusti, Dispens. IpsV 108 9 8J

Die Jovis, septimo die Augusti, ibidem,.. 104 14 3

Die Veneris, octavo die Augusti, ibidem,.. 100 3 9£

Die Sabbati, nono die Augusti, ibidem,.. 108 10 6£ ADHUNC IPPESWICHE. Die Dominica, decimo die Augusti, ibidem, Dipens. 105s. 3d. Butill'. 19: 7:11. Garder, 16:1: 7. Coquina, 34:19: 2. Jullia, 19:1:0. Scutilla, 6:5:0. Salsar, 23s. Aulse et Camera, 53s. 3d. Stabulum, 19:8: 8£. Vadea, 10£. Elimosina, 4s. Tot. £134:9: 4.

It is peculiarly gratifying to see with what exactness the royal accounts were kept even in those early days, to the nicety of a fraction or single halfpenny!

It is probable that when the queen sailed down the river, on the 17th of July, that she landed on the Essex coast, and visited Colchester; for Mr. Nichols observes, in his notes, "that she was at Colchester the latter end of July, and thence she went to Ipswich." Here her majesty took a great dislike to the imprudent behaviour of many of the ministers and readers; there being many weak ones among them, and little or no order observed in the public service, and few or none wearing the surplice. And the Bishop of Norwich was thought remiss, and that he winked at schismatics. But more particularly she was offended with the clergy's marriage; and that in cathedrals and colleges, there were so many

wives, and widows and children seen; which she said was contrary to the intent of the founders, and so much tending to the interrupt ion of the studies of those who were placed there. Therefore she issued an order to all dignitaries, dated Aug. 9th, at Ipswich, to forbid all women to the lodgings of cathedrals or colleges, and that upon pain of losing their ecclesiastical promotions. This precious proclamation may be seen at full length in "Strype's Life of Parker. " And thankful ought the clergy to have been for this careful anxiety of the maiden queen for their comfort, character, and morals. There was an act likewise passed, in the thirteenth year of her reign, which empowered and directed the bailiffs to cause such an augmentation to be made to some of the poorer livings in Ipswich, as might be agreed upon by the most respectable inhabitants, as " meet for the maintenance of the minister." It does not appear that the inhabitants of this loyal town exhibited any extraordinary symptoms of exultation at this gracious visit of her majesty, for we can discover no account of pageants, processions, or rejoicings. She visited them again, in 1565, when we may suppose that the corporation became imbued with a portion of her sacred majesty's wisdom; for, shortly after, the following pious injunction appeared in the court books: — "Twelfth of Elizabeth, July 5.— Whereas, the common and poorer sort of people in the town are grown to excess of apparel, to the ruin, decay, and impoverishment of the town, against the commandment of the queen, in contempt of the laws, to the increase of wickedness and sin whereby everybody shall fall into the displeasure of almighty God. It is, therefore, ordered that every person carrying on any mystery or occupation, shall not allow their apprentices, servants, or journeymen to wear certain stuffs or woollen clothing, &c. &c. as herein specified, on pain of imprisonment; and the constables shall bring all such persons offending before the bailiffs for the time being!"

Though we are in duty bound to admire the prudential foresight of our ancestors, and their careful consideration for the salvation of the poor, it is to be hoped that we may pardonably rejoice at living in those times when the fair inhabitants of Ipswich, of every rank and condition, may clothe their persons in whatever they think most becoming to the beauty of their features, or the elegance of their forms. So far did the vigilance of the corporation at that time extend, that the most minute offence against delicacy was liable to punishment; for it was decreed, as it had often been before, that hogs traversing the streets were a public nuisance; and that if any inhabitant should allow any duck or drake to be in the channel, that the sergeant of the admiralty should take these feathered offenders into custody, and sell them, half for his own use, and half for the town. It is, we hope, not derogating too much from the dignity of history, to say, that our sapient magistrates made *ducks and drakes* of justice upon this occasion, and that there was a great deal of *quackery* in the whole transaction.

In the twelfth year of this reign, Robert Inglish, of Magdalen College, in respect of his poverty, and being a toward young man, shall have a yearly exhibition of 53s. 4d. out of the foundation: and this was the *first exhibition* from Ipswich school. At the same time an order was made and published for the better order of the Grammar School, and the master, usher, and scholars, according to the charter thereof. These regulations were afterwards guaranteed by the queen, and the salary of the master and usher settled by her determination, in the charter dated March 18th, 1565.

In the thirteenth year of this reign, a statute of parliament was passed, called " An Act for Paving the Town of Ipswich;" and it was commanded by king Charles II. in his charter dated 1685, that the corporation should act in all things duly as this statute commands.

In the year 1578, much difference of opinion arose in the minds of the inhabitants respecting the advantages of establishing a mart for general business in the town; several representations were made to the government respecting it, and two or three tracts on the subject are preserved amongst the Lansdownc MSS. in the British museum, but they throw very little light on the matter.

An order of the great court appears in 1583, for half a tun of wine, as a present to Lord Wentworth, on his first coming to Nettlestead, after his accession to the title. And, in 1585, he was presented with a hogshead of wine, two gallons of claret, and a gallon of sack.

In the sixteenth year of Elizabeth, John Clenche, esq. was, from Midsummer next, to bear the name of recorder of the town, and therefore to solicit the town causes at London; and he shall dwell in the town, be sworn a freeman, and his yearly fee shall be £13:6:8. This is the *first* mention of a *recorder.*

In the eighteenth year of Elizabeth, Dr. Norton is retained ordinary preacher in this town, to be continually resident herein, and shall have £50 stipend, payable quarterly, beginning his work at Easter next. And this is the *first* regular institution of the *present town lectureship,* though there had been a town preacher before.

In the twenty-fifth year of this reign, a person libelling the bailiffs was fined £40, and another was fined £10 *for his-paynes;* and, for the like offence, Edmund Gooding was ordered to come to such punishment as Judge Clenche shall think fit; by which it appears that calumny and detraction were much afloat, or that our worthy magistrates were particularly tenacious of their honour.

In the thirty-first year of Elizabeth, ten pounds were demanded by Mr. Garneys, for die pay of certain horses which went out of the town to Tilbury, for the use of the queen's majesty; and it was ordered that it should be levied on the inhabitants, by a collection of a fifth part of the subsidy granted to the queen.

In the thirty-seventh year of Elizabeth, we have to note an instance of the gallantry of the corporate body, for a silver standing cup, value £10: 13: 8, double gilt, was presented from the town to Sir Philip Parker, on the marriage of his daughter. They, at another time, presented him with half a tun of claret; and, in 1593, a hogshead of claret, for his friendship to the town.,

On the third of January, in the thirty-eighth year of Elizabeth, an order was issued for the fitting out two ships for the general defence of the realm:—the bailiffs to proceed to London to get an order for raising the money in the shire. The names of the first two vessels that were furnished were the " William," of Ipswich, 140 tons, thirty men, Barnaby Lowe commander; and the " Katherine," of Ipswich, 123 tons, thirty men, commanded by Thomas Grimble: they acted as coasters in the fleet opposed to the Spanish Armada, in the division commanded by Lord Henry Seymour. In the year 1591, in a MS. account, preserved in the Cotton library, of the number of ships in the different ports on the eastern coast of the kingdom, Ipswich had six vessels, employing 190 men; Woodbridge six, with only 18 men; Aldborough fifty-four, with 120 men; Dunwic-h fourteen, with 80 men; Southwold twenty, with 100 men; and Yarmouth fifty-five, with 541 men: by which it will be seen that the tonnage of the other vessels bore no proportion to those of Ipswich. In 1596, in the expedition against Cadiz, consisting of upwards of ninety sail of ships and transports, under the command of the earl of Essex, and Charles Lord Howard, of Effingham, lord high admiral, the "Corslet," of Ipswich, carrying 40 mariners and 100 soldiers, Captain Herrick, and the " James," of Ipswich, with 44 mariners and 100 soldiers, Captain Devrie, were attached to the lord admiral's squadron. It appears that Sir Richard WingTield lost his life fighting valiantly on land, on this occasion.

In 1711, the "Ipswich," a seventy-gun ship, was in port at Woolwich—where she was built is uncertain; she was taken to pieces in 1727, and rebuilt in 1730. This was, most probably, the ship of the same name and number of guns, with a crew of 446 men, Captain George Townsend, that formed part of the combined fleet of the English and Dutch, when they insulted and annoyed the whole coast of France, in the year 1696.

The "Ipswich" is also mentioned as being in active service from 1704 to 1711. She is again mentioned at the conclusion of the war, 1748; and was broken up between that period and 1756.

In 1605, James I. confirmed all former charters by an inspeximus dated at Westminster, April 3rd, in the second year of his reign. This was also done by Charles I. March 11th, 1634, in the tenth year of his reign.

In 1618, a charge of 30s. is entered, for a person going with a horse which the king of Denmark sent to his majesty, James I.

In 1641, the earl of Coventry, lord keeper of the great seal, paid a visit to Ipswich, and was escorted in and out of town by the corporation and the train-bands.—In the chamberlain's accounts, is a receipt from Goodman Mumfrye, "for his boye's drawing bloud of the maide in the house, 3s. 4d."

The "Annals of Ipswich," by Bacon, supply materials, collected from official documents, up to the year 1649; which documents are now, most of them, lost or destroyed, except the charters which are preserved in the treasury; and we next come to the examination of the court books of the corporation, which commence with the year 1643, so that, fortunately, no chasm intervenes. We must, necessarily, put this part of our narration somewhat into the form of a journal, in order to preserve the regularity of dates; and we must likewise detail what some perhaps will think rather too minute particulars of the proceedings of the corporate body; but as we expect, of course, that every free burgess of Ipswich will be anxious to possess himself of our valuable work, w e must endeavour to cater for the appetites of all our numerous readers; and as we well know that some of our brother burgesses would sooner part with their life than with their *freedom,* it is but right to pay due deference to men of such exalted purity and principle; and, in spite of the injury done to our sight in deciphering some of the almost hieroglyphical writing of our forefathers, we have extracted w-hat we conceived might be matter of interest; by which it will appear that

our ancestors were quite as fond of *quo warrantos* and *writs of mandamus* as their successors are at the present day; and we conceive that this part of our history of the corporation will be the more interesting, as it has never before appeared in print.

In 1643, a number of the burgesses were fined 2s. 6d. each for not attending at a great court; whereas they are now paid 2s. 6d. each for their attendance.

In 1648, great alarm was excited on this coast by the depredations of pirates; the train-bands and auxiliary horse and foot were drawn out of the town to Cattawade bridge, and the town was guarded by seamen. At this time there was a great scarcity of corn in this part of the kingdom, being so dear that the bailiffs, &c. sent to London for a supply of grain for the consumption of the poor inhabitants of the town.

But little of note is to be met with respecting the town during the time of the Commonwealth. There is a very scarce pamphlet in the library of Lambeth palace, respecting the Protector having sent down two anabaptist preachers, Knowles and Griffin, to Ipswich, dated January 22nd, 1648; and another tract, in the British museum, dated 1641, relating to the conduct of some domineering lordly prelates who had introduced some abominable practices here, to undermine the church. And we have seen an order signed by Oliver, Protector, for an embargo upon all the shipping in the port, and for impressing seamen, directed as under.

"6th Feh. 1654.

To Bailiffs of Ipswich,

And all other Officers of that Port, These,

Ipswich.

For the special service of the State.

Hast.

Hast.

Post Hast."

And several of his dispatches were indorsed with —

' Hast.

Post Hast.

Hast for your life." 1654. Great damage having lately befallen to the town by fire, it is ordered that all straw-kilns

in this town shall be suppressed. John Camplin, a foreigner, was admitted a free burgess, on paying a fine of £20; which proves that the honour of being a freeman could then be had for money.

August 20th, 1657, the different town marshes were let for £122, which appears a large sum at that period, and we know not how much they are since increased.

At a great court, November 4th, 1658, we observe the following judicious orders for the regulation of speech, which are not unworthy of attention even in these enlightened times:—" Ordered that no person shall speak in the great court, but shall first come and direct his speech to Mr. Bailiffs, and not to speak above once or twice to any one business without licence of Mr. Bailiffs; and no person to speak whilst any other is a speaking, upon pain to forfeit, for each offence, twelve pence. And that no one is to depart the court till the business is finished, without licence from the bailiffs, upon pain of forfeiting one shilling and sixpence."

December 16th, 1658, it is ordered that £40, arising from Mr. Snow's and Mr. Tyler's charities, be expended in the buying of books and apparel and binding out, as apprentices, eight poor boys, after being two years at the grammar school, that is to say, to each of them £3. We suppose that this is now only applicable to the boys at Christ's hospital.—This year the duke of York, afterward James II., visited the town, and a dinner was provided by the corporation for him and his suite.

May 20th, 1660. At this court it is ordered that a present of £300, out of the treasury of this town, and as much more as can be obtained by the voluntary subscription of the freemen of this town, be presented in gold, or some thing else, at the discretion of the persons here-under named, to our gracious sovereign lord, king Charles II., as a token of the duty of allegiance of this town; and that the Bailiff Sorrel, Mr. Robert Sparrowe, Henry Cosens, Thomas Wright, and Robert Clarke, shall carry and present the same; and that Mr. Nathaniel Bacon,

Mr. Francis Bacon, and Mr. John Sicklemore, and such others as Mr. Bailiff and Mr. Sparrowe shall think fit, shall go along with them to his majesty, and that their charges shall be borne by the town. And that Mr. Nathaniel Bacon, Mr. Francis Bacon, and Mr. John Sicklemore, shall consider whether an address in writing, or by word of mouth, shall be delivered at the same time to his majesty; and, if in writing, then to draw the same, and Mr. Francis Bacon to sign the same, in the name of the bailiffs, burgesses, and commonalty of this town.

A subscription was set on foot which amounted, we suppose, to something like £50; for at this same court we find the corporation borrowed £250 of four individuals, upon the security of the marshes called "Portman's Meadows." And that most likely, on presentation of the gift, Mr. Bailiff Sorrel preferred delivering an oral address, for he received the honour of knighthood upon this memorable occasion, as we find *Miles* attached to his name ever afterwards.

In November, this year, we find only one bailiff, and he served alone till the 29th of September following; which may be accounted for by the following extract:— "Whereas Mr. (now elect) Aldtis being sent for to come and take his oath of bailiff of this town, he not being well sent word he could not come up; whereupon the court doth order that Mr. Aldus shall take his oath at the next petty court." But we suppose he did not recover, for his name does not appear afterwards, and Mr. Lucas Jones served the office alone.

In the year 1663, an order was made for the treasurer and chamberlains to pay for a pulpit cloth and cushion for the Tower church; and likewise for the entertaining of the Bishop of Norwich.

At another court, Andrew Sorrel, esq. and John Robinson, gent. are chosen portmen, in the room and place of Robert Jennings and Henry Whiting, discharged by his majesty's commissioners for not subscribing according to the act for the regulation of corporations. Four other members of the corporation were discharged for a similar reason.—At this court the right honourable Joannes, earl of Suffolk, lord lieutenant of the county, is elected high steward; and a yearly annuity of £10 is granted him.

At a great court held May 7th, this year, is the following order:—" Agreed by this court that every freeman of this town shall subscribe the declaration for the removing of the covenant, which declaration is expressed in the act of parliament made the thirteenth year of his majesty's reign that now is entitled 'An act for the well ordering and regulating of corporations;' and if any refuse, he shall have no right in any great court to be holden for this town, until he have subscribed the same." At the end of the court book is the following form of declaration.

"I, A. B. do declare that I hold that there lies no obligation upon me, or any other person, from the oath commonly called 'The solemn League and Covenant;' and that the same was in itself an unlawful oath, and imposed upon the subjects of this realm against the known laws and liberties of this kingdom.

May 1th, 1663. RICHARD PEYTON."

And after the date of June 16th, 1663, are the signatures of thirty-seven free burgesses — five of whom set their marks. On the 8th of September following are seventeen other signatures — three of whom set their marks. On the 27th of February, 1664, eight more signatures — one with a mark. On the 29th of September, 1667, three more. And so late as the 13th of May, 1679, are the signatures of Miles Wallis and E. Gravenor.

On the first leaf of the book is an entry, dated October 18th, 1691—" That this book was exhibited to Mr. Robert Clarke upon the examination to the third interr. on the accounts thereto, by William Flack, J, Freeman, J. Harrison, and James Gibson, commissioners.

In this year, 1663, is inserted the following curious order of the court:—" Ordered that for the better preservation of children which are walking or playing in the common streets of this town, that every person coming with cart or tumbril, shall, for the time coming, lead the horse of such team in such manner that one wheel may roll on one side of the channel, and the other on the other side: and such as offend herein shall forfeit 12d. for the use of the poor. And no person shall ride upon any cart or tumbril in this town, under pain of forfeiting 12d. for each offence."

At this court, 1664, John Wright and Richard Drayle are discharged from being portmen, for not subscribing the declaration; and several other burgesses on the like account. And the following order is issued:—" Whereas the ancient government and order of this town hath been, in these late distracted times much broken and altered; and, for the establishing of some of the said ancient orders, for the better governing of the town, it is ordered and agreed as follows. First, that the bailiffs, portmen, town clerk, and twenty-four men, shall, for the time to come, appear at every great court, assembly) and sessions, with their maces, in their black gowns, upon pain that the portmen shall forfeit, for every default, each of them make 3s. ; aad for the town clerk and four-and-twenty, 2s. to be levied by distress: the months of June, July, and August, as to the wearing their gowns in assemblys, only excepted, in regard of the heat of the weather." Here follows a string of resolutions respecting the attendance of the corporate body at church, with the fines for absence without leave of the bailiffs.

In this year the portmen and twenty-four men are ordered to fill up their respective numbers. And it is ordered that any officer of the corporation found in any ale-house playing at cards, dice, hide tables, or other unlawful games, shall lose his place, and be further dealt with at law, as a great court shall think fit. By which it will be seen that these worthies in office were kept strictly to their good behaviour.

In the year 1665, Mr. Bailiff Sparrow e is ordered to prepare a banquet for the duke of York, and to entertain him at his house: for which he was paid.

At this time no one could open a shop

in the town, except a freeman, without paying a fine of one shilling. And no mechanic could exercise his trade or calling, unless he paid sixpence to the corporation. And a committee was annually appointed, to see that the fines were duly collected.

In the year 1666 it was "Agreed that, in regard that the town is visited with the sickness, there shall be no fair kept the fourteenth day of this inst. September. Agreed that in regard of the increase of the plague and pestilence, causing great misery amongst us, and the major part of the inhabitants being out of town, that the rates made cannot be gathered, the charges bein so great that this town is not able to relieve them; and there be right certificates made to the justices of the peace of this county, to assess the inhabitants within five miles, for and towards this place. The court doth therefore agree to borrow of Mr. Robert Sparrowe, Mr. John Wright, Mr. Henry Cosens, and Mr. Robert Clarke, £300, for a year; and to give them security by Handford Hall lands. And that the mortgage of the said lands, now had for their security, shall be sealed at this present court; and, accordingly, is sealed." The magistrates did not neglect their fellowtownsmen at this melancholy period; for, at this time of affliction, a man and woman were appointed to search for persons havin the plague, and to render them what service was possible. All public funerals were prohibited, and the bell was to toll only a quarter of an hour before any burial took place; and every precaution was taken to prevent the spreading of the contagion.

At this period the Quakers suffered much persecution in various parts of the kingdom. The five following persons, of that sect, were imprisoned at Ipswich; viz. William Brown, Edwd. Milksopp, Thos. Milksopp, James Tailor, and John Tomson. And there is a letter in the possession of Mr. Batley, from Robert Duncon.-who had been more than once bailiff of the town, dated Feb. 6th, 1666. The direction is torn off, and it is not known to whom it was addressed: but the writer begins by styling the person " Friend and observing that he is informed that the liberating these poor people rests entirely with him: he therefore conjures him to be merciful, for that rigorous persecution for religion's sake was not likely to procure the favour of almighty God in staying the ravages of the plague, and that it could not be necessary for political security; for he understood that, at York, the archbishop had greatly exerted himself with the justices there, and had procured the liberation of the Quakers that had been imprisoned in that city: and he intreated that he might not be allowed to plead in vain.

On the first of August, 1668, Charles II. paid a visit to the Lord Hereford; and dined at Christ's Church. On his arrival, he was waited upon by the body corporate; who were escorted by the militia companies then in the town, as far as the court yard; when the bailiffs entered the house, with their maces under their arms, and, on their knees, presented them to his majesty; who took them, and returned them to the bailiffs; who, after kissing the king's hand, retired. His majesty departed immediately he had dined 5 when the bailiffs and the corporation, bareheaded, and mounted on horseback, accompanied by a large train of gentlemen, escorted the king as far as Broke's Hall; when his majesty left them. They returned to the town, and entertained the king's retinue who were left behind, at dinher. And the chief gentlemen of the household applied to the bailiffs for certain *fees of homage,* which amounted to £39:12:8; which, of course, they cheerfully paid, for the honour of kissing the hand of this ' merry monarch;' who suffered his servants to be as thoughtlessly profligate as himself. The bailiffs had also to pay extravagantly for ale, sack, ahd other refreshments, for the life-guards and train-bands who escorted the king.

In 1672, it is agreed that the council-chamber, and rooms near and under the same, shall be pulled down; and shall be rebuilt, at the charge of the town, as wide and as large as the common hall, and larger: and that the bailiffs, with sundry persons named, shall agree and treat with any persons respecting it, and make report of the same.

In 1674, an order of court is made to receive the sum of £104, due from the city of Bristol, since 1659, on account of Sir Thomas White's charity. An order was also made, that Mr. Robert Clarke shall have allowed him twenty nobles, for the great trouble he has had in quartering the soldiers.

This year, upon the petition of many poor people to Mr. Bailiffs, who have quartered sundry seamen, humbly requesting their aid in the endeavouring to obtain the money due to them for quartering of such seamen, which amounts to about £1200, this court doth agree that, at the charge of the town, application shall be made to his majesty in their behalf.

In the year 1675, Andrew Sorrel, esq. died in his bailiwick; and John Wright was chosen bailiff in his room, to serve till Michaelmas.

The following is an extract from the journal of Phineas Pett, afterwards Sir Phineas Pett, and commissioner at Chatham. It was a detail of his proceedings in company with Sir Anthony Deane, lent. in a journey made into the counties of Suffolk and Norfolk, for the buying up all such timber and plank as they found fit for his majesty's service, towards building thirty ships, by act of parliament, the 29th of May, 1677.

"After we had done at Harwich, we went over to Shotley, in Suffolk, to Sir Henry Felton's. When we came thither, my lady acquainted us that Sir Henry was very ill, and could not be spoke with; which, we conceived, was rather his backwardness not to speak with us; for that my lady told us Sir Henry thought himself not engaged to sell us the timber, and could have more for it; upon which we desired to know his pleasure, by Saturday, at Ipswich,

"Friday, 1st of June. We met with Sir Francis Mannock, at Ipswich, and contracted with him for his timber, being sixty large trees, at £3: 4: 0 per load, on the place.

"Saturday 2nd. In the morning, we visited the shipwrights' yards, to buy what timber we could light on: which was done accordingly. In the afternoon we contracted with Sir Henry Felton for his timber, at Shotley, Playford, and Buckleston. We also received an account from Mr. Cary, Mr. Gingy, and Mr. Cooper, of what provision they had found in the country.

"Monday 4th. We went from Ipswich to Woodbridge; where we agreed for a quantity of four, three, and two-inch plank. Called on the Widow Gulledge, and marked out several pieces of compass timber; which we bought of her. We also bought of Henry Cole, a parcel of four and three-inch plank. In the afternoon we went to Otley, to view Sir Anthony Deane's timber; and gave directions for carriage, and coverlin. From thence we went to Wickham, and lay there that night.

"Friday 15th. We went from Redgrave to Thornhall, to Capt. Paul Buckman, where we viewed 170 top trees, which we conceived would make 240 load of timber: it is very good and sound — few boughs fit for service: it is fifteen miles from Ipswich: he would sell them standing—asks £600, as he says it was valued at: we bid him £35 per load on the place—he would not take it: at last he promised to consider of it,, and meet us at Ipswich, on Monday, and, if he can, to agree for it. From thence we went to Sir Charles Gaudy's, at Crowfield Hall, and lay there that night.

"Saturday 16th. We went over the grounds of Sir Charles Gaudy, and viewed his grove: promised faithfully he would sell to his majesty, next spring, 300 or 350 of his best trees in the grove, at the market price, goodness considered, but would set no price now, only assures us, if he lives, we shall have it. From Crow's Hall we went to Otley; where we found the carriers carrying away a stern post for the new ship at Harwich, and the rest converting on the ground as fast as could be. From thence we departed, and lay at Ipswich that night.

"Sunday 17th. We rested at Ipswich.

"Monday 18th." After some agreements for planks, &c. he proceeds—" We spent the rest of the day in filling up warrants for impressing of men, and

for land carriage, to the justices of the peace, whither timber is to be carried, and writing letters unto the board. Lay at Ipswich that night.

"Tuesday. This morning we agreed with one Moor, at Ipswich, to carry what timber his vessel can stow, into Harwich, at 2s. 6d. per load. In the afternoon I departed from Ipswich, for Lee, in Essex, and Sir Anthony Deane for Harwich. I agreed with Sir Anthony Deane for his timber at Otley, for 55s. per load, delivered at Ipswich, at 47s. on the place. About 7 at night I got to Colchester, where I lay, at the King's Head, that night; and from thence returned with Sir Anthony to London."

In the seventeenth year of Charles II. 1678, in order to rectify some irregularities, and settle some disputes which had arisen in the preceding times of confusion, particularly with regard to the election of portmen, and the twentyfour chief constables or common council, he granted a charter in which he confirmed the high steward, the twelve portmen, the twenty-four chief constables, the recorder, and town clerk, for the time being, by their names; and directed, that upon the death or removal of one or more of the portmen or chief constables, that the vacancy should be filled up by the rest or residue, &c. of their respective bodies. This charter is very long, and confirms all the preceding charters, except the express directions which are given for the election of the different officers of the corporation; and is the charter under which the business and acts of the corporation are now done and executed.

1679. Agreed, that whereas there was absolute necessity for new building the mill at Handford, and of repairing the mill at Stoke — which, by estimation, will come to £250 — this court agrees to borrow of Mr. Town Clerk, the sum of £200, for one year; for which he shall have a mortgage of Handford Hall lands, by way of lease, for ninety years, to be sealed at some petty court; the money to be disposed of in the building of the mill, and other town business, as the bailiffs shall think fit to order.— And at this court it is agreed that the

right honourable the earl of Arlington shall be admitted a free burgess.

In 1682, Christopher, duke of Albermarle, was elected a free burgess. Sir John Barker, lord of the manor of Walton and Trimley, enfranchised all the copyhold lands formerly given to the town by Mr. Smart.

1683. The twenty-four men not attending the assembly, to forfeit three shillings and sixpence.

April the 3rd, 1685, an address was ordered to be presented to his majesty, by the bailiffs, Sir John Barker, and as many of the portmen as please, declaring their abhorrence of " that model of treason, anarchy, and confusion, styled an association, lately produced at the trial of the earl of Shaftesbury;" and likewise offering their lives and fortunes, in support of his majesty's sacred person, his heirs, and lawful successors.

On the 13th of July, this year, the following address was presented to his majesty; which we insert at length, on account of the curiosity of iucLiction.

"*To the King's most excellent Majesty.* Oread Sovereign,

We, the bailiffs, burgesses, aud commonalty of the ancient corporation of Ipswich, have heard of the late detested conspiracy against the precious life of your sacred majesty, and your dearest brother—whether with greater amazement or abomination, we cannot say — but, sure we are, it is and must be the eternal shame and reproach of that party and sort of men amongst whom such villany and misconduct 6nd nursery and encouragement, as could not be satisfied with the blood and gore of one king of blessed memory, but were proceeding (in a short ration of the same age) to gorge their cannibal appetites upon a second. The natural consequences of this hideous parricide must have been (in all respect of reason) the spoiling your majesty's three kingdoms of their present tranquility, plenty, ease, government, and excellent religion, and turning them into so many great shambles, and being of utmost ruin and confusion. A reflection hereupon (we trust) will establish your majesty's liege people (except those whose malice is desperate) in principles and practices of loyalty, and obedience to authority. For ourselves, we first thank, with solemn adoration, the great King of angels and men, for favouring and vouching his own ordinance, as well by former as by this new signal deliverance of his Anointed. Our fortunes aud live, (which, had the conspiracy taken its horrible effects, might, by this time, not have been our own) we, next, repeatedly vow and prostrate to the service of your sacred majesty, your heirs and successors, and the defence of the government, as now established, in church and state: which we shall be always ready religiously to make good against all fanatical associations, or other rebels whatever. In testimony whereof, we have annexed our common seal, this thirteenth day of July, in the five-and-thirtieth year of your majesty's gracious reign,—whom God almighty long aud long preserve."

On the 29th of September, Mr. Richard Kedder, minister of St. Martin s Oustrip, in London, was chosen town preacher, with a salary of £120 a year. But it appears that this court was not legal, tor Mr. Kedder did not hold the preacher's place under it; for, on the 7th of January following, Dr. Mapletoft was elected. At the same time, Mr. Charles Wright was chosen one of the bailiffs, in room of Mr. John Wright, deceased.

1685. At this period the affairs of the corporation were in an intricate and distracted state—which was not peculiar to this borough—for, from their constant jarrings and litigations, the government took an opportunity of threatening many of the boroughs in the kingdom with the severity of the king's displeasure; and the corporation of Ipswich, intimidated by proceedings instituted against them in the King's Bench, followed the example of many other towns, and gave up their charter to the king. And at a great court, the 26th day of March, 1685, it was agreed to surrender the charter of the corporation into his majesty's hands, and petition for a new charter; and that certain persons should draw up a petition to be presented.

Upon Mr. Bailiff Wright's request to be discharged of his bailiffs place, for special reasons by him offered to this court, he is, accordingly, discharged from his bailiff's place from this day.

On the 2nd of April, the following petition was read:—

"TO THE KING'S MOST EXCELLENT MAJESTY.

"*The humble petition of the Bailiffs, Unryesses, and Commonalty of Ipswich, in all humility sheweth to your sacred Majesty,*

"That they are, with great regret and sorrow, sensible of their many miscarriages in the government of your said town, and in the misuse of those great favours and privileges which your majesty's royal predecessors have so freely conferred upon them, and, that by such miscarriages they have justly incurred your majesty's displeasure. Having, therefore, had so many comfortable experiences of your majesty's goodness and benevolence to all your subjects, the petitioners, with all submission, throw themselves at your majesty's feet, humbly begging your gracious pardon, and willingly resigning their charter and privilege into your majesty's hands, who so freely bestowed them; dutifully, also, imploring your wonted kindness and favour to this your ancient corporation, that your majesty may be graciously pleased to consult the reasonable and good government of the said town, and provide for the due disposal and employment of those many gifts and charities as herewith, by the bounty of many benefactors, it hath been intrusted. By which your majesty's most clement favour, you will, thirdly, oblige your humble petitioners, not only to be very tender of all your favours and bounties, but, as their bounden duty is, to be ever faithful and constant in their loyalty and allegiance to your sacred majesty, your heirs and successors, And ever to pray."

Agreed, that the petition now read shall be sealed with the common seal of this town at this court; and, accordingly, it is sealed: and that Sir John Barker, bart., Sir Robert Broke, bart., Capt. Neave, and John Blomfield, gent., are deputed to present this grant, and surrender it to his majesty, or to such person or persons as his majesty shall appoint to receive the same.

On the 28th day of July, a new charter was received; and the following persons were appointed, by name, by the authority of this charter, to fill the offices of the corporation.

With others named, but not present. Sir Henry Felton, bart., and John Burrough, were appointed bailiffs under this charter.

Sir Rohert Broke, hart., *Recorder.* Christopher Milton, *Deputy Recorder.* Thomas Brook, *Town Clerk.*

This charter, dated July 8th, 1685, deprived the freemen of all their rights and privileges, and vested the whole command of the corporation in the bailiffs, portmen, and common-council; and power was reserved, that the crown might, by an order of council, turn out any of the portmen or common-council, when and as often as his majesty or his successors might think proper; which power was, several times after, put in force. Though the burgesses received this charter, and acted under it, for three years, until 1688, yet the surrender of the town was not enrolled, nor was any judgment entered upon record upon the *quo warranto* brought against the corporation in the reign of king Charles II. Therefore, at the time of the landing of the prince of Orange, James II. by a proclamation and act in council, dated at Whitehall, the 17th of October, 1688, annulled it, and restored the corporations to their ancient charters, declaring the several deeds of surrender as informal and illegal. In consequence of this proclamation, the bailiffs, portmen, and twenty-fourmen who had acted under the charter of the 17th of Charles II. resumed their functions and filled up their bodies, respectively; the rights of the fre.e burgesses were restored, and from these portmen, and these twenty-fourmen are the present portmen, and the present twentyfour-men derived: and under this charter are the affairs of the corporation conducted. The principal officers of the corporation now are, two bailiffs, a high steward, a recorder, twelve portmen, of whom four are assistant justices, appointed by the bailiff's when they are sworn into office, a town-clerk, twenty-four common-council-men, two of whom are coroners, twelve of them head-boroughs or chief constables, and three clavigers; also a town treasurer, and two chamberlains. The corporation have likewise fifteen inferior or livery servants, consisting of five musicians, four Serjeants at mace, two beadles, a common crier, a water-bailiff, a gaoler, and a bridewell-keeper. Their functions, and the power of the bailiffs, &c. will be more particularly defined in that portion of the volume describing the present state of the town.

There is also a court of Small Pleas, for the town and borough of Ipsw ich, which has peculiar powers. This court, by prescription, has cognizance of all debts to any amount; but, until the reign of Henry III. not one record of the court of pleas can be found, owing to the flight of John Blake, a perfidious town-clerk, who carried away the same; so as, of all the pleas in former times, not more than four small rolls, and those in the latter part of the reign, are now left.

The first entry found is in the thirty-ninth year of Henry III. "A debt acknowledged before the bailiffs in court, and, for non-payment, a distress to be taken by the bailiffs' order, of all goods and chattels in the liberty of Ipswich belonging to the debtor; and under penalty of £5 to the bailiffs' use, if it be not payde."

"34th Edward I. An action of debt between Robert Tillet and Roger Patchett, merchants, for 17 marks, Cs. 8d., commenced originally, and was tried in the town court without the king's writ, and the king's writ comme, and injoin execution." And in the writ it is expressly mentioned, that the trial was according to the custom of the town without the king's writ.

From this time processes have been uniformly granted by the bailiffs, for debts to any amount, originally, and without the king's writ. Affidavits to hold to bail are taken before the bailiffs for the time being, and writs are granted by the town-clerk, in the name of the bailiffs. There are four attornies of this court.

In the 13th of George II. an act was passed for allowing magistrates of boroughs to exercise the same power of levying the Marshalsea rate in their jurisdiction, as had, the year before, been granted to the county magistrates. It! is hardly necessary to premise, that this rate is levied upon the inhabitants in general, for defraying the expenses incident to the erection and government of prisons — maintaining and removing prisoners—repairing of bridges — billeting of soldiers, and carrying their baggage from one town to another, coroners' fees, &c. &c. There is no peculiar privilege or power, in this respect, attached to the borough of Ipswich; but no order can be executed under this act, except by the authority of the magistates present'at the general sessions of the peace for the borough; and as the present four assistant justices form a permanent majority, they have the power, and'exercise it accordingly, of filling up all the appointments—such as jailor, surgeon, and chaplain to the prison, treasurer to the Marshalseaj &c. &d. in the manner most agreeable to themselves and friends.

The Court of Requests was instituted by an act passe'd in 1807, and consists of the corporate body, and fifty-six other inhabitants; who meet every Tuesday, on the town hall, and take cognizance of all debts not exceeding £5. There" is no appeal from their decision. This court not only applies to constant residents, but it is immaterial where the debt accrued due, provided the debtor is a trader, of in any Way a dealer in the town at the time he is summoned.

The extensive privileges and jurisdiction of the cOrporation have been before enumerated and explained; and there were several ancient usages and customs peculiar to the place, all of which have fallen into disuse, except the following, which have sometimes been acted upon.

Upon an alienation of seisin of tenements, in the said town, delivered to a purchaser, the wife of the vendor may come into court, and being solely examined before the bailiffs, may acknowlege that alienation to be done with her consent; and that recognizance being enrolled, operates as a fine, and passes the estate of the feme covert.

All those that have lands and tenements in the town, whether male or female, who can reckon, count, and measure, having completed the age of fourteen years, may give his or her land or freehold, or sell it, or let it, and of his or her right, quit claim for evermore, as if he or she had accomplished the age of twenty-one years.

A woman covert may be compelled to answer in a plea of trespass, on pain of imprisonment, in like manner as she would were she sole, so that the trespass be personal and touch not freehold.

Most of the privileges and exemptions from tolls, &c. of which our worthy free-burgesses are so wont to boast, have, from the lapse of time, and enacting of new laws and regulations, become nearly nonentities, and of little service or utility.

Either from a desire of condensing their power into few hands, or from some extraordinary error or neglect, the portmen did not fill up the vacancies that occurred from time to time in their own body, till they were reduced to seven; when, some time after the death of Mr. Henry Seekamp and Mr. John Spooner, two of their number, in 1820, they proceeded to choose Sir William Middleton, bart., and Mr. Stephen Abbott Notcutt, in their room; but it was determined in the court of King's Bench, that the words in the charter of the 17th of Charles II., where it is stated, "that any vacancy occurring in the number of the twelve portmen, shall be filled up by the rest or residue, or the greater part of them," meant the majority of the number twelve; and as, at the death of the two before-mentioned gentlemen, the number of portmen was reduced to five — four only of whom concurred in that election — the majority of twelve was lost, and, in consequence, they had not the power of choosing any new portmen; therefore, the election they had made was null and void. Thus the charter must, in a few years, naturally expire, for there will not be a sufficient number of portmen left to constitute a great court for transacting the business of the corporation; when it will be necessary to procure a writ of mandamus to fill up the number, or a new charter must be obtained; in which case it will be desirable for both parties to prevent the non-resident freemen from interfering in the election for the officers of the corporation, for the system of bringing them annually from all parts of the country, has, of late years, been carried to a ruinous extent; and it would likewise be proper to prevent any person from obtaining his freedom by servitude, unless he had duly and truly served his apprenticeship to a free burgess residing within the liberties of the borough, for the freedom being now obtained by apprenticeship to a free burgess, resident or non-resident, it opens the door to much fraud and abuse, and many have procured their freedom in a surreptitious and unlawful manner. This might, even now, be, in a great measure, prevented by not granting the freedom by servitude, unless the indentures were enrolled and registered in the town clerk's office within a stated time after the indenture was executed. The freedom is likewise acquired by patrimony, all the sons of a free burgess being entitled to their fran4 chise, unless born before their father had taken up his freedom at a great court; but it would surely be better to enact that all the sons of a free burgess should be entitled to their freedom, whether their father should have taken up his freedom or not, for it appears unjust to deprive a child of the advantages of his birth-right for the omission of an act which, perhaps, his father might have had no opportunity of performing; and which has happened, in several instances, where a soldier or sailor has been absent, fighting the battles of his country. All the sons of the gallant Sir Philip Broke have lost their franchise in this manner.

At the time of the Revolution, Lord Dumbarton's regiment, 1300 strong, was quartered here; and they marched out of the town, towards Scotland, with their arms and four pieces of cannon. King William immediately sent two Dutch regiments and a regiment of horse in pursuit of them. The officers were exceedingly desirous to fight it out, though the Dutchmen were four times as strong; but the soldiers, after some little parley, quietly marched back again, and submitted to king William.

At this period there appeared to be no regular time for choosing the bailiffs; for several elections took place in the years 1687 and 1688.

By virtue of a letter from his royal highness the prince of Orange, dated the 29th of September, 1688, it was agreed that Sir Henry Felton, bart., Sir John Barker, bart., and Peyton Ventris, esq. , be put in nomination for burgesses in parliament: and on a poll being demanded, the numbers were as follow:—

Sir Henry Felton. hart 53

Sir John Barker, hart..... I 7O

Peyton Ventri, esq 169

Whereupon, the two latter were declared duly elected: and here we have the first instance of a contested election for representatives for the borough. Thus the gauntlet of contention was thrown into the midst of the corporation, and many a battle has ensued, hardly fought, and *dearly* won, and, we are sorry to say, that, in several instances, not without the shedding of blood. Mr. Ventris was, soon after, made a judge; and Sir Charles Blois wag elected in his room.

January 16th, 1689, Charles Lord Cornwallis was chosen a free burgess. On the 18th of February following, an election for burgesses to serve in parliament took place; and, on a poll being demanded, the numbers were —

Sir John Barker, hart 143

Sir Charles Blois, hait 110

John Hodges, esq 49

Charles Whittaker, esq... 103

Whereupon the two former were declared duly elected.

September 8th, 1690. Agreed, that the bailiffs that are to be chosen this day, shall be out of four portmen and two free burgesses. And, upon choice, there being a poll demanded, the poll is as followeth:—

Mr. Tye had 38 votes, heing a portman.

Mr. John Bloinfield 39 ditto

Mr. John Burrough 2 ditto

Mr. William Neav-e 3 ditto

Mr. Richard Puplett 112 votes, heing a freeman.

Mr. Rohert Manning 110 ditto

Here we have the first instance of anv of the twenty-four men becoming bailiffs; they had, previous to this time, been chosen from the portmen. And in this the first contest for bailiffs, the free burgesses carried it with a high hand against the portmen.

On the 9th of December, this year, a committee was appointed to receive proposals respecting the linen manufactory; and it was agreed that the town shall furnish the linen corporation with a convenient work-house for carrying on the trade, gratis; and they shall have such work-house, rent-free. And if the said corporation should think fit to set up a bleachery in or near the town, that the town will furnish them at a reasonable rate. And that the common hoymen shall he obliged to tarry the goods belonging to these trades, at very moderate and reasonable rates. And that Mr. Snelling shall go to London to treat with the corporation of the linen manufacture.

It was agreed, July 31st, 1690, that several persons named shall go about the town and gather the voluntary sums of money the inhabitants shall give for defraying the expense of the assizes, to be held here the 7th of September next; and that a committee be appointed to enquire what is fit and requisite to allow the judges at their coming to this town. And, also, to examine into the charter of king Charles II. concerning the election of officers, and to make report thereupon. And, on the 13th of August, it was agreed that a booth shall be built for the judges of the assize, by Mr. Norris, to be thirty feet wide, and the length proportionable — to be paid £8 for the same. That the judges that come the circuit shall be at Mr. John Sparrowe's house; and Mr. Sparrowe to have £5 for the lodging of the judges paid him by the treasurer of the town. And that the bailiffs do take care for the treating of the judges with respect, and to do as they shall think fit and reasonable therein.

The bailiffs, with a great train of gentlemen, met the judge and escorted him into the town.

Sept. 6th, Edward Nevill Knight, one of the barons of the exchequer, and judge of the assizes, is chosen a freeman.

June 30th, 1691. Agreed, that the bailiffs, Mr. Recorder, and Mr. Town Clerk, are desired to make such allowance of meat, fish, bread, and beer, for the reception of the judges, as they shall think fit, at the charge of the town; and that Mr. Sparrowe shall be allowed £5 for lodging the judges, and their servants, at the next assizes. And that the council-chamber and booth shall be made ready, and half the charge to be borne by the town.

July 8th, Mr. John Blomfield and Mr. William Tye were discharged from their office of portmen, for neglect and non-attendance. Charles Lord Cornwallis was chosen high steward. Agreed, that the charges that were laid out for the entertaining the soldiers that came from Holland, and were forced to this town, shall be allowed by Mr. Bailiffs. Great sickness, or some epidemic disease, perhaps something like what was prevalent in our army at the time of the Walcheren expedition, prevailed amongst these troops; and a house formerly the Elephant and Castle, was fitted up as an hospital for their reception: a great mortality took place whilst they remained here: and there is a tradition that an elevated piece of ground behind the shire-hall is the place where the bodies were deposited; and, on recently digging the foundations for some houses now erecting by William Lane, esq., our present bailiff, a great many human bones have been found, not lying in regular order as in consecrated ground, but transversely, in various directions, as if they had been promiscuously heaped together. It has likewise been stated that this was one of the burial-places for those persons who died of the plague; but we are inclined to think that the magistrates would not have suffered the bodies of those w ho died of such a pestilential disease to be buried in the

very heart of the town. It is certain that great quantities of bones have been discovered on this spot; and the probability is, that they are the remains of the Dutch soldiers.

On the 26th of May, 1692, it was ngreed to present a petition to His Majesty, respecting the repairing of the custom-house. July 24th, lord chief justice Holt was chosen a freeman.

November 28th, 1693, it was agreed that fifty families of French protestants that manufacture lutestring, shall be admitted inhabitants in this town; and they shall have 20s. each family; and the charges of coming to the town shall be found by the town: and they shall have a chnrch minded for them, and allowance for their minister of £20 a-year, for two years; and that they shall not be rated nor put into any office for seven years: and that Mr. Snelling shall go to London to treat with the Frenchmen about this business.

This year an order was issued from government, for the town to fit out a ship of war; but they were unable, for lack of money and mariners.

King William was at Ipswich, this year; and it cost the town £30: 19: 5 for his entertainment.

16th of May, 1695. Agreed, that the address to His Majesty, now read, for his safe deliverance from his enemies that would have murdered him, shall be forthwith sealed with the common seal of this town, and sent up to London to the recorder, to be by him presented to His Majesty. The right honourable the Lord Cornwallis shall be desired, by letter from the bailiffs, to assist the recorder in the delivery thereof.

Agreed, that any freeman suffering any foreigner to sell upon his premises, any grocery, books, pictures, or other wares, he shall forfeit his freedom; and any innkeeper suffering the same, shall forfeit his licence.

The following was the population of Ipswich at this period, as taken upon an act of parliament for burials, marriages, and births. By which it appears that the male population of the town was nearly double that of the female.

In the reign of William III. there resided

at Ipswich, a family which, from the number of peculiarities belonging to it, was distinguished by the name of the " odd family." Every event remarkably good or bad happened to this family on an odd day of the month, and every member had something odd in his or her person, manner, and behaviour;— the very letters in their Christian names always happened to be an odd number— the husband's name was Peter, and the wife's, Rabah;—they had seven children, all boys, viz. Solomon, Roger, James, Matthew, Jonas, David, and Ezekiel;—the husband had but one leg, his wife but one arm, Solomon was born blind of one eye, and Roger lost his sight by accident, James had his left ear bit off by a boy in a quarrel, and Matthew was born with only three fingers on bis right hand, Jonas had a stump foot, and David was hump-backed;—all these, except the latter, were remarkably short, while Ezekiel was six feet one inch high at the age of nineteen 5—the stump-footed Jonas and the hump-backed David got wives of fortune, but no girls in the borough would listen to the addresses of their brothers;—the husband's hair was as black as jet, and the wife's remarkably white, yet every one of the children's hair was red;—the husband was killed by accidentally falling into a deep pit, in the year 1701, and his wife refusing all kind of sustenance, died five days after him, and they were buried in one grave;—in the year 1703, Ezekiel enlisted as a grenadier, and although he was afterwards wounded in twenty-three places, he recovered;—Roger, James, Matthew, Jonas, and David, it appears by the church registers, died in different places, and were buried on the same day, in the year 1713, and Solomon and Ezekiel were drowned together in crossing the Thames, in the year 1723. Such a collection of odd circumstances never before occurred in one family. This account is taken from an odd corner of an old newspaper, and we cannot any further vouch for its authenticity; there can be no doubt but that it is altogether odd, and we think it would be still more odd if it were true.

September 8th, 1696, an order w as made for the better regulation of the market; and that no person should expose any eatables for sale, except in the market.

1697. Ordered, that an address to His Majesty be sealed with the town seal, and be sent to the burgesses to be presented to the king, they desiring my Lord Cornwallis, high steward, to introduce them. A long address on the blessings of the peace derived from His Majesty's great wisdom and prowess in arms, dated 9th of December 1697, was presented. 1698. It is ordered that the intended shire-house shall be erected and built on the ground behind the hospital; and that a committee shall be formed for treating and . agreeing about the building, and for procuring subscriptions, and using all other proper ways and means for the erecting the said shire-house. Sir Samuel Barnardiston, who was member for the borough at this time, contributed largely to the subscription. But we cannot find that the assizes were ever held in this building except once, in the year 1740, when the town of Bury suffered dreadfully from the small-pox. 1699. Several persons were admitted to their freedom this year, on the payment of £5. 1702. A committee was formed to view the reed-ground by Stoke bridge, to see how it could be improved to the best advantage of the town.

It is agreed that an act of parliament shall be applied for, for the better regulating and employing the poor, and for granting other advantages to the town.

A loyal and dutiful address was presented to the queen, on her accession to the throne.

Richard Phillips was fined £100 for neglecting his duty as a portman, but was afterwards excused on account of the service he had since done the town.

In 1703, a number of persons were, at different times, fined and sued for neglecting or refusing to act in their office of portmen.

It is agreed, that to-morrow being the 5th of November, shall be observed in such manner as Mr. Bailiffs shall direct; and the charge thereof to be paid by the chamberlain.

It was agreed that Mr. Bailiff Gravenor is desired, at his going to London, to attend the lord high steward and the burgesses of the town, and to pray their favour in endeavouring to obtain the present assizes to be held in this town. They were not held here more than three or four years, and there is no account of the cause of their being removed to Bury, but we suppose it was owing to the interest felt by the lord lieutenant, the duke of Grafton, for that town.

A committee was formed to regulate the fees for goods brought or carried out of the town-house or this port. Which town-house meant the *custom-house,* for it was, formerly, so called. A long string of orders was issued for the better regulation of the corn and coal-meters and porters, and to prevent the frauds that had been practised.

Henry Sparrowe was fined £20, and discharged from his office of portman, for non-attendance and neglect of duty.

On Richard Phillips and Cooper Gravenor going out of office this year, it was agreed that they should have such security given them as their counsel shall advise, to indemnify them and their officers in all differences between them and the town.

Many gentlemen in the town and neighbourhood were, about this time, presented with their freedom; and the disputes in the corporation were carried to great lengths.

At a great court, the 9th of June, 1704, it was agreed that Mr. Richard Puplett had committed several breaches and misdemeanours in his office of town clerk; and it appearing to the court that he was never duly chosen into the said office; and on a poll being demanded, to determine whether he should be discharged or not, a majority of forty-two appearing against him, he was discharged accordingly, and Mr. Edmund Harvey elected town-clerk in his room. A long letter was read and ordered to be sent to Charles Whittaker, esq., recorder, desiring him to shew cause why he had neglected to hold the session of Oyer and Terminer, as he ought to have done; also to shew cause why he kept and retained in his custody, certain charters, books, and deeds, belonging to the town; and why he had taken part with suitors and delinquents, and had given his opinion against, and had condemned the conduct of the bailiffs in the discharge of their duty, and had refused to give his advice when asked by the bailiffs and portmen; and, lastly, to shew cause why he should not be discharged from his office of recorder of the said town of Ipswich; and on the 8th of September following, his answer not being deemed satisfactory, it was put to the vote, and decided by a majority of 69, that he should be discharged from his office of recorder. He was discharged accordingly, and Leicester Martin, esq. elected in his place.

On the 13th of November, 1704, it was ordered and agreed, that an address be presented to his Majesty by the high steward of this town, "on the remarkable successes of the forces under the command of Charles, Duke of Marlborough and Sir George Rooke."

On the 22nd day of December, it was ordered that a nightly watch should be established from this time to the 2nd day of March, and that four persons of the east ward, and two persons of the other three wards shall be obliged to watch in person, in their turn; and that every one refusing to watch in person, shall forfeit one shilling.

It appeared that Richard Puplett and Charles Whittaker had each of them obtained a writ of mandamus against the corporation, to be restored to their offices.

It was agreed that Mr. William Betts should be paid what may be considered reasonably due to him for defending the town upon the mandamus brought against them by Richard Puplett and Charles Whittaker.

On the 7th of February, 1704, five persons were admitted to their freedom, on paying £5 each, which seemed to be now a common custom.

On the 12th day of June, at this court, it is ordered and agreed, that steps shall be taken to apply to the Earl of

L

Dysart, and Mr. Pooley, to procure the next assizes to be held at this town, and a committee was formed to go about the town to collect subscriptions.

On the 25th day of June, 1706, at this court, it is agreed, that Thursday next being the day appointed by proclamation for a public thanksgiving for the happy success of His Majesty's forces under the Duke of Marlborough, in Flanders, and the Earl of Peterborough, in Catalonia, shall be observed with all decency, and the charge thereof to be paid by the treasurer and chamberlains.

It was agreed, that a sum, not exceeding £600, shall be forthwith borrowed, at interest, upon Handford Hall, for and towards payment of damages and costs of suit, recovered and decreed to Samuel Caley, and, that the security of the lender shall be under the common seal of this town.

By this it will be seen, that more than a century back the corporate body were deeply involved in those mazes of litigation from which they have never escaped.

At this time it appeared usual for one of the bailiffs to attend the judge at the assizes at Bury, at the expense of the town.

On the 26th of September, 1706, it was ordered and agreed, that every person admitted to his freedom of this town, claiming it by service or patrimony, shall pay 3s. 4d. to Christ's Hospital; and those admitted by purchase shall pay 6s. 8d.; and those who are presented to it shall pay 10s. each to the said hospital. And this is a custom which ought not to have fallen into disuse.

On the 23d of October, 1706, whereas, it appears by the ancient records of this town, that every iron-bound cart of foreigners that shall come upon the common quay, to load or unload any manner of merchandise, hath formerly paid, and now ought to pay, two-pence, for every such cart, and a penny for every bare cart, and a halfpenny for every man's burthen, it is now ordered, that the said duty or custom be demanded by the water bailiff, or his deputy, and that the money so gathered shall go towards the repairs of the common quay.

It is agreed, that Cooper Gravenor, esq. do forthwith get the common quay so far repaired as to prevent further damage. By this we may suppose that some extraordinary high tide had occasioned injury to the quay and wharfs.

An order was issued, that all butchers should bring their meat into the market, to be publicly examined, before it was offered for sale at their shops or houses, as a great deal of unwholesome provisions had been exposed to sale, particularly swine's flesh, which was prohibited by act of parliament, at certain seasons of the year, as detrimental to the health of her Majesty's liege subjects.

Ordered, that no person be allowed to take, with nets, or any other engine, any fish out of the river belonging to this corporation, before the bailiffs, for the time being, have first fished the river, upon pain of forfeiting, for each such fishing, 20s.

On the 22d of April, 1707, a writ of mandamus was received, commanding the bailiffs to restore Charles Whittaker, esq. to the recordership of the corporation; the said writ of mandamus being read in open court, "he is accordingly restored to the said recordership by us, as much as lieth in our power;" when he was immediately served by Mr. Thomas Stisted, town clerk, in open court, with a summons, to shew cause, on or before the 7th day of May next, why he had been guilty of the said misdemeanours, as before named, and why he should not be discharged from his office.

On the 7th of May, 1707, it was agreed, that Charles Whittaker, having been served with the said summons, and not having returned a satisfactory answer, it is ordered and agreed, that the said Charles Whittaker is discharged from the office of recorder, and William Thompson, esq. is elected in his stead.

Whereas, Richard Puplett, Mr. Henry Hill, Mr. Henry Sparrow, and Mr. Thomas Bowell, have exhibited a bill in chancery, touching the building the shire house, in this town, against the corporation, and Cooper Giavenor, gent., and Joseph Clarke, gent., it is ordered, that Mr. Stisted be chosen solicitor in defending the same, and that his charges shall be reimbursed by the corporation. It is ordered, that £1,000 be borrowed for one year, and that Handford Hall, and the land and appurtenances thereunto be made a security for the same.

When we see the vast sums that have been expended in suits of law, by the corporation of Ipswich, for more than a century past, we are inclined to applaud the wisdom of the corporation of Edinburgh, who will, upon no consideration whatever, admit a lawyer to be one of their body. Four more gentlemen were elected freemen, and it must be confessed that our forefathers were at this time exceedingly lavish of these presentations. Every year an order was issued for observing the 5th of November with all due solemnity.

On the 29th of July it was ordered, that the charges of the coroners of this town, and the witnesses obliged to attend at Bury assizes, to prosecute Elizabeth Cooke, for the murder of a bastard child, shall be paid by the town.

On the 1st of March, 1707, is this memorandum in the court book:—This court was broke up, and no minutes taken, because the town clerk was not at it, and Mr. Snelling objected against Mr. John Harrison taking the business of the court, he being no freeman. This is important, as we have lately had two town clerks who were not free burgesses.

September the 19th, 1707, a vessel belonging to Richard Cole, jun. was seized as a deodand, by the coroner, in consequence of one Thomas Robinson falling from the sprit, upon the deck of the said vessel, and was killed, but the bailiffs, &c. wishing to be favourable to the said Richard Cole, ordered the vessel to be restored, on paying a fine of 20s. At this court it is agreed and ordered, that Mr. Serjeant Whittaker shall not be restored to the office of recorder of this town, but that a return shall be made to the writ of mandamus now read in court, as counsel shall advise. And it is ordered and agreed by this court, that William Thompson be confirmed in the office of recorder, for his natural life.

The bailiffs ordered their seat in the Tower Church to be hung with black, and the town servants to be put into mourning, on account of the death of Prince George, of Denmark.

Nov. 12, 1708. Whereas, there are several great debts due from this town, which, if not suddenly paid, will create and raise considerable costs and expenses in law. It is therefore necessary to consider of a ready way for paying these debts respectively. A committee was therefore appointed, to examine and state an account of town debts, and to enquire by what means such difficulties were formerly got over, and by what means the present debts may be answered and paid to the persons respectively, to whom they are due and owing, whether by *scottant* or *lottant,* or otherwise, and report thereof at the next great court; at which court it was ordered, that for the payment of the charges of suits contracted in and about the necessary defence of prosecution for the rights and liberties of the town: it is by this court granted, ordered, and agreed, that all freemen of this town shall be *scottant* and *lottant,* for and toward payment of the same, (as respectively they were parties obliged by the free man's oath) and as in former times hath been used: and that the said free men shall severally and respectively be assessed, allotted, and charged discretionally, by such persons as (at the next great court to be held in this town) shall be nominated, elected, and chosen assessors, for raising a sum of money, not exceeding £600, for the purposes aforesaid. What would the freemen think of such an assessment, now-a-days? Great exertions were made by the corporation in getting in all monies due to them, for rents, fines, and forfeited bonds; but, on the 10th day of January following, it was considered absolutely necessary to augment the sum to be raised, to pay off the town debts, from £600 to £1,600.

On the 10th of February, 1709, it was agreed, that the present bailiffs shall have the management of the public thanksgiving day, upon Thursday next, for the success of her Majesty's forces, and those of the allies, in taking the town and fortress of Lisle, relieving Ghent, Bruges, &c., as to them shall seem meet, at the charge of the town.

In 1709, the Duke of Marlborough visited this town, and was presented with the freedom of the borough, and an entertainment was provided for him at the expense of the corporation.

August 4th, 1709. In consequence of a letter from the Duke of Grafton, a committee was appointed to enquire and find out ways and methods for receiving, placing, and employing, within this town, certain families of the poor distressed Palatine German Protestants, if possibly it may be done, in compliance with her Majesty's gracious intention towards that people. In answer to the letter, the committee declared, that this town, by reason of decay of trade, and having no manufactory to employ these poor people, and the great burden and increase of their own poor inhabitants, they could not receive them, but that when a brief shall be tendered for their relief all due care shall be taken to excite the inhabitants of the town to a liberal contribution.

At this court the freedom of the corporation was offered to the Duke of Grafton.

26th May, 110. Hugh Wright paid a fine to be discharged from serving the office of guildholder, and it was resolved that no further election of guildholders shall be made for the year ensuing.

About this time a number of persons were fined for not serving the office of guildholder, which, owing to the falling off of the trade, the holding of the feast was probably attended with too much expense, and we are led to believe that the guild feast was soon after laid aside.

October 9th, 1710. The following gentlemen were put in nomination, as candidates to represent the borough in the ensuing parliament:—viz. SirWm. Barker, bart.,Wm. Churchill, esq., William Thompson, esq., recorder, and Orlando Bridgman, esq. A poll was demanded for them severally, which was granted; but, before the poll commenced, Richard Puplett, esq., Robert Snelling, gent., and several other freemen, did severally request and insist upon it, that their respective dissents from, and protests thereunto, be entered against all and every the vote or votes of such honorary freemen of this corporation, who were only presented with their freedom, and who had, nor have, no right thereunto by patrimony, service, or purchase, nor who were, or are, resident within the said town, that shall be given at this election, for any one or more of the said candidates; which request the bailiffs complied with, and ordered the same to be entered, and it was entered accordingly, and then proceeded to the poll, which was as follows:—
8ir William Baiter, hut., in all, including upwards of 50 honorary freeman $

William Churchill, esq 258

William Thompson, esq 2»5

Orlando Bridgman 172

The majority was declared to be for Sir William Barker, with the honorary freemen, and for William Churchill, esq.: and without the honorary freemen, for the said WilUam Churchill and William Thompson, esq., but the two former sat out the sessions, and were again elected in 1713.

On the 15th of June, 1711, the feuds of the corporation seem to have increased; for, at this court, six of the portmen, and 17 of the twenty-four men and others, entered their protest against the proceedings of the court, as illegal, and withdrew, when it was voted by the floor, or the whole of the remaining freemen present, which amounted to 156, that it was a legal court, to all intents and purposes, and they proceeded to vote the freedom of the corporation to no less than 52 gentlemen of the county, and some of London, among whom are seven baronets.

August 7. A protest is entered by four of the portmen, and several of the twenty-four men, against the legality of this court. The bailiffs were indemnified against the suits that were proceeding against them in the courts of law. Nine persons were admitted to their freedom, on paying £5, and thirty-five more gentlemen, and three clergymen, were voted in as freemen of the borough.

September 8. The greater part of the portmen, and twenty-four men entered their protest against the freedom of those gentlemen who had been admitted at the two previous great courts; and a poll being demanded for bailiffs, the numbers were—

Mr. Bowel 240

Mr. Hill 241

Mr. Day 243

Mr. Quia tin 239

A scrutiny was demanded on the part of Mr Quintin and Mr. Hill, and scrutators appointed, who met on the 10th inst.; and those for Mr. Quintin objected to all those gentlemen who had obtained their freedom by presentment, at the two last great courts; and those on the part of Mr. Hill objected to all those gentlemen who had been made free by presentment, within the last ten years. Mr. Day and Mr. Hill were eventually appointed.

Sept. 15th. Eight more gentlemen were presented with their freedom, and eighteen persons were admitted by purchase.

September 18th. Mr. Maston and Mr. Pew, clavigers, refuse to attend and deliver up the keys of the treasury, wherein the common seal is kept, they are discharged, and two other persons chosen: and it was ordered that the two locks of the treasury door should be taken off, and new ones put on. Eight persons are admitted to their freedom, on paying £5 each.

January 11. It was ordered and agreed, that the town marshes shall be added as a security with Handford Hall, for the sum of £1,200., to be borrowed for the purpose of paying what appears to be due to Mr. Hooke, on his suit in chancery against the corporation.

May 12, 1713. Agreed, that the manner of the observance of the proclamation for the peace between her Majesty and the most Christian King, shall be left to the bailiffs, at the charge of the corporation.

September 3, 1713. William Churchill, esq., William Thompson, esq., Richard Richardson, esq., and Orlando Bridgman, esq., were put in nomination, as candidates to represent the borough in the ensuing parliament; and a poll was demanded, when the said Mr.

Richardson and Mr. Bridgman protested against and objected to the votes of such persons who were presented to their freedom at a great court pretended to be held on the 15th of June, 1711, and at another great court pretended to be held on the 7th of August following, or at any other great court pretended to be held since June 15, 1711, and disclaimed all such votes as illegal, except they have their freedom by service or birthright. Mr. Thompson, for himself, and Mr. Churchill, requested that their protest should be entered against all gentlemen who are called honorary free burgesses, and pretend to their right of freedom by votes of great courts at any time, for the space of ten years, before the said 15th of June, 1711. After some debate and struggle it was agreed that one person, not a freeman, should be appointed for each candidate, to see that the poll was fairly taken. Before the poll was declared, each member took the oath of qualification, as necessary by a late act of parliament. The numbers were as follow:—

Mr. Churchill 265

Mr. Thompson 270

Mr. Richardson 204

Mr. Bridgman 2IS whereupon the two former were declared duly elected.

September 29th, 1713. Mr. John Pemberton and Mr. Cross were discharged from their office of portmen, for non-attendance upon great courts, when duly summoned.

November 3d, 1713. Fourteen gentlemen, six of them resident at Bury, were presented with their freedom. Agreed, that all such persons who in contempt of the several orders and bye laws of this corporation, keep open shops, or traffick and trade in this borough, shall be forthwith fined, as counsel shall advise.

August 12th, 1714. John Clarke, gent., one of the portmen, left the court in contempt, and did not return to take the oath required by act of parliament.

September 8th. Sir Dudley Cullum, bart., and twentythree other gentlemen were sworn in as freemen of the borough.

September 21st. An address was read, and ordered to be presented to his

Majesty King George, on his accession to the throne. Mr. Jonathan Quintin and Mr. Isaac Sutton were severally served with a summons to shew cause why they should not be discharged from their office of portmen, for having contemptuously withdrawn themselves from a great court, held June 15th, 1711, and from another great court, held the 7th of August; and on account of their absence from two other great courts held in September following, by reason of which departure and absence, all the freemen made at the said courts were declared to be illegally made by the honourable the House of Commons, at the late hearing of the merits of the election for the said town; and that their misbehaviour, in this respect, was contrary to the duty of the office of portmen; and their answer not being deemed satisfactory, they were discharged accordingly: as also was Mr. William Tye, for absenting himself from many great courts, for four years past.

January 28th, 1715. William Thompson, esq. recorder, and William Churchill, esq., were elected members for the borough, without opposition. Six gentlemen were presented with their freedom.

June 13th. Whereas, it has been represented to this court, that certain persons pretending to be headboroughs, have ordered, or granted, or pretended to order and grant to Robert Edgar, gent. , a right to a certain quantity of town ground, against the place where the said Robert Edgar hath pulled or taken down part of a messuage situate in the Highstreet, called Brook-street, in this town; which agreement this court declares null and void; and that neither the bailiffs, portmen, or headboroughs, or any of them, jointly or severally, have any legal right or authentic usage or custom, to grant, make, or confirm any title or interest of, in, or to, any part or parcel of town waste, soil, or ground, to any person or persons whomsoever; and that the same is to be first proposed to be deliberated upon, and agreed, at some great court, consisting of the bailiffs, burgesses, and commonalty of the corporation of Ipswich, and not otherwise, or in any other manner howsoever. But it is ordered, that in consideration of two guineas in gold, paid by the said Robert Edgar, he shall be allowed to lay the foundation of his new wall nine inches further into the common street, the right of the bailiffs, burgesses, and commonalty being by him acknowledged; and that he shall be allowed to erect pales all along the front of the said house in Brook-street, and that he shall be allowed to build a porch to the said house, on paying £5 for the use of the corporation.

September, 8, 1716. Whereas, the town house, wharf, warehouse, and river Orwell, with the several duties and fees annexed, and therefrom arising, have been always received and taken as part of the fee farm, for which the bailiffs, burgesses, and commonalty of this town, do pay an annual rent of £60 into his Majesty's court of exchequer; and whereas, the said duties and fees have been paid, without interruption, beyond the memory of man, it is ordered and agreed, that all the said duties and fees must and shall be maintained and preserved, and shall be henceforth strictly enforced and collected; and that all such persons as shall attempt to withhold and frustrate this intention, by landing merchandise at private quays, shall be proceeded against, as counsel shall advise.

April 10th, 1717. Agreed, that great care and due methods be taken to recover the charter of King Edward IV. and all other charters or writings of or belonging to this corporation, that are out of the town treasury, or mislaid; and that where any such charters and writings are wanted, and cannot be recovered by endeavour and search, that new copies or transcripts and exemplifications be taken from the records, at the charge of this corporation, without let or delay.

November 28th. One hundred and fifty pounds was agreed to be paid to the proprietors of the conduithead, late Mr. Caley's, for supplying the town with water; about which great pains were taken by the bailiffs, and a piece of land adjoining is hired of Mr. Bailiff Cohnan, for the purpose of forming a reservoir,

laying down pipes &c., and the whole was managed under the direction of Mr. Colman.

December 9th, 1719. It was resolved, that making the river navigable from this port to Stowmarket would be prejudicial to the trade of Ipswich.

October 18th, 1720. Thursday next, being the king's coronation, shall be kept in such a manner as the bailiffs shall direct, at the charge of the corporation.

May 16th, 1721. Agreed and ordered, that £50 be given as a gratuity to Mr. Nottingham, who was an instrument in bringing about a release that was given to Mr. Stroud, respecting the Handford Hall estate: and it was agreed and ordered, that Mr. Bailiffs shall have liberty to *treat* the said Mr. Stroud and Mr. Nottingham, or either of them, whenever they come to see the corporation, at the discretion of the said bailiffs, and at the expense of the corporation. The persons in power had actually agreed to sell the Handford Hall estate, and it would have been lost to the corporation, but for this timely negotiation.

September 8th. John Marlow, gent., and William Churchill, esq., were elected bailiffs.

On the 29th of September, Mr. Churchill was discharged from the oice of bailiff, at his request, and Mr. John Steward was chosen in his room.

Mr. Marlow was discharged from his office of bailiff, and, for his contempt of the court, fined £50, when Mr. Steward and Mr. Gravenor were sworn in.

October 10th. This court doth agree, that Mr. Gravenor, by procuring Mr. Steward to be sworn on the 29th of September last, did save the corporation from being dissolved; that Mr. Marlow's discharge was not regular; that he do remain bailiff, with Mr. Steward, and take the oath immediately. This court doth order the following speech, spoken by Cooper Gravenor, gent., now in court, shall be recorded in the great court book, which follows in these words:—

"Gentlemen, "I presume you all know, and I hope you will believe, that the inducement I had to offer my service

on the 29th of September, was (as I really intended it) in that emergency, to draw the new-elected Mr. Steward to the hall to be sworn, and thereby prevent the dissolution of the corporation, by the absence and refusal of those who were chosen to accept the office, which succeeded accordingly, and I hope will not prove such an obstruction of another being elected, as to create a forfeiture within the act of parliament; and that it will appear that I did not offend either against the government or the act. Gentlemen, I am advised, and do agree, that my election is void in law, and, consequently, my oath which I hare taken; that Mr. Marlow's discharge was not regular, and consequently his fine was not regular, and I desire that you will agree, and order that Mr. Marlow's fine and discharge, being irregular, be repealed, and discharged and vacated; that my election is void, that Mr. Marlow remain bailiff, having been chosen on the 8th of September last, for the year ensuing, and thathe be sworn and declared bailiff, with Mr. Steward, by whose being sworn in the 29th of September, the corporation is saved."

November 27th, 1722. A loyal address was presented to His Majesty.

June 17, 1723. Goodchild Clarke was admitted to his freedom, on paying a fine of £5, having served Mr. Nathaniel Burrage, late town clerk, only five years; and two other persons were admitted, on paying a small fine, having served only part of their apprenticeship, and twelve other persons were admitted, on paying a fine of £10 each: by which it may be seen that it was formerly much easier to obtain the honour of being a free burgess than at the present day. At this court it was stated, that Mr. Cooper Gravenor had been possessed of the town-house crane, and crane house, and of a quay or wharf called the town quay, under a pretended lease, subject to the payment of £50, yearly, as rent of the aforesaid premises, and hath not paid or accounted with this corporation for any part of the said rent for thirteen years, and is also indebted to the corporation, on several other accounts, in divers sums of money; and whereas, the present bailiffs have, in a friendly manner, requested the said Cooper Gravenor to pass and settle his accounts, which he has refused to do; and having got into his power, or custody, several charters, court books, papers, and records, belonging to the corporation, which he refuses to deliver up: it is agreed, that a suit or suits be commenced against him, at the expense of the corporation, when, on the request of Mr. Gravenor, it was put to the vote, and the resolution was carried by one hundred and sixty four votes for it, and only a solitary vote against it, Mr. Edward Bird. Glad enough must the corporation have been to get rid of such a troublesome subject, for they were involved in a continued scene of confusion, broils, and litigation, during the twenty years Mr. Gravenor was amongst them. They seemed now to have settled down into something like a calm, and continued to proceed for several years in an uninterrupted routine of regularity.

July 31st, it was agreed, that to-morrow being the accession of His Majesty King George II. to the throne, be celebrated by drinking His Majesty's health on the town hall, as usual.

August 2d, 1723. Being advised, by counsel, that no freeman can be evidence in the case between William Salter, and Cooper Gravenor, to be tried at Bury assizes, it is Ordered and agreed, that the several persons named be disfranchised, to give evidence at the trial, and five persons Were Ordered to be, and were disfranchised, accordingly; and, on the 8th of September these five persons were re-elected free burgesses, and sworn in accordingly. Cooper Gravenor exhibited a bill in chancery against the corporation, on pretence of having expended the amount of his rent, &c., for the benefit of the corporation: an anBWer was ordered to be put in.

April 26th, 1726. It is agreed, that upon payment of £200 by Cooper Gravenor to the corporation, that all differences, suits, and demands existing, or that have existed between them, from the beginning of the world to the present, shall cease, and be put an end to, and that on his payment of the money,

the common seal shall be set To this agreement.

It seems that our worthy ancestors, not being yet enlightened on the subject of free trade, on the 18th of

August, 1727, they published a most lengthy document against any person, not a freeman, exercising any trade or calling, or opening a shop, for any business whatever, without leave or licence, under a penalty of 20s.; that he shall be subject to a fine not exceeding 3s., and not less than 6d. for every day he shall have so acted.without leave and licence; and any person who shall use or exercise any art, trade, or mystery, or manual occupation, shall pay a sum not exceeding Is., and not less than 2d. for every day he shall have so acted; considering that great injury had arisen to the freemen, and to the trade of the town, in consequence of the evasion of this bye-law: trifling as the sum was that would be raised by such a law, it excited great odium in the feelings of strangers, and we are persuaded that trade flourishes much more without any such invidious restriction. This law was afterwards altered, that the fine should be so much per week. It appears that strangers and foreigners, not regarding this act, the corporation again issued long orders respecting it, and determined that the fines to be paid by the offenders shall be sued for, or levied by distress.

January 27th, 1729. Forty-six persons were admitted to their freedom, by patrimony and servitude; and, upon a writ being received to elect a member to represent the borough in parliament, in the room of Sir William Thomson; and the oath being administered to the bailiffs against bribery and corruption, two candidates were proposed, and a poll demanded. The numbers were, for.

John dheppnrd, esq 837

Philip Broke, esq 286 w hereupon the latter was declared duly elected.

Feb. 19th, 1730. Again this odious proclamation against the freedom of trade makes its appearance, and

M again and again it is evaded: but there is more good sense in the following order:—"That a boat be bought, at the charge of the corporation, for col-

lecting the duties on the anchorage and ballast, and the profits of the fishery within the admiralty jurisdiction of the borough."

September 8th, 1731. Whereas, the several persons named were formerly admitted freemen of this corporation, and there having arisen some disputes respecting the legality of their freedom, and their right of voting as such, now this court, to prevent all disputes and questions that may hereafter arise thereupon, doth re-choose and establish all the said persons to be freemen of this corporation, and doth now give to each of them the privilege and freedom thereof, to all intents and purposes: and hereupon fifty gentlemen were admitted to their freedom.

December 10th, 1731. It was agreed and ordered, that £50 be deposited in the hands of Francis Child, esq. then lord mayor of London, towards defraying his expenses of carrying on the suit of this corporation, jointly with other corporations, against the city of Bristol, for recovery of the improved value of Sir Thomas White's gift. At this time the headboroughs were surveyors of the town, and made their report respecting the highways, buildings, and nuisances.

January 29th, 1732. Twenty-one gentlemen were admitted to their freedom.

September 8th, 1733. It is agreed, that Laurence Rainbird, miller, be allowed to take down the windmill by him lately erected in the town marshes, in his occupation; and that Thomas Flintoft, miller, have liberty to erect a windmill on the town marshes, in his occupation, and to take down the same before the expiration of his lease of the same marshes. It is agreed, that opinions be taken of Mr. Attorney General and Mr. Sergeant Eyre, in relation to commencing suits against persons trading in the borough, not being free.

April 25th, 1734. The four following candidates were put in nomination to represent the borough in parliament; viz.—

William Wollaston, esq. I Samuel Kent, esq.

Edward Vernon, esq. Philips Cuhnan, esq.

when a poll was demanded, and a majority of legal votes was declared by the bailiffs to be for the two former, who were thereupon declared duly elected; but the numbers on the poll are not stated. Great preparations had been made on both sides for this contest, and it was carried on with much bitterness and animosity. Admiral Vernon was a great favourite of the people, but the freedom of his speeches in parliament had dipleased the ministers. The portmen were supported by the interest of the government, but the common council, or the blue party, relied on the justice of their cause, and the popularity of the admiral. So high did party run, that no remark upon the election, or detail of the circumstances attending it, are to be met with in the Ipswich Journal of the time. The election happened on a *Sunday,* in consequence of which there was a vast influx of country people on the Cornhill, and from the following circumstance, the passions of the populace were highly inflamed: an attempt was made, on the evening previous to the election, to get at some freemen secured in Mr. TufTnell's house, who then resided in St. Clement's, where the office of the gas works lately was. By the sudden and violent shutting of the door, a gentleman's foot was crushed between the door and the threshold, where he was kept in great torture for a considerable time. The populace without did all they could to relieve him, and m doing this forced out one of the pannels of the door. At last, a man named William Roberts, proposed to try whether the gentleman's foot could not be slipped out, if he left his shoe behind; and while this man was stooping down to loosen the shoe, he received, from some person inside the house, two stabs in his body, one of which proved mortal.

January 14th, 1736. His Majesty King George II. landed at Lowestoft; and between six and 6even o'clock in the evening, a messenger arrived at Ipswich, with the news that the king would be there that night; on which the corporate body assembled in their formalities, and proceeded to the north gate, to receive him; but the crowd was so great that they were obliged to retreat to the White Horse, where they attended him, as he alighted from the carriage. He immediately proceeded up stairs, into the great dining-room, whither they were admitted, with several of the clergy, andajiad all the honour of kissing the king's hand. Mr. Bailiff Sparrow addressed His Majesty, in a short but appropriate speech, and, His Majesty being much fatigued, they soon after retired. This same gentleman was honored by a singular mark of attention from George I.; who sent him, in the last year of his reign, a very fine portrait of himself, painted by Fountaine, which is now in Mr. Sparrow's house, in the Buttermarket, in return for a marchpane of extraordinary dimensions. This confectionary composition was made of cuke, pistachio nuts, sugar, sweetmeats, and comfits, and is thus alluded to by Sir Philip Sidney:—

"Along whoae ridge such hones are met,
Like comfits round in *marchpane* set."

The wand of office which Mr. Sparrow bore before Geo II. is also carefully preserved. The messenger who was gone forward, left orders for a coach and chaise, with four horses each, to be hired here, and as many dragoons as could be got together, to attend. His Majesty entered the chaise a little before twelve, amidst the loud acclamations of the crowd. Before he reached Copdock, the night became so dark that lights were considered necessary, to enable the royal *cortege* to proceed on their journey. The courier who preceded the carriages enquired of the landlady of the White Elm if she had any flambeaux, or could procure any. On her replying that there was nothing so Frenchified in the neighbourhood, she was asked if she had any *links.* "Aye, that I have," said she," and some as good as His Majesty, God bless him, ever saw, in all his life;" and, with great satisfaction and importance, she immediately produced a long string of Suffolk sausages, to the great amusement of the standers by. His Majesty stopped at the Swan, at Stratford, where he laid himself down upon a bed for three or four hours, and about six o'clock took coach, for London, and arrived at St. James's palace at two in the afternoon. At what a different rate of rapidity has our present Sovereign, George IV., travelled the same road!

June 12th, 1736. A grand entertainment was given to the gentlemen of the neighbourhood, when the first display of fireworks ever seen in this town was exhibited, to celebrate the king's accession to the throne. This month a most violent storm of wind arose, that untiled most of the houses in the town, and did great damage in the neighbourhood.

On the 8th of September, 1736, John Sparrow, esq., and Edward Lynch, esq., were duly elected bailiffs for the year ensuing; but, upon the 29th of September, inst. the said Edward Lynch went out of town, to avoid being sworn into the office, when he was fined £80 by the court, and a writ of mandamus was procured, to compel him to serve, and to legalise the transaction; and on the 22d of November following, he was swor n in, with Mr. Sparrow, and they served the office of bailiffs accordingly.

May 8th, 1741. Edward Vernon, esq., vice admiral of the blue, Samuel Kent, esq., and Knox Ward, esq., clarencieux king at arms, were put in nomination, as candidates to represent the borough in parliament; a poll was demanded, when the numbers were as follow:—

Edward Vernon, esq 527
Samuel Kent, esq 298
Knox Ward, ecq 824 whereupon a scrutiny was demanded by Mr. Ward, to be decided on the 13th inst.; and it was declared that the two former were duly elected. By the number voted at this election, it will be seen how greatly the freemen had increased; and on this 13th inst., no less than fifty-three persons more were admitted to their freedom, by patrimony, and servitude; from this time, the admission by purchase has been seldom resorted to.

Strong apprehensions were entertained as to the safety of some of the portmens' persons. Upon the first intimation of this, Admiral Vernon, accompanied by several other gentlemen, immediately went to the house where they were assembled, and, under his protection, escorted them to the town hall. The gentlemen who were in the admiral's interest, many of whom were magistrates, and persons of consequence in the neighbourhood, took their posts at the bottom of the stairs leading up to the town hall, and in different parts of the Cornhill, to prevent riot, and to keep the peace, which was effectually done through the day, but this was construed by the other party into an undue exertion of influence, and that the blues carried their point by the strength of their purse. The blues retorted the same charges against the yellows, and long and bitter was the paper war carried on in the London papers, each one charging the other with corruption; but we, who know the immaculate purity of the electors, may conclude, with Peachum and Lockit, when quarrelling about their honesty, that they were probably both in the wrong, and that the less that is said about it the better. Unfortunately, another man, of the name of Cooper, lost his life during this contest; so that we may be said to live in quiet and peaceable times, compared to this era of outrage and violence.

October 6th, 1743. A committee was appointed to examine into the management of the gifts and charities belonging to the corporation, for these last thirty years; and on September 27th, 1744, a report from this committee was read, containing many long and judicious regulations for the better management of Christ's Hospital, and the other charities of the town; more particularly that called Tooley's Foundation, into which no persons not belonging to the town, nor those who have other means of subsistence, ought to be admitted; but this rule has never been properly attended to. The committee was continued for another year, and discovered that an improper expenditure had been made of the money belonging to the lending fund; for about the year 1675, when Mr. Neave was treasurer of the lending fund, it appeared, by his accounts, that the corporation took of this lending cash, to pay off their debts, £529: 9s.

In October, 1745, a subscription was set on foot, in the county of Suffolk, in aid of government, for the suppression of the rebellion. The Duke of Grafton subscribed £1,000, and five other noblemen and gentlemen £500 each. The gentlemen of the town of Ipswich were conspicuous for their loyalty on this occasion, and the whole sum subscribed amounted to £16,318: 10: 6.

A dutiful and loyal address was read, on the success of His Majesty's arms at Cape Breton, the happy influence of his counsels abroad, and his safe arrival in his own dominions at home; and at the same time expressing a just abhorrence against the wicked and traitorous attempts of those ungrateful and rebellious people who are now in arms against His Majesty's person, family, and government, carried on, supported as it is by that proud and imperious monarch, the French king; and after very long and fervent wishes for his preservation, it concludes with stating, "that their latest posterity shall, with pleasure, tell how George the Second reigned, and how his people loved him." It was ordered to be presented to His Majesty by the members for the borough, and the recorder.

July 1st, 1746. A committee, consisting of several clergymen and gentlemen, was formed to enquire into the government and jurisdiction of the grammar school, according to the charter: and, on the 4th of November following, a long string of resolutions, for the management and discipline of this school was read and approved of, as drawn up by the committee; but, like many other ingenious theories, they could never be put in practice, but must be left to the discretion of the master, whose qualifications should be carefully ascertained, before he is elected to the situation. Very few of these regulations have ever been attended to, except those respecting the plentiful number of holidays the boys were to be allowed. Of the exhibitions, which are of the most importance to the interest of the school, nothing is said.

1747. This year, Nathaniel Cole, gent. , died in his bailiwick, and Michael Thirkle, esq., wiis, on the 28th of December, sworn in in his room. The farm

in Whitton was advertised to be let, to the best bidder: and surely this is the best way of making the most of the corporation property, and avoiding the odium of undue preference or favouritism. 1749. John Margerum, esq., died in his bailiwick, and on the 23d of July, Samuel Kent, esq,, was chosen in his stead.

September 29th, 1750. The beadles are abated 20s. for this year's rent, in consideration that the fish market is reduced to little or no value. Again, at this time, we see the wholesome practice of *advertising* the town marshes to be let on lease to the best bidder.

On the 22d of May, 1751, the common seal was set to an order for the consolidation of the parishes of St. Clement and St. Helen into one rectory, pursuant to the statute.

September 8th, 1753. Sixty-four persons were admitted to their freedom, by patrimony, and servitude; and, on the 29th inst., forty-seven persons were admitted; and, on the 18th of April, 1754, fifty-two persons were admitted.

September 8th, 1754. A contest took place for bailiffs; and, on a poll being demanded, the numbers were, for

HamphyRant,e« "?Portn«n.
William IIammond, gcnt... ѕм 3
Thorn.. RIchud.cn, gent... 362 ..
John Gravenor, gent 363

But the presiding bailiffs did not consent to the two latter being sworn in, and hero beginneth another schism in the corporation, for it was deemed necessary to obtain a writ of mandamus, to compel the presiding bailiffs to swear them into the office, which was done accordingly, on the 8th of January, 1755. We suppose that Mr. Gravenor, one of the then bailiffs, inherited some of the spirit of his father, the flame of discord raging furiously in the corporation; for, at a great court, held the 19th day of June, 1755, no less than one hundred and twenty seven gentlemen of the county, and of various other places, were presented with their freedom, on paying five guineas each: amongst whom were eight baronets and thirty-five clergymen: and it was agreed, that the money raised by these admissions should be applied in defence of any suit or prosecution that might be brought against the then bailiffs, or against James Wilder, one of the justices of the peace of the town of Ipswich; for, it appears, he was the only portman present. At this court there were fourteen of the twentyfour men, and only fifty-two freemen on the floor. This appears to be a continuation of the contest for power between the portmen and the twenty-four men. It was formerly the custom to fill up the vacancies in the body of portmen from the twenty-four men, or common council, which had been of late neglected. And they have ever since been in constant opposition to each other, and ranged themselves under the banner of their respective parties, distinguished by blues and yellows. An advertisement appeared in the Ipswich Journal, called "A final Answer to Mr. Thirkle's final Advertisement, respecting the disputes of the Corporation." We make the following extract:—" That the gentlemen who had the lead in governing the town have been charged with assuming more power and authority than by the constitution of the borough they are, or ought to be, invested with. They have been charged with not holding great courts at proper times, and with disobeying and disregarding the orders of those few courts they did hold." The election for bailiffs having recently taken place, thia reflection, of course, applied to their predecessors in office. In the next paper are more last words of Mr. Michael Thirkle, addressed to the Rev. Richard Canning, in which he says, that " It still remains a doubt, whether the great talents providence has so amply endowed him with, might not be more usefully employed than in the care of the corporation; and whether it would not be more becoming his character to write and preach sermons, than to throw out censures and threats, in public papers, against persons who so little regard them."

An order was issued from the great court, that their thanks should be given to Mr. Vernon, for his constant attendance, and steady, uniform, and constitutional behaviour in parliament. Mr.

Samuel Kilderbee was elected town clerk, in the room of Mr. Peter Clarke, and was sworn in a free burgess, and acted immediately. On the 8th day of September, 1755, the aforesaid Mr. Wilder was the only portman present, with nineteen of the twenty-four men, and eighty-one on the floor. Larke Tarver and Thomas Bowell, gents., and Michael Thirkle, jun., and John Sparrow, esqrs., were nominated for bailiffs, when the two former were declared unanimously elected. The several other portmen were summoned to attend, which they refused to do, and on the 29th inst. Mr. John Sparrow was given till the 14th day of October, to shew cause why he should not be discharged from his office of portman; and on that day, John Sparrow, Michael Thirkle, Sir Richard Lloyd, Humphrey Rant, Samuel Kent, Goodchild Clarke, William Hammond, Ellis Brand, George Foster Tuffnell, and John Firmin, were all discharged from their office of portmen, on account of nonattendance upon the several great courts, for the space of one year: and the following gentlemen were elected portmen, by Mr. James Wilder, the sole remaining portman— Thomas Richardson, John Gravenor, Larke Tarver, Thomas Bowell, Samuel Hamblin, William Trueloye, sen., Thomas Bunnell, William Hammond, John Dade, Charles Walford, and Robert Edgar, esq.; and the first nine were immediately sworn into their office.

January 29th, 1756. The scarcity and high price of corn was a subject of general complaint throughout the kingdom, but it was the peculiar happiness of the county of Suffolk to enjoy peace and plenty; and it was recommended to the richer inhabitants of Ipswich to purchase sufficient corn to last both them, and their poorer neighbours, till the next harvest, or the evil effects of scarcity would be soon felt here. This prudent foresight was but of little avail, for, on the 9th of September following, seTcnteen men and women were tried for riotously assembling and taking flour, by force. At this time the small pox made frightful ravages in the town and neighbourhood.

On the 6th of April, an address was ordered to be presented to His Majesty, on the critical situation of public affairs, and on the late unprovoked attacks that had been made on His Majesty's dominions by our perfidious neighbours, in full peace. On the 29th of September a committee was formed, for putting in force some judicious regulations respecting the supply of water for the town; and likewise to examine into, and report upon the accounts of the treasurer and chamberlains, for the last twenty years past: and, on the 15th of October, 1756, we have the first statement of the accounts of the corporation, regularly balanced and entered at full length in the court book, which every freeman has a right to see. Surely praise is due to any set of men, of whatever party, that would persevere in such a wholesome and satisfactory practice. On the 19th of November, 1756, is entered a long list of instructions, I from the court, to their representatives in parliament. They are of a very free and spirited description; and, amongst other things, protest against the introduction of foreign subsidiaries, instead of arming our countrymen for the defence of the land; wishing not only for a change of men, but a change of measures; to introduce a bill for triennial parliaments; to establish a well-regulated and constitutional militia: and they press upon their representatives to support these measures, to the utmost of their power; concluding by particularly suggesting to Admiral Vernon, to recommend the necessity of fighting admirals, to lead on our fleets, to support the honour of the British flag. So strangely do circumstances alter political feeling: these sort of radical sentiments emanated from the blues, who have long supported the principles of the high tory party. We believe that these instructions were drawn up by the late Rev. Richard Canning, who was at the time an active man in the corporation, and to whom the public is indebted for searching into the nature and situation of the charities of this town. In this month the militia were first embodied, and 903 men out of 960, the quota for the county, took their oaths accordingly. Admiral Vernon died, aged 73, and Thomas Staunton was elected in his stead, without opposition, December 7th, 1757.

May 2nd, 1758. Judgment having been given against the then portmen, they were discharged from their office, and the old portmen reinstated in their places.

November 20th, 1759. An address was read, and ordered to be presented to His Majesty, on the late glorious successes of our arms in every quarter of the globe. After enumerating the several advantages gained, and lamenting the fall of the gallant Wolfe, at Quebec, it concludes with a most loyal and dutiful prayer for the life of His Majesty, written in language far superior to the generality of borough addresses, and was ordered to be presented by the members. And on the 1 st of November, 1760, another dutiful and loyal address was ordered to be presented to His Majesty, King George III., on his accession to the throne.

September 22d, 1761. This being the day of His Majesty's coronation, the corporation attended at church, in due form, with a procession of the woolcombers, and the day passed over with unusual demonstrations of joy, concluding with an illumination, and a ball in the evening.

October 19th, 1761. An address was ordered to be presented, on His Majesty's marriage.

September 29th, 1762. An address was ordered to be presented on the birth of the Prince of Wales. It is to be observed, that none of the portmen, except Mr. Wilder, had been present at any of the great courts held from the time they were reinstated into their office, until the 27th of December, 1762, when Lord Orwell was chosen member for the borough, without opposition.

January 15th, 1762. This day His Majesty's declaration of war against Spain was proclaimed by the magistrates, with all due solemnity.

May 7th. In the paper of this date, is an account of a most extraordinary case of affliction in a family at Wattisham, attested by Dr. Wollaston, of Bury, and various magistrates, in which a family, consisting of a mother and five children being first seized with a pain in one of their legs, they all of them, in the course of a few days, lost the use of their lower limbs; a mortification ensued, and it was necessary to perform amputation upon the whole of them: and, what is remarkable, during this affliction, they all of them appeared to be in perfect health, and suffered very little pain. A collection, made at Ipswich, and other places in the county for them, amounted to £178: 15: 5.

On the 8th of February, 1763, Mr. Samuel Kilderbee, and ten other persons, requested to be discharged from being free burgesses, on their own petition, for the purpose of giving evidence in a cause respecting the corporation, and they were discharged accordingly. On the 4th of May following an address was ordered to be presented to His Majesty, on the salutary and honourable peace.

February 24th, 1764. Three quarters of an acre of ground, in a field near the river Orwell, about a mile from this town, sunk four feet perpendicular, in a short time. It is supposed to have been occasioned by the springs having been encreased by the late heavy rains.

On the 8th of September, 1765, a poll was demanded for Mr. Peter Clarke, who was opposed to Mr. Kilderbee, for the town clerkship. The numbers were, for

Mr. Kilderhee 218
Mr. Clarke 94

Sept. 29th, 1766. Two of the seceding portmen made their appearance.—On the 31st of October provisions were very scarce, and corn remarkably dear. Several persons assembled in the market, and compelled the dealers to sell their butter at sevenpence-halfpenny the pint. They threatened to pull down the granaries and mills. A subscription, for the purpose of purchasing wheat for the poor, was set on foot in Ipswich and the vicinity, and amounted to upwards of £1,000; and they were furnished with wheat at 4s. 6d. per bushel, which was at that period a great price; but if any riot took place, this supply was to cease.

The people suffered great distress and privation, on account of the scarcity. The exportation of grain was stopped, by order of the government, at this and the neighbouring ports. At this time advertisements appeared from Mr. Gravenor and Mr. Staunton, respecting the election of the one hundred and twenty-seven honorary freemen, the one asserting and the other denying that Mr. Staunton was the planner and contriver of it: and disputes in the corporation were carried on with great violence and ill-will.

January 13th, 1767. A mandamus was read, ordering Thomas Staunton, esq., to be admitted a free burgess, he having been refused, though duly elected, and be was sworn in accordingly. On the 13th of February sundry persons protested against the legality of the court, there being no portmen present.

September 8th. It was agreed, that the one hundred and twenty-seven honorary freemen made, or pretended to be made, at a great court held, or pretended to be held, on the 15th of June, 1755, were illegally made, such court being illegal on account of there being only one portman present; and it was thereby ordered that they be struck out of the books of the corporation. Fortyeight persons were admitted by patrimony and servitude, and here again the portmen gained the ascendancy.

November 13th. The honourable William Tollemache, second son of the Earl of Dysart, declared himself a candidate to represent the borough in parliament. From this time, the exertions made by both parties surpass any thing we know of elections at the present day. The money expended upon this memorable contest between Staunton and Wollaston, and Tollemache and Cruttenden, was far superior to the expenses of modern times. An advertisement appears, stating that the bailiffs refused several persons, whose names are thereunto signed from being sworn in as freemen, though regularly entitled to their freedom. Others again, for and against the advantages and disadvantages of honorary freemen. On the 12th of Feb. following, Edward Holden Cruttenden declared himself a candidate, in conjunction with Mr. Tollemache; and party spirit raged more violently than ever. Meetings and processions were numerous, and great convulsions arose. The newspaper was filled with replies and rejoinders, in the shape of advertisements, and the election took place on the 16th of March. Previous to this election, many of the freemen lived at Finborough Hall, or Helmingham, at which places they took up their residence, for days and weeks together. Open house was kept for months at these places, and at various taverns in Ipswich; dinners, feastings, and entertainments were the order of the day, and Bacchus presided over the orgies of the night. Balls were given, on both sides, to the freemen and their wives and daughters; and the candidates and their friends, of both sexes, were emulous in their civilities and condescension; and we remember an honest gardener's daughter, of this town, giving us a lively example of how she swam along through the mazes of the dance, and figured in with Colonel Wollaston, or the honourable Mr. Tollemache, through the 'Jolly Haymakers,' and the ' Soldier's Joy.' For our own parts, we regret that we never witnessed the humours of an election ball.

March 16th, 1768. Thomas Staunton, and William Wollaston, esqrs., Wilbraham Tollemache, and Edward Holden Cruttenden, were put in nomination for representatives of the borough, when, on a poll being demanded, the numbers were, for

Mr. Staunton.... Si7
Mr. Wollmton... 317
Mr. Tolleuiache... 289
Mr. Cruttenden... 2S7

Thus ended the glorious contest of 1768.
p
September 8th, 1769. A contest for bailiffs took place, when the numbers were, for

March 25th, 1770. The corpse of the right honourable Lionel, Earl of Dysart, high steward of the corporation, lay in state, at the Cross tavern, in this town, on the w.ay to Helmingham. The Cross tavern was then the principal inn in the town, and stood where Mr. Neale now resides, on the Cornhill, comprising not only that house, but the other adjoining to and over the entrance to the opening leading to the Tower Ditches, still called the Cross-yard.

April 20th. William Wollaston, esq., was appointed colonel of the East Suffolk militia, in the room of Lord Orwell, resigned.

September 7th. Robert Wollaston and Thomas Hallum, esq., were elected port men, in the room of James Wilder, and the late Michael Thirkle, esq.

December 28th. A dreadful storm and hurricane of wind happened: much damage was done, and many ships lost off the coast, near Lowestoft, Harwich, and other places. Much distress arose amongst the poor, this winter, on account of the inclemency of the season, and great collections were made for their relief, at Ipswich, and in the neighbourhood. On the 25th of February, the thermometer was down to nineteen, Fahrenheit's scale.

March, 1771. Several persons were served with quo warrantos, to shew cause why they acted as free burgesses. On the 29th, James Wilder, portman, died. This was the man who undertook to choose eleven portmen, on his own individual responsibility,and presided alone, at the time the objectionable one hundred and twenty-seven honorary freemen were made. Thomas Rainbird was sworn in as a free burgess, by order of a writ of mandamus.

April 3d, 1772. Corn became exceedingly scarce and dear; and a subscription was set on foot, to furnish the poor with wheat, at 18s. a coomb. The populace stopped some carts proceeding to London with dead calves, and sold the veal for 2£d. and 3d. the pound. They were guilty of several outrages upon the vendors of provisions, which induced the bailiffs and magistrates, by public advertisement, to entreat the dealers to supply the market, as usual, and that they should be carefully protected from any harm and insult for the future. Butter was sold at the expense of the corporation, for 6d. a pound, to the poor.

May 22nd. A most extraordinary act of generosity and honour occurred here, worthy to be related.-A gentleman having been, for three or four years, in possession of a considerable estate, under a devise, accidentally discovered that the will had been improperly attested, and that thereby the estate descended to the heir at law, who lived in this town; he came hither, from a distant part, related the circumstance of the case, and surrendered the estate: but the rents and profits, which he also offered to account for, were, with gratitude, refused by the legal owner.

July 3rd. Fourteen horses were entered for the races this year, and every day the heats were most severely contested. Owing to the influence of Sir Charles Bunbury, Ipswich races, at this period, were attended by a great concourse of persons of fashion, and excited great interest in the sporting world.

September 18th. In consequence of a number of persons being brought into the town, for the purpose of inoculation for the small pox, all the principal surgeons agreed, by advertisement, to refrain from the practice. A general meeting of the inhabitants took place on the town hall, when the bailiffs, portmen, and the churchwardens of each parish, determined to set their faces against inoculation, as tending to encrease the small pox, by reason of the probability of contagion,

March 14tb, 1773. It was determined, in the Court of King's Bench, that a pretended great court, held in the year 1755, at which a number of freemen were made, was illegal, only one portman being present June 18th, it was determined, in the Court of Common Pleas, that the deputy postmaster at Ipswich had no right to demand any more than the legal postage, and that he could not compel the inhabitants to send to the post office for their letters.

May, 1774. A dreadful mortality raged amongst the cattle, in the neighbourhood of Ipswich, in consequence of a contagious distemper, by which hundreds were carried off: an order was issued by the county magistrates, for all persons to shoot or kill, immediately, every beast so affected, to slash the hide from head to tail, so that it could not be made use of, and to bury the whole carcase four feet below the surface of the earth.

August 22d. The Earl of Bute passed through this town, on his way to Landguard Fort, to observe the experiments trying there, under the direction of General Williamson, for making shot, weighing forty-two pounds, in t he shape of a pear, by which a saving of one-third of powder is effected. September 7th, forty-one persons were admitted, by patrimony and servitude.

October 8th. A contest for members took place.

February 17th, 1776. The petition of John Spooner was presented, by Robert Manning, that he might be a free burgess, on paying a reasonable fine; and on its being put to the vote, his petition was carried by sixtyfive to six, and he was admitted accordingly, on paying five guineas; and, we believe, he was the last man admitted by paying a fine.

At this time, great distress was felt by the poor, from the scarcity of provisions and inclemency of the season; and large collections were raised in Ipswich, for their relief. Smuggling and highway robberies were carried on to a great extent, in this neighbourhood.

November 1st, 1777. A subscription was entered into for writing up the names of the streets, according to the suggestion of Mr. Pennington, who was engaged in a survey of the town, for the purpose of publishing a map of Ipswich.

December 12th, 1778. In consequence of a scuffle which ensued between the press-gang and a party of men assembled at the Green Man, in this town, Mr. Thomas Nicholls, the master of the Ram inn, who interfered, was so ill-treated, that he languished till the next morning, when he died; and the coroner's inquest brought in a verdict of wilful murder against two midshipmen and fifteen of the press-gang, who were committed to the borough gaol: they were tried in the Court of King's Bench, at Westminster, June, 1779, and acquitted.

September 7th, 1780. Seventy-two persons were admitted to their freedom. On the 9th inst. four candidates were put in nomination for members for the borough:— the numbers were—

Thomaa Staunton, esq....... 341
William Wollsaton, esq..... 346
Joshua Grighy, eaq 253
William Middlcton, eaq 847 whereupon the two former were declared duly elected.

September 8th, 1781. A contest for the bailiwick took place, when the numbers were—

William Clarke, nq 166
William Wollaston, esq... 166
Mr. Christopher Rolfe 109
Mr. Rohert Manning, 106

August 4th, 1782. In consequence of the high sheriff's advertisement, a number of gentlemen, freeholders, &c. assembled at Stowmarket; when Sir John Rous proposed that the county should undertake to build a man-of-war, of seventy-four guns, for the service of the public; which being seconded by Sir Charles Davers, and unanimously agreed to, a subscription was immediately set on foot, and the sum of £17,441: 6: 9 was subscribed within a few weeks: but the committee being sensible that the exertions of the county of Suffolk, alone, could be of but little avail in increasing our navy, it was agreed that the ship should not be put upon the stocks till twelve other counties should have entered into similar associations. Ipswich contributed largely to the subscription, which, on the whole, amounted to upwards of £20,000; but no other counties following so laudable an example, the scheme fell to the ground.

On the 4th of March, 1783, an address was ordered to be presented to His Majesty, on the blessings of peace. And, on the 27th of January, 1784, another address was presented, congratulating him upon the dismissal of his late ministers.

On the 3rd of April, 1784, three candidates were put in nomination, for members for the borough; when, on a poll being demanded, the numbers were, for

John Cator, esq 297

William Middleton, esq 460
Chas. Alexander Crickitt, esq. 7 whereupon the two former were declared duly elected. Mr. Crickitt exerted himself, on this occasion, in favour of the admission of those persons who had for some time been kept back, and thirty-two persons were admitted to their freedom. On the 25th of June following, thirtythree more freemen were admitted, by patrimony and servitude; for we seem now to have nearly got clear both from honorary freemen, as well as those by purchase. At the last election, on the 3rd of April, there was an understanding between some of the leaders of the corporation, that something like a compromise should take place, and it was agreed that each party should return a member; but it was supposed that there was some tampering or collusion, respecting money matters, with Mr. Cator, which came to the knowledge of Mr. Crickitt, who arrived on the town hall, with his seven voters, a few minutes previous to the time fixed for the election. He afterwards presented a petition against Mr.Cator, on the grounds of bribery and corruption, when Mr. Cator's election was declared null and void: and, on the 25th of June, Mr. Crickitt offered himself a candidate in the blue interest; on which occasion he was opposed by Robert Thornton, esq. ; and, on a poll being demanded, the numbers were, for

Charles Alexander Crickitt,esq. 353
Rohert Thornton, esq 183
when the former was declared duly elected: and the following minute was entered in the court book: —" That the thanks of this court be given to Mr. Crickitt, for his noble and spirited exertions in detecting and exposing a most dangerous species of bribery and corruption, the disgrace of human nature, and the acknowledged means of destroying our excellent and long-admired constitution." On the 8th of September following, there was a contest and a poll for the water-bailiff and the town crier; which was decided in favour of the blue party: and the bailiffs, and Mr. Batley as town clerk, came in on the blue interest with little or no opposition.

On the 8th of September, 1785, it was proposed that William Lynch, esq., John Kerridgc, esq., Robert Trotman, esq., and Charles Squire, gent., be presented with the freedom of the corporation; which was put to the vote, and decided that they should be admitted, by a majority of seventy-five. A committee was appointed to inquire into the accounts, property, and revenue of the corporation, from the 16th day of October, 1748; and in the report which they made, November 3rd, 1786, it is stated that, at Michaelmas preceding, the demands on the corporation, unpaid, amounted to £440: 13: 5J, and a mortgage of £3,000, at five per cent, interest; that the annual receipts of the corporation were £890, and that the payments will generally amount to about £608, leaving only a surplus of £132 to answer all repairs and contingent expenses. They suggested that it was desirable to appoint persons to superintend the management of the estates and farms, that attention should be paid to the water rental; and it was resolved, that it appears to the court, from the state of this report, that economy was necessary to be used, in the expenditure of the revenue of the corporation.

On the 18th of August, 1786, the following address was ordered to be presented to His Majesty, on his escape from the attempt of Margaret Nicholson to stab him with a knife, whilst presenting a petition:—

"TO THE KINO'S MOST EXCELLENT MAJESTY.

"*The humhle Address of the Bailiffs, Burgtssess, and Commonalty of the ancient Borough of Ipswich, in Great Court assembled.* "We, your *Majesty's* dutiful and loyal subjects, the Bailiffs, Burgesses, and Commonalty of the ancient Borough of Ipswich, beg leave humbly to offer to *your Majesty,* our sincere and hearty congratulations on *your Majesty's* providential escape from the late esperate attempt made upon *your Majesty's* sacred person; au attempt which at once endangered *your Majesty's* life, and the happiness of all *your Majesty's* subjects.

"Fully sensible of the innumerable blessings we enjoy under *your Majesty's* mild government, we fervently pray that *your Majesty's* most valuable life may be preserved many years, and that *your Majesty* may long reign over a free, happy", and loyal people.

"Given under our common seal, the 18th of August, 1786"

Which address gave rise to the following *jeu (T esprit:—*

"*The humble Address of Georr/e Parish and Edward Bell, Esquires, Bellmen of the Borough of Ipswich, in full Pots assembled.*

"The BeHmen of Ipswich, unwilling to be outdone in loyalty to *His Majesty,* have composed an address equally as full of *majesty* as that presented by their worthy masters to *His Majesty,* of which the following is an exact copy:—

"To *His Majesty* most excellent,
With humble duty we present,
In lines replete with *majesty.*
As lights upon the starry sky,
Your Majesty to congratulate,
In being sav'd from th' attack of late—
The attack against your royal life,
By woman's hand and blunted knife.
How could she dare to lift on high
Her hand, to stab *your Majesty?*
That wicked hand, with rage so fierce,
Your Majesty's kind heart to pierce.
'Twas happy for *your Majesty*
That Providence was standing by,
Or else perhaps *your Majesty*
Might have receiv'd a blow so sly.
As would have kill'd *your Majesty.*
What sorrow would the land o'erspread,
T have heard *your Majesty* was dead!
Your subjects would have wept full sore,
T' have seen *your Majesty* no more.
Our thanks unfeign'd we send on high,
To Him who sav'd *your Majesty;*
Q
  And hope that he will hear our cry,
And long preserve your *Majesty.*
"Given under our great seal,
The lanthorn, staff, and midnight bell."

September, 1787. John Howard, the philanthropist, paid a visit to this town, and staid two days inspecting our gaols, of which he expressed the highest satisfaction.

October 26th. A smack from this port, to London, laden with upwards of four thousand coombs of barley, sprung a leak whilst riding at anchor, two miles below the Horns: the men cut the cable, in order to run her aground, but she, unfortunately, fell on her side, and sunk upon a sand-bank, leaving not more than two feet of her mast above water. One man was drowned.

December 15th, C. A. Crickitt, esq. was elected recorder of this borough; on which occasion it is customary.to give billets of 2s.6d. each, to every freeman, to be spent at a public house; but he humanely and judiciously varied this plan, and gave six bushels of coals to every poor freeman, indiscriminately, who should apply, and upwards of two hundred persons were thus seasonably relieved.

April 25th, 1789, was observed here as a day of general thanksgiving for His Majesty's recovery.

On the 11th of May, an address was ordered to be presented to His Majesty, on his recovery from his severe indisposition: and likewise an address of thanks to the right honourable William Pitt, for his unwearied attention to a faithful discharge of his trust, during His Majesty's illness. On the 14th inst. a general illumination took place.

September 26th. Lord Mazarene, who was liberated from the Grand Chatelet at Paris, in June last, in which place he had been confined near thirty years, arrived at the Great White Horse, accompanied by his lady, ond the Marquis of Polladore and his lady; and the next day they visited the old and new gaol, in this town. It would have been natural to suppose, that a gaol would be the last place his lordship would have wished to visit.

March 13th, 1790. At this time Sir John Rous, bait., SirT. C. Bunbury.bart. , and Sir Gerard William Vanneck, bart. , announced their intention of becoming candidates to represent the county of Suffolk in parliament. Though this is not strictly relative to the history of the borough, yet, as the election took place here, and the Ipswich Journal was crowded with advertisements and squibs, respecting this remarkable con-

on the behalf of the two former gentlemen, it was agreed by all the candidates that it should commence immediately. Scrutators on both sides were appointed, and, on the next day, to which the court was adjourned, the numbers were declared to be, for

Mr. Clarke 285

Mr. Wollaston 284

Mr. Truelove 286

Mr. Kerridge 285 whereupon, the bailiffs, Mr. Henry Seekamp, and Mr. John Spooner, thinking it their duty to declare an election of two bailiffs, that the charter of the corporation might not be forfeited, declared Mr. Peter Clarke and Mr. Wm. Truelove duly elected. Before the declaration of the election, Mr. Kerridge demanded to be declared duly elected, for that he had a majority of legal votes, several persons having tendered their votes for Mr. Truelove and Mr. Kerridge, whose names were not entered on the poll: he afterwards obtained a writ of mandamus, and Mr. Clarke was *ousted.*—A contest for town clerk also took place, when the numbers were, for

Mr. William llatley 294

Mr. T. F. Notcutt 270

On the 29th of September, the thanks of the court were unanimously given to the Rev. John King, for his long and faithful services as lecturer to the corporation. A contest took place for the lectureship, when the num bers were, for

Rev. Thomas Hallmn 322

Rev. Mr. Bolton 315

Majority, 7 hine.

For the water-bailiff:—

Chriatopher Prentice 317

William Johsrni 316

Majority, I yellow.

For the town crier:—

William Blieheodeu, jun 121

William Hlichenden, ua..... 314

Majority 7 yellow.

For the guide to Christ's Hospital:—

Samuel Hainhlin *313*

Thomas Studd 31.1

Majority, 8 hlue.

This contest was carried on with great violence, uproar, and confusion.

On the 7th of June, 1792, an address was ordered to be presented to His Majesty, on issuing his royal proclamation against those wicked and seditious writings which had of late been printed and circulated with malevolent intentions against His Majesty's government, and stating that the loyal and dutiful subjects of the ancient borough of Ipswich were ready, with their lives and fortunes and best strength, to unite with His Majesty in endeavouring to repel the wicked attempts of all whose aim was to subvert our most excellent, happy, and glorious constitution—the admiration and envy of surrounding nations.

On the 8th of September, 1792, the blues succeeded to all the places in the corporation, and maintained their uninterrupted sway for upwards of twenty-eight years.

November 13th, 1792. At the time of high water, a number of sailors assembled on the Common Quay, for the purpose of demanding an advance of wages, and forcibly took away some men who had agreed to go on board Captain Hadley's vessel. The magistrates interfered, and they dispersed. They, however, assembled again in the evening, in greater numbers, when three of them were taken up, and underwent an examination, but, upon security being given for their good behaviour, they were dismissed. The magistrates met on the town hall, on Thursday; when the men belonging to Captain Hadley attended, and acknowledged their readiness to proceed to sea with him. The constables went to see them safe on board; but they were no sooner there, and the peaceofficers departed, than the rioters forcibly took the men away, and, further, would not suffer the ship to depart. The magistrates finding mild measures useless, called in the assistance of a party of dragoons, and, with a great number of the gentlemen of the town, headed by the colonel of the dragoons, proceeded down St. Clement's, and took three of the ringleaders into custody, and committed them to gaol; when the remuinder of the sailors quietly dispersed.

On the 29th of December, this year, resolutions, stating that this corporation would use every possible means to suppress all unlawful and seditious assemblies within the borough, and to bring to justice every disturber of public tranquility and order, were ordered to be inserted in the public papers.

On the 5th of April, 1793, it was ordered and agreed, that the representatives of the borough be requested to oppose the bill for paving, lighting, cleansing, and otherwise improving the town, in its progress through the House of Commons, as tending to encroach upoii the rights and privileges of the corporation.

Iti this year, 1793, an act of parliament was obtained for "paving, lighting, cleansing, and otherwise improving the town of Ipswichand commissioners were appointed to carry this act into execution: and, on Monday, August the 5th, the first stone of the new pavement was laid, at the Bell corner, near the Cornhill.

In consequence of an encampment at Harwich, the wherries from this place were crowded to such excess,

R that they were, daily, obliged to leave passengers behind; and between twenty and thirty open boats have been known to leave Ipswich in a day, for the conveyance of passengers to Harwich..

The body of Lieut. Lionel Tollemache, the last male heir of this ancient family, who was slain by a shell before Valenciennes, passed through this town, in the way to Helmingham, August 17th.

On the 1st of January, 1794, it was agreed dial Messrs. Thomas Fulcher and Benjamin Nathaniel Folkard, should have leave to inclose part of the salt water river; and that a lease of ninety-five years should be granted them, at the rent of 50s. a year, for the part to be inlosed, namely, three acres and thirty-six perches at 26s. 6d., and two acres, two roods, and twenty-four perches at 23s. Cd. It was also proposed that a lease should be granted to Mr. George Gooding, of the old shambles, for sixty years, at the yearly rent of £20; he undertaking to erect a new building, at his own expense.

On the 10th of February, 1794, the

first stone of the rotunda, to be built on the scite of the old shambles, was laid by J. Kerridge, esq. and William Norris, esq., bailiffs. This building was so expeditiously erected, that a concert and ball was performed in it, August 12th, in the same year; at which five hundred persons were present.

On the 31st of March, 1794, a letter was read, from the commissioners under the act for paving the streets, stating that, by right of their powers to remove all obstructions, they could order the stairs leading up to the town hall to be taken down, but that they wished to act with the concurrence of the corporation, and requesting that they would give orders for their removal. Upon which it was determined by the court, that the commissioners had no legal right or power to cause these stairs, leading to the town hall, to be taken away; not, however, restraining themselves by this resolution, in some future more favourable circumstances, from removing those stairs for the sake of general improvement.

This month, March, a subscription was opened for the relief of the wives and children of those soldiers and sailors who might lose their lives in defence of their country.

May 27th. At a meeting of the inhabitants, on the town hall, Sir Robert Harland, bart., in the chair, it was resolved to form a volunteer corps, according to the act of the 17th of April, for the internal defence of the country, to be called " The loyal Ipswich volunteer corps."

On the 11th of June, the news of Lord Howe's victory over the French fleet was received; when the town was most brilliantly illuminated.

On the 8th of September, a slight contest for bailiffs took place:—

Mr. Trotman 169
Mr. Walford 182
Mr. Spooner 95

On the 29th of September, a resolution to the following purport was road in court, and unanimously agreed to:— That we, the bailiffs, burgesses, and commonalty of the town and borough of Ipswich, in great court assembled, understanding that other towns in Great

Britain have come forward to strengthen the hands of government, and, taking into consideration the offer of Major Robinson, of His Majesty's late reduced Horse Grenadier Guards, to raise a corps for the service of government, under our patronage, consisting of thirty-two Serjeants, thirty corporals, twenty-two drummers, and six hundred private men, to be called "The Ipswich regiment," do unanimously consent thereto, and determine that this resolution shall bo addressed to the right honorable General Jeffery, Lord Amherst, commanding His Majesty's forces, &c, requesting him to move His Majesty to grant a letter of service to Major Robinson, to raise tins corps, to be called "The Ipswich regiment." This resolution was transmitted in writing to his lordship, accordingly, but was never carried into effect

On the 21st of January, 1795, the Princess of Orange, hereditary prince, &c. passed through this town, in their way from Yarmouth; and, on the following day, arrived His Royal Highness the Duke of York, who had been to Yarmouth, by the way of Norwich, to receive these illustrious visitors, and by that means missed them.

In consequence of a rapid thaw, and the frost setting in severely the same evening, on the 7th of February, between thirty and forty persons were seen skaiting through the principal streets of the town.

About this time, great distress arose amongst the poor in this town, in consequence of the enormous price of grain and potatoes: new wheat was sold in the market, from 48s. to 50s. per coomb, and potatoes at 7s. per sack. And, in April, an order was published by the magistrates of the borough, in which it is recommended to their representatives to aid in the promotion of any plan for removing the public distress; particularly for the inclosure of waste lands, and the employment of the poor.

September 29th. An order was published by the bailiffs, stating that the frequency of oaths, as required to be taken by law, tends to decrease their efficacy, and to increase the crime of per-

jury, they recommend to their representatives to support an act for the repeal of many of these oaths, now become useless and unnecessary.

So populous and busy had Ipswich become at this time, that constant hints were given in the papers, for persons to observe the same rule in walking the streets as is customary in London, in order to prevent confusion.

November 13th. An address w as ordered to be presented to His Majesty, stating that this corporation contemplated, with real concern, the publication of principles disloyal and seditious, by a factious few; and they pledge themselves to use every legal exertion against such offences and such offenders.

On the 27th of May, 1796, and following day, sixty-two freemen were admitted. On the 28th, three candidates were put in nomination for members; when, on a poll being demanded, the numbers were, for

Mr. Middle ton states, in his advertisement, that he was anxious to preserve the peace of the town undisturbed; but, in consequence of Mr. Crickitt introducing a stranger, he throws himself upon the support of the independent

July, 1797. His Royal Highness Prince William of Gloucester, takes up his residence here, as commanderin-chief of the eastern district; and was at the races, which were most fashionably attended.

February 20th, 1798. A meeting of gentlemen took place on the town hall, for the purpose of entering into a subscription for the general defence of the country, when a considerable sum was immediately subscribed.

July 20th, 1798. On the resignation of the Rev. John King, as master of the grammar school, the Rev. Rowland Ingram was chosen in his room. — A committee having been appointed for the management of the water rate, it was determined that no more leases should be grantcd; that a new rent roll should be made out, and that a col lector should be appointed. On Tuesday, October 16th, 1798, there was a grand free burgesses.

ball and supper, in commemoration of Lord Nelson's brilliant victory. About eight o'clock, Lady Nelson's arrival was announced by the ringing of bells and the loud huzzas of a vast concourse of people in the street. Her ladyship was introduced into the ball-room by Admiral Sir Richard Hughes, bart., and Admiral Reeve, who conducted her to the top of the room, attended by the Rev. Mr. Nelson, the venerable father of the admiral, followed by Captain Bourchier, leading up Miss Berry, sister to Capt. Berry, of the vanguard. The room was lighted up with transparencies, and variegated lamps interspersed amongst a variety of evergreens, which had a beautiful effect. Upwards of three hundred persons of distinction and fashion were present, and the evening passed off with universal hilarity and eclat.

February 2d, 1799, a remarkable fall of snow happened, by which the roads between this town and Yarmouth, were rendered utterly impassable, and the mail coaches were detained more than a day.

June 1 st, Lord Duncan and his daughter paid a visit to Admiral Reeve, of this town.

November 9th. At this time our army, from Holland, marched through here, in different divisions, in a most miserable and wretched state of sickness and distress. Severe privation was occasioned amongst the poor, from the scarcity and high price of provisions: great collections were made for providing them with nutritious soup, and otherwise affording them relief.

May 29th, 1800, the following address was ordered to be presented to His Majesty:—

"Most gracious Sovereign,

"We, the Bailiffs, Burgesses, and Commonalty of your ancient and loyal town of Ipswich, first offering our sincere acknowledgments to that divine power by whom kings reign, for preserving your Majesty in the late atrocious attempt on your sacred person, beg leave to express our cordial congratulations to your Majesty, upon an event so important to the whole realm; trusting that the preservation of your

valuable life will insure us, in common with all your Majesty's subjects, a continuation of the blessings which we derive from your gracious government and illustrious example.

"Given under our common seal, on the anniversary of the restoration of royalty, 29th May, 1800."

On the 6th of July, Horatio Lord Nelson was chosen high steward of the borough, in the room of Lionel, earl of Dysart, deceased.

August 19th, the Turkish ambassador and suite passed through this town, on the way to Yarmouth. About two miles from Colchester, one of the carriages broke down; when His Excellency ordered the whole party to stop, and retired, with his attendants, into an adjoining wood; where a canopy was thrown across some trees, under which he regaled himself with his pipe, for upwards of two hours, while the carriage was repairing.

September 20th. Much rioting took place about this time, in consequence of the high price of provisions. An attack was made, by the mob, upon Mr. Rainbird's mill: a full account of which will be seen in the account of St. Peter's parish.

On the 8th of November, Lord Nelson, with Sir Wm. and Lady Hamilton, passed through this town, and stopped at the Great White Horse, on their way to London.

October 13th, 1801, a general illumination and great rejoicings took place, on account of the signing of the preliminaries of peace.

The population of the town in the year 1755, was —

Males 7 826 Female" 4298
J29K 12124

And, in the year 1801,—
Males,.... 6150 Feinata,.... 6211
6211
11061

In the first statement, the number of the males is nearly double that of the females 5 but, in the last, the fair sex greatly preponderate: the population, however was considerably decreased.

July 5th, 1802. Sir A. S. Hamond, bart., and C. A. Crickitt, esq., were re-

elected members for the borough, without opposition.

February 8th, 1803. William Middleton, esq., was elected member of the borough, without opposition, in the room of C. A. Crickitt, esq., deceased.

July 14th. A loyal and dutiful address was ordered to be presented to His Majesty, concurring in the necessity for the declaration of war with France.

August 26th. The dukes of York and Cambridge arrived at Ipswich, and reviewed the troops of the garrison.

September 8th. A slight contest for bailiffs took place:—

Rohert Trotman, eaq 154
Mr. Simon Jnckman,.... 1S7
Mr. Rohert Manning,.... 48

December 19th. A new set of colours was delivered to the Ipswich volunteers, by William Middleton, esq. This corps, under the command of Colonel Neale, offered their services to the amount of two hundred men, to take any part of the garrison duty, to march to the neighbouring coast for fourteen days, or, in case of actual invasion, to march to any part of the kingdom where they might be wanted.

April 9th, 1804. The loyal Ipswich volunteers, under the command of Colonel Neale, marched into Hadleigh, on permanent duty for twenty-one days. And, again, in 1805, they were on permanent duty, for the same period, with the garrison, at Ipswich; and frequently received the thanks of the reviewing generals, for their soldier-like conduct and behaviour.

The races, this year, were productive of a remarkable degree of interest, independent of the regular plates, for which finer running was never seen. Many matches were made amongst the officers of the garrison, and afforded unusual sport. Lord Charles Fitzroy, with a liberality honourable to his character, ordered sixty guineas, which he won by a sweepstakes, to be distributed amongst the wives and children of the men composing his own brigade. And we repeat that it is the duty of every well-wisher to Ipswich, to use his utmost exertions for the restoration of the races to their former excellence and splendour.

January 14th, 1805. The officers of the district performed the play of The Castle Spectre, and the farce of The Apprentice, for the benefit of the Ipswich Public Dispensary; which produced to the charity £140. And, in the following month, they played She Stoops to Conquer, and a farce, in aid of the Norwich Theatrical Fund: an appropriate address was written for the occasion; and the receipts of the house were upwards of £100.

April 4th, 1805. It was determined that several clauses in the bill brought into parliament, for improving the port of Ipswich, would, if suffered to pass into a law, in the state it then was, materially affect the chartered rights and interests of the corporation; and it was ordered that a petition be presented to the House of Commons, praying to be heard by counsel, against the said bill, in order to get these objectionable clauses expunged or amended.

September 1st, 1805. An extraordinary heavy fall of rain was experienced here; the water, in many of the s streets, being two or three feet deep; and much damage was done in warehouses and cellars.

October 15th, 1805. His Royal Highness the Duke of York arrived in this town, and slept at the residence of Lord Paget, the present Marquis of Anglesea. The next morning the following troops were inspected by His Royal Highness, on Rushmere Heath: — the Royal Berkshire, Shropshire, R. E. Middlesex, Hertford, and W. Suffolk regiments of militia; a detachment of the Royal Artillery, Royal Horse Artillery, R. N. British Dragoons, (the Greys) and the 7th and 21st Light Dragoons, amounting to 8000 men. The review took place during a heavy rain, amidst a multitude of spectators.

November 29th, 1805. The ceremony of introducing St. Andrew into this town, was observed by the Scots Greys, in garrison here. A soldier of the regiment represented the venerable saint: he was mounted on a fine grey horse, and wore a bear's-skin cloak and a long white beard; he had a roll of paper in his right hand, and a cross affixed to his breast; two men led his horse, and a guard of twelve soldiers, in the Highland dress, with their broad swords drawn, kept off the crowd: the procession was proceeded by the band of the regiment, who played several national airs, this being St. Andrew's day.

On the arrival of the news of the victory of Trafalgar, large collections were made at all the churches here, in aid of the patriotic fund at Lloyd's; but the rejoicings were greatly damped by the loss of the gallant hero, Nelson, who was peculiarly connected with this town, as high steward, and whose amiable lady had long resided in its immediate vicinity.

December 18th, 1805. An address was ordered to be presented to His Majesty, congratulating him upon the victory over the combined fleets of France and Spain, at the battle of Trafalgar; and condoling with him, in the deepest and most heartfelt sorrow, on the death of the illustrious Lord Viscount Nelson.

On the 20th of February, 1806, the election for a member of parliament for the county took place here; when T. S. Gooch, esq. was chosen, without opposition, in the room of Lord Brome, who became Marquis Cornwallis.

July 11th. A violent thunder-storm lasted two hours: the lightning fell upon a stable in St. Margaret's parish, by which two horses were killed, and a man and several horses considerably injured.

September 8th. Sixty-seven freemen were admitted. A warm contest took place for bailiffs; the numbers being, for

Mr. Kenidge 227
Mr. Trotinan 229
Mr. Spooner 290
Mr. Foreett 284
For the town clerk:—
Mr. William Batley.... 262
Mr. Brame 255

On the 3rd of October, the Duke of York, accompanied by the Duke of Cambridge, reviewed the troops in garrison here and at Woodbridge, on Rushmere Heath.

On the 29th of October, the election for members of parliament for the borough came on; when, on a poll being demanded, the numbers were as follow:— when the two former were declared duly elected. Capt. Stopford being absent, on His Majesty's service, he was represented by his friend Capt. C. Cunningham; who was chaired in his naval uniform.

On the 2nd of November, Sir T. C. Bunbury, bart. and T. S. Gooch, esq. were here chosen members for the county, without opposition.

On the 4th of May, 1807, and following day, sixty-eight freemen were admitted. And, on the 8th inst. four candidates were put in nomination for members; when, a poll being demanded, the numbers were, for

Sir Home Popham, knt S97
Roht. Alexander Crickitt, eaI. 388
Richard Wilson, eaq i»7
R. H. A. Bennett, C«i 920

Previous to this, all elections for the borough had been concluded in one day—this lasted two days. Sir H. Popham was chaired in his full naval uniform, preceded by six officers of the navy, and attended by an immense concourse of people. Seven hundred and eighteen persons voted at this election; which was a greater number than on any former occasion.

May 14th. Sir T. C. Bunbury, bart. and T. S. Gooch, esq., were elected members for the county, here, without opposition.

October 5th. The Duke of York, accompanied by the Dukes of Cambridge and Cumberland, with a long train of nobility and general officers, reviewed the troops in garrison here, on Rushmere Heath. At this period, Ipswich was in the zenith of its glory. Every building, cottage, or apartment, that could be hired at almost any price, was occupied by persons belonging or attached to the garrison. Martial fetes and exhibitions were the order of the day. The agriculturists vied with the military in the liberality of their expenditure. Trade and commerce nourished in an extraordinary degree, and handsome fortunes were realised by many of the inhabitants.

On Tuesday, November 3rd, about

three o'clock, Louis XVIII. king of France, arrived at the Great White Horse, in this town, on his way from Yarmouth, attended by Prince de Conde, Comte d' Artois, Due de Bourbon, Due de Grammont, and suite; and, after changing horses, set off for Gosfield Park, in Essex, the seat of the Marquis of Buckingham.

On the 8th of September, 1808, an humble address was presented to His Majesty, to congratulate him on the glorious victories lately obtained by the Spanish and Portuguese patriots.

April 21st, 1809. The portmen of this borough having signed a requisition to the bailiffs, to hold a great court, for the purpose of addressing Mr. Wardle; and having proposed and seconded a motion for that purpose, it was rejected by a considerable majority: and resolutions to the following effect were carried:— That it is the opinion of this court, that it is highly improper to countenance public meetings for the purpose of returning thanks to any individual member of the House of Commons, however meritorious his exertions may have been in the public cause, when such thanks cannot be bestowed but at the hazard of the public tranquility: and that this court have the firmest reliance on the wisdom, energy, and integrity of His Majesty's ministers. Which resolutions were ordered to be inserted in the public papers.

October 25th, 1809. A loyal, dutiful, and congratulatory address was ordered to be presented to His Majesty, on this propitious day, being the fiftieth anniversary of His Majesty's reign. Great rejoicings took place in the town; and a large subscription was raised for the poor.

In February, 1810, a petition was presented to parliament, by R. A. Crickitt, esq., that the assizes may be held alternately at Ipswich and Bury, and was lost by a very small majority. The gentry and inhabitants of this eastern district of the county ought not to rest satisfied till this object is accomplished.

In June, this year, a violent storm of hail and rain occurred here, which, in many parts, completely flooded the town, and great damage was done to goods in cellars and warehouses. At Mr. Chapman's pinery, upwards of four thousand panes of glass were broken.

August 8th, 1811. Eighteen persons requested to be disfranchised, in order to give evidence in a cause respecting the corporation, at the assizes at Bury. They were afterwards admitted again to their freedom, and received the thanks of the great court for their services.

August 15th. It was ordered that the bounds of this corporation, as well by land as by water, be gone every seven years; and that the perambulation of the same shall take place between this day and the 29th of September next. It was likewise ordered, unanimously, that the Right Honourable the Earl of Dysart, elected high steward of the borough, be presented to the freedom of the corporation. And it was also ordered that a committee be chosen to prepare rules and orders for the regulation of the fishery of the river Orwell; and some regulations were made respecting the dredging for oysters, but not for any plan for enlarging and extending the fisheries in general, such as might be of essential advantage to the town: and which we still hope to see carried into effect in a way hereafter pointed out.

On Thursday, September 12th, 1811, the troops in garrison here and at Woodbridge, were reviewed on Rushmere Heath, by the Prince Regent, attended by the Dukes of York, Cumberland, and Cambridge, and a number of distinguished persons. After the review, His Royal Highness, with his brothers, rode through the town to the cavalry barracks, in St. Matthew's; where they partook of an elegant breakfast, provided by Lieut.-General Baron Linsingen, at which many gentlemen of the town and neigbourhood were introduced to His Royal Highness; after which he proceeded to Colchester.

On the 29th of September, an address was ordered to be presented to the Prince Regent, testifying the satisfaction of the corporation, on the re-appointment of the Duke of York as commander-in-chief.

May 19th, 1812. An address from the inhabitants of the town in general, was presented to the Prince Regent, expressive of their regret and horror at the assassination of the Hon. Spencer Perceval.

July 2nd. The corporation waited upon the Earl of Dysart, at his seat at Helmingham, and presented him with the freedom of the borough, in a box made of oak from his lordship's park, beautifully inlaid with gold.

August 20th. A brilliant and general illumination took place, in honour of Lord Wellington's victory over the French, at Salamanca, &c.

On the 5th of October, thirty-one freemen were admitted. Robert Alexander Crickitt, esq., and John Round, esq., were chosen members for the borough, without opposition.

Nov. 25th. His Royal Highness the Prince Regent, accompanied by the Duke of Clarence, arrived in this town, and were entertained at dinner by General Linsingen. There was a concert at the assembly-rooms; at which many of the principal families of the town and neighbourhood were invited: their Royal Highnesses left the room at eleven o'clock, and proceeded to Copdock White Elm, where they slept; and their dormitories are still distinguished by the names of "The Regent" and "The Clarence," and were always pointed out with pride by the loyal landlord, James Martin, who was then " mine honest host" of the Elm.

January 15th, 1813. A petition was ordered to be prerented to the House of Lords, against any further concessions to the Roman Catholics.

February 19th. The eccentric but benevolent James Webb, esq., arrived in this town; and crowds of poor and afflicted persons assembled round the door of the Golden Lion, where he took up his abode. He relieved a great number of distressed objects; he also left £100 with Messrs. Alexander, to be distributed among the poor of the twelve different parishes; he gave £30 to the poor debtors, in the gaol here; to the Friendly Society, £10, and to the Female Society, £5: altogether it was ascertained that he distributed upwards of

£450 in this town.

October 28th. His Royal Highness the Prince Regent arrived here, on a visit to Baron Linsingen. Dinner was served up at seven o'clock; and the different bands attended. His Royal Highness expressed himself so well pleased with his reception and accommodation, that the next day, after inspecting the cavalry, he again dined with the baron, in company with several gentlemen of the neighbourhood, who had the honour of an invitation; many of whom will never forget the glorious conviviality of those days: and the house in the Tower Lane, the residence of Mrs. Studd, will for ages be pointed out as the spot where George IV. threw aside the formality of state, and so happily blended the monarch and the gentleman, as to win the hearts and affections of all those who were present on the occasion.

November 30th. An address was ordered to be presented to the Prince Regent, on the recent and repeated victories of His Majesty's arms, and his illustrious allies'; congratulating him upon the emancipation and liberation of the United States of Holland, from tyranny and oppression; and of the reinstatement, in His Majesty's electoral dominions, of its former mild and beneficent government.

January, 1814. The E. Suffolk local militia, under the command of Col. Vernon, quartered at Ipswich, offered their services to march to any part of England; and it is somewhat remarkable that this fine body of men mustered stronger than any regiment of local militia in the kingdom. A subscription was entered into, for the purpose of relieving the poor, at this inclement season, and upwards of £700 were collected: five thousand applications were made for relief.

In February, a large sum was raised for the distressed inhabitants of Germany: the corporation subscribed £20, and the Quakers collected, amongst themselves, upwards of £130. The sum of £100 was also collected at an assembly, for the relief of the widows and children of soldiers killed in Lord Wellington's army; for which he returned his public thanks, expressing his high sense of gratitude for the donation. It is a striking feature in the character of the residents of this town and neighbourhood, that upon all occasions of calamity and distress, they come forward with unexampled liberality and benevolence; and there are more charitable institutions of various descriptions in the town, than in any other place of similar population.

May 30th. A meeting took place upon the town hall, to consider of a petition to both houses of parliament, to postpone any alteration in the corn laws; and it was afterwards signed by upwards of two thousand persons.

June 13th. An address was ordered to be presented to the Prince Regent, on the glorious termination of the war with France.

June 25th. A general illumination took place here, on account of the peace; and, at the expense of the Society of Friends, an excellent dinner of roast and boiled beef was given to all the poor children of the different schools,

T amounting to one thousand and thirty-six. The tables were set out in the new market-place—which was decorated with flowers and shrubs; and it was altogether a most pleasing and interesting exhibition, worthy of the kind and benevolent feelings of the donors. The Society of Friends in this town are always conspicuous for their aid, in any thing tending to promote real utility and benevolent feeling.

July, 1814. A petition was presented from the inhabitants of Ipswich, against the slave trade.

On the thanksgiving day for peace, a subscription was entered into for enabling the poor to partake of the general joy, and tickets of the value of 16d. each were distributed to upwards of seven thousand persons.

January, 1815. A meeting took place on the town hall to present a petition to parliament against the renewal of the property tax; though we believe it is now the general feeling that a fairly modified property tax would be one of the most effectual means of relieving the exigencies of the country; and we are convinced that the present premier is the only man competent to accomplish it.

July 20th. The bishop of Norwich preached a sermon at St. Mary Tower Church, for the benefit of the society for the relief of the widows and orphans of clergymen; and afterwards presided at a large party at dinner, at the Bear and Crown. He also accepted the office of patron of the Ipswich Female Asylum.

November, 1815. A meeting was held on the town hall to take into consideration the best means of preventing the spreading of the small-pox, which had been very fatal in the town, notwithstanding the benefit of vaccination.

November 20th. A congratulatory address was ordered to be presented to the Prince Regent; and it was agreed and ordered that the bailiffs, who were William Biitley and James Thorndike, esqrs., the town clerk, William Barnard Clarke, Edward Bacon, and John Denny, esqrs., as a deputation of this corporation, do wait upon His Royal Highness, at the seat of the Most Noble the Marquis of Hertford, at Sudbourn Hall, in this county, and present the same. To which His Royal Highness returned the following most gracious answer:—

"*To the bailiffs, hurgesses, and commonalty of the town and horough of Ipswich.*

"Gentlemen,

"I thank you for your loyal and dutiful address, and for the expression of your attachment to His Majesty, to my person, to my family, and to my government.

"The triumphs that have crowned our efforts for the reestablishment of civilized Europe, are mainly owing to the zeal and firmness with which I have been supported; and, however deeply I must deplore the pressure which the nation has borne with such unexampled cheerfulness, I am highly gratified in the reflection that our envied and happy constitution remains unimpaired, and the country's grandeur has assumed a character beyond all former periods of our history.

"I desire to assure you, gentlemen, of my best wishes for the prosperity, welfare, and happiness of your most ancient and loyal town and borough."

And it was agreed and ordered that the thanks of the corporation be given to the Most Noble the Marquis of Hertford, for his politeness, attention, and hospitality to the deputation that presented the address. The members of the body corporate were highly gratified with their reception. This visit has been celebrated as follows:—

"TO MRS.

"On a tour, my dear Mary, in Suffolk I've been,
And at Sudbourn beheld a delectable scene;
Where the Bailiffs of Ipswich, that loyal old town
Having heard that his Highness the Regent was down,
Came in form to present an address to the Crown.
Id attendance the Marquis and General wait,
And the Regent received them with dignified state.
The address was then read, but not strictly in order,—
It was read by the Town Clerk, and not the Recorder.
Then the Regent, with grace, condescension, and ease,
Such as, spite of the Chronicle, Englishmen please,
Which the prince and the gentleman clearly display,
And, while duty commands, makes us wish to obey,
His high satisfaction was pleased to express,
With their dutiful, loyal, and well-timed address;
And by way of a compliment, due to their wives,
Proposed giving them titles to last both their lives.
But their Worships the Bailiffs, tho' greatly delighted
With his Highness's offer, declined being knighted,
But remained to regale, by the Marquis invited;
And, with each flowing bumper and delicate bit,
Drank his health, and applauded his wine and his wit:
And, having dispos'd of the splendid collation,
Away went to Ipswich the whole corporation.
"P.S.—What prodigious high honours some people arrive at!—
Mr. Square, after all, saw the Regent in private;
Who graciously asked him, with confidence treating,
When Colchester Oysters were fittest for eating;—
With a very low bow, said the eloquent Member,
Please your Highness, they're best in the month of December.'"

February, 1816. It was agreed at a general meeting of the inhabitants, to petition the parliament against the renewal of the tax on income.

May 13th. An address was ordered to be presented to the Prince Regent, on the marriage of his daughter, the Princess Charlotte of Wales, to Prince Leopold of Saxe Coburg.

April 29th, 1817. A violent gale of wind happened here, by which several vessels were driven from their moorings in the river; some chimneys were blown down, and considerable damage done in the neighbourhood.

In August, this year, "The Orwell" East Indiaman was launched from Mr. Jabez Bayley's ship-yard at Halifax: a full account of which is given in the description of the banks of the river Orwell.

December 18th. An address was ordered to be presented to the Prince Regent, humbly and sincerely condoling with him on the death of the Princess Charlotte of Wales. An address of condolence was also presented to Prince Leopold of Saxe Cobourg, on the same melancholy event.

June 16th, 1818, and following day, seventy-nine freemen were admitted. Four candidates to represent the borough in parliament, were put in nomination; and, on the 22nd inst. the numbers on the poll were declared to be, for

Rohert Alexander Crickitt, esq 425
William New-ton, eaq 422

Henry Baring, eaq 389
Sir Will iain Bolton, 362

Such were the exertions made by both parties to bring the voters from the most distant parts, that this election continued for six days; and on the third day, Mr. Baring was at the head of the poll. A scrutiny was demanded on the 1st of July, and the numbers were, for

Rohert Alexander Crickitt, esq 394
William Newton, esq 387
Henry Baring, eaq 356
Sir William Bolton, 33a whereupon R. A. Crickitt and William Newton, esqrs., were declared duly elected. — When Mr. Baring paid a visit to Ipswich, at the races, he was met at Copdock by a party of fifty persons on horseback, and the populace drew his carriage into the town.

On the 14th of December, 1818, an address was presented to the Prince Regent, on the death of her most gracious Majesty Queen Charlotte.

March, 1819. A petition was presented to both houses of parliament, in favour of a revision of the criminal laws.

June 16th. A large party of Mr. Baring's friends dined together at the Bear and Crown, to celebrate the anniversary of his becoming a candidate for Ipswich. And, on the 2nd of July, the blues had a public dinner at the White Horse, in commemoration of the return of Mr. Crickitt and Mr. Newton, to parliament. These gentlemen were present, and presided on the occasion.

September 29th, 1819. Mr. Thomas Duningham petitioned for his freedom, by apprenticeship to Edwd. Bacon, esq. , banker; but it was objected to, upon the plea that a banker was no trade or mystery, and that it was contrary to usage for any person to be bound apprentice after the age of twenty-one; and it was also confessed that he was bound for the purpose of obtaining his freedom. It was, however, brought before a court of justice, and determined that it was a *bona fide* apprenticeship, and a verdict was given in his favour.

Jan. 20th, 1820. His Grace the Duke of Wellington passed through this town, on his way from Lord Granville's at

Wherstead Lodge, to Lord Suffield's, and paid a visit to Admiral and Mrs. Page, with whom he had returned from India.

Feb. 2nd. The proclaiming the accession of George IV. took place here, as the county town, by the undersheriff; and, on the following day, by the bailiffs for the borough, Messrs. James Thorndike and J. E. Sparrow; when the proclamation was read on the Market Hill and the Common Quay: when a sumptuous collation was prepared on the town hall, at the bailiffs' expense.

On the 17th of March, four candidates were put in nomination as representatives of the borough, and a contest the most strenuous and protracted of any that had ever taken place in this town commenced. More virulence and ill-nature appeared on this occasion than usual, and each party energetically braced themselves for the fight; and, after continuing the contest for six days, the numbers on the poll appeared as follow:—for

William Haldimand, esq 483
Thomas Barrett Lennard, esq... 482
Rohert Alexander Crickitt, esq. 474
John Round, esq 468

A scrutiny was demanded, and after it had been carefully gone into, the numbers were, at its conclusion,

Rohert Alexander Crickitt, esq. 4so
William Haldimand, esq 428
Thomae Barrett Lennard, esq... 427
John Round, esq 424
Majority for Mr. Crickitt,.... 2
Majority for Mr. Haldimand, l

And, at the latter end of April, Mr. Crickitt was chaired at Ipswich, attended by a procession of his friends of the blue party. The true-blue ladies of Ipswich presented him with a set of colours: and the procession terminated with a dinner, as is usual upon such occasions.

At the conclusion of the scrutiny, Mr. Haldimand addressed a letter to his constituents, thanking them for their support, and congratulating them upon their victory in favour of independence, but regretted that the result had excluded his friend, Mr. Lennard, from acting with him as his colleague, but stated that he

meant to petition the House of Commons, which he did; when Mr. Crickitt finding that several bad votes had been given in his favor, declined defending it; and the following determination put an end to the dispute:—

"*Home of Commons, June Hth,* 1820.

"A petition having been presented against Mr. Haldimand's return, and also one against Mr. Crickitt's return, and the petitioners ou the part of the latter gentleman having agreed to withdraw their petition, and allow four votes to be struck off Mr. Crickitt's poll, Mr. Haldimand and Mr. Lennard were, this day, declared duly elected."

When this decision was made known at Ipswich, the joy and exultation of the yellow party knew no bounds: the most extensive preparations were made, to give eclat to the chairing of their members; and the most splendid procession took place that had ever been witnessed on a similar occasion; of which we shall only attempt a brief description, — for a full account we must refer our readers to the *Suffolk Chronicle Extraordinary,* published July 20th, 1820. An extensive range of hustings was erected in the middle of the Cornhill, for the accommodation of the ladies; who, by their presence, to the number of about four hundred, gave interest and animation to the scene. In Westgate-street, an arch adorned with laurels, flowers, and ribands, was thrown across the road, and bore the inscription "Welcome." The houses of many individuals were fitted up in an appropriate style; and the front of the Golden Lion was converted to a temporary alcove, displaying the word "Victory" in the centre. The procession was appointed to assemble on Crane Hall Hill, by nine o'clock, as a place of rendezvous; from which having met the members, it was to proceed through the town by a circuitous route. Long before this hour, the leading streets were lined with spectators; and fresh groups of persons from the neighbourhood continued to arrive in all directions. Several bands of music contributed greatly to the effect. The cavalcade was nearly a mile and half in length; and, for numbers, magnificence,

and arrangement, surpassed the most splendid example of former times. It was led by a man of large stature clad in bright armour. Near Messrs. Alexanders bank, a temple of Fame, rising twenty-two feet high, from the shoulders of the bearers, joined the procession. This structure, in addition to the names of Lennard, Haldimand, and Baring, bore those of many distinguished persons by whom the cause of independence was supported. On each side were two profile paintings of Fame in flying posture, bearing white flags, with the motto "Ipswich is free." Soon after two o'clock, the members ascended their triumphal cars; each of which consisted of a cupola, supported by eight pillars, raised upon a platform of spacious dimensions, and carried by thirty-two men. As soon as the members had seated themselves in their chairs, they were lifted up amidst the acclamations of the multitude, and taken slowly along round the Cornhill, and from thence through the principal streets, till they regained their former station. In Tavernstreet, on their return, a figure of Justice, on a pedestal, with a sword and scales, and surmounted by a white flag, bearing an appropriate motto, was also displayed. About five o'clock, the ceremony of chairing concluded, and the members having alighted at a house on the Cornhill, and severally delivered an energetic address, they then proceeded to the Golden Lion, preparatory to the dinner. Accommodation was provided for three hundred and fifty guests; and the Free Grammar School-room was fitted up at a considerable expense, for this occasion,—where an excellent dinner was provided.

Thus ended the most splendid electioneering exhibition ever witnessed at Ipswich. A state of the poll was printed and published by both parties; and, by way of preface to that of the yellows', a long statement of the proceedings of the election was entered into, and much abuse was hurled upon Mr. Crickitt, and the conduct of the bailiffs as returning officers, for their gross evasion and partiality: and the whole was written with bitterness of feeling and sarcastic severity. This called forth a reply from the bailiffs, in" vindication of their conduct and character, from the malicious and unjust aspersions which they said had been undeservedly cast upon them: it appeared in the shape of a pamphlet, and was signed by them, as bailiffs, James Thorndike and E. Sparrow, dated September 2nd, 1820.

We do not pretend to judge of the merits of the case, nor shall we involve ourselves in electioneering disputes, but we cannot but observe that the attack is written in a strain of personal severity hardly justifiable from a triumphant anonymous writer, and that the returning officers, who have committed their names to the public, have justified themselves in a much milder tone.

August 15th, 1820. A singular circumstance occurred on the road from Colchester to Ipswich:—the stage waggon belonging to Messrs. Betts and Bury, of this town, was observed by the driver to be on fire at the top; who, with great presence of mind, instantly aroused a man, woman, and two children, who were asleep; and he extricated the horses, as there were several packages of gunpowder amongst the luggage: he had scarcely accomplished this, when the waggon, with its whole contents, was blown up with a tremendous explosion: scarcely an article was saved,—but no lives were lost. It was supposed to have been occasioned by the lightning, which had been very vivid that evening.

September 8th. The blue party were certainly defeated, by the decision of the House of Commons in favour of their opponents, at the last election for members, but they were not disheartened, for they rallied again on this occasion, and the most warm and animated contest took place; when the numbers, at the close of the poll, were as follow:— t

William Brame, e«4 495 Bailjff

W. B. Clarke, e 485 $

William Hammond, eaq 485 Town Clerk.

William Batley, eaq 465 gjff-
John Denny, esq 462
S. Jaekaman, esq 462 Town Clerk.

On this occasion, the members and the late candidates took an active part: voters were brought from the most distant parts of the kingdom, and as many were polled as at the preceding general election. All this took place in one day; which proves the folly of protracting the voting for members for five or six days, and which might, by consent of both parties, be for the future easily avoided.

On the 29th inst. the minor officers of the corporation w ere warmly contested; but the yellow interest prevailed, except in one instance, which was that of the water-bailiff. The blues, however, had a public dinner at the White Horse, and appeared to be neither dispirited nor dismayed.

November 18th. The town hall was illuminated, in consequence of the decision of the House of Lords, respecting Queen Caroline, and the town was partially illuminated.

December 12th, 1820. A meeting was held on the town hall, for presenting a petition to His Majesty, for the dismissal of his ministers; and to present a congratulatory address to the queen: which, after a tumultuous debate, was carried by acclamation, in consequence of the hall being occupied by a promiscuous crowd, and not by resident householders, as intended. The party against the measure withdrew to the White Horse, drew up a protest against the proceedings, and published a loyal address to His Majesty; which was afterwards signed by a great number of the inhabitants.

January 7th, 1821. The Duke of Wellington took up his freedom on the town hall, and, being Sunday, proceeded to the church of St. Mary at the Tower, attended by the whole body corporate, in grand procession. He walked between the two bailiffs, W. B. Clarke, esq. and B. Brame, esq., accompanied by Lord Granville and Admiral Page. After the service he partook of some refreshments at the house of the worthy admiral, and soon after departed with Lord Granville for Wherstead Lodge.

Wilbraham, earl of Dysart, high steward of the borough, died in March, 1821. He was a great loss to the town

and neighbourhood, for his benevolent and amiable disposition rendered him the patron of the arte and sciences, as well as the friend and benefactor of the poor. He was the firm supporter of the true-blue interest at Ipswich; and was universally beloved and lamented by persons of all parties. And, on the 23rd of March, his remains passed dirough this town; when the procession was headed by his lordship's tenants, followed by the bailiffs, and common-council of the borough, in eight coaches. A great number of horsemen and gentlemen's carriages followed the hearse; forming altogether a most splendid and imposing cavalcade.

The population of Ipswich, in June, 1821, being an increase, on the whole, of 3727, since 1811; the females still bearing the larger proportion. The number of houses, at this time, was 3378.

June, 1821. A charitable bazaar was opened at the old assembly-room; when £84 was collected for the poor, by the sale of fancy articles manufactured by the ladies of the town and neighbourhood. This plan has been adopted annually, with great benefit and advantage.

July 2nd. A meeting of about seventy gentlemen in the yellow interest took place at the Bear and Crown, to celebrate the anniversary of the return of Messrs. Lennard and Haldimand. Mr. Lennard presided at the dinner; and the party afterwards joined a number of the free burgesses, who supped on the town hall.

July 19th. The day appointed for the coronation of George IV. was observed at Ipswich with much general rejoicing. Many public dinners took place, particularly one of the common-council and the friends of the blue party, at which Mr. Crickitt presided. A ball and supper at the new assembly-rooms were numerously attended; and there was a general illumination in the evening. But, strange to say, the bailiffs and portmen, as the chief magistrates of the corporation, issued no orders respecting the observation of the day, nor attended church in their official capacity, but actually threatened a prosecution against the editor of the Ipswich Journal, for having lamented this extraordinary circumstance.

September 8th. On this occasion, an offer was made by the common-council, to the leaders of the yellow party, that if they would pledge themselves not to attempt to make any honorary freemen, the blues would offer no opposition to their election of bailiffs and town clerk; but no such pledge was given, and a warm contest took place: and what appears to us very injudicious, the Duke of Wellington was proposed as a candidate for the office of high steward; and, contrary to all precedent, this high and hononrable office, which had, on all former occasions, been unanimously presented to the person who was selected for this honour, was made to depend upon the issue of a poll, and by that means subjected the greatest man in the kingdom to an inglorious defeat; and as this was done without His Grace's consent, it could not be very agreeable to his feelings, for the numbers were as follow:

Sir Rohert Hailand, hart 401 High Steward.

Sir Williain Middleton, hart... 397 ,,..
..

F. F. Seekamp, eaq 397 J
S. Notcutt, eaq 392 Town Clerk.

The Duke of Wellington, S25 High Steward.

William Batlcy, esq 329 BIijff
J. E. Sparrow, esq 327
S. Jackaenan, esq 332 Town Clerk.

September 13th. A beautiful lndiaman, named " The David Scott," was launched at Mr. Bayley's Halifax shipyard; and, a few days afterwards, another lndiaman, 1350 tons burthen, was launched from the same yard, called "The William Fairlie."

November, 1821. A meeting of the inhabitants was held, at which it was stated that £1,100, in £25 shares, had already been subscribed towards a botanic garden, and that about £900 more was still wanting to carry the plan proposed into execution; and we yet hope to see this accomplished at some future time.

May 17th, 1822. A meeting was called, by the bailiffs, on the town hall, to take into consideration the sufferings of our fellow-subjects in Ireland; and a considerable sum was subscribed for their relief.

September 8th. We now come to a very critical crisis in the affairs of the corporation. It was, after some discussion in private, agreed between the leaders of both parties to make a certain number of honorary freemen on each side; and, in the midst of much noise, discordance, and confusion, the following gentlemen were elected:— YELLOWS. BLUES.

John Aldrich
Jain e Maedonald, M. P.
Samuel Alexander
Edgar Rust Buchanan
Richaed Crawley
Jeremiah Head
Eleazar Lawrance
William Pearson
William Smart
Henry Alexander.
  Henry Bristo
John Cohhold, jun.
Thomas Cohhold, Harwich
T. R. Drake
Charles Gross
William Sparrow
James Wenn
Iohn Bond.

By this it is shewn that the boasted rights and privileges of the free burgesses of Ipswich are held by a very precarious tenure, and can at any time be easily invaded.

September 14th. About this time, a parcel containing bank notes, of the firm of Messrs. Alexander and Co., to the amount of £31,192, was abstracted from the coach by which it was sent from London. The firm immediately altered the appearance of their notes, which were worked in red ink instead of black; and they called in all the black notes that had been previously issued; by which ingenious contrivance, they rendered the plan of negociation which our modern abstractors resort to of but little value; and it is supposed that the eventual loss was not more than between two and three thousand pounds. A reward of £5,000 was offered, but no discovery was ever made.

On the 29th inst. the minor offices of the corporation were strongly contested, and the blues succeeded in carrying two out of the three. This election took place on a Sunday; and, though we do not pretend to be very precise, we are confident that it never was contemplated by the granters of any charter, that it was necessary to so strictly abide by the letter of the law, that a contested election for the minor officers of a borough should take place on a day set apart for far different purposes.

March, 1823. A meeting took place on the town hall, for the purpose of petitioning-the legislature against the coast duty on coal; which petition was unanimously agreed to. Also a petition against the Insolvent Debtors Act was presented to the House of Commons, from this town.

April, 1823. An opportunity of trying the relative strength of the two opposing parties, occurred in the choice of a person to fill the office of collector of the duties on coal. The right of voting is confined to residents who can prove themselves worth £1,000, or who rent premises of £50 per annum. The contest was as warm and spirited as a borough election; and, at the close of the poll, the numbers were as follow:—

Mr. Aethur Barker, 1(1
Mr. George Coe 1.51 the blues carrying the election.

August 21st. The Suffolk Pitt club held its anniversary meeting here; when a temporary building was erected in the garden formerly occupied by the late Rev. J. Edge; which was lighted with gas, and decorated with evergreens and flowers, and had a beautiful effect. This was one of the most splendid and numerously attended public dinners that had ever taken place at Ipswich.

September 8th. The busy note of preparation had been for some time heard in the circles of the contending parties. Mr. Gross, and several of the honorary freeman, had already been elected common-council-men, and two new candidates for office appeared on the yellow side. From the very respectable character of all the individuals, offensive personal remarks were more than generally avoided, though a considerable portion of political warmth and animosity was freely indulged in. After an arduous and fluctuating contest, the blues were again triumphant; for, at the close of the poll, which was kept open till halfpast eleven o'clock at night, the numbers were, for

William Barley, esq 449

John Aldrich, esq 450 J

S. Jackaenan, esq 451 Town Clerk.

Williain Pearson, esq £ Bailifls

Richard Crawley, esq 435$

S. A. Notcutt, esq 432 Town Clerk.

Our pen is nearly worn out with detailing the continued contests for every place and office of the smallest importance in the town; but as they are interesting to persons on the spot, it is our duty to record them. And, on the election of an additional collector under the paving and lighting act, a poll was demanded, and the numbers were, for

Mr. J. B. Lawrance 193

Mr. Thomas Brady, 178 the blues still keeping the ascendancy.

The alarum bell was again rung; for, in February, 1824, we find *rules nisi* were granted by the Court of King's Bench, calling upon John Aldrich and James Macdonald, esqrs., to shew cause by what authority they claimed to be free burgesses of Ipswich; and these notices were afterwards extended to the sixteen other honorary freemen. It seems that these honorary freemen had been proposed to the great court and elected in *couples,* instead of having been proposed separately, and that the legality of the court was called in question, in consequence of Mr. Notcutt acting as town clerk as well as portman, it being necessary that two portmen should be present, when it appears there was only one besides Mr. Notcutt; and it was therefore contended that he could not preside on the bench as portman, and fill the office of town clerk at one and the same time. Great chagrin and disappointment were evinced by these gentlemen, who had recently tasted x the sweets of office, and "had borne their blushing honors full upon them" for so brief a space of time. The election of Mr. Aldrich, as bailiff, would become null and void, and the charter was

in danger of being lost. "The oharter in danger" became the watch-word of alarm amongst the freemen at large, and both parties accused each other of this dreaded event; but which, we think, is devoutly to be wished, for the affairs of the borough cannot be easily legalised till it actually does take place.

July 5th, 1824. A meeting of the friends of the yellow party, to commemorate the return of their representatives, was held at the old assembly-room, at which Mr. Leonard presided; and a resolute determination to retain their pre-eminence was the general feeling of the company.

September 8th. The yellows had made great efforts to carry the election for bailiffs. The London voters on their side had been brought down, and both the members personally attended. But, on the presumption that Mr. Aldrich's election would be declared illegal, the blues offered no opposition, and Mr. Seekamp and Mr. C. C. Hammond were chosen bailiffs, and Mr. Notcutt town clerk, amidst much clamour and confusion. At a great court held a few days afterwards, much warmth and recrimination took place respecting leases and mortgages; but the business was afterwards explained by a public advertisement, in a very satisfactory manner.

September 29th. The minor officers of the corporation were elected by the yellows, without opposition. Each party had a public dinner; where their respective friends mustered in great numerical strength. The yellows, as an extraordinary circumstance, proposed the health of the premier, Mr. Canning; and the blues were in high spirits, and seemed fully prepared for a contest at the ensuing general election.

November 13th-In the Court of King's Bench, the King *v.* Sir William Middleton, bart., and Stephen Abbott Notcutt, gent. This was a rule calling on the defendants to shew cause why an information, in the nature of a *quo warranto,* should not be exhibited against them, for illegally assuming to be portmen of Ipswich. The rule was made absolute, and those gentlemen were obliged to disclaim and be discharged from

the office of portmen. On Saturday, also, the Attorney General moved for *quo warranto* informations against the then bailiffs and town clerk, by their own consent. Judgment had been signed against all the honorary freemen.

Thus absurdly do our fellow-townsmen suffer the lawyers to fatten on the feuds of the corporation, and remain as far from legalising their transactions as they were before they had expended their money.

December 27th. A meeting of the committee of the County of Suffolk Shipwreck Association was held at the Great White Horse, Ipswich; when it was satisfactorily stated that a very considerable fund had been raised, and many resolutions were passed to further the intentions of this praiseworthy and excellent institution.

June, 1825. The late bailiffs having disclaimed, the town was left under the jurisdiction of the two remaining portmen, till a new election could be made, under a writ of *mandamus* lately issued. An assembly of the burgesses took place July 21st, on the town hall, at which William Batley, esq., the only good bailiff, presided. He stated that this assembly was held in obedience to the writ of *mandamus,* for the purpose of electing two bailiffs to serve for the remainder of the year, till the 29th day of September next; and that he had no doubt but that such persons returned this day, would be legally and validly elected; when Mr. Seekamp and Mr. Hammond were rechosen, without opposition.

The statute made in the ninth year of Queen Anne, ch. 20, respecting the election of bailiffs and mayors acting as returning officers, expressly states, "That no person or persons who hath been in such annual office for one whole year, shall be capable to be chosen into the same office, for the year immmediately ensuing." Nevertheless, on the 8th of September, the then bailiffs and town clerk started again as candidates, and a protest was entered against them, signed by several freemen, upon the ground that the bailiffs ought, by the charter, to be chosen annually, and that they were incompetent, as returning officers, to elect themselves; however, they were returned by the following majority, as appeared at the close of the poll:—

Mr. Seekamp,.... 4 67 Bilill»
Mr. Hammond,.. 449)
Mr. Notcntt, 465 Town Clerk.
' 5, J Bailiff..
Mr. Cohhold,.... 424 *S*
Mr. Jack, in an 420 Town Clerk.

Great exultation arose amongst the yellows, who now considered themselves securely seated in power, and that the independence of the borough was at length completed. The blues contended that their discomfiture arose from some vacillation in their committee that occasioned a misunderstanding amongst the voters, and which they were determined to avoid on another occasion. All the minor offices were filled by the yellows, on the 29th, without opposition. Each party had their public dinner, and each declared themselves prepared for a contest at the ensuing general election.

December, 1825. At this time of general panic, the inhabitants of this town promptly entered into an agreement to support the banks, and to give them their entire confidence and credit; which saved them from a run, and enabled them both to remain firm and secure.

April 29th, 1826. In the papers of this day, Mr. Lennard announced his intention of resigning the honour of representing Ipswich in another parliament, and Colonel R. Torrens declared his wish to be returned, as member, with Mr. Haldimand—who says, in his address, that " he shall be proud and happy to take Colonel Torrens by the hand." And, no doubt, they expected to walk quietly over the course. But, on the 27th of May, Charles Mackinnon and Robert Adam Dundas, esqrs. announced their joint intention of entering the field in the blue interest. The busy note of preparation was now heard on either side; and, on Monday, June 12th, the election commenced.

This contest was disputed with the most determined pertinacity, for six

days; and, on the first day, the yellows took the lead by a majority of twenty-two, and kept a-head till the final close of the poll, on the Friday afternoon, at three o'clock; when the returning officers declared the numbers to be as follow, and that Mr. Haldimand and Colonel Torrens were duly elected:—

Mr. Haldiinand 4»«
Colonel Torrens, 495
Mr. Mackinnon, 488
Mr. Dundas, 488

But there were six men who had been occasionally employed in the Customs, as *glutmen,* as they are called— in reality, temporary labourers when a press of business happens—seven men employed in the preventive service, and three others, whose votes were rejected by the returning officers; who, altogether, rejected sixteen votes that were tendered for Messrs. Mackinnon and Dundas, which, had they been accepted, would have turned the scale in favour of the blues. Upon this and other grounds, a petition was presented to parliament, to eject the members returned; which was done by the decision of the House of Commons, February 23?d, 1827.

On Tuesday, June 20th, 1826, the election of members for the county took place at Ipswich; when Sir Thomas S. Gooch, bart. and Sir William Rowley, bart. were chosen without opposition.

September 8th. At this time, some of the leaders of both parties had agreed to a compromise, and that one blue and one yellow should be proposed for the office of bailiff; that the present town clerk should remain for the ensuing year, and that a blue town clerk should be chosen the year after. This plan, it was thought, would put an end to dissension, and settle all disputes; but it would be as easy to still the waves of the ocean, as to calm the turbulence of party spirit, or silence the voices of Ipswich freemen: for when Mr. Hammond was proposed as bailiff, by the yellows, and Mr. Batley by the blues, and Mr. S. Notcutt to remain as town clerk, the blues proposed J. C. Cobbold, esq. and William Lane, esq. as bailiffs, and Mr. Charles Gross as town clerk. This was done by a party of the blues acting in

opposition to those of their leaders, who wished for a compromise. Mr. Jackaman was proposed as town clerk, by Mr. Denny, in the blue interest, and Mr. George Gooding, by Mr. R. King, as bailiff in the yellow interest; but Mr. Jackaman, finding the tide of popular opinion against him, in about half an hour withdrew his name. A poll being demanded, the numbers were, for

J. C Cohhold, «, "Bailiffs.
W. Lane, esq. 234 $
Charles Grow, esq 242 Town Clerk.
William Hammond, esq 134 ,,.,.,,
William Batley, esq *7A $* 8. A. Notcutt, esq 133 Town Clerk.
Mr. George Gooding, 4 Bailiff.

It was observed, at the conclusion of this contest, that the blues had carried the election by such an overwhelming majority, that it must be considered as a death blow to the yellow interest; but, no such thing! for, on the 29th, a warm contest took place for the minor offices of the borough, viz.—the water-bailiff, guide to the hospital, and town crier. The fate of the day was, for some time, doubtful; but the Ipswich steamer having been engaged to bring down a number of London voters, they arrived in time to turn the balance in favour of the yellows; for, at the close of the poll, the numbers were as follow:— YELLOWS.

Breckles,.. 827 Cork,.. 3-11 Nunn,.... S31 BLCES.

Johon,.. 259 Baker,.. 215 Wilkinson, 256

The yellows thus obtained a temporary triumph, and demonstrated to the public, that a steam engine may be used with great effect at a contested election.

On Monday, January 22nd, 1827, a great court was held; when an address of condolence, on the lamented death of His Royal Highness the Duke of York, was ordered to be presented to His Majesty.

In the Court of King's Bench, the King *v.* Slythe, an application had been made, and a rule granted, for a *quo warranto,* calling on the defendant to shew by what authority he exercised the right of free burgess of Ipswich, he having been admitted to his freedom by two bailiffs of the borough who had not been duly elected themselves; when the court were of opinion, that having a right to be a free burgess, it mattered not whether the bailiffs who had sworn him in had been duly elected themselves. The motives for this proceeding have been stated as very illiberal; but we consider that it was highly desirable to set the question at rest, for all those young freemen, of both parties, who had taken up their freedom under the same circumstances, would have been for a long time in a state of disagreeable uncertainty.

February 23rd. A letter was sent, by Colonel Torrens, to the committee of the House of Commons appointed to try the merits of the Ipswich election, stating that he and Mr. Haldimand meant to offer no opposition to the petition against them; and it was agreed by their solicitor, that the first ten names on the pauper list of the yellows should be struck off without proof, when the committee declared that C. Mackinnon, esq. , and R. A. Dundas, esq., were duly elected.

On the 18th of April, Messrs. Mackinnon and Dundas, made their triumphal entry into this town, in grand procession, attended by an immense multitude of persons on horseback as well as foot, and a long line of gentlemen's carriages and vehicles of all descriptions, decorated with ribands, and accompanied with banners, bands of music, and every thing conducive to the splendour of the procession. After the ceremony of chairing had taken place, upwards of three hundred gentlemen sat down to an excellent dinner which was served up in a temporary building, erected for the purpose, on the waste ground opposite to the Great White Horse. This room was fitted up with evergreens, banners, and inscriptions, and lighted by a gaslight chandelier suspended in the centre. The whole of the decorations, exhibiting great taste, were under the direction of Mr. Brooks, giving great satisfaction to the exulting party assembled; and, certainly, it was the most splendid exhibition of triumph ever displayed by the "True Blues;" who, according to the speeches of their orators, at the dinner,

were now firmly in possession of the borough.

On Sunday, May 13th, the bishop of Chichester administered the rite of confirmation to upwards of two thousand young persons, in the churches of St. Mary Tower and St. Margaret, in this town.

June 12th and 13th. A charitable bazaar was opened, at the Old Assembly-room; when the articles exhibited for sale, produced £137.

June 19th. A grand selection of sacred music was performed at the Tower Church, in the morning, and in the evening at the Theatre, by the Musical Society of Ipswich; assisted by Mr. E. Taylor, from London, with several other celebrated provincial singers, together with our favorite native songstress, Miss Goward. The performances went off smoothly, and were well attended and strongly patronised by the gentry of the neighbourhood; but, notwithstanding the receipts were intended for the benefit of the different charities of Ipswich, such is the expense attendant on these exhibitions, that but little benefit accrued.

July 23rd. Agreeably to the standing order of the great court, that the boundary of the jurisdiction of the corporation, by water, should be sailed every seventh year, the bailiffs, recorder, steward of the admiralty, the clerk of the admiralty court, and the greater part of the corporate body, with the persons summoned to serve on the jury, proceeded down the river, and held an admiralty court on St. Andrew's Sand, beyond Harwich; where William Batley, esq. the steward, in an admirable speech, clearly pointed out the duties of the jury, and the importance of the rights connected with this jurisdiction, which had, at various times, been confirmed for many centuries. Considering the great privileges which the corporation enjoys from the exercise of this power, we trust that this septennial proceeding will never be neglected; and, at the earliest opportunity, we hope that the boundaries of the corporation will be perambulated by land.

September 8th. After a comparative

calm of several months, it was supposed that the election of bailiffs would

Y have passed over without opposition; but the following gentlemen were put in nomination, and at the close of the poll the numbers were — YELLOW.

F.F.Beekamp,,,

Joseph Pooley, eaq 247

E. Lawrancc, esq 242 Town Clerk.

BLUE.

John Denny, «q J Bailiff..

J. E. Sparrow, eaq 216) 8. Jackaman, eaq 216 Town Clerk.

Thus, we see, the yellows again acquiring a considerable majority; which was in consequence of their having freighted "The Suffolk" steamer with a valuable cargo of free burgesses, — who arrived in Ipswich about eight o'clock at night, and secured the triumph of their party. There was one remarkable feature in this election, that the leaders, on both sides, were at length sensible of their former folly in giving large sums of money to the voters, and took the most effectual method to prevent bribery and corruption, by offering no temptation.

October 12th. Mr. Green made an ascent with his balloon, from a meadow near the gas-works, in view of the greatest concourse of spectators ever assembled in this town, as it was the first time that such an occurrence had taken place here; and it certainly creates a peculiar sensation in the minds of the gazing multitude to behold a human being soaring in mid air, suspended, as it were, by a thread, between heaven and earth, till he dwindles to a speck, and is lost to the human eye, by being enveloped in clouds. How much it is to be regretted that this sublime discovery has never yet been productive of utility, and that the daring adventurers are so ill-repaid for their hazard and their labour.

January 2nd, 1828. A novelty in Ipswich — a grand fancy ball — took place at the Assembly-rooms, here; at which upwards of three hundred of the gentry of the town and neighbourhood were present, arrayed in the various costumes usually to be seen on such occasions.

February 2nd. The *rule nisi* for an

information which was procured in Michaelmas term, was made absolute against Mr. E. Lawrance, as being incompetent to hold the town clerkship, in consequence of his not being a free burgess.

February 21st. The tragedy of " Douglas" and the drama of "The Shepherd of Derwent Vale," were performed at this theatre, by youthful amateurs, for the purpose of augmenting the funds of the institution for the relief of the sick and aged poor, and the receipts were upwards of £100.

March 5th. An extraordinary high tide occurred here, which overflowed the Common Quay, and entirely covered the marshes above Stoke bridge. From the wind blowing a strong gale from the N. W. on the preceding night, it occasioned this accumulation of water, and forced the tide to rise to its height about two hours before the regular time, that is, by twelve o'clock, and was near five feet higher than a regular spring tide.

April 16th. Died, Joseph Pooley, esq. aged 68, one of the bailiffs of this town, during life esteemed for his integrity, and whilst in office as chief magistrate, for an active and able discharge of his public duties. An unusual degree of sympathy and regret was felt at his decease; and he was attended to the grave by the whole body corporate, in their robes of office, and followed by a number of gentlemen, his personal friends. The bells of all the churches tolled during the morning, and the windows of the shops and private house were generally closed.

June 7th. The Court of King's Bench granted a writ of *mandamus* for the election of two burgesses to serve the office of bailiffs, now vacant; for Mr. Seekamp, the colleague of the late Mr. Pooley, had disclaimed, considering that being reelected under the writ of *mandamus* would legalise any informality that there might have been in his previous election; and, on the 17th inst. the election took place, Mr. Hammond, as senior portmen, presiding; when F. F. Seekamp, esq., and C. C. Hammond, esq., were proposed by Mr. Brame, in

the yellow interest, and W. Batley, esq. , and B. B. Catt, esq., by the blues on the floor; when, after a very short contest, the poll was closed at one o'clock, in opposition to the protest of many of the freemen, and the numbers were, for

Mr. Seekamp, 97 J Mr. Batley, 60
Mr. Hammond, 97 Mr. Catt, 59

September 8th. At a great court held this day, Wm. Lane and B. B. Catt, esqrs., were elected bailiffs without opposition, and J. E. Sparrow, esq., town clerk. Thus the blues appear to have obtained quiet possession of power.

November 21st. The members of the Friendly Society held their eighteenth anniversary, upon the town hall; and the following statement will evince the peculiar excellence of this benevolent institution: — 984 bushels of coals have been carried to the houses of one hundred and twenty-three aged persons, the majority of whom were above seventy-five years of age—one at the advanced age of a hundred,—1174 bushels of coals, 60 sheets, 135 calico garments, 232 flannel ditto, 67J yards of flannel, and 9 yards of calico. The total number relieved by this society last year, were 203 perrons hetween 65 and 75 years of age, 90 ditto 75 and S5 ditto ie ditto *f,* ond 100 ditto

December 19th. The tenth anniversary of another excellent institution, called the Penny Club, took place here; which exhibited the pleasing spectacle of between five and six hundred children, all habited in comfortable garments, in consequence of the judicious expenditure of the funds of this society, arising principally from the savings of the poor.

Thus endeth our chronological chapter of the history of the borough, up to the end of the year 1828. In relating the circumstances connected with the various contested elections, together with the feuds of the corporation, we have endeavoured to steer clear of party prejudice, feeling confident that our statement is impartial and correct; and we shall notice any event of importance that may occur previous to the conclusion of this work, in the chapter in which we shall hereafter speak of the

present state of the town.

ANTIQUITIES, CHURCHES, AND RELIGIOUS EDIFICES.

It is, of course, an author's desire to please all classes of his readers, as far as in his power; but it is to be feared that here is but little to gratify the taste of those who prefer the blue mould, or rather the green rust of antiquity, to a sound, solid brick building; for Suffolk brick is much in repute, being considered of a very durable nature, and, as an article of home manufacture, has been very much encouraged at Ipswich; for, except the churches, there is not, we believe, a stone building in the town. Gilpin, the great father of the picturesque school, condescended to notice only one object as worthy of his remark, and that was the poor old Market Cross; which is now, alas! to be numbered with the things that were. The eye of the artist, who had rather behold the mouldering ruins of the ivy-mantled tower, than a snug, comfortable habitation, will certainly be disappointed; but still there are many beautiful and romantic scenes to be met with in the vicinity of this town, calculated to satisfy the most fastidious observer, and such as our own Gainsborough delighted to paint. Whether the castle which stood on the spot still called the Castle Hills, on the high ground not far from Brook's Hall, can claim the honour, with Walton Castle, of having been built by those politic invaders who did not, like the Danes, conquer to destroy, has never been ascertained; and as we know of no coins or relics that have been found, to give a plausible colouring to the fact, we must give up the point of its having been a Roman fort, or that there ever was a Roman station here. All that is known of this castle is, that when the Normans had possessed themselves of England, the Conqueror, to awe the people into subjection, built, among other castles, one at Ipswich; which Hugh Bigod, earl of Norfolk, maintained, for some time, against King Stephen, in the behalf of Henry Fitz-Empresse, but was, at length, obliged to surrender it: however, afterwards, in consequence of this Hugh Bigod's disaffection, who took part with his sons against Henry II. , this monarch, in the year 1176, caused it to be destroyed, and no vestiges of it remain; but, upon digging a few feet below the surface of the earth, relics of an ancient building have frequently been found.

The town was formerly surrounded by ramparts and a ditch; which had been, more than once, demolished by the Danes; but which were repaired and fortified in the fifth year of King John, as appears from the following extract from Doomsday Book:—

Anno 5'. regis Joannis, 1203. Facta fuerunt magna fossata Villa Oippovici per praefatum Regem et Auxilium totius patriae et Comitate Cantab rigise.

This is six hundred and twenty-five years ago, but the line of the *fossa* is clearly marked; and on what are still called the Tower Ditches, and St. Margaret's Ditches, fragments of this fortification may yet be seen.

To this rampart were attached four gates, which served as entrances into the town, and were called, from their situation, after the four principal points of the compass; and from these gates were named the four *letes* or *wards* into which the place was divided. And, in Ipswich Doomsday, is the following account of the division:— East-gate *lete* reaches fiom North-gate to the stone cross in Brook-street, called St. Lewis's Cross; so down Tankard-street, till you come to the common ditch, next to the friars' preacher's wall; with Carr-street, Thingsted or St. Margaret's Green, and the lane leading to Little Bolton, and Caldwell or St. Helen's-street. West-gate *lete,* from North-gate, by the Archdeacon's House, till you come to the corner of the street leading from Brook-street to the Fish Market; and so by the same market, (which was at the east end of St. Lawrence' church-yard, in White Hart Lane,) on the right hand, to the further corner of St. Lawrence' conduit-house, and to the Corn-hill, on the north side of the street, till you come to the West-gate, with the suburbs that be without the gate. South-gate *lete,* from West-gate, on one side of the high-street, till you come at St. Mildred

Church, (the old town hall) and so upon the right hand on one part of the street, till you come to Woulfern's Lane, in the parish of St. Peter, almost against the west end of the said church-yard. North-gate *lete* contains all the rest of the town, with the suburbs beyond Stoke bridge, and, besides the Key, with St. Clement'8-street. A fifth has also been mentioned, called Lose-gate, which stood on the bank of the Orwell between the Common Quay and Stoke bridge, where there was a ford over the river. From this it may be seen that nearly the whole of the parishes of St. Austin, St. Clement, and St. Helen, with a great part of St. Margaret and St. Matthew, were not included within the ramparts or in the *letes* or *wards,* but were called the suburbs of Ipswich, in old writings.

Nine churches are mentioned in Doomsday, afterwards mcreased to twenty-one; but there are now only twelve, which are those of

St. Matthew St. Nicholas St. Clement St. Mary at the Elms St. Peter-St. Helen

St. Lawrence St. Mary Stoke St. Margaret

St. Stephen St. Mary ut the Key St. Mary at the Tower and, within the liberties of the borough, those of Thurlston, Whitton, and Westerfield.

The first church that meets the eye of a stranger, from the London or Norwich roads, is that of St. Matthew. It has no beauty to recommend it, but it is situated on a rising ground, and the churchyard is a delightful spot;— to some people who, like Goldsmith's wounded veteran, "always like to lie well," this may be a matter of importance.

So fond are we of copying our neighbours the French, in every thing relative to folly or to fashion, that it extends even unto death; and, because they have, with their usual frivolity, planted and ornamented a cemetery in the neighbourhood of Paris, and endeavoured to make even a receptacle for the dead, gay, airy, and fashionable, so some people in this country have taken it into their heads to be very fastidious about the pleasantness of their buri-

alplace. Such persons may be exceedingly well acommodated in St. Matthew's church-yard.

St. Matthew's has always been termed a rectory, and the incumbent instituted as such, but the great tithes now belong to the family of Fonnereau, although the advowson to the living is in right of the crown. The present worthy incumbent, the Rev. William Layton, has been rector of this parish upwards of fifty years.

This parish once contained four churches or chapels, long since demolished. These were, All Saints', St. George's, St. Mildred's, and St. Mary's.

The scite of All Saints' cannot now be ascertained, but z it is supposed to have been upon a piete of ground near Handford bridge, which is part of the glebe appertaining to the rectory of St. Matthew. All Saints' church was consolidated with.St. Matthew's, before 1333.

St. George's Chapel was used for divine service so late as the middle of the sixteenth century, in the time of Henry VIII.; when Mr. Bilney, who suffered martyrdom, was there apprehended as he was preaching in favour of the Reformation: and so enraged were the monks against him, that they twice plucked him out of the pulpit there. But he escaped out of their hands, and still kept on preaching, till, in a sermon at Christ's Church, in this town, he gave so great an offence to the Popish clergy and people, that they took and imprisoned him. He ably confuted Friar Brasterd, respecting the mediation of saints; but he was accused as a heretic, removed to London, and was executed there.

Considerable remains of this edifice were left till within these few years, having been used as a barn, but they have lately been pulled down, and a handsome row of houses, called St. George's Terrace, erected on the spot.

November 1st, 1764. A fire broke out at a barn, formerly St. George's Chapel, and consumed all the hay and corn on the premises. It was occasioned by a boy knocking his torch against some pales adjoining to the barn. This boy had been attending a funeral—for, at this time, it was customary to bury the dead by torch-light—and, in consequence of this accident, it was recommended that the custom should be abolished.

St. Mildred's Church was one of the most ancient buildings in Ipswich. Part of it had been converted into what was the Old Town Hall, the foundation and walls of the church forming the principal part of the front of the building, under which were three rooms or vaults; and, contiguous to the hall, was a spacious council chamber, with kitchens below, formerly used at the leasts of the merchants' guilds. This portion of the building w as. rebuilt, or thoroughly repaired, at the restoration of Charles II. The brick building at the end of the hall appears to have been erected about the year 1449.

The prior and convent of the Holy Trinity, in the year 1393, granted to the burgesses of Ipswich a piece of ground in the parish of St. Mildred, twenty-four feet long and eighteen wide, the north end abutting on the Cornhill. On this ground the edifice in question was erected; and there is an order made at a great court, in the twentysixth year of Henry VI., that all the profits of the escheator and justice of the peace, should be applied towards the expense of the building at the end of the Hall of Pleas: therefore, this structure must be one of the oldest brick buildings in the kingdom, as the date assigned to its erection is earlier, by some years, than the period considered as the era of the introduction of that material.

In 1812, the front of the Old Town Hall was pulled down. It was a homely, uncouth specimen of architecture; and the ascent to the spacious apartment where public business was transacted, was by a flight of stairs, clumsy, steep, and dangerous. The materials with which the walls were composed, were so tenaciously cemented together, that it was with difficulty they could be razed for the purpose of erecting a new front; which was copied from a design of Palladio, and executed under the direction of Mr. Benjamin Catt. It is ornamented with four Ionic pillars, twenty-six feet high, supporting a pediment, and reaching from the base to the entablature of the building; to which are added two pilasters, of the same order, on each side. It has two stories, and there are thirteen windows in the front; which extends about seventy feet in length, next the Corn-hill. The exterior has, altogether, an elegant appearance, and does credit to the architect. The first stone of the new front was laid by Edward Bacon, esq., on the 4th of June, 1818; and the inscription on it is as follows:—

"THIS STONE WAS LAID THE 4TH OF JUNE, 1818.

« Edward Bacon,?,
"John E. Sparrow, S
"B. B. Catt, Architect."

But so much more difficult is it to build up than to destroy, that the intended alterations of this building have never been completed; and, for want of funds, the interior remains in a deplorable, half-finished state,—a reproach to the corporation. For our own part, we do not coincide with those exceedingly meek-spirited politicians who contend that party spirit has been the ruin of the town; on the contrary, we are convinced that the nicety of the balance has tended to excite emulation — that the town *has* improved and flourished, and *will continue* to improve and flourish under *its* strong and stimulating influence. Ft arouses in the mind of every man, a sense of his own rights; it keeps the place from stagnating into careless indifference respecting justice and liberty, and we are bold to assert, that a great deal more good than harm arises from the legitimate and appropriate direction of the spirit of party. But there are times when this feeling requires to be moderated, for the general good; and surely it would be desirable to lull the turbulence of contention, into peace, for a short period; and, instead of lavishing away money in useless annual contests, expend it for the purpose of completing the town hall; which would then afford admirable accommodation for all the purposes of the corporation, would benefit both parties, and be an honour to the town.

As the subject of' Antiquities is included in this chapter, we shall step a little out of the parish, and now speak of the Old Market Cross; which stood upon the Cornhill, within a few yards of the Town Hall, opposite to King-street. In 1812, it was deemed necessary, in furtherance of the improvements that were then taking place, to pull down this picturesque and ornamental structure; which was effected with considerable difficulty, as the timber, and every part of it, were in excellent preservation. As a relic of antiquity, we cannot but regret its loss. It was erected by Edmund Daundy, in 1510; and the following notices respecting it, from the town treasurer's book, may not be uninteresting:—" Benjamin Osmond, by will, dated June 1619, gave £50 towards building the cross. In 1628, £34 was paid to the town, in lieu of £50 which was given by B. Osmond, towards the building of the new cross. Paid to Thomas Allen, in part of the framing of Uk; cross, £10. More paid to said Allen, in full, of £38, for framing the said cross." Several entries are to be seen respecting the timber taken from Ulverstone, for the use of the cross, and of the sums paid by the corporation to Tfcoley's charity for it. May 10th, 1660, the cross was ordered to be beautified, for the proclamation of King Charles II. , and five or six great guns to be provided at the Common Quay, and to be discharged at the same time. April 12th, 1694, it was ordered that a new Justice be set upon the cross, and the cross repaired, at the charge of the town. April 15th, 1723, it was ordered that the town treasurer repair the Market Cross, at the charge of the corporation; and, this year, the thanks of the corporation were ordered to Francis Negus, esq., for his present of the statue of Justice, which was brought from his seat at Dallinghoe. This gentleman represented the borough in the parliaments of 1717, 1722, and 1727. The arms on the cross, above each pillar, were those of Ipswich, of the families of Daundy, Bloss, Long, Sparrowe, and the two tradesmen's marks of C. A. and B. K. M.

The cross was a large octagon building of wood, supported by eight stone pillars, a circular roof, terminated in the centre with a spiral point carried to a considerable height, surmounted with a small stone cross upon which stood a well-executed figure of Justice, w ith her usual attributes. The building was twenty-seven feet in diameter, and about fifty feet from the ground to the top of the figure.

Several drawings of this building have been taken, and several different engravings of it have appeared; the largest and best of which is the one published by Mr. Raw, executed by that ingenious artist the late Mr. George Frost, of this town: in which a correct view of the Old Town Hall is also introduced. The view of it in our publication is from the pencil of the same artist, when the Rotunda was standing.

The demolition of the Cross is thus lamented by an Ipswich bard:—

"No more the traveller shall its dome admire,
Its patron Goddess, with her scales and sword;
With Wolsey's Gate no more its name inspire,
Nor to the moralist a theme afford.

"From forth its canopy no more shall sound
The trump of war, with terror's fierce acclaim;
Nor pomp heraldic scatter pleasure round,
And to the joyous crowd sweet peace proclaim.

"Peace to its manes? doom'd no more to live,
Unless in Memory's ever fading page;
The mournful Muse this verse alone can give—
A feeble record for remoter age."

A number of different poems on the same subject have been published, both pathetic and satirical.

There is another excellent engraving of the Cross, from a drawing by the before-mentioned Mr. Frost, in the East Anglian, in which a view of the Old Shambles is preserved. These shambles, or butchery, was a commodious but ug-

ly structure, built of wood, and said, probably on account of the purposes to which it was appropriated, to have been erected by Cardinal Wolsey: but, in the reign of Queen Elizabeth, there is an order of the great court for repairing or rebuilding the Shambles, and that timber should be cut down and carried from the Ulverstone estate for that purpose; therefore we cannot suppose this to have been necessary, had this edifice been erected so recently as the time of Wolsey. It formed three sides of a square; in the interior of which was held what was then called the Herb Market. — The following is a faithful representation of this building.

Upon this scite, about twenty-five years ago, an extensive circular building was erected, called the Rotunda, intended for a market-house, and was fitted up with shops, and apartments above. It was built by Mr. G. Gooding, and had this singularity, that not a nail was used in its construction. It was afterwards divided into numerous small partitions, and was so crowded with inhabitants, that, from the want of a free circulation of air, it became a nuisance, and was pulled down. The present Corn Exchange was erected in its stead; and the figure of J ustice was transferred from the Market Cross, to decorate the front of this building, with a golden sickle and wheat ears substituted for the sword and balance. This transformation gave rise to the following impromptu:—

"Long in Ipswich Market-place,
Astrea look'd, with languid face,
Upon the proud Agrarian race,
Broken her sword, her scales uneven;
Resolved that corn again shall rise,
Ceres the lofty space supplies,
And holds her sample to the skies,
    While scorn'd Astrea flies to heaven.
"

The history of this figure of Astrea reminds us of the doctrine of metempsychosis, or transmigration of souls. The original destination of this deified substance was that of decorating a gentleman's grounds, under the semblance of Flora. Having for some years watched over the loves of the plants, she was removed, (it is presumed for her ser-

vices,) invested with the insignia of Justice, and raised to the top of the Market Cross; and happening to possess an elegant exterior, she had afterwards a sickle and wheatears placed in her hand, was called Ceres, and took her natural station upon the Corn Exchange, — where it is hoped she may long remain, an emblem of peace and plenty.

"When Ceres reign'd on earth, in Nature's prime,
Nor scales nor weights debased the golden time,
Vindictive then no sword did Justice bear,
To take the life that mercy lov'd to spare:
    Peace beam'd around, sweet plenty crown'd the swain,
And joy and gladness blessed the fertile plain.
Herald to times like those, the goddess smiles,
Displays the rich reward, the fruits of honest toils."

We are sorry to see that, at the present moment, this figure is without her sickle and wheat-ears; and it is ditScult to know whether this goddess, thus divested of her attributes, may be considered as Flora, Astrea, or Ceres. The first stone of the Corn Exchange was laid by E. Bacon, esq., in 1810, with the following inscription:—

K Bacon, Esq.
S. Saffobd, Esq. J
    G. GOODING, Bmlder

Previous to the erection of the Corn Exchange, a meeting of the merchants and dealers in corn and flour, took place, and they were consulted respecting the plan best adapted to their convenience; and an agreement was entered into, that they were to pay three guineas annually for the use of the stand with which each individual firm was to be accommodated: and at a meeting of the agriculturists, it was determined also by them, that they would pay annually a small sum each, for the convenience afforded. This income, it was supposed, would pay the corporation £10 per cent, for the money they had expended in the building; but, from mismanagement and misunderstanding, no rent has been paid, and the Corn Exchange is now let to an individual for £42 per annum; having thus been a heavy loss to the corporation.

On the 29th of April, 1818, a fire broke out, at about two o'clock in the morning, at the Bear and Crown inn, in St. Matthew's. The fire raged with great violence, and seven valuable horses perished in the flames. In a few days, upwards of £270 was subscribed for the relief of those persons whose property was destroyed by the fire.

A. A

St. Mary's chapel, commonly called Our Lady of Grace, stood at the N. W. corner of the lane, without the gate, which to this day goes by the name of Lady-lane. This chapel was famous for an image of the Blessed Virgin, much resorted to; and to which, in old wills, many pilgrimages were ordered to be made: and it was styled *Our Lady of Ipswich*. This venerated image shared the fate of other relics of superstition; for it was conveyed to London, and publicly burned. The scite of the chapel is now covered with buildings.

It was to this chapel that Cardinal Wolsey ordered an annual procession to be made by the dean of his college, on September 8th, being the nativity of the Virgin Mary, the tutelar saint of Ipswich: and no doubt the benign influence of this guardian saint of the town has had its due effect upon the chastity and virtue of its highlyfavoured inhabitants. In "Grove's Dialogue b Wolsey and Cardinal Ximenes," published in 1761, is a plan of the streets through which this procession passed. The image of Our Lady of Ipswich is mentioned as a notorious object of idolatry in the Homilies of the Church of England. It must have been a religious house of note at an early period of our history; for an old MS. mentions, upon what authority we know not, that in the year 1297, Elizabeth, the daughter of Edward I., was married to John, Count of Holland, at the chapel of Our Lady of Ipswich.

In the year 1515, Mr. Edmund Daundy erected fifteen alms'-houses now standing in Lady-lane, for the poor of this parish, and gave, by his will, wood to each of his alms'-houses, "besides Our Lady of Gracebut the revenue for the support of these houses is lost. Mr. Benjamin Osmond, by his will, dated the 30th of June, 1G19, left £350 to the bailiffs, &c. — 50 towards building the Cross, and the rest towards erecting a residence for, and the maintenance of, four poor persons of St. Matthew's parish. In the year 1651, John Crane, esq. of Cambridge, left, by will, 40s. for the preaching of a sermon every five years, in the parish church of St. Matthew, on the 25th of October; being the parish wherein his father was born. In 1698, Mr. Henry Skynner, portman, gave £100 to be laid out in the purchase of land, the rent of which to be expended in bread for the poor of this parish: and, accordingly, eight shillings'-worth of bread is distributed every Sunday. In the same year, Mr. Thomas Bright left £100 to buy lands for the purpose of maintaining two boys from this parish, at Christ's Hospital, in this town. In 1717, Mr. John Gibbons, by will, dated April 9th, gave a house to be sold, and the money arising from it to be laid out in the purchase of land, the rent of which is thus expended:—£1 to the rector, for an annual sermon; £40 to the charity school of Grey-coat Boys and Blue-coat Girls, and £20 for clothing for sundry poor persons of St. Matthew's parish. There are several other minor bequests; the produce of which is expended in bread, and in otherwise relieving the pbor.

In St. Matthew's church-yard, beneath an altar monument, lie the remains of the late Lord Chedworth; and, on a tablet in the church, is the following inscription: — THE RIGHT HONOURABLE JOHN (HOWE) LORD CHEDWORTH, BARON OF CHEDWORTH, IN THE COUNTY OF GLOUCESTER,
WAS BORN AUGUST 24th, 1745,
DIED OCTOBER 29th, 1804.

He succeeded his uncle Frederic-Hemy, October 6th, 1781, and dying a hachelor, the title hecame extinct. He was a nohleman of superior ahilities, well versed in every hranch of elegant and polite literature; an ahle, active,

and upright magistrate, intimately acquainted with the laws and constitution of his country; a strenuous supporter or civil and religions liherty;
firmly ultached to the principles estahlished at the Revolution, and a sincere heliever in the truths of christianily.

His lordship's grandfather, John Howe, esq., was elevated to the peerage, in 1741. The eldest son of this gentleman married a Suffolk lady, the daughter of Sir P. P. Long, bart., and dying, as well as his next brother, without issue, the title devolved to John Howe, esq., issue of the third son, the Rev. Mr. Howe, by the daughter of Thomas White, esq., of Tattingstone Place, near Ipswich. This lady, after the death of her husband, fixed her residence here, and thus laid the foundation of her son's partiality to this town; from which he seldom was absent, except when attending to his duty in parliament. He was designed for the profession of the law; which he relinquished, on his accession to the title. He, for many years, officiated as chairman of the County Quarter Sessions at Ipswich: in which capacity, and as a magistrate, he displayed great legal knowledge, impartiality, and discrimination: and it was observed by the late Lord Chancellor Thurlow, that Lord Chedworth understood the laws of his country better than any county magistrate in the kingdom. His lordship died unmarried, and was buried, by his express desire, in the same vault with his mother. He was mild and amiable in his disposition, but of harmlessly eccentric habits; and, from the retired manner in which he passed his days, he died possessed of much greater wealth than he was himself aware of. He bequeathed property to the amount of £183,000, besides a very large sum to his residuary legatee, in legacies, to various persons not at all related to him, and not moving in his sphere of life; and many of the inhabitants of Ipswich were considerably enriched by his bequests. This testamentary disposition of his fortune was opposed by his relations, on the plea of insanity; but was afterwards established by the legal tribunal to which it was referred. His estates in Gloucestershire were brought to the hammer, in 1811, and sold for the sum of £268,635.

In "Dowsing's Journal," it appears that they brake down thirty-five superstitious pictures, three angels with stars on their breast, and 'crosses, at St. Matthew's. Within this church, directly opposite to the entrance by the southeast door, are two somewhat singular monuments, very similar to each other, and about the date 1630; representing, in tolerable sculpture, coloured, the effigies of the father and mother of each family, with a number of their sons and daughters, all kneeling in the attitude of prayer; and, to denote the grand-children, several infants, in swaddling clothes, are laid at the feet of their respective mothers. One of these monuments is to the memory of Mr. Christopher Cock, formerly a portman of this borough: he had six sons and seven daughters: he died 1629, aged sixty. The other is to the memory of Arthur Penning, of Kettleburgh; who was high sheriff of the county, in 1607; and who had issue by his wife Elizabeth, daughter of Thomas Croft, esq. of Saxmundham, fourteen sons and four daughters: he died 1631, aged sixty-five.

"His faith hy love he did express, His love hy works he did approve; The poor man's luynes did him hless, The rich and pour did him love.

"His faith hy works he daily did declare,
His life for death he did himself prepare;
Now heing dead, the world sings of his praise,
And fame proclaims his works to future days."

There was a marble in this church under which were deposited the remains of Dr. John Bailey, who was incumbent there in the time of Henry VIII., and contested with Cardinal Wolsey about alienating the great tithes, which were then worth two hundred marks per annum: there belonged to it, St. George's chapel, and the Lady Grey's chapel, and St. Peter's church, the rector allowing to a minister to officiate, £3 per annum. Dr. Bailey died three years before Henry VIII. The brasses are all off this stone, as well as many others.

In the chancel in the middle aisle, is a stone on which is,

"Here lyeth the hody of EDWARD SHErPARD, CENT.; who departed this life, the 8th day of Septemher, 1680.

"He lived heloved, and died lamented.
Few men's death so much resented."

On the north side of the communion table:—

"THOMAS BRIGHT, GENT., late hailiffand portinan of Ipswich, departed this life, the 5th of July, 1698, aged 62. Alo his wife and son.

Mr. Foster was minister of this parish, in the time of Kings Charles and James, and died a reverend old man.

On the north-east side of the churchyard, is a handsome vaulted tomb to the. memory of Henry Seekamp, esq.; who died August 19th, 1819, aged 75, portman and assistant justice, and twice bailiff of the corporation. He was conscientious, benevolent, and humane, always easy of access, zealous and unremitting in his duties as a magistrate, and it may be truly said of him, that he delighted in *doing justice.*

In this church-yard is a monument to the memory of Sir William Innes, bart., of Balveny, N. B.: he died March 13th, 1817, in the 100th year of his age. Lady Innes, his wife, died May 15th, 1770. They are both buried in the family vault of Thomas Hodges, esq. of this town; whose daughter Lady Innes was.

Thomas Seckford, master of requests to Queen Elizabeth, founder of the alms'-houses at Woodbridge, and representative for Ipswich in 1563, *did build a fair house in this parish.* In 1631, it was in the possession of Anthony Cage; in 1039, it was sold by Sir Thomas Bandish, knt., to Sir Robert Hitcham, bart. ; in 1652, it was in the occupation of Sir Thomas Bedingfield, and was at that time sold by the representatives of Thomas Knapp, to Sir John Barker, bart., of Trimley, who represented the borough in four different parliaments; he sold it afterwards to John Sicklemore, esq., who was member for Ipswich in 1G61. It is mentioned, and a south view of it given, in Ogilvy's map of Ipswich, as Squire Gaudy's house; after that time it was possessed by Thomas M. Gibson, esq.; it then became the property of the late Edward Hazell, esq.; from whom it descended to William Rodwell, esq., the present possessor; who has lately repaired and fitted it up with great taste and splendour. It had, formerly, two lofty towers at each end, with a turret of considerable height, surmounted with a vane on each. It is called, in the title deeds, Seckford House, or the Great House in St. Matthew's.

Broke's Hall is within this parish, and the hamlet so called takes in part of this, and part of the parishes of Bramford, Whitton, Thurlston, and Westerfield. It is said, in Doomsday, that " King Edward gave Brokes, a member of Ipswich, to Alric of Clare, then of the yearly value of ten pounds, and R. Bedile holdeth it of the Countess of Clare, by the service of one knight's fee. " Broke's Hall farm, on which there is a handsome brickbuilt house, is now occupied by Mr. John Orford; who pays, annually, £26:13:4 to Christ's Hospital. The family of De Bois was owner of Broke's Hall, in the year 1282; and Boss Hall, in this parish, now occupied by Mr. Kersey, took its name from this family.

As we enter into this parish, by the London road, on the left-hand side, is Handford Hall, a handsome newlyerected farm house, occupied by Mr. Henry Waller; whose family has had it for many years. The farm belongs to the corporation, and contains one hundred and sixty-eight acres, let upon lease, at the yearly rent of £220. It is well known as the spot where the Lamb-fair is kept; which much enhances the value of the occupation. This fair is held on the 22nd of August, lasts three days, and is frequented by all the growers, and agriculturists in the district. Lambs are sent from many miles distance; particularly from the large breeders in Norfolk, Lincoln, and Cambridgeshire. The number of lambs this year, 1828, was computed at upwards of 130,000; but, in the year 1791, there were upwards of 200,000:

and the celebrity of this fair is equal to any of the kind in the kingdom.

Proceeding on, towards the town, we pass over Handford Bridge, of a single arch, over the Gipping; but, owing to the lowness of the road on the west side, works connected with the bridge were obliged to be extended to a considerable distance, in order to preserve it from the frequent inundations, in a rainy season.

On the 20th of February, 1771, a post-chaise, from Colchester, was overturned by the rapidity of the stream, near Handford bridge, and carried twenty yards by the current. The two horses were drowned, but the driver and two gentlemen, passengers, were saved.

In February, 1814, it was announced, by public advertisement, that the road at the foot of Handford bridge was rendered impassable, in consequence of the damage done by the floods.

This bridge was built about 1793, by the late Mr. Fulcher, at the time when the Gipping was made navigable to Stowmarket. This navigation is sixteen miles in length, and has fifteen locks, each sixty feet long, and fourteen wide. The total expense was £26,380. The charges for the conveyance of goods, are one penny per ton per mile, from Stowmarket to Ipswich, and half as much from Ipswich to Stowmarket. Great trade is carried on through the medium of this canal, to the evident advantage of the interior of the county; for vast quantities of grain, &c. are shipped at Stowmarket, and coals, with a great variety of other heavy goods, are sent back in return, and circulated, at a moderate expense, through all parts of the western division of the county. We are happy to state, that the shares pay more than five per cent. for the money employed, and that the concern is in a very flourishing condition. It is gratifying to our feelings, when we can announce the success of a public spirited work like this, as it encourages others to attempt similar undertakings.

After passing over the bridge, at a few paces to the right, we come to the Royal William inn, kept by Mr. William Wollard, an ingenious and well-informed practical gardener. In the year 1823, he, in conjunction with some of his brother gardeners, and a few gentlemen who were lovers of horticulture, instituted an annual exhibition of fruit, particularly gooseberries, and ridiculously enough christened themselves "The Gooseberry Society." Again we say, that there is more in a name than absolutely meets the ear, for under this appellation the fraternity very slowly increased; but, in the year 1826, a gentleman of the town, whose spirit and liberality are equal to his wishes to do good, observed that it was impossible for any gentleman to enrol his name as member of a society so absurdly denominated, without the hazard of being called gooseberry fool,' as he walked along the street; and he suggested that it should hereafter be called the " Ipswich Horticultural Society," not confining themselves to gooseberries, but to offer prizes, generally, for the cultivation of horticultural productions. This was immediately done, and some few judicious regulations drawn up, and made public; when offers of subscriptions, which are confined to five shillings, poured in from all quarters, — that is, persons sent in their names, as each individual must be

B B proposed by a member, at one meeting, and voted in at the next. The number of subscribers now amounts to upwards of 200, including many of the neighbouring nobility, gentry, and clergy, as well as agriculturists, florists, and practical gardeners. The prizes vary from seven shillings to twenty shillings, according to the nature, quality, and superiority of the article produced. There are four quarterly exhibitions in the year, and the show of fruit and flowers, at their exhibition meeting, September the 15tL, 1828, was one of the most excellent and gratifying description. The prize-fruit and flowers were arranged in booths which surround an extensive bowling-green, and excited the admiration of a great number of both ladies and gentlemen, who attended as spectators. After the show, an excellent dinner is always provided, at a moderate charge, and each individual pays for whatever liquor he likes to indulge in; which enables the man who has cultivated, with his own hand, these productions so grateful to the sight and the palate, to sit down, with honest pride, at the same table with his superiors. It is this association of gentlemen with the humbler classes who have distinguished themselves by their industrious ingenuity, that gives a peculiar zest to this truly English institution. From the garden is a fine open view of the surrounding country: it is an agreeable promenade for the ladies who honour the exhibition with their presence; and surely nothing can be more appropriate than their appearance on such an occasion, for even amongst all these choice and beautiful productions of nature, they are themselves the loveliest flowers of the creation. Upwards of seventy gentlemen sat down to dinner at the last meeting, and a number of names were proposed as subscribers: the whole proceedings did honour to the committee, and their able and talented chairman, William Rodwell, esq. And thus, principally from the exertions of Mr. Buchanan, of Stowmarket, and a few spirited individuals, has originated one of the most useful and agreeable institutions in Ipswich We now come to a subject of so much importance, that I must treat of it in the first person singular; and I shall, I trust, be excused for handling it somewhat diffusely;— it is on the *mineral springs* which abound in this town, but more particularly in this parish; and to which I am most earnestly anxious to draw the public attention. I shall, therefore, in the first place, insert, *verbatim,* two letters that appeared in a very ingenious publication, called the East Anglian, printed at the County Press, here, in the year 1814.

"TO THE EDITOR OF THE EAST ANGLIAN.

"Sir,

"Having been favoured with an opportunity of inspecting a collection of curious *excerpta, memoranda,* &c. chiefly relating to the county of Suffolk, I was induced to transcribe the following remarks; and I forward them to you, for insertion in The East Anglian, should they be approved, in the hope of obtaining some additional information on the subject.

"' *Inqvirenda; about* IPSWICH SPAW WATERS, *hy Experiments and Observations from them made.*

"'As to the Ipswich Spaw, seeing Mr. Boyle, in his Memoirs thinks fit the *Scituation of the Spring* should be observ'd: 'As whether the Spring-head do chiefly regard the *East,* the *West,* the *North,* or the *South* And whether the Water be found in a Plain, or Valley; and if not, Whether it arise in any Hillock, Hill, or a Mountain.' p. 18. I say, seeing he looks upon this to be an *Inquirendum* about *Mineral Waters* springing out of the Earth (tho' I think it a Curiosity of no great Moment to discover the Goodness or Badness of Mineral Waters.) I have thought fit to let my reader know, that the *Ipswich S"paw* runs directly *South* and arises from a pretty large Hill, just adjoining to it, from whose Declivity it issues out, as those Springs are observed to do, which produce the *German Spaw,* which around *Liege* are many, and on which grow several woods, so that the Scituation seems not to be much unlike that of the *German Spaw,* if any Advantage from thence may accrue.

"' This *Ipswich Spaw* runs generally very clear, but do's not seem to have a Transparency equal to *Common Water* flowing from *some* Springs, because it is impregnated with the *Mineral Salt* from the Earth, which in just reason, I conclude to give it a less Transparency than the former; which Earth is of a black Colour, and denotes to me the *Sulphurs* conjoyn'd with the *Salt,* beforeeraention'd, which I doubt not to prove by some of the following Experiments. It is scituate on such a Declivity that violent Rains seldom prejudice the Waters, or weaken their strength; tho' slow Rain and Snow, do's in some measure, soaking into the Hills above it, and mixing with the Mineral Waters; yet never so, as wholly to diminish their Tinging Quality with Powder of Galls, equal, *even then,* to the best Flask of *German Spaw* that I have met with. In the Winter Season, they smell in the Source very Sulphureous, as Mr. *Boyle*

has observed of the *Tunhridge Waters,* and seem to be stronger of the Mineral Spirit at that time, than in an hotter Season. If you put your Head over the Well, you find the Place very warm, and the Waters never subject to freeze in the hardest frost that may happen. So that I cannot see but that these Waters have all the principles in them, that may make them very Valuable; at least, as valuable as any Water whatever of the same Nature. These Waters, after 3 or 4 Days standing in the Well, seem to grow *foul;* for which reason it is empty'd at least thrice in the week, which I cause to be done, not only for the more cleanly drinking them, but also to dis. cover what sort of Matter it was that render'd the Waters so turbid, as they appear'd, and I found it to be a kind of *Ferruginous Ore,* not much unlike yellow Oker, tho' not so deep colour'd; but like that found in the Bottoms of some *German Spaw Water Flasks,* which subsided to the bottom of the Well. Wherefore I cannot but conclude, that these *Ipswich Spaw Waters,* answer in every Point, as to their Composition, as I may well call it, the Goodness of the *German Spaw,* or *Tunhridge* Wells; and, IF DRANK ON THE PLACE, much Superior to any *German Spaw,* brought into *England."'* "From the above (which I copied *verhatim,* retaining the old orthography, punctuation, tc.) it appears, that the town of Ipswich formerly possessed a mineral spring, of considerable virtue. Can you, Sir, or any of your Correspondents, inform me, whether the spring be now known; and, if known, whether its waters be ever taken medicinally, and with success?

"The fragment, I am informed, from which I transcribed the above, was part of a very rare pamphlet, entitled '*Hydro-Sidereon;'* but, unfortunately, its title-page and imprint have been lost; and, consequently, I have no means of ascertaining who was the author, or what was the date of its publication. The passage which I have given, is followed by a series of experiments on the water: should they be deemed worth insertion, I will transmit them to you, in abstract, or in detail, as may best suit. I am, &c.

"M. D.
"Bury St. Edmund's, Feb. 10th, 1814."
"TO THE EDITOR OF THE EAST ANGLIAN.
"Sir,

"In answer to the inquiries of your Correspondent, M. D. respecting the existence of mineral waters in Ipswich, I beg leave to trouble you with the following particulars, for the accuracy of which I can vouch, from my own knowledge of the facts.

"Between thirty and forty years ago, the late Mr. Isaac Brook, cooper, father of Mr. Brook, grocer, now of this town, accidentally discovered a mineral spring, in a piece of ground on the west side of St. George's Lane, St. Matthew's. The well (now the property of Mr. Dykes Alexander) is still to be seen; and it is arched over with brick, and might be easily re-opened.

"Mr. Brook, in digging for water, with the view of forming a reservoir for the supply of his house, met with this spring. Finding the water to be ungrateful to the taste, and, as he supposed, unfit for culinary purposes, he was much disappointed. He brought me a bottle of the water, which, conjecturing to be a mineral nature, I submitted to the usual tests.

"Drs. Venn, Bigsby, and Coyte, were present at the analysation; aud they were unanimously of the opinion, that the water was equal to the Bath waters. In consonance with that opinion, when Medcalf Russell, esq. who then lived at the Chantry, near this town, was recommended, by his London physician, to drink the Bath waters, those gentlemen proposed to him a trial of the Ipswich miner;' water. He assented, and his recovery confirmed their judgment of its efficacy. Many other persons also participated in the benefits resulting from its use.

"In consequence of the proved virtue of the spring, it was proposed to the leading persons in the town, at that time, that measures should be taken to give celebrity to the waters, in order that company might be induced to resort hither. With this view, the erection of a warm, and of a cold bath, was further suggested. These propositions, however, were resisted, on the ground, that, although in some respects, their adoption might benefit the town, the advantages would be more than counterbalanced, by the advance that would be occasioned in the price of provisions.

"On the justness of this argument, I have nothing to remark; nor do I know what might be the fate of similar proposals, were they now to be submitted; but it is, perhaps, worth while to state, that there is, in this town, as fine a warm spring, adapted for the supply of a bath, as can be imagined.

"It seems highly probable, that mineral springs abound in the town and neighbourhood of Ipswich. About thirty years ago, when St. Matthew's gate was pulled down, a slight distance below the surface, several masses of ferruginous matter were found; indicating the existence of a metallic vein in their vicinity.

"That there are medicinal earths, and springs, in Ipswich, is evident also from the following circumstance. In the yard of the borough gaol, there is a spring, the water of which is very fine and clear; but highly impregnated with vitriolic magnesia; resembling, and possessing the properties of, the well-known Epsom water.

"I am, &c.

"H. SEEKAMP.

"Ipswich, March Xbth, 18H."

In addition to these, is a mineral well, on the premises of Mr. Dykes Alexander, at the entrance of the town; and likewise another on Mr. Richard Alexander's ground, close by. There is also a well, situated at the cottage adjoining to the house formerly the Shears public-house, in St. Margaret's parish, the water of which is strongly impregnated with iron and sulphur, it constantly overflows above the surface, and never freezes. The well mentioned n the East Anglian, is in the garden situated on the left hand of Globe-lane, the property of Mr. Dykes Alexander, now in the occupation of Mr. Jefl'eries, nurseryman: it is covered with a brick arch, the entrance to which is by several steps, crumbling to decay, leading down to a room, of considerable dimensions, that surrounds the well; and the water

is so strongly impregnated with some mineral substance, that it is never used even for watering the garden.

The fact being clearly established, that several mineral springs do actually exist, and are easily accessible, it is, surely, desirable to bring them into use; for the present age is too enlightened for a moment to apprehend that an influx of visitors would enhance the price of provisions. Of late years, whenever a prospect has arisen of any improvement likely to conduce to the general good, public spirited individuals have always been found, ready to give effect to such a speculation: I therefore feel confident that this opportunity will not be neglected; for I am convinced that these waters might, at a very trifling expense, be rendered of essential benefit to the town. Their efficacy has been satisfactorily proved, by the most respectable testimony, in the case of the late Mr. Russel; and if the matter were taken up by the leading medical men of the town, and, on analysing the waters of the different springs, and ascertaining their peculiar properties, they would, individually, recommend them in those cases where such remedies are usually employed, I am certain that Mr. Alexander would throw no obstacle in the way of such an application of them, that they might be readily brought into public repute, and into general use; and, if proper methods were taken to give them publicity, I doubt not but that the Ipswich waters would soon become as famous as those of Bath or Cheltenham; for here we have the advantage of combining the qualities of both: and, from the salubrity of the air, and situation, together with the beautiful rides and walks in the vicinity, no town in the kingdom is a more delightful residence for invalids. And, in addition to the use of the baths and the waters, those who occasionally require the bracing influence of the seabreeze, could readily enjoy it, by a trip to Felixstow, or in an excursion to Harwich, along the sinuous and picturesque course of the Orwell.

This is not one of those speculations that would require thousands to bring it to bear, but might be accomplished by a

little strenuous exertion, without scarcely the possibility of risk. And, if, by my humble efforts, 1 should be fortunate to attract attention to this subject, and could see this project carried into effect, I should rejoice in having been instrumental to what would be of service to thousands of my fellow-creatures, and of positive permanent advantage to my native town.

Some of the water has been sent to London; and is now in the hands of an eminent chemist, for the purpose of analisation. He states that it is of the class designated *chalybeate,* with a small proportion of *saline;* and, as far as his examination has gone, there appears no doubt of its being eligible for the purposes of medicine. But as it necessarily requires a considerable time before a mature report can be made of its exact properties and qualities, a correct account shall be given in the last chapter of this publication.

At the top of St. Matthew's-street, on the right hand, are the Horse Barracks, as they are called. They were built in the year 1795, by Mr. Richard Gooding; forming three sides of a square. The mess-room and officers' apartments, in the centre, are unconnected with the sides; in which are lodgings for the men, and stabling for the horses. The building will hold about three troops: and Ipswich is generally the head-quarters of the regiment. They stand on an elevated, airy spot, considered remarkably healthy; for we believe that there have been but two or three instances of any commissioned officer dying there since they were erected, about twenty-four years ago, when the Queen's Bays first occupied the building. The military are very partial to Ipswich, as quarters; for they, generally, are much noticed by, and associate in a friendly manner with, the gentry of the town and neighbourhood.

Between forty and fifty years ago, West-gate, or Saint Matthew's gate, as it was frequently called, was standing entire, across St. Matthew's, or West-gate-street, formerly called Bargate-street, and Gaol-street, just before you come to the Three Feathers public house. In the twentyseventh year of Henry VI., an order of the great court was issued for a common gaol for the town, to be erected at St. Matthew's gate; and, at the same period, the gate was rebuilt, and made a gaol, at the voluntary expense of John de Caldwell, bailiff and portman: and in the will of Walter Velvet, dated January 11th, 1458, is this bequest:

"Item lego ad fabricationem nnius pontis inter capellam beatae Marise et Prisonam Domini Regis cum aliquis alius fabricari velit, aut fabricari faciat."

Notwithstanding a gaol for the town was afterwards built, a vault or cell in one of the towers of the gate, was used as a dungeon, or ' black hole,' as it was called, until the demolition of the gate itself. In the rebuilding of the gate, the original stone foundation was left to the height of about fifteen feet above the ground, upon which the new brick additions were laid; so that we may conclude that it retained nearly the same form as the ancient struc c c ture. It was formed of two projecting towers, with rather a lofty arch in the centre; above which was a room or rooms, covered with a sloping roof, a little higher than the side towers. The roof was surmounted by a small wooden turret or belfry; and in front of the building was a large clock, commonly called the town clock. There is a painting, by the late ingenious Mr. Baldery, representing a ' Distress for Rent,' in the back ground of which is St. Matthew's gate; and it is one of the best representations we remember to have seen. There is also a view of it published in the fifth volume of " Grose's Antiquities." Our wood-cut represents it as it appeared on entering the town from the London road.

At the east corner of the lane, just within the gate, on the spot where Mr. William Hamilton's house now stands, was the town and borough gaol. The keeper's house fronted the street, and behind it was the debtor's courtyard, ninety feet by twenty-seven. At the west end of the building, was a neat chapel: where a regular chaplain officiated, with a salary of £30. This prison was, for many years, kept by Mr. John Ripshaw, a man of

Herculean mould and strength. He was an adept in the art of self defence, skilled in all manly games and athletic exercises; and, though of rough exterior, was of a remarkably mild and humane disposition. And John Ripshaw was a striking instance that a man's conduct may render the most disagreeable office respectable.

In St. George's-lane, opposite the place where St. George's chapel formerly stood, is Salem chapel; which was opened on the 11th of June, 1812. It was built at the sole expense of Mr. Joseph Chamberlain; who, after having expended £1,200 in its erection, generously conveyed it to trustees, for the use of the Particular Baptists. It is a brick building, measuring forty-five feet by thirtyfive, and capable of accommodating nearly four hundred persons.

In a south-east direction, at a little distance from St. Matthew's, is the small church of St. Mary at the Elms, one of the four churches at Ipswich dedicated to the Holy Virgin, and is, probably, built on the scite of the dilapidated church of St. Saviour. It was given to Trinity Priory, by Alan, the son of Edgar Aleto, and his son Richard; but there seems to have been no grant of the impropriation, since the dissolution of the monastery. It is a mean building, with a tasteless red brick steeple attached to it. It is a curacy; patrons, the parishioners.

Against the wall of the chancel, is a monument to the memory of William Acton, portman; who died in 1616, aged 76. This was erected by John Aeton, his son, who resided at Bramford, and was high sheriff for the county, and from whom the present family are descended. The statue of the wife of John Acton lies at the bottom of this monument, with the following inscription:—

"Memoriie Gvlielmi Acton viri justici timentis Drain, suis semper henefiei, praetantisuue molt&s eleemosynas, que ohiit Novem. 29, 1616,.Ctatis 76, honum illud certamen deoertavit, cursmn conenminavit, et fidmn servavit: Vo lcctores idem agite, sagite. Parentavit Johannes Acton pictatis ergo."

There is likewise the following in-

scription:— "Under a marhle in the chancel, lies WiLlIAM LYNCH, a clothier,
a man of good fame: he died in 1659:

"Whose hounty to the poor did those things give,
Which in their wants did often them relieve:
He felt affliction great, till he lay down,
A mortal life, for an immortal crown."

Over the chancel door is a square white marble tablet, over an oval one, with inscriptions to the memory of William Lynch, esq., several times bailiff of Ipswich, as well as various branches of the Lynch family.

In the church, under a marble, lies Thomas Johnson, a clothier, who died 1618.

Near the pulpit is a richly-ornamented marble monument, bearing the arms of the Hambys. Robert Hamby, gent., attorney at law, died October 3rd, 1735, aged 51; and his wife Frances died June the 1st, 1740, aged 59. After a long and just eulogium on the character and benevolence of both, it concludes with —

"Their works do follow them. Rev. xiv. IS."

On the north wall is a marble slab,

"In memory of Samuel REEVE, ESQ. Vic Admiral of the White; who died suddenly, May 5th, 1803, aged 70. He was exemplar)-in the duties of his profession — a man of strict prohity — a valuahle friend— and a hrother justly heloved, and most gratefully rememhered.''

Opposite to the church-yard, a neat brick building is erected, bearing, over the entrance, the following inscription:—

"Mrs. Smith's Alms Houses, erected in the year 1780, for the henefit of twelve poor women, of honest life and conversation, of the age of fifty yean and upwards, heing communicants of the Church of England, as hy law estahlished."

In 1720, this Mrs. Ann Smith, of London, widow, left, by will, £5,000 for this purpose; but there being a deficiency in the assets, after adjusting all claims, the Court of Chancery appointed £4,432: 6: 2 to be laid out in South Sea Annuities; and the ministers of the parishes of St. Peter and St. Mary at the Elms, were appointed trustees. This is one of the few instances of modern date, of an individual leaving money for erecting a building for a charitable institution. We have, now, no Greshams, Seckfords, Tooleys, or Smarts, anxious to hand down their names, as charitable benefactors, to futurity. This liberal age seems to act upon the more provident principle of the Irishman who observed, that "as posterity had never done anything for him, he did not see why he should do anything for posterity."

In 1635, Mr. William Hunt gave £100 to the town of Ipswich, to be lent to five poor tradesmen, in the parish of St. Mary at the Elms, at 4 per cent., for five years; the interest to be paid to the churchwardens, to buy shirts and shifts, to be distributed to the poor of the said parish: but of this the corporation received no more than £60.

We have not to record the names of many great or exalted characters which this parish has produced; hut the following account exhibits such a striking instance of the vicissitudes of fortune, that it might appear to be fabulous, had it not been attested by the evidence of Edward Bacon, esq., of this town, who is well acquainted with the veracity of the particulars. Some years ago, a pauper of the name of Jacob Dedham, *alias* Caulins Jaun, left the parish workhouse of St. Mary at the Elms, with but one solitary shilling in his pocket, given him by the churchwarden. By some means or other he contrived to get a passage out to India, either as a soldier or sailor. This self-taught genius was a quiet inoffensive man, but was possessed of keen and quick penetration. He discovered a talent for drawing; and having attracted the attention of some persons in power, he was taken into the engineering department, and being employed as a spy, he assumed various disguises, and was instrumental in rendering great service to Lord Cornwallis; w-ho was so sensible of the value of his communications, that he always intended to have placed him in independence; but his noble pa-

tron dying before Caulins returned to England, his services were overlooked or forgotten. After traversing our eastern territories, in various directions, and meeting with many singular adventures, he married the widow of a Nabob, immensely rich, and lived in the height of luxury and splendour. He was thoughtless and improvident, and probably not more correct in his transactions than some other East India Nabobs have been; but he did not escape the shafts of envy or detraction, and, from some suspicions attaching to his character, he was compelled to fly from the country, and leave his wife and his wealth behind, thinking himself fortunate to escape with his life. He returned to England; and, after being reduced to the most abject poverty, wretchedness, and disease, he once again arrived at Ipswieh, in a state of beggary and starvation; and was actually found one morning asleep in the porch of St. Mary at the Elms' church. From his disgusting appearance, he was refused admittance into the workhouse, was carried before the magistrate as a vagabond, and gave an account of himself that was not believed. But, from the local knowledge which Mr. Bacon had of India, he was fully convinced of the truth of his narration; and, with the humanity which is so conspicuous in his character, interested himself warmly in this singular adventurer's behalf. He was relieved, clothed, and restored to health and comparative comfort; and maintained himself for some time, decently, by his pencil. He was employed by Mr. Bacon, to take a view of the town of Ipswich; which is now, with several other of his drawings, in the possession of the Rev. Richard Cobbold:—this view, though evidently not the production of a professional artist, is executed with an extraordinary degree of accuracy and precision, is a very pleasing picture, and a curious specimen of what may be effected by a person who had never been taught the rudiments of the art. After residing here for some time, his passion for adventures once more revived, and he proceeded to some port, where he engaged again to work out his passage to India;

but he had scarcely got on board to take possession of his birth, when he accidentally fell into the hold of the ship, and was killed upon the spot. Thus strangely ended the more strange life of Caulins Jaun, the workhouse wanderer from St. Mary at the Elms.

We now proceed through Little King-street, into the Old Butter-market, where we enter St. Lawrence parish. St. Lawrence is said, in Doomsday, to have possessed twelve acres of land. Norman, the son of Eadnoth, gave this church to Trinity Priory,—to which it was impropriated; but, as there was no grant of its impropriation, at the dissolution of the priory, we may conclude that there was then no land belonging to the church. A convent of Carmelites, or White Friars, was established here, in 1279, by Sir Thomas Loudham. It was of considerable, extent, reaching from St. Nicholas'-street, to St. Stephen's lane, taking in a portion of the Old Butter-market; and some part of the building was afterwards appropriated to the purpose of a county gaol, and was situated in what is still called the Old Gaol Lane, abutting upon Mr. Barnard Clarke's garden. Some fragments of the building are yet to be met with in this garden; which is opposite to the west entrance into the New Market. Some years ago, on excavating the earth for the purpose of laying the foundation of Mr. Bowman's brewery, great numbers of human bones were dug up; so that, doubtless, here was the cemetery of the convent. Sir Thomas Loudham, the founder, and John Loudham, esq., were buried in the conventual church; also John Barningham, a person very learned, who had studied long at Oxford, and among the Sorbonists at Paris: he wrote divers books, and died a wondrous old man, January 22nd, 1448; and had been prior of this convent. Several of the priors were much distinguished for their learning.

The present church was begun by John Bottold; who died in 1431, and is buried in tho church, with this inscription:—

"Suhjacet hoc lapide John Bottold vir prohus *ipst,*

latins eocleaue primus inceptor fuit iste, Cujus anima, Domine, miserere tu hone Chrute.

Ohiit M.CCCC.XXXI. Litem Dominicalia G."

The chancel was built by John Baldwyn, draper; who died in 1449; and whose name is in the stone work, under the east window, accompanied with a pair of shears, indicative of his profession. This stone has been ridiculously plastered over.

About this time, several legacies were also left for the erection of the steeple: which, we believe, is the highest in the town.

In 1514, Edmund Daundy, then representative for the borough, and one of the most respectable men of the town, founded a chauntry in this church, for a secular priest to officiate at the altar of St. Thomas, in behalf of himself and his relations — among whom he reckoned Thomas Wolsey, then Dean of Lincoln, and the dean's parents, Robert and Jane Wolsey, deceased. To this priest and his successors, he gave his house, in this parish, for a residence, and his lands in Sproughton, Stoke, and Alnesborne, for a maintenance. Mr. Daundy died in 1515, and is buried in the chancel.

A chauntry was a sacred edifice, generally placed in separate chapels, or at altars, within cathedrals, monasteries, and parish churches, endowed with possessions for the payment of mass to be sung for the soul of their founders or their kindred; but they were destroyed in all the churches visited by Wm. Dowsing and his merciless coadjutors. We may form some idea of the richness of this particular endowment, from the following document: "In the church chest of this parish, shuffled in among other papers, a receipt was found some years ago, given by Edward Grymeston, to Lionel Talmage and William Foster, esquires, John Holland, and Matthew Goodying, bailives of Ipswich, (commissioners for the sale of church goods, within the said town,) acknowledging these particulars, viz. thirty-eight pounds seven shillings and fourpence, in ready money, arising from goods already sold by them; four hundred, three-

score, and seventeen ounces and a half, of plate; eight copes of cloth of gold and tissue; two vestments of cloth of gold and tissue; and two tunicles of cloth of gold and tissue, to be delivered over to the use of the king's majesty, by the said Edward Grymeston: dated 28th May, in the seventh year of Edward VI. 1553."

John Clyatt, port man, who died 1529, is buried in the church; and a monument to the memory of John Moone,

D D gent., portraan, is erected in the chancel, — who died February 17th, 1585.

In the narrow passage nearly opposite the pulpit, on a brass plate is inscribed —

"Here lieth the hody of GEORGE SPARROWE, late a citizen and grocer of London, eeroud on of William Sparrowe, one of the portmen of IpRwich; who departed out of this life, the 11th day of Dec. 1599."

On a small brass plate:—

"A. M. 8PARROW/E, Portman, 1614."

In various parts of the church, are stones with inscriptions to the memory of many of the Sparrowe family; who seem to have been more intimately connected with the corporation of Ipswich, than any family on record; and, for centuries, resided in diis parish. In 1665, lived John Sparrowe, gent.: his father, grandfather, and great grandfather, his grandmother and great grandmother's fathers, were portmen, and his mother was daughter of the recorder; his father built the great house in Thurlston, still called the Sparrow's Nest; and on the entrance to the family vault, in this church, these words are inscribed:—

"NIDUS l'ASSERUM.'

There is also a monument to John Sparrowe, esq., many years magistrate of the town and county, and thirteen times bailiff of this town; who died 24th of December, 1762, aged 73: and various individuals of the Sparrowe family, since that time.

In the chancel is a monument to the memory of John Pemberton, portman, the founder of the charity for the benefit of the widows and orphans of clergymen; who left, with other bequests, a

sum to be distributed amongst the poor of this parish: he died March 3rd, 1718.

Against the south wall, in the middle of the church, is & white marble monument, to the memory of Francis Colman, many times bailiff of Ipswich, and a considerable benefactor to this parish. And, directly opposite, against the south wall, is a marble pillar monument, to Elizabeth his wife; through whose instigation, it is stated that he left certain sums to benevolent purposes.

mong others, we notice the following inscriptions:—

"Sacred to the memory of EDWARD CLARE PARISH, ESQ.; who died Jan. 3, 1764, aged 60.

"Also Elizabeth Parish, hi wife; who died 10 Jan. 1776, aged 68.

"Also his daughter, ANNA PARISH, and several others of the family."

"Here resteth the hody of LAURENCE STISTED, GENT.; who died June 4, 1675, aged 70.

"Also his daughter ANNA, wife of Edward Reynolds, portinan; who died July 31, 1674, aged 26."

"Here resteth the hodys of THOMAS lV'ES, GENT., who died May 3, 1662, and BEATRIX, his wife, who died Dec. 16, 1631."

Under the gallery:—

"Here lieth, for a hlessed resurrection, the hody of Mr. John BurROUGH, late portinan of this town; who died July 26, 1695, aged 6b. Also his wife and grand-daughter."

By the gallery stairs:— "In memory of Johannes Baptista Oytrecht, M. D., and

Oculist; who died Jan. I8, 1787, aged 63.

"It was his greatest pleasure to relieve the afflicted poor; which he always did *grati"'*

On a small brass plate, near the communion table:—

"Here lieth STEVEN Copping, the Sonne of George Copping, who departed this life, the last daie of August, Ano 1620."

At the entrance of the church, under the steeple, on a flat stone:—

"wm. Truelove died 20th June, 1766, uged 72. He was five times hailiff of Ipswich."

The late William Truelove died August 25th, 1798, and was buried in the above-mentioned vault, with his father; but without any inscription. He was four times bailiff; and was one of the original founders of the Blue Bank.

The following persons are also buried in the church, but the inscriptions are now obliterated:—

"John Walworth, Gent., died X. April, 1488. Clementia Walworth, widow, died 1437. Margaret Walworth, wife of William Walwoilh, late of Ippeswyche, gent., died April 1, 1460."

On the north side of the church-yard, is a vaulted tomb to the memory of Mr. Samuel Thorndike, who was six times bailiff of Ipswich; he died December 25th, 1819, aged 62. Also to his son, Lieut. James Thorndike, of the Royal Artillery, who died August 7th, 1814; and many of the Thorndike, Frewer, and Mayhew families, are buried in this vault.

In 1598, Elizabeth Walter, widow, of London, left, by her will, £50: which sum, together with £30 from some of the parishioners, was expended in the purchase of a house abutting on the church-yard, the rent of which was to be appropriated to the maintenance of a godly learned preacher in the parish of St. Lawrence. This house is kept in repair by the parishioners, and the minister used to receive the whole rent, without any deduction; but, for years, the custom was, for the parishioners only to allow something occasionally: however, at the present time, the will of the donor is strictly adhered to, and the minister receives the whole rent.

Mr. John Burrough, of London, by will, dated March 22nd, 1613, gave to the bailiffs, &c. of Ipswich, £100 to be laid out in land which would fetch the annual rent of £5, to be distributed to forty poor persons of the town, on every Good Friday, in St. Lawrence church. Land was bought at Westerfield, and let upon a lease for a hundred years, at no more than £5. The funds of this charity have increased so much, that upwards of three hundred poor persons annually receive three shillings and sixpence each.

In 1080, Mr. William Sayer, portman, gave one hundred pounds, by will, to the bailiffs and five eldest portmen, to the intent, that, out of the interest thereof, bread should be provided for the poor, and distributed at St. Lawrence' parish, in the forenoon of every Sabbath.

In 1720, Mr. Francis Colxnan, portman, left a piece of land, of six acres, in the parish of St. Helen, to the corporation, for one thousand years, on condition of their paying £8: 2: 0 to eleven trustees, inhabitants of St. Lawrence' parish, for the purpose of supplying the poor with bread and clothing, annually, to that amount.

The parish of St. Lawrence is what is called a perpetual curacy, in the gift of the parishioners. It was augmented by Queen Anne's bounty, from Michaelmas, 1748; and, in 1751, lands in St. Mary Stoke, were judged proper to be purchased, for the augmentation of the churches of St. Lawrence and St. Nicholas: but the governors refused to go through with the purchase of those lands, unless the bailiffs and portmen should enter in some of their public books, an agreement that the rates which had been usually made, for the last seven years, for the maintaining the ministers, as well as for the repairs of the churches of the said parishes, shall not be taken away, lessened, or abated, in consequence of such augmentation. This agreement was assented to, entered in the Assembly Book of the corporation, and confirmed by a decree of Chancery, April 23rd, 1774.

In 1808, a contest took place for the election of the curate; when the numbers were, for the

Rev. R. L. Page, A.B *H*

Rev. *i.* Ford, A. M. (the present incumhent) 44

The Rev. Richard Canning, M. A., a gentleman of distinguished character and ability, editor of the second edition of Kirby's Suffolk Traveller, and compiler of the account of the Ipswich Charities, was forty years minister of this church; and died June 9th, 1775. He was a man of very superior literary attain-

ments, and well versed in every thin relative to the history and antiquities of Ipswich.

The Rev. Thomas Lee, D. D., was curate of the parish for several years; and died June, 1824, aged 66. He was president of Trinity College, Oxford; and served the office of vice-chancellor, from 1814 to 1818. He was a man of superior learning and accomplishments, tempered with peculiar suavity of manners, and was universally beloved and lamented.

In the year 1804, Sir Robert Kerr Porter, who was then a captain in the Westminster Militia that formed part of the garrison here, being on terms of great intimacy with the late Rev. Dr. Lee, who was minister of St. Lawrence at that time, he was induced, as a compliment to his friend, to present the parish with the picture of' Our Saviour discoursing with the Doctors in the Temple,' that now covers the whole of the west end of the building, and forms so conspicuous an ornament to St. Lawrence' church; but the extra projection of the upper gallery tends much to injure its effect. This painting, though hastily executed, shews the strength and colouring peculiar to Sir Robert's style: it has thus been described by a poetical traveller:—

"At St. Lawrence' a beautiful painting we saw,
Of Our Lord to the Doctors expounding the Law.'
Captain Porter, (they talk of it much to his praise,)
Completed this picture in less than six days."

In September, 1795, an organ was introduced into this church, and a new gallery erected between the nave and the chancel; and it is altogether very neatly fitted up.

Previous to repairing the altar-piece of this church, an exceedingly well painted picture was removed from the church. It represented King Charles I. lying in state, in his ermined robes, with the crown and sceptre placed upon his breast: the features are forcibly delineated, and exhibit die livid hue of death: at his feet is a graceful figure of an angel blowing a trump,—and may be supposed to be sounding the requiem of the martyred king, or summoning him to bliss, at the day of resurrection. The following inscription appears, in large gold letters, on a black ground, at the bottom of the picture:—

"Within this Sacred Arch doth lye
"Of royalty One Bo Exact

The quinteMence of Majesty That praise come short and doth detract

Which heing Sett more Glorious Shines If you would see hiin to endure

The hest of Kings hest of Divines Behold him in his poitrailure

Brittain's Shame and Brittain's Glory If such another you would find

Mirrour of Prince's Compleat Story It innst hy Angels he designed."

The painting is considerably defaced, but the design and colouring are good, and the perspective of the building wherein the tomb is placed, is well defined and preserved. The whole picture and inscription measure ten feet in height, by nine feet. It is now in the possession of Mr. Piper, bookseller.

The meetings of the Mechanics' Institution are held in this parish, in a large room on the premises of Mr. Piper. This institution owes its existence to a prospectus which was issued by Mr. Raw, in the winter of 1823—*i:* in which is suggested the desirableness of forming a society which should have for its object, the information of mechanics, which was thought to be attainable by enabling them to have the use of books, at a small expense, to a much greater extent than their own individual means would reach. Nothing further was done until towards the close of the year 1824; when an individual, who, from peculiar circumstances, was unable to take any active part in the business sooner, determined to try what could be effected; and, after consulting with several persons who were supposed to be friendly to the diffusion of knowledge, a meeting was convened on the Town Hall, on Tuesday, November 23rd, 1824, for the purpose of forming an institution for the spread of scientific information amongst the artizans and mechanics of the town and neighbouihood. William

Batley, esq., one of the common council, was called to the chair, and opened the business in a masterly manner. The large council chamber was completely crammed. One of the papers printed in the town, thus notices it:—" The public meeting on the Town Hall, in this place, on Tuesday last, was most numerously attended; and all the resolutions were unanimously passed. We hail this event, as the harbinger of a more general spirit of unanimity in the town. It is a rare thing, at Ipswich, to find men, on any subject, all of one mind; but, happily, they seem to be so in this matter; which is indeed of very great importance, both as it regards the welfare of a numerous and most useful class of men in society, and the best interests of society itself. One hundred and seven persons have already enrolled their names as members: which number, we have no doubt, before the end of the year, will be considerably increased." — The circumstance of every member of a literary society then existing in the town taking an active part in the promoting and establishing the Mechanics' Institution, affords a gratifying proof how well calculated mental pursuits are to expand the mind with benevolent and kindly feelings towards those who have not possessed the same advantages.

After this auspicious commencement, the committee of the institution took a room in St. Matthew's, which had been formerly used as a school. And, on the 17th of February, 1825, Mr. Vaux delivered the first lecture to the new society, on the council-chamber of the Town Hall; subject, " Pneumatics."

During the time the society occupied the apartment in St. Matthew's—which was not convenient—lectures were only delivered occasionally. The committee, however, soon determined on engaging the room now occupied by the institution: which, from its central situation, is better adapted to the purpose. After the removal to the present premises, a number of gentlemen engaged to deliver a series of gratuitous lectures, once a fortnight, on various subjects: which has been the practice from that time to the present. Non-snbscribers are admit-

ted to the lectures, on paying a small fee. Since the introduction of lectures at stated times, the society has evidently beeu increasing in utility; one decisive proof is, the great additional number of volumes which are now circulated among the members. Since its establishment, in 1824, the donations of books to the institution, from various g'entlemen of the town and neighbourhood, are very considerable, both in number and value; and it now possesses a library containing of upwards of six hundred volumes, besides a number of tracts and pamphlets not yet bound up.

The museum belonging to this institution, contains a number of valuable specimens of natural history, geology, arts, and manufactures: all of which are donations to the society, from members connected with, or gentlemen residing in, the neighbourhood. A book is kept at the museum, in which the several articles are described; together with the names of the donors.

The following is an extract from an old document in the museum of the Mechanics' Institution. $t is chiefly in the old black letter, and is entitled

E E A Complaint against such as favoured the Gospel at Ipswich, exhihited to Queene Mnrie' Counsaile sittyng in Commission at Beckle in Suffolke, the 18th May, Ann. 1.1.18, hy Philip Williams, Foot e man, John 9teward, and Matthew Bntler, worae for the purpose."

It contains a list of eighty-one names of persons, male and female, arranged under separate heads, mentioning the parish in which each individual resided, as follow:— "The names of nch as fled out of the Towne and lurked in secret places.

"The names of such aa have not received the Sacrament.
"Names of such as ohserve not ceremonies.
Names of Priests' Wives who have had access to their hushands.
"Names of maintainors against the complaint.
"Their requests to punish and convent certaine, whose ensample might reverse other from theiT opinions."

The first head relates only to the year 1556, but the remainder to 1558.

Nearly opposite to this spot, is a rude carving in wood, on the corner of Mr. Conder's house, about eight feet from the ground, of which we have given a representation. Many of the corners of the houses in Ipswich were, formerly, ornamented in the same manner, with some fanciful or allegorical figures:—

In the Old Butter-market, in this parish, is one of the greatest architectural curiosities in Ipswich: it is the house now in the possession of Mr. J. E. Sparrow, town clerk for the borough, and coroner for the county. It was built in 1567, by a person of the name of Clyatt, for Mr. Robert Sparrow; who was several times bailiff of Ipswich: and it has never been inhabited by any other resident than of the name of Sparrow. On the second story there are four bay windows in the front—which is about seventy feet next the street; and on the base of each of these windows are respectively sculptured the emblematical figures of Europe, Asia, Africa, and America, with their peculiar attributes. Above these windows is a considerable projection, extending the whole length of the front, forming a promenade, on the outside, nearly round the house. On the roof are four attic windows, forming so many gable ends, and corresponding with those beneath them. Over these upper windows are figures of Cupids in different attitudes: and the whole exterior of the building is profusely ornamented with animals, fruit, and flowers, with wreaths of roses and other devices relative to the armorial bearings of the Spauow family. No chimnies can be seen from the street. On the west end of the house, facing St. Stephen's lane, is represented an uncouth figure of Atlas with a long beard, kneeling on one knee, and supporting the globe on his shoulders. At the corner, a little below this, is a pastoral scene; consisting of a figure sitting under a tree, surrounded by sheep: another figure, a shepherd, is approaching him, with his hat in one hand, and a crook, which projects from the wall, in the other: he is leading a flock of sheep; and is in the attitude of addressing the person who is seated beneath the wide-spreading beech. It is not, however, easy to determine, from the foliage, whether the tree is meant for a beech, an oak, 01 an elm: but there is little doubt but that the artist, being seized with a fit of classical enthusiasm, intended this effort as an illustration of the discourse between Tityrus and Melibceus, in the first eclogue of Virgil.

We are induced to believe that the ornaments on this house are all emblematical: and we may infer, from this last composition, that the wool trade then flourished in Ipswich, and was of great importance; and the other decorations in front, are intended to imply that it was carried on with all quarters of the globe.

In the centre of the house, in the front, the royal arms of Charles II. are largely displayed; and executed in a better style than the rest of the ornaments. Several of the rooms in the interior are panelled with oak, and exhibit perfect and curious specimens of the caning in wood at that period. On one side of the court-yard or square, is a gallery over a colonnade supported by pillars. The drawing-room, in the part next the street, is forty-six feet in length by twenty-one feet, lofty in proportion; and is the largest room in any private house in the town. There is an apartment in the roof of the back part of the house, the entrance to which was ingeniously concealed by a sliding panel: it has only one small window, and that cannot be seen from any other part of the premises. It had been fitted up as a private chapel or oratory: and there is a tradition in the family, that Charles II. was concealed in this room, some time after the battle of Worcester. There is no written evidence to be found, or any demonstrative proof of this fact; but it is certain that there are many circumstances tending to place beyond a doubt, that there was a peculiar and intimate connexion between this monarch and the Sparrow family; for there were, lately, here, no less than three original portraits of King Charles II.; and there are several of various individuals of the Stuart family, and many other excellent portraits by Vandyke, Kneller, and Lely, scattered through the different apartments: and there are still in the possession of the Sparrow family, two beautifullyexecuted miniature portraits of the king and Mrs. Lane, splendidly set in gold; which were, it is said, presented by this sovereign to his host, when he left the place of his concealment; and the royal arms of Charles II., on the front of the house, tend still further to corroborate the conjecture.

This edifice, after a lapse of two hundred and sixty years, is in excellent preservation; and is well worth the attention of the curious. Several good views of it have been engraved, particularly one designed by Mr. William Sparrow, which ornaments our work; and another very beautiful one, in the "Excursions through Suffolk," published in the year 1818.

In this narrow street, in the open air, the provision market was formerly held, and but scantily supplied. But in 1809, five public spirited individuals undertook to erect a new market, at their joint expense. A piece of land, not far from the old spot, was purchased, and a new markct-placo completed, November, 1811. It is composed of an outer and inner quadrangle; round each of which runs a range of buildings, supported by stone columns, that afford accommodation and protection from the weather, to the persons attending the market. The different stations allotted to the vendors, are numbered; and'they pay a small annual or weekly rent. In the centre of the interior quadrangle is a fountain, the pedestal surmounted with a pyramid of Portland stone, forming an obelisk about twenty feet high; on each side of the pedestal, a basin is cut into the solid stone, and supplied with water from a lion's head above: thus the supply of water is made to contribute to the ornament as well as convenience of the market, but it ought to be better attended to. The whole undertaking cost about £10,000, was executed from the designs of Mr. William Brown and Mr. B. B. Catt, architects, of Ipswich; and does credit to their abilities. Adjoining is a large inclosed space, for the cattle market: which is an excellent arrangement, in a populous town. There is a small supply of provisions and vegetables, on Wednesday; but Saturday is the great market day for all kinds of provisions, and for goods of every description; and the assemblage of vendors from the neighbouring towns and villages, is so great, that it is not uncommon to see the articles, even of haberdashery and millinery, spread out for display upon the ground: the whole exhibiting a scene of bustle and animation, worthy the observation of strangers. It has been thought, by some, that this influx of promiscuous dealers is somewhat prejudicial to the resident shopkeepers of the town, and takes away some of the ready money they might otherwise receive; but we are inclined to believe, that the general good far outbalances any partial evil. The town is much indebted to the original projectors; who are amply repaid by the profits arising from their speculation. One of the five shares was lately disposed of by auction, and sold for £2,460.

In this parish, in the Old Butter-market, at the corner of the Old Jail-lane, the Ipswich Journal is printed, and published every Saturday, by its estimable and benevolent proprietor, Mr. Postle Jackson. This is one of the oldest and most respectable provincial papers in the kingdom. It was first printed in the year 1720, by John Bagnal, in a small quarto sheet, on coarse paper; price, three halfpence. The first Ipswich Journal is preserved; but the oldest we have seen, is dated the 23rd of May, 1724. Some of the early numbers are ornamented with a view of Ipswich, rudely cut in wood; and many of the advertisements are headed by a wood-cut, indicative of the article advertised: and what is singular, the early papers which we have seen, contain not a word of local intelligence,— neither deaths, marriages, or births, are announced. It was first called the Ipswich Journal; then, for some little time, the Ipswich Gazette; and then, again, resumed its original appellation: and we have a pa-

per before us, dated February 22, 1735, which is called the Ipswich Weekly Mercury; and has the following curious imprint:—

' Ipswich: printed hy T. Norris, in the Cross Key Street, near the Great s White Horse Comer: where Advertisements are taken in, and hy the men that sell this paper: at the said Office may he had Lcmmons hy Wholesale and Retail, and where all sorts of Blank Warrants are printed and sold."

The only advertisement this paper contains, is as follows:—

"ADVERTISEMENT. "SUFFOLK."yyHF. REAS his Majesty's Writ under the Seal of *Great* Britain is i.sned forth and directed to the Sheriff of the said County to elect and make choice of a Knight to serve in Parliament for the same County in the room and place of Sir Rohert Kemp, Bart, lately deceased. This is therefore to ppve notice that the next County Court will he holden at Ipswich in the said County of Suffolk, on Wednesday the.'ith day of March next, at which time *for the safety of the Electors of the said County upon a pluce called Great Boughton at or near the said toivn of Ipswich,* the said Sheriff will proceed to Election pursuant to the said Writ."

This must evidently have been an opposition paper; for w e have seen the Ipswich Gazette, printed by John Bagnal, of the same date, wherein the foregoing advertisement appears, with another of a meeting at Stowmarket, recommending Sir Cordell Firebrace, bart., as a proper person to succeed Sir Robert Kemp.

As a further corroboration of w hat we have previously advanced, we extract the following advertisement, *verbatim,* from the Ipswich Journal, dated from Saturday, May 16th, to Saturday, May 23rd, 1724. By which it will be seen, that there was, formerly, more than one spring from which the medicinal waters, in this town, were produced:—

"The Ipswich Spaw Waters is now opened by Mrs. Martha Coward, and Attendance will be given every Morning at the Bath on St. Margaret's Green,

from 6 to 9 at One Penny per Morning, and Two Pence for each Palk carried off."

In one of the papers, about this time, is an advertisement of the New Fly Post Coach, that will set out from Ipswich early in the morning, and arrive in London in the evening of the next day, " *If God permit.'""*

April 8th, 1756. At this time it was in agitation to lay an additional duty of a halfpenny on newspapers,—which then paid only one halfpenny; and "likewise an additional duty of one shilling on advertisements,—then only two shillings each: which the editor of the Journal declared that he was not able to pay.

September 2nd, 1769. William Jackson having purchased the moiety of the Ipswich Journal, of Mrs. Elizabeth Craighton, the partnership between them was dissolved; and it was, afterwards, printed by him only. This lady died in February, 1796, at the advanced age of ninetytwo.

December 2nd, 1774. A dispute arose between Mr. William Jackson, the proprietor of the Journal, and Mrs. Craighton and Mr. Shave; and a new paper was expected to be published: and on the 17th of Dec. the Ipswich Journal was printed by William Bailey, for the benefit of the creditors of Mr. William Jackson; who had agreed to pay Mrs. Craighton an annuity of £20 a year; whioh they refused to continue. Mr. Shave did publish a paper; and, for some time, there were two Ipswich Journals, both purporting to be the original:—this paper was entitled "The Original Ipswich Journal. Saturday, Dec. 24th, 1774;" and so continued till March 22nd, 1777: when the creditors paper was discontinued, and the other continued to be published in the names of Shave, Craighton, and Jackson. A paper war took place between the two editors: and the following; effusion having some humour, we are induced to extract it:—

' Upon the whole, Mr. Shave's best apology is no better than Benedict's in the play; who observes, that, when he said he would die a bachelor, he did not think he should live till he was married. Whether Mr. Shave's new wife— for he declared himself wedded to his New Paper—will prove so good a fortune as he flatters himself, time only will shew. The creditors, however, are determined to support their legal contract to the *Good Old Lady,* the *Original* Ipswich Journal, with their interest and fortune, until Mr. Shave can procure her *Bill of Divorce* from the public."

September 10th, 1818, the late Mr. Stephen Jackson died, at the age of seventy-one: he had been forty-three years proprietor and editor of the Ipswich Journal.

In the Old Jail-lane, the Wesleyan chapel, a substantial brick building, was erected in 1816: and is calculated to hold eight hundred persons.

Just behind Mr. Sparrow's house, a little south from St. Lawrence' church, stands the church of St. Stephen. It is a rectory; and the revenues are so small, that it is generally held by sequestration: but m the year 1140, it was in the presentation of Sir Andrew de Bures; of the Cavendishes in 1400; of Sir Gilbert Debenham in 1487; then the family of Brewes, till it came to Sir Edmund Witypoll; and went, as well as St. Peter's, with the Christ's Church estate.

It is a singular fact, that, in the year 1635, an order was made for the officers of St. Stephen's parish to make a

F F rate for the aid of the mamtenance of the poor.of St. Nicholas'; the said St. Stephen's parish having no poor of its own. So strangely do some of the parishes in this town intersect each other, that there is a piece of ground extending from the glebe land adjoining to St. Helen's church, to the corner of Water-lane, in the Woodbridge road, that is in St. Stephen's parish, whereon a number of miserable huts were erected at the time the barracks were there; which brought such an accession of settlers, who have since become burdensome to the parish, that the poor rates of St. Stephen are n,ow as high as those of any parish in Ipswich.

At the entrance into this church by the south-east door, is a monument, in coloured marble, to the memory of Robert Lcman, who served the office

of sheriff of London, and of Mary his wife: they both died on the same day, September 3rd, 1637. The figures are kneeling on each side of an altar, with the effigies of one son and four daughters, in the same attitude, beneath. The following strangely inelegant inscription is attached:—

"Beneath this monument intomhed lye
The rare remark of a conjugal lie
Rohert and Mary who to hew how neere
They did comply, how to each other deare
One loath hehind the other long to stay
(As married) died together in one day."

In the middle of the church, is one brass plate, with an inscription in black letter, that has escaped the ravages of the spoiler: an attempt has been evidently made to take it away, as part of it is broken off: it is simply, "William Sherman, grocer, of Lundun, U84"

"Ro. UIPFS, Merchant, died 1624.

"Rven dust as I am now Po thou in time shall he
Such one was 1 as thou
Behold thyself hy me."

"ELIZ. Girps, fair wife, died 1644."

"john Reynolds, Gent, and Elizabeth hiswife. He gave ahout £500 to charitahle uses; ho wa horn 1571, ami died Mar. 28, 1648"

It is somewhat remarkable, that in this little parish are buried three noted physicians. On the north side of the communion table is a large stone on which is sculptured,

"Here resteth the hody of HENRY REDDISH, Dr. in Physic, who married the duughterof Harhottle Wingtield, of CraAeld, Eqr. in Suffolk; he died Sep. 14;— cSalutis 1663 "Anno *I JFAatia HO* Etiain media inoriantur/'

"Here lieth the hody of JOHN BARKER, M. D. Fellow of the Royal College of Physicians, London, and physician to his Majesty's Forces in the Low Countries, horn Ap. 18, 1708 died Jan. 31, 1748—9."

On the north side of the wall, is a neat marble tablet

"To the memory of JOHN G'LUBBE, late u very eminent Physician in this place: he died *25* April, 1811, aged 7O.

He will he long rememhered in Ipswich, for his skill, prohity, and Immunity."

"Here lieth the hody of EDMUND JENNY, ESQ,. who lived on eaith 75 year, and departed to a hetter life 4th June, 1624."

"GEORGE Raymond, one of the Common Council of Ipswich, he died 1617." Faith, Piety, and upright life, in tin-life did him grace.

Christ aith, and God's undouhted word, say such in heaven have place."

Between the communion table and the vestry:— "In memory of MARY, relict of Philip CaYter, Gent, who departed this life May 11, 1771, aged *4* 8 yean.

"Farewell vain world, I've had enough of thee.
And now am careless what thou sayeet of me;
Thy smiles I court not, nor thy frowns I fear,
My cares are past, my head lies quiet here,
What faults you've seen in me, take care to shun,
And look at home, enough is to he done. "

Near the chancel door:— "Here resteth the hody of MARTHA, the beloved wife of Ralph Noose, ot Ipswich, meichant, who departed this life Mar. 13, 1657, aged.'i4.

"Yet she's not dead, she lives where she did love,
Her memory on earth, her soul ahove."

"Likewise the hody of the aforesaid Ralph Noose, who died Jan. 10, 1663, aged 67."

"Also his son, RlCHARD NO08E, who died Ap. 3, 1668, aged 30."

On the south wall is a tablet

"To the memory of Robt. Collins, Esq. late of this parish, who died 18 Sep. 1809, aged 51."

Sir Anthony would have had two stately mansions so close together; for the Coach and Horses inn abuts upon the premises then occupied by Sir Anthony, and would have left no room for the extent of ground usually attached to such residences. We, therefore, think that the *Coach House,* or *Coach Houses,* has been confounded with the Coach and Horses; and that Brandon House—

if ever it was in Brook-street at all— occupied the scite on which the houses have been built extending from the corner of the Old Butter-market, to the passage leading to Saint Stephen's church-yard; for thirty years ago, the premises now occupied by Mr. Dickerson, were then the *Coach House,* or rather *Coach Houses,* attached to the adjoining mansion, then occupied by the late Mrs. Parish.

In the Tankard public house, some curious remains of the decorations of Sir Anthony's mansion still exist, particularly in a large room on the ground floor; the oak wainscot of which— beautifully carved in festoons of flowers, and a variety of devices — was formerly gilt, but is now painted blue and white. The ceiling is of groined work, carved, and wrought something after the manner of Henry Vllth's chapel at Westminster. In various compartments of this ceiling, numerous coats of arms are sculptured, and have been emblazoned in their proper colours: most of which are defaced, but still several of those of the Wingfield family, encircled with the motto of the Order of the Garter, remain in tolerable preservation. This room is twenty-seven feet long, sixteen feet nine inches wide, and only nine feet five inches high. The ceiling is divided into panels sixteen inches and a half square; there are twelve of these in the length of the room, and eight in the breadth: each panel is bordered with a band, and alternately emblazoned with a coat of arms, or filled up with a projecting ornament, in the shape THE NEW YORK PUBLIC LIBRARY ASTON, LENOX AND

TILDES FOUNDATIONS.

of an inverted pediment, with concave sides, richly carved, and pendentive six inches from the ceiling: each of these projections terminates nearly in a point, tipped with a leaf or rose. There is one large beam intersects the ceiling, in the centre, the whole length of the room, and two smaller transverse ones — one of them a little deviating from its original horizontal position.

Whatever defect there may be in the description, has been amply compensat-

ed by the accurate and beautiful engraving from a drawing by Mr. H. Davy; which at once stamps him as a master of his profession.

Over the fire-place is a basso relievo, rudely carved in wood, and colored in a tasteless style. On our inspection of this curious relic, it was melancholy to note how the figures have been mutilated, beheaded, and defaced. We were told that this wanton mischief was principally perpetrated by the military, when this was a garrison town: and we were rejoiced to find that the sober citizens of Ipswich were not guilty of such an outrage against decency and taste.

The interpretation of this sculpture has been thus given, agreeable to the generally received but ridiculous tradition, that it represented the battle of Bosworth Field. "Leicester town, in one corner; several warriors in the centre; Sir Charles William Brandon, standard-bearer to the earl of Richmond, lies dead by his horse, and on the other side the standard; at a distance is the earl with the crown placed upon his head by Sir William Stanley; in another is Leicester Abbey—the abbot coming out of the porch to compliment the earl." Now one would think that this was clear enough, but the magic wand of another conjuror turns the whole picture into the Judgment of Paris, and its consequences, in five compartments. "In the first," says this writer, " he appears seated, habited in the Phrygian robe and bonnet, amusing himself with his lute, when the three goddesses present themselves. The next scene is his adjudgment of the prize; when Juno, as Queen of Heaven, leads the way, followed by Venus disclosing all her charms, and Pallas with the Gorgon's head and *Mgis.* Paris, won by the attractions of the Goddess of Love, and her assistant son, who hovers above in the air, decrees to her the prize which he holds in his hand. We next view him armed *cap d piè,* reclining perhaps at the foot of the statue of his patroness, meditating his conquest; his lance lying beside him, and his horse standing saddled and bridled. The reclining warrior and the horse are the only figures in the piece,

that could possibly suggest the idea of the battle of Bosworth Field; but the latter might, with as much propriety, have been taken for the Trojan horse, as for that of Richard III. or Paris for that king. Below, in the left corner, we see Paris and some of his friends, with horses, preparing to carry oft' Helen; and, in the distance, they appear offering up their vows in the temple of Venus, or perhaps solemnizing their nuptials, while the horse or horses are waiting without."

Were we not aware into what absurdities antiquarians will run, when led astray by conjecture, we should have thought it impossible that two persons could have given such different descriptions of one and the same thing; but in this, as in all other doubtful cases, we recommend our readers to see and judge for themselves. There is no appearance whatever of a warlike engagement. There is no other figure of an armed man but one; who is reclining on the ground, with a lance lying by the side of his horse, and, according to the perspective, many yards in length. Now, as one soldier cannot make a battle, it clearly has no reference to the desperate conflict between Richard and Richmond. There are three female figures that cannot be mistaken, as they are portrayed in the denuded state in which the three goddesses in question are usually represented, are distinguished by their several attributes, and certainly could have no business in Bosworth Field. The principal figure, completely equipped in black armour, is reclined at the toot of what is termed in the description, " a statue to his patroness; but which is, clearly, a pyramidical altar of considerable height, with a figure of a youthful bacchanal on the top, holding a bunch of grapes in one hand, and a goblet in the other, raised, as we may suppose, to do honour to the nuptials of Paris and Helen; which lady, from the delicacy of a bride, does not any where make her appearance. The artist, as was not uncommon in those days, has fallen into a palpable anachronism, by making the instrument on which Paris is amusing himself, exactly like a Spanish guitar. He is playing to three female figures, who are dancing as they approach him; and are, evidently, intended to represent the Graces, as introductory to the approac h of the Goddesses, and not the three goddesses themselves, — who appear in the second compartment. There is a town in the back ground, which it is difficult to determine whether it is in the clouds or on the earth, and may as well be meant for Troy as for Leicester. How the first *writer* could have run into such an egregious error, can only be accounted for upon the charitable supposition that he never saw the piece. We, therefore, with some little reservation, decidedly agree with the description of his opponent, which appeared in the Gentleman's Magazine, 1796.— Fresh depredations are daily committed upon this curious relic, and it will soon have to be numbered with the things that were.

We flatter ourselves that our readers will be much gratified with the following original lines, from the elegant pen of Bernard Barton:— SUCH were the rooms in which, of yore, Our ancestors were wont to dwell;

And still of fashions known no more,
Even these ling'ring relique« tell.

The oaken wainscot richly grac'd
With gay festoons of mimic flow'rs,
The armorial bearings, now defac'd,
All speak of proud and long past hours.

The ceiling, quaintly carv'd and groin'd, With pendent pediments revers'd,
A by-gone age recals to mind,
Whose glories Song hath oft rehears'd.

And true, though trite, the moral taught, And worthy of the Poet's rhyme,
By ALL that can impress on thought,
The changes made by Chance and Time.

These tell "a plain, unvarnish'd tale"
Of Wealth's decline, and Pride's decay;
Nor less unto the mind unveil
Those things which cannot pass away.

And truths which no attention wake,
When Poets sing, or Parsons teach,
Perchance may some impression make,
When thus a PUBLIC-HOUSE may Preach.

Adjoining to the Tankard, is the Theatre: on whieh spot was a Catholic chapel, for Judge Milton — the brother of the illustrious poet of that name — in the time of James II. The Norwich company played Henry VIll. August, 1759, at the theatre in Tacket-street: previous to which, pi ay 8 were acted at a temporary theatre in the Griffin yard, and sometimes in the Shire Hall. We copy the following advertisement, in the Ipswich Journal, dated November 30th, 1728:— FOR l'HE BENEFIT OF MR. PLAT, MRS. BUCK, AND MRS. Pi.OMEK.
Neeer acted hen.
BY THE NORWICH COMPANY OF COMEDIANS.
At the Shire Hall in Ipswich, on Monday next, heing the 2d of Decemher, will he acted a Comedy called
THE CHANCES; OR, HOOD LUCK AT LAST.
Written tij tke late Duke of Buckingham.
The Parts to he ptay'd as follows,—
Duke of Ferrara hy Mr. James,
Petruchio, Governor of Bologna, Mr. Bowman, Don John h) Mr. Frizhy,
Don Frederic hy Mr. Marshal, Don Antonio hy Mr. Paul, Perez hy Mr. Buck, Anthony hy Mr. Morris; 1st Constantia hy Mrs. Frishy, 2d Con-Untia hy Mrs. Buck, Landlady h) Mrs. Homer, Estifania hy Mrs. Bray.
Willi several entertainments of singing and dancing hy Mr. Plat, Mr. Cliurg, and Mrs. Jackson, particularly the 24 Fidlers, the Satire upou all Trade's, and a new drinking Song never sung in this town hefore.

Being a yearly Benefit, and positively the only one in Town.
Tickets to he had at Scrutton's Coffee House.
Beginning positively at 6 o'Clock.
Vicat Res.

The present building was erected on the scite of the old theatre, in the year 1803, by subscription of fourteen shares of £100 each; which entitled the holders to 5 per cent. for their money, in addition to a silver ticket, admitting them to each night's performance.

This town has reason to be proud of having first appreciated the merits of the renowned David Garrick; who, un-

der the assumed name of Lyddal, made his first dramatic attempt, before an Ipswich audience, in the character of *Dick,* in the "Lying Valet," in the year 1739; and, two years afterwards, on the 19th of October, 1741, he made his first appearance in London, at Goodman's Fields, in the character of Richard III.

Dunstal's company, from London, played here in 1739: and most of the performers of eminence have passed the ordeal of our critical audience.

Before provincial managers adopted the custom of bringing down the London *stars,* to enlighten their rural hemisphere, the Norwich company was excellent, and the theatre at Ipswich well attended; but now, unless when some celebrated London actor condescends to favour us with his performance, for half the receipts of the house, there is nothing but "a beggarly account of empty boxes." This was not the case in the time of the elder Brunton, who played Evander, and the Roman Father, with such judgment and effect, to his eldest daughter's Ephrasia, and Horatia, in the year 1785. This lady afterwards became Mrs. Merry, and went to America: from whence she never returned. Next to Mrs. Siddons and Miss O'Neil, she was, ceitainly, the finest tragedian of the day.

For the many years that the company was under the management of Mr. Hindes, he set his face against the *stars,* and the theatre flourished; but the times are changed;—the lateness of the modish dinner hour is prejudicial to the play-house; and it is to be lamented, that the regular drama is not better encouraged. The present respectable manager, Mr. Smith, is unwillingly compelled to give way to the prevailing taste for mummery and show; and Shakspeare and Otway are superseded by Punch and the Man Monkey.

But we now come to a more pleasing object of consideration,— that charming little actress, Miss Goward. She was born at Ipswich, the 22nd of November, 1805; and, at the age of twelve years, she attracted the notice of the late Mrs. Cobbold: from whom she ever after received the greatest kindness, instruction, and encouragement. At fifteen, she was placed under the care of the late Mr. Henry Smart, the brother of Sir George Smart; who took great pains with his fair pupil, till the time of his death; and his widow faithfully and effectually completed the task. At the age of sixteen, Miss Goward made her first appearance on any stage, at Yarmouth, in the character of *Lucy Bertram;* from whence she went to Dublin: on her return, she played four nights at Ipswich; where she was received with enthusiastic applause, and recited a beautiful and appropriate address, written for her by Mrs. Cobbold, with great feeling and effect. She then joined the York company; and afterwards played at Norwich: from whence she went to London; where she made her first appearance at the English Opera House, on the 2nd of July, 1825, as *Rosina,* in the farce of that name, and in *Little Pickle.* Her timidity, for some time, quite overcame her; but, encouraged by the most enthusiastic applauses, she went through both the characters with complete success. She went from the English Opera House, to Covent Garden; where she has remained ever since, and is now decidedly and deservedly an established favourite with the public. Her voice has great sweetness and flexibility, but has not pow(er sufficient to constitute her a first-rate female singer. As an actress she copies from nature, and can display archness and vivacity, as well as sensibility and pathos. Her person is *petite,* and her features expressive; her figure altogether is lovely and agreeable, and her conduct and character are equal to her talents and her charms: and if she continue the career of improvement she is now pursuing, Ipswich will have to boast of having given birth to one of the brightest ornaments of the stage. She has lately married to Mr. Keeley, the celebrated comedian, of Covent Garden; who is as great a favourite with the public as herself: and there is such a striking similarity in their persons, talents, and pursuits, that we are induced to observe, with the poet,—

"Ah! sure a pair were never seen
So justly formed to meet by nature."

On Saturday, July 13th, 1799, on the last night of the company's performance for the season, an alarm of fire was given by some persons who were intoxicated; when the terror and confusion became so great, that several persons jumped from the gallery and the upper boxes, into the pit: but, happily, no lives were lost, nor did any serious accident happen. In August, 1816, the present theatre had a narrow escape from fire, when Mr. Mason's workshop, adjoining, was burnt to the ground: the flames destroyed some part of the dressing-rooms, but the main building was preserved.

The parishes in Ipswich, are, in some cases, so blended with each other, that, from its immediate vicinity, we have been induced to notice Tacket-street Chapel here; though it is, in fact, within the boundaries of St. Margaret's parish

On the same side of the way, not far from the Theatre, in Tacket-street, is the Independent Meeting-house, a substantial brick building, fifty-five by forty-four feet: it has three galleries, and will seat about eight hundred persons. In the year 1686, a few serious christians hired a building which stood in the Green Yard, in the parish of St. Peter, and converted it into a meeting-house. They invited the Rev. John Langston; who had been ejected, at the Restoration, from his living in Gloucestershire, to become the minister of their newly-formed church; and he was elected into the office, on the 2nd of November, in the same year: he was much persecuted for his opinions, but he was a learned and pious man; and there is a good painting of him in the vestry of the meeting-house. He was succeeded, at his death, in January, 1704, by the Rev. Benjamin Glandfield; who died in 1720. The congregation had greatly increased under his ministry; and in 1718, an extensive piece of ground was purchased, and in 1720, the present building was erected. The «uccessor of Mr. Glandfield, was Mr. Thomas Milway; who died May 21st, 1724. He was succeeded by the Rev. William Notcutt; who was followed by Dr. William Gordon: who, after continuing here ten years, removed to London. In 1763, the Rev. David Ed-

wards became pastor of this church, and remained here till 1791; when some disagreement took place between him and the congregation, and he left them, and retired to Wotton-UnderEdge, in Gloucestershire; where he died, May 30, 1795. On his removal, several of the congregation seceded, and established themselves in a place of worship, in Dairy Lane; where they have had a succession of pastors to the present day. In October, 1792, the Rev. Charles Atkinson was ordained to the pastoral office, in Tacketstreet; where he still remains, highly esteemed and respected: but being advanced in years, he is assisted by the Rev. William Notcutt, the great grandson of the beforementioned William Notcutt.

The Rev. William Notcutt was born at Wrington, near Bristol, in Somersetshire, in the year 1672. He was placed under the tuition of the Rev. William Payne, of Saffron Walden; and commenced preaching in 1705. He was chosen to succeed Mr. Milway, at Tacketstreet, December 10th, 1724; and was pastor of that congregation, nearly thirty-two years: he lived but a short time after his resignation; and, at his death, was buried in the ground belonging to the meeting-house, with the following inscription on his tomb:—

"The Rev. Mr. Wm. Notcutt died July 17, 175«, aged «1 years.

"Or temper heavenly, and of soul sincere,

In converse plea8ing, and in conduct clear,

In all a pastor's various work approv'd,

By numhers hlest, and e'en hy al l helov'd,

With every gentle, social virtue drest,

Of smiling patience e'en in death possess'd.

All these were Notcutt's honours thro' his stay

In these low regions, till he dropt his clay, *And* soar'd triumphant to the realms of day.''

He was an amiable, zealous, and learned man. He was the author of no less than one-and-twenty religious tracts: the most popular of w! ich was his last, "*A Dying Pastor's Legacy to his People*" 1724.

We do not pretend to understand the theory of dreams; but there are such extraordinary coincidences connected with some which have been well authenticated, as to puzzle the most enlightened philosophers to account for: and we give the following recital as correct, because the family is too conscientious and respectable for their authenticity to be doubted:—

Mrs Notcutt, the wife of the above-mentioned gentleman, died December 27th, 1755, at the age of 77. While she and her husband resided at Tbaxted, and before they had any idea of removing from thence, Mrs. Notcutt dreamed one night that they went to live at Ipswich; and the house in which she imagined they resided, was so impressed upon her mind, that when she actually went there, some years afterwards, she had a perfect recollection of it. She also dreamed that as she was going to a parlour, her nose began to bleed, and that it would be found impossible to stop the blood, until she had lost so much as to occasion her death; which event would happen forty years from that day. As her mind was deeply impressed, she wrote down in her pocket-book, the day of the month, and the year in which her dream occurred. In process of time, they went to reside at Ipswich; and Mrs. Notcutt, on removing to her new habitation, was surprised to find it correspond exactly with the one she had seen in her dream; and also the very same closet in going to which she thought the fatal accident happened. But parental duties, together with the busy concerns of life, engaging her attention, these circumstances were soon forgotten; and the closet was frequented for a number of years, without any fear of the accomplishment of her dream. On Christmas-day, 1755, as she was reaching a bottle of drops from the closet, to give to Mr. Notcutt, who was confined on his couch in the room, her nose began to bleed. Finding, after some time, that all the means to stop the blood proved ineffectual, her dream came to her recollection; and she requested one of her attendants to fetch her pocket-

book, directing where to find it. Upon examining, they found, to their unspeakable surprise, that it was exactly forty years from the time her dream had occurred. All methods were tried, but without effect: and as the medical attendant entered the room, she said to him, " You may try to stop the bleeding if you please, but you will not be able." So it proved in the event. Every part of her dream was fulfilled; and she languished from Thursday till Saturday,—when she breathed her last.

There is a convenient house and garden adjoining the building, for the use of the minister: and there is a spacious burying-ground, in which several distinguished individuals are interred: amongst which we noticed the following:—

"Rev. Wh. Gordon, D. D. died 1Mh Oct. ior, aged s7."

This gentleman was remarkable as having been the private secretary to Washington, for several years, during our contest with the United States.

"Susanna Harrison died 3d August, 17M, aged 32.

"During twelve years affliction, she discovered a gracious spirit; and was the Author of 'The Songs in the Night.' She heing dead, yet speaketh."

This woman, uneducated, and in an humble sphere of life, was confined to her bed for many years. She bore her affliction with pious resignation; and amused herself with the composition of poetry, consisting principally of

H H religious effusions: which, from many of them being written in the intervals of pain, when she could not sleep, she called them "Songs in the Night. " Among the numerous productions of her pen, there is occasionally a piece imbued with an enthusiasm that appears something like genius. The work was printed at Ipswich, in 2 vols. 12mo. about the time of her death, and met. with a good circulation among religious people.

"John Rodbard, M. D. mo." He was many years an eminent physician in this town.

"REV. Wm. Jrb Vis, mne *teen* yeare Paetor of the Congregation of Protec-

tant Disseoten, in the pariah of St. Nichouu, died 2lit March, I797, aged *72."*

"Wm. Clarke, Esq. died rth May, I791."

He was five times bailiff of Ipswich.

"Peter Clarke, Esq. died Nov. no4, aged t." He was five times bailiff of Ipswich.

"Rev. John Wright died Novemher 10th, 1800."

He was the author of a volume of sermons against popery —printed at Ipswich.

We shall next notice the church of St. Nicholas. It was impropriated to St. Peter's priory: on the dissolution of which, it was granted to Webb and Breton. It is not mentioned in Doomsday; and was, probably, erected on the scite of the dilapidated church of St. Michael: which is said, in that record, to have had eight acres of land. The present church is conjectured to have been built with some of the old materials: which is rendered more probable, from a stone at the west end of the south aisle, on which is a rude representation of St. Michael encountering the dragon. Of another stone, exhibiting the figure of a boar, it is more difficult to give any thing like a satisfactory account: an inscription, nearly defaced, above the animal, is thought to have been *In Dedication Ecclesie Omnium Sanctorum:* but why or how it came to be placed in its present situation, no one can conjecture.

Cardinal Wolsey's father bequeathed, in his will, six shillings and eightpence to the high altar of St. Nicholas, and forty shillings to the painting of the archangel there. The following intelligence respecting this picture, is from an eye-witness: — About twelve or thirteen years ago, some workmen, in taking down an old monument of the Esdaile family, for the purpose of erecting a gallery, discovered, on the wall of the north aisle of the church, a painting, extending for several feet: of which they informed some of the neighbouring residents; and this gentleman, who, with many others, saw it at the time, says that it was of considerable extent and size— supposed to be the figure of St. Michael, rudely executed on the wall itself, and coloured in distemper.

St. Nicholas is a perpetual curacy, in the gift of the parishioners. A neat little organ has lately been introduced in the new gallery. Over the communion table is a good copy of a picture by West, of our Saviour breaking bread with his disciples, at Emmaus, after his resurrection: the colouring is rather too glaring, and the figures too large for the situation in which it is placed, being within a few yards of the ground: it, however, does credit to the artist, Mr. J. Smart, of this town; who painted it in 1807. There is a neat window of stained glass, above this picture. The altar-piece is appropriately decorated: and the church is, altogether, very neatly fitted up. In the vestry, there is a beautiful plan of the parish, with a view of the ruins of the Grey Friars' Priory; a sketch of the porch door; the stone on which is the figure of St. Michael and the dragon, as well as that of the boar; together with the arms of the present minister, the Rev. Mileson G. Edgar, and those of the families of note connected with the parish, brilliantly emblazoned in their proper colours: it is executed with peculiar delicacy and correctness; and was presented to the minister and parishioners, by a gentleman of the parish.

At the east end of the south aisle, there is a white marble monument to the memory of Charles Whitaker, esq.; who was recorder, and member of parliament for Ipswich, the last year of William III. and the first year of Queen Anne's reign, 1701 and 1702.

On a stone in the church, is this simple inscription: —

"THOMA8 BLOYS, Oct. 14, H2."

"Here lyeth the hodyea of WILLIAM BLOYS, merchant, uortman of tiiia town, and ALICE hia wife; who were married together 49 year. He died the 23d of Jan. 1607, heing 81 yean of age; and the «aid Alice the 3d of Nov. 1608, heing 82 yeara of age."

"Here lieth the hody of Wjl. BnlDON, ofthitown, died I Ith of Dec. 1610.

'lndutrv

Whwe

Mr. Lany, who was recorder of Ipswich, married the widow of Mr. Bri-

don.

"Here reeteth the hody of Mary DE-PDEN, wife of Nicholae Philip, of this town, merchant; who died Oct. 3, 1642. "

She was accounted the unparalleled beauty of her age. Her husband, after her death, was made portman of Ipswich.

It is remarked by an old writer, that, " in November, 1657, the brass was off almost all the old marbles; but there was a fair marble in the middle alley, between the church doors, which, it is supposed, was placed there by Cardinal VVolsey, for preserving the memory of his father and mother:" and it is most likely that here their remains are deposited. This stone now forms a step at the entrance of the church, at the porch door.

In the yard, near the church door, was a large marble tomb, raised up w ith arches, breast high:— "Roger and Winifred Cutler, under one stone we two have interred EZEK1EL, JOSEPH, BENJAMIN, WINIFRED oar choicest food.

"Ac earth to he committed to the Earth

Lord save our «ouls and fit us for our death

Soul fear not death, nor tremhle for the pain

Christ is in life our hope, in Death our gain.

About the stone is a Death's head in every corner, and *Kai.* Cry Joseph.

South ide. What shall 1 cry Benjamin.

H'et end. All flesh is grass Winifred.

North iide. And the goodliest of it as the flower of the field.

Witness my Spring, which did ten Christides keep.

Vet in my prime died, and dying steep. Ezekiel.

In the north aisle:—

"In memory of Wu. BEESTON Coyte, M.D.; who died March 3, 1810, aged 69. Likewise Sarah his wife, and three children."

On the south side:—

"In memory of the Rev. James Coyte, Clerk, 97 years Minister of this parish, and Rector of Cantley, in Norfolk, died June 13th, IBI2, aged 63. Also of ANNE

his wife, who died Feh. I8, 1890, aged 60."

On the north side of the communion table:— "Here resteth the hody of SIR Peyton Ventris, late one of the

Justices of His Majesty's Court of Common Pleas, Westminster; who departed this life the 6th day of April, 1691, An. jfitatis."

He represented the borough in parliament, 1688.

In the yard, near the south-west porch:—

"Rout. Hewke, 26th April, I SOS.

"This world's a city full of streets,

And Death's a market-place where all men meets.

U life were merchandize, that men could huy,

Rich men would ever live, and poor men die."

In the yard, on the north side of the church, is a handsome vaulted monument to the memory of James Hatley, esq.; and of his daughter, Dame Judith Laurie, wife of Lieutenant-General Sir Robert Laurie, bart., who died January 25th, 1824

Mr. Ury Topley died March 23rd, 1759, aged 75. He was clerk and sexton of this parish fifty-three years; and his father thirty-six years. He was buried, according to his own desire, in the steeple, under the great bell.

In repairing this church, in 1827, five urns or jars formed of common earth,, each of them one foot deep, and three feet in circumference, were found imbedded in the wall of the church, in a strait line, very near together. One of them is now in the possession of Mr. R. Clamp, who was churchwarden of this parish; and it is in good preservation. They were entirely empty, and exhibited no symptoms of having contained any bones or ashes, or any other substance whatever.

In the year 1645, Mr. John Cutler left by will, his house in St. Nicholas, to this parish: out of the rent of which should be paid £5 per annum, for bread for the poor, and the remainder to be appropriated to the repairs of the church, and to the minister; likewise £10 per annum out of an estate called Blofield's, at

Trimley, now belonging to the earl of Rochford. In 1687, Captain Nicholas Kerrington, of Wapping, in Middlesex, by his will, dated the 19th of July, bequeathed £5 per annum, to be laid out in bread for the poor of this parish. There are some other trifling bequests, but none worthy of record.

The following notices of some persons of repute; who formerly resided in this parish, are worthy of attention:—

In this parish, in 1655, Francis Bacon, esq. a counsellor at law, fifth son of Edmund Bacon, of Shrubland Hall, esq., lived in a house which he bought of Capt. William Bloys, — whose father built it. Mr. Bacon married Katherine, daughter of Sir Thomas Wingfield, of Letheringham, knight. His estate was about £500 per annum. He was a magistrate of the county of Suffolk; and, in 1657, master of requests.

John Sicklemore, esq., counsellor at law, lived in an house, hy some called Middle House, being about the middle of the town. His father—who built that house— and his grandfather, were both portmen of Ipswich. His first wife was Anne, daughter of Pitilip Bedingfield, esq. of Ditchingharn Hall, in Norfolk: his second wife, Martha, eldest daughter of Nicholas Bacon, of Shrubland Hall, esq.

Benjamin Cutler, gent., son of Robert Cutler, a portman of Ipswich, and brother of Thomas Cutler, esq. some time justice of the peace for the county of Suffolk. His estate about £160 per annum.

William Cage, esq., portman of Ipswich, lived in this parish, in the time of Kings Charles II. and James II. His country house was at Bui stall. His estate, with his wife's, between *4* and £500 per annum.

Edward Man, of Ipswich, counsellor at law. His estate upwards of £200.

Nicholson, esq. about £400 Gosnold, gent. a farmer of the Customs.

The parliamentary visitors, in 1649, broke down six pictures, and took up three brass inscriptions: which is much to be regretted; because, in all probability, they would have thrown some light upon Wolsey's ancestors, who were buried in this church: for, on the south side of the passage leading from St. Nieholas'-street to the churchyard, stands the house in which tradition reports that Cardinal Wolsey was born. It was, formerly, inhabited by a Mrs. Edwards; but is now in the occupation of Mr. Vaux, surgeon. The house has been rebuilt, and modernized; but, on the premises, are walls which must have formed part of an ancient edifice of some importance; and there is nothing to corroborate the common report that the cardinal was the son of a butcher, for his father was most respectably connected, and related to Mr. Edmund Daundy, one of the first men in the town. However, the occupation of Wolsey's father matters but little; for Cavendish, who was the servant of this mighty prelate, states that he was a poor man's son, of Ipswich; that is, it must be considered that his parent was of comparatively humble origin, for he was wealthy enough, at his death, to bequeath money, in his will, to religious purposes: and though there is nothing to prove that he was a butcher, there is nothing to refute it; therefore, it is most likely that the generally-received opinion is correct.

Opposite to the lane leading from the south side of this churchyard—partly in this parish, and partly in St. Peter's — stood the mansion granted in the reign of Edward VI. to the bishop of Norwich, by the appellation of *The Lord CurzorCs House.* The mansion was, formerly, called the King's Hospital; it having been applied to that purpose, during the Dutch wars. It was subsequently known as the Elephant and Castle; and was afterwards long used by the late Mr. Trotman, as a malt kiln. The strong and stately brick porch belonging to this edifice, was demolished in 1760. Persons still living, remember it projecting a considerable way into the street; and under which horsemen used to ride. The main building was pulled down some years ago: when it appeared that the rooms were of large and lofty dimensions; and one banqueting room in particular, was richly carved, and profusely ornamented with many coats of arms of the Curzon family—who resided here in the thirteenth year of Henry VIII.; for both Lord Curzon, and Sir Robert Curzon, knt. were amongst the commissioners then appointed to inquire into the extent of the liberties of the borough; and about forty years ago, a Mr. Curzon—one of the same family— occupied the house in which Mr. Rodwell now lives, in St Matthew's. The street has been widened here, and no vestige of this once superb structure now remains.

By a stat ute of the twenty-sixth of Henry VIII., Ipswich was appointed for the seat of a suffragan bishop; and this house was appropriated for his residence. Thomas Manning, prior of Butley, consecrated by Archbishop Cranmer, in 1525, was the first and last suffragan bishop of Ipswich: after his decease, it was granted to the bishop of Norwich.

In this parish, westward of the church, on the bank of the river Gipping, stood a convent of Franciscan Grey Friars Minors, founded in the reign of Edward I. by Lord Tiptoth, of Nettlestead. A small portion of this edifice is yet to be seen, as here represented, in a garden belonging to Mr. Bird:—

Very little more is known of this establishment, than that Lord Tiptoth, with many of his family, were buried in the conventual church: amongst whom are the following persons of distinction:—

Sir Rohert Tiptoth, and Dame Una, his wife. The heart of Sir Rohert Vere, the elder. Margaret, Countess of Oxenford, wife of Sir Rohert Vere, the younger, Earl of Oxenford. Dame Elizaheth, wife of Sir Thomas Mord, daughter of the Earl of Warwick. Sir Rohert Tiptoth the younger. Margaret, wifeof Sir Johh Tiptoth. Rohert Tiptoth, esq. Elizaheth Uflford. Elizaheth, Lady Spenser, wedded to Sir Philip Spenser, daughter of fir Rohert Tiptoth. Philip, George, and Elizaheth, children of Sir Philp Spenser. Jane, daughter of Sir Hugh Spenser. Sir Rohert Warkesham, and Daine Jone, his wife. John, son of William Claydon. fir Thomas Hunlill, kni. Dame Elizaheth, wife of Sir Walter

Clopton, of Hadley. Sir William Laynham. Sir Hugh Peach, and Sir John Lovelocks, knts. Item, the hearts of Dame Petronill Ufford, Dame Beatrice Botcler; Dame Quatefteld; Dame Margery, aunt to Sir Rohert Ufford; Dame Alice, widow of Sir John Holhrook.

The family of Tiptoth failing of male issue, in the fortysixth year of Edward III. the estate of Nettlestead came, some time afterwards, into the possession of Lord Wentworth: and Nettlestead Hall is noted as the birth-place of his daughter Henrietta-Maria, the beautiful and beloved mistress of James, Duke of Monmouth; and whose romantic history is feelingly depicted by the late Mrs. Cobbold, in an elegant little poem, called "The Lily of Nettlestead." Bernard Barton thus speaks of the gateway, still remaining:—

"Thou art noble yet, for thy ruins recal The remembrance of vanish'd glory;
And time, which has levell'd the ancient hall,,
Still spares thee to tell of its story.
O'er thy crumbling arch the sculptur'd shield,
In spite of Spoil's bereavement,
Is left as a relique, on which are reveal'd
The insignia of bold achievement."

Saint Nicholas'-street Chapel is the first which was erected in this town by Protestant Dissenters. For a long time previous to its erection, a number of serious christians were accustomed to meet together for divine worship: but it was not until some years after that notable era in ecclesiastical history, the 24th of August, 1662— on which day no less than two thousand two hundred and fifty-seven ministers were ejected from the Church of England, for nonconformity—that the dissenters of this town were enabled to establish a regular congregation. We have no authentic record of any minister having been regularly appointed as pastor, until 1672; when King Charles II. granted indulgence to the nonconformists. Immediately on the issuing of this grant, they invited to this office, the Rev. Owen Stockton, A. M.; who had been ejected from his benefice at Colchester. He af-

terwards preached three years in his own house, to all that came to him, till the town was visited with the pestilence; when, others flying, he offered the magistrates to stay and preach for them, if they would allow him the liberty of a public church; which, notwithstanding the great necessity of the people, was denied him. Hereupon, he removed to Chattisham: from whence he had a call from a congregation at Colchester, and another at Ipswich. That he might answer both, as far as he was able, he undertook half the service of each; and, with other ministers, divided his services between them as long as he lived. He died of a fever, September 10th, 1680; being about fifty years of age. He was the author of " *A Scriptural Catechism, and a Treatise of Family Instruction;*" "*A Rebuke to Reformers* "*Counsel to the A fflicted, occasioned by the Fire of London* " *Sfc. Sfc.*

Mr. Stockton was succeeded, at Ipswich, by the Rev. John Fairfax, A. M. ; who had been ejected from the rectory of Barking. After he was ejected from his living, he continued to reside at Barking; and preached to a society of nonconformists there, until his death. By reason of this engagement, he could not undertake the charge of the congregation at Ipswich, otherwise than in part, as his predecessor had done; and, like him, was assisted by other ministers.

In the year 1687, the congregation hired a house for their religious meetings, in the parish of St. Nicholas, near the place where the Elephant and Castle stood. There they were acustomed to meet, until the 26th of April, 1700; on which day, the present chapel in Nicholas' street was opened for public worship, by Mr. Fairfax; who, on the occasion, preached a sermon on Ex. xx. 24; which was afterwards printed, and dedicated to Sir Thomas Cuddon, chamberlain of the city of London.

Mr. Fairfax did not live long after this chapel was erected. On the 11th of August following, he died at his house, in Barking, aged seventy-seven. His printed works are " *The Life of the Rev. Owen Stockton, A. M. with his Funeral Ser-*

mon "*Primitive Synagogce, a Sermon preached at Ipswich, on the opening of Nicholas Street, Chapel;* "*A Sermon on the Death of the Rev. Matthew Newcomen, A. M.*"

Among the ejected ministers who assisted Mr. Fairfax, in Ipswich, may be mentioned the Rev. John Butler, and the Rev. Tobius Legg, A. M.

Mr. Butler was ejected from the rectory of Feltwell, in Norfolk. After his ejectment,he for some years preached very seldom; and was prevailed on to travel to Smyrna. At his return, after remaining some time at Harwich, he removed to Ipswich; where he preached occasionally, and in the country around. He died in 1696, in the eightyfourth year of his age.

Mr. Legg was ejected from the rectory of Hemingston. He was forced, by the corporation act, to choose another settlement; where more than twenty years, he preached in his own house, almost every Lord's-day; not receiving or deriving any pecuniary remuneration for his labour, although he had a large family of children. He met with such general love and respect, that when other ministers suffered, he was connived at. He embraced all opportunities of preaching publicly. He died at Ipswich, in the year 1700, aged seventy-seven.

Early in the year 1701, the Rev. Samuel Baxter, A. M. the eldest son of the Rev. Nathaniel Baxter, A. M.—who was ejected from the vicarage of St. Michaers-upon-Plyer, in Lancashire—was invited from Lowestoft, to succeed Mr. Fairfax in Ipswich; where he continued for thirtynine years, until death put an end to his labours, on the 13th of July, 1740, in the seventieth year of his age. In the year 1725, the Rev. Samuel Say, the son of the Rev. Giles Say—who was ejected from the living of St. Michael's, in Hampshire—was invited from Lowestoft, where he had exercised the ministry for eighteen years, to become co-pastor with him. In this situation, Mr. Say continued until 1734; when he was appointed successor to Dr. Calamy, in Westminster.

On Mr. Say's removal to Westminster, the Rev. Thomas N. Scott—the well-known translator of the book of Job, in verse—who had succeeded him at Lowestoft, was invited thence, to succeed him also at Ipswich. In the first instance co-pastor with Mr. Baxter, and afterwards his successor, he exercised the ministry in this congregation forty years: after which he removed to Napton, in Norfolk; where he died, in the year 1774. In 1767, the Rev. William Wood, F. L. S., from Stamford, in Lincolnshire, undertook the pastoral charge of this congregation, in conjunction with him. He remained here only three years, until he removed to Mill Hill Chapel, in Leeds; where he succeeded Dr. Priestly. Then the Rev. R. Lewin, from Debenham, was appointed co-pastor with Mr. Scott; but after the lapse of a little more than three years, he accepted an invitation from a congregation at Liverpool. Soon after, the Rev. James Pilkington, from Derbyshire, was appointed in his room. Two years having elapsed, he resigned the pastoral charge of the congregation. He died in this town, on the 15th of September, 1804, aged fifty-two years; and is interred in the burialground attached to the chapel. He was the author of a history and description of Derbyshire, 2 vols. 8vo.

When Mr. Pilkington resigned, the congregation was obliged, for the space of one year, to procure supplies: among whom may be mentioned the Rev. Robert Alderson; who, afterwards, was, for several years, one of the ministers at the Octagon Chapel, in Norwich, and subsequently was appointed pastor of a congregation at Filby, in Norfolk; where he continued for some years, until after the death of his wife; when he turned his attention to the law: and is now recorder of Ipswich.

In the month of January, 1778, the Rev. William Jervis —who had been for some time minister of a congregation at Devizes, in Wiltshire—accepted an invitation from this society, to become their pastor. He continued amongst them, until the 24th of March, 1797; when he died, aged seventy-two years.

After the death of Mr. Jervis, the Rev. Samuel Parker —then minister of Cose-

ley, in Staffordshire—was invited to Ipswich; and remained here till 1803.

Mr. Parker was succeeded by the Rev. Thomas Rees, F. L. S. (now Dr. Rees) from Caermarthen Academy. He was here only two years, until his father's death; when he was invited to succed him at Gellionen, in Glamorganshire. He thence removed to Stoke Newington, and is now minister of Stamford-st. Chapel, in Southwark.

In 1805, the Rev. Thomas Drummond—who had, for some time, been the minister of a congregation at Filby, in Norfolk—accepted an invitation from this society, to become their pastor. He resigned in 1813.

Soon after Mr. Drummond's resignation, the Rev. Isaac Perry removed from the pastoral charge of a congregation in Norwich. Mr. Perry remained here until 1825.

After Mr. Perry's removal, about two years elapsed without any stated minister being chosen. Early in 1827, the Rev. John Philp— who had been, for some time, minister of a congregation at Whitchurch—-was appointed. His labours in the ministry were very soon intercepted by the hand of death; for he died August 1827, aged about twenty-eight years.

In the autumn of the same year, the Rev. Andrew Melville, A. M., from the County of Downe, was appointed minister of this congregation; and still remains in that situation.

In 1712, Mr. Edward Gael bequeathed the sum of £100 to be placed out at interest, in aid of this chapel.

In 1743, Mr. Samuel Parish bequeathed to the Dissenters' Charity School, in Ipswich, the sum of £40, to be disposed of for the benefit of the said school. He also bequeathed the sum of £100, the interest thereof to be applied towards the support of the minister for the time being, for ever; unless it should happen, by any succeeding troublesome times, that this chapel should be appropriated to other purposes than the worship of almighty God, and the society, by such means, should be broken and dispersed, then, and in such case only, he required the trustees for the time be-

ing to dispose of the said £100, to such of the society as they should think to be the greatest objects of charity, and to as many of them as the sum would allow.

In 1786, Mr. John Leggett, bequeathed to the trustees of this society, the sum of £100; the interest thereof to be paid towards the maintenance of the minister for the time being, for ever. He also gave to the governors and trustees of the charity-school of the Protestant Dissenters, in Ipswich, called the Green Sleeves, the sum of £100, to be applied for the benefit of the said charity.

In 1799, Mr. William Dymock bequeathed the sum of £100, stock, 3 per cent. reduced annuities, at the decease of Mrs. Elizabeth Carver, upon trust, that the dividends should be received by the minister of this chapel for the time being, for ever.

In 1809, Dr. Rodbard bequeathed the sum of £200, the interest to be applied towards the repairs of the chapel, for ever.

This chapel is a large square building, with a spacious gallery on three sides; and on the south side is a handsome pulpit, the balustrades of the stairs leading up to which are beautifully carved in oak,—as well as some of the external ornaments over the doors: the roof is supported by four massive pillars in the centre; and opposite the pulpit is a splendid brass chandelier, of large dimensions. A neat little organ is erected, and was opened the 17th of March, 1799. The building is calculated to hold twelve hundred persons; and the congregation now profess Unitarian principles.

There is a circumstance connected with this chapel, that is somewhat remarkable. In the year 1779, when William Clarke, esq. and Joseph Clarke, esq. were bailiffs, being both Dissenters, the corporation attended this chapel, with their usual formalities; but the maces were not allowed to be carried further than the door, as the place was not dedicated to religious worship, according to the doctrines of the established church. The seat which was fitted up for the reception of the bailiffs, &c was situated at the south-east corner of the gallery, and was separated from the rest by a glazed partition; which was pulled down a few years ago.

The new chapel in St. Nicholas'-street, nearly opposite to the old one, was opened for worship, on April 29th, 1829. The morning sermon was preached by the Rev. H. I. Roper, of Teignmouth; and the evening sermon by the Rev. James Stratten, of London. The purchase of the ground, and the erection of this structure, was effected by Thomas Wilson, esq. the treasurer of Highbury College, London: whose object was, to promote the spiritual welfare of an increasing population, and the better to accommodate a congregation who had previously occupied a small chapel in Dairy Lane. The style of architecture adopted in this building, is somewhat approaching to the Gothic; and the interior is fitted up with more taste and elegance than any other dissenting place of worship in the town. It is lighted with gas; and has, altogether, a very pleasing effect. It is calculated to hold about seven hundred persons. The congregation are Independents.

Proceeding, in a strait line, from St. Nicholas'-street, we presently come to St. Peter's church, a neat building, with a handsome flint steeple. St. Peter's had, in the Confessor's time, large possessions: for, in Ipswich Doomsday, it is stated, " It had six caricutes of land, eight villains, twenty bordarii, and two mills; of these Earl Roger claimed one hundred acres, five villains, and one mill, in right of the King's manor at Bramford. Five villains of the said manor witnessed for him; but the half hundred of Ipswich witnessed that they belonged to the church in the time of the Confessor, then valued at one hundred shillings, now at £15." It is further said, " That to this church belonged five burgesses, and twenty acres

K K of land within the borough." It was afterwards impropriated to the priory of St. Peter and St. Paul; which stood contiguous to the churchyard, and was founded in the reign of Henry II. by Thomas Lacy and his wife, for Black Canons of the order of St. Augustine. This establishment had extensive pos-

sessions for the churches of St. Edmund a Pountney, St. Austin, St. Mildred, St. Nicholas, St. Mary at Key, St. Peter, Thurlston in Ipswich; and of Cretingham, Crew, Wherstead, Dokesworth, and the manors of St. Peter's in Ipswich, Harold in Burstall, St. Peter in Cretingham and Hintlesham, and the tithes of St. Matthew in Ipswich, Letheringham, Thorpe, &c. with revenues in many other parishes, were impropriated to this priory. Letheringham Abbey was a cell to this house.

This Order was suppressed in 1527, by Wolsey; who, desirous of bestowing some marks of regard on the place of his nativity, and of erecting there a lasting monument of his greatness, resolved to build and endow a college and grammar-school, to serve as a nursery for his new college at Oxford. For this purpose, he obtained bulls from the Pope, for the suppression, and letters patent from the king, for the scite and estate of the priory of St. Peter and St. Paul: where, in the twentieth year of Henry VIII. he founded a oollege, dedicated to the honour of the Blessed Virgin; consisting of a dean, twelve secular canons, eight clerks, and eight choristers, with a grammar school; and, for its further endowment, he procured part of the possessions of the late monasteries of Snape, Dodnash, Wix, Harkesley, Tiptree, Romborough, Felixstow, Bromehill, Blythburgh, and Mountjoye. The patent for this college is dated 1529. The first stone was laid by John Longland, bishop of Lincoln,— who was confessor to Henry VIII. On this occasion, a grand procession was made through the town, from the college to the church of Our Lady,

Not more than three years elapsed before the cardinal's disgrace. Shortly afterwards, this noble foundation was razed to the ground; and the scite, containing six acres, was granted, in the twenty-third year of Henry VIII. to Thomas Alverde, and in the ninth year of James I. to Richard Percival and Edmund Dunield. Nearly a century ago, the first stone was found, in two pieces, worked up in a common wall in Woulfern's Lane, with a Latin inscription to this effect:— In the year of

Christ, 1528, and the twentieth of Henry VIII, King of England, and on the 15th of June, laid hy John, Bishop of Lincoln."

No part of this college now remains, except the gate; which stands adjoining to the E. side of St. Peter's churchyard. This gate, with the exception of a square stone tablet on which are carved the arms of Henry VIII., is entirely of brick, worked into niches, wreathed pinnacles, flowers, and other decorations, according to the fashion of that time. It is supposed by several writers to have been the great or chief gate, for, say they, as the cardinal, by setting the king's arms over a college cf his own foundation, meant to flatter that monarch, it is not probable that he would put them over any other part than the principal entrance. If this conjecture be correct, the specimen but ill accords with the character given of the college by the writer of Wolsey's secret history; who says that it was a "sumptuous building." and, indeed, the cardinal himself, in a Latin preface to Lilly's grammar, then lately published, styles it" no ways inelegant. " Its insignificance is the more remarkable, as, at that period, architects were extremely attentive to, and expended great sums in, the construction of gate-houses; which they generally made superior in magnificence to other parts of the edifice; and this was particularly observable in all the buildings erected by this ostentatious prelate. Fuller says that " King Henry took just offence, that the cardinal set his own arms above the king's on the gate-house, at the entrance into the college. This was no verbal, but a real *Ego et Rex mens,* excusable by no plea in manners or grammar, except only by that which is rather a fault than a figure, a harsh downwright *hysterosis*but to humble the cardinal's pride, some one afterwards set up on a window a painted mastiff dog, gnawing the blade-bone of a shoulder of mutton, to mind the cardinal of his extraction; it being utterly improbable, as some have fancied, that the picture was placed there by the cardinal's own appointment, to be to him a monitor of humility." If what Fuller says has any reference to the college at Ipswich, it cannot relate to the gate in question, nor had the monarch any cause for offence; for the cardinal's arms do not appear. As to what has been asserted, that it was not probable that Wolsey would place the king's arms anywhere but over the main entrance, we think it likely that the royal arms would be placed in various parts of the building. We cannot bring ourselves to believe that the chief entrance to a college which occupied six acres of ground, would be by such a pitiful piece of architecture as this gate; for the haughty cardinal must have bowed his head on entering, and it is not wide enough to admit a carriage of any description: and as there is Wolsey's own evidence that the old church of St. Peter was taken down, for the purpose of enlarging the scite of the new buildings, we are led to suppose that the front of the college was fronting to the west; and it is not at all probable that, in the demolition of the building, the main entrance should be the only portion left standing; on the contrary, it would, most likely, be the first part that was pulled down. Therefore, we are decidedly of opinion, that the gate now standing, was the entrance to some quadrangle of the edifice, appropriated, perhaps, for the residence of the students; and it would have been no disgrace to the king, in thus placing his arms over such a portion of a seminary of learning.

A writer, half a century ago, observed that this gate was nodding to its fall; but though it is a little out of its perpendicular, it may last for a century to come. A great variety of different views of it have already been engraved: we have given an engraving in which its present appearance is well preserved. We are glad of an opportunity of inserting the following original stanzas, which have been furnished us by Mr. James Bird, of Yoxford:—

Thou crumbling relic of the ancient time!
Ere sure decay subdues thy aged brow,
What if I lug thy Reverence into rhyme?
Thy founder, Wolsey, cannot hear me now!
No! if my strain be lowly, or sublime.

He is unconscious, and as deaf as thou!
Ye heed no more of what a scribbler tells
Than doth the *Orwell—or St. Peter's* bellb!
Fair Portal! oft thy *Cardinal*, of old,
Hath slyly counselled with our great king, Harry,
Whene'er he longed for Woman in his hold,
Whether to snap her head off, or to marry!
And, though they spared not in their project bold,
How oft Man's hopes of lasting bliss miscarry!—.
Thy Wolsey played with edged-tools in his pride,
And HARRY played the Tyrant—and then died!

Where are the footsteps which of yore were seen
Within thy courts?—and where the allotted places
Of busy Canon, Clerk, and reverend Dean,
And tuneful Chorister?—and where the traces
Of ruminating Students, pale, and lean,
With hollow downcast eyes and pensive faces,
Poring on Metaphysics, Logic, Grammar,
Spurring their brains with Alpha—Beta—Gamma!

All, all are gone, with *Cardinal,* and *King.* And thou, old Portal! art but left to show.
That withering Time, with his relentless wing.
Sweeps, like a pestilence, o'er all below!
And that his power, omnipotent, will bring,
As onward fast his wasting waters flow,
Man and Man's works unto the dust, and leave
No stone to moulder, and no eye to grieve!

This parish is a curacy, in the gift of the Rev. Charles William Fonnereau, LL. B.

The steeple of this church is lofty and handsome, and has lately been repaired with great judgment. The following notice respecting it, is somewhat curious:— *Copy of a Manuscript found in the Library of Samuel Dowsing, of Stratford, written by his Father, William Dowsing; and was afterwards sold to Mr. Huse, a Bookseller in Exeter Cluxnge, London, Sept. 6th,* 1704.

"A Legacy left by the Will of Wm. Stile, dated 28th April, 1463. Item, to the making of the Steeple of the Parish Church of St. Peter, Ipswich, 6s. 8d.

"Also Margery Alexander, by Will dated 2d Sep. 1465. Item, I give towards the making of a Steeple to the Church of St. Peter, 3s. 4d.

"Maltilda Scaspy, the 9th Dec. 1476, also to the making a Steeple of the said Church, I bequeath Is. 8d.

"Wm. Blake, the 15th Feb. 1476, I also bequeath to the Steeple, 6s. 9d."

There are but few monuments of any note. We observe the following inscriptions:— "John Knapp, 2d May, n04." "JOHN ALDUS, Portman, 16 Sep. 1661, aged *a."*
"Robert Trotman, Esq. Jan. 31, 1803."

He was high-sheriff for Suffolk, in 1783; and seven times bailiff of Ipswich. His liberality and benevolence will not soon be forgotten.—There is a monument also to his father and mother; and one likewise to Mrs. Trotman, his wife, and several of their children.

There is a flat stone to the memory of Sir Manuel Sorrel, knt. portman, Oct. 14, 1669, aged 68. He left, by his will, forty shillings to be distributed in coals, annually, to the poor of this parish; and likewise the conduit in St. Peter's-street, for the supply of water to the neighbourhood: and the house now occupied by Mr. Richard Crawley, pays £2: 10: 0, annually, to the churchwardens, for this purpose. Sir Manuel Sorrel received the honor of knighthood from King Charles II., when, at his return to the throne of his ancestors, a gift was presented to him, from the town of Ipswich, by the said Sir Manuel,—then senior bailiff.

In this churchyard, on the north side:—

"Abigail, wife of David Vlaford, 26 Aug. 1810, aged *to.*

"She was, hut words an wanted to say what—
Say what a woinau should he, and she was that."

"Jeremiah Webster died Oct. 31, 1824, aged 27.

"Stop mortal, and depart not from this stone
'Till you have pondered well where I am gone.
Death quickly took my sense and strength away,
And laid me down in this dark hed of clay.
'onsider of me, and take home this line—
The grave that next is opened, may he thine."

The journal of Dowsing and the visitors, saith, "At Peter's was on the porch, the crown of thorns, the sponge, and the Trinity in stone, and the rails were there; all which I ordered to break in pieces." Here is an ancient stone font, of curious workmanship, that has escaped the hand of these fell destroyers.

In 1772, Isaac Blomfield, late of Mildenhall, left by will, estates to the minister and churchwardens, for the poor of this parish. The hereditaments so devised, are novv, used for a workhouse: for which the overseers pay *to* the minister and churchwardens, the yearly rent of £5. There is the date of 1637, now on the front of the house.

In 1723, Mrs. Mary Chappie, widow, left several tenements to the minister and churchwardens, the rents of which to be distributed amongst the poor, according to their discretion.

In 1756, Mr. John Blythe left a yearly annuity of twentysix shillings, to be distributed in bread. There are no other bequests, except that of Mr. Thorne, mentioned in the gifts to St. Nicholas.

On the 24th of July, 1772, a violent storm of thunder and lightning, with a heavy shower of rain, occurred; when a ball of fire fell upon St. Peter's steeple, and shattered a large piece of oak which supported the weathercock, struck down several stones, and defaced some figures on the dial-plate, without doing further harm.

A melancholy accident happened near Mr. Crawley's premises, in August, 1806:—a number of workmen were employed in building an arch for a wine-vault of considerable extent; when, on about two-thirds of it being completed, the frame upon which it was raised was removed, and the arch fell in with a tremendous crash, carrying down part of the adjoining buildings, as well as a portion of the churchyard wall. Several persons were buried in the ruins; and the master bricklayer, Mr. John Scarlett, and his son, a boy of six year9 old, lost their lives.

In St. Peter's-street, directly opposite to the steeple of this church, on the spot where Mr. Colchester's house now stands, was a building that fell down about seventy years ago, said to have been used as ussembly-rooms, before the Old Assembly-room in the Tower-lane was erected.

In 1655, Colonel William Bloys lived in this parish. His estate lay chiefly in and about Grundisburgh.—Also in the same parish lived Abigail his sister, the relict of John Hodges, esq. late of Woodbridge; who was justice of the peace for Suffolk, and serjeant-major of a regiment of Suffolk men, commanded by his brother, the aforesaid Colonel Bloys, at the siege of Colchester.

At a little distance from St. Peter's church, we come to the spot where the river Gipping empties itself into the Orwell. This river — from which Ipswich derives its appellation—is here formed into a considerable basin, or dam, that turns the spacious mill belonging to the corporation, now occupied by Mr. Calver and Mr. Rouse. The Gipping takes its rise from three different fountain heads;—the one at Wetherden, another at Rattlesden, and the third near the village of Gipping by Mendlesham, the three streams all uniting at Stowmarket, twelve miles from Ipswich. The banks of this stream—particularly between Handford mill and Handford bridge—are exceedingly picturesque and beautiful; and have been thus spoken of by a native poet:—

"Meandering Gipping, loveliest stream That ever roll'd its limpid flood Through many a rich sequester'd mead,
And many an overhanging wood,
"I owe thee much; thy gentle tide Deserves what I can ne'er bestow,
To flow along immortal lines,
As sweetly as thy waters flow."

We shall endeavour to give an account of an event which occurred at the above-mentioned mill, some years ago:—In the year 1800, at the time when provisions were at an extraordinary high price, the poorer classes of society suffered much in consequence: and the populace of this town hit upon a notable expedient to remedy the evil. They went into the market, and unceremoniously seized the butter and other articles, for themselves; and all sorts of commodities speedily disappeared. The consequence was, that, the next Saturday, there were no provisions in the market at all: the dealers, of course, being afraid to come to the town. The offenders were very leniently dealt with by the magistrates, from a general feeling that they were much aggrieved. A violent prejudice existed against all dealers in corn and flour: the millers, in particular, were personally threatened; and several, fearful of their lives, actually left their residences.

This fermentation amongst the populace, at length reached to an alarming height. On the 15th of September, this year, a great body of men, women, and children, with cries of " Bread! Bread!" proceeded over Stoke bridge, for the avowed purpose of demolishing a mill then belonging to Mr. Savage; but, rinding an attack upon a wind-mill rather a Quixotic attempt, they retreated without doing any further injury than slightly damaging the sails. They then returned back, and took possession of the water-mill, and a large quantity of flour therein. Mr. Rainbird, the occupier, durst not make his appearance: and the men working in the mill were speedily ejected. The mob appeared to be confounded with their own success; for they seemed to have had no previous arrangement, nor any persons willing to act as leaders in the work of destruction. But things assumed an alarming aspect. Curses deep and loud, were heard, and cries of "Down with the mill! Set fire to the premises!" issued from the crowd; which had gradually increased to a fearful multitude. Had they at once proceeded to action, there was nothing to prevent them: and no one can tell where the mischief might have concluded. But, during the fortunate interval of delay, the alarm was given; the bailiffs and magistrates assembled on the Town-hall, and a number of the more respectable inhabitants were sworn in as constables; the Volunteers were immediately under arms: and all proceeded to the scene of action. The constables entered the mill, and soon cleared it of its troublesome inhabitants. Their resistance was not desperate. The women were most tenacious of possession, and were not to be ejected till they had discharged a most outrageous volley of abuse. Oaths, screams, and flour were bandied about in all directions; and many a stout-hearted citizen emerged from the mill, with his face as white as a sheet. On the outside, the magistrates were violently attacked with stones, brick-bats, and other offensive missiles. The riot-act was read by Mr. William Batley, who was then town-clerk; and a brick, which was thrown within an inch of his head, had nearly put a period to his elocution. The volunteers, after fruitlessly endeavouring to disperse the people, were posted in the garden, on the little island opposite the mill. The mob, which were constantly accumulating, had got possession of the road, and all the approaches to the place. Their threats and violence were increasing: when it was deemed expedient to send for a troop of cavalry, from the barracks. The rioters had taken possession of St. Peter's churchyard; which, from its elevation, completely commanded the street: and when the cavalry approached, they were received with a tremendous shower of bricks and stones, by which they were much annoyed; but after they had cleared the street, they were ordered to charge upon their assailants in the churchyard; when the multitude fled in complete confusion,— hundreds of them tumbling head over heels amongst the tomb-stones, vociferating for mercy, as the broad-

swords of the soldiers were flourished *in terrorem* over their heads. More fright than injury was sustained by the populace, thus speedily overthrown; and though there were no lives lost, sundries of them were literally sent to their graves. The military, who behaved with praiseworthy moderation, soon dispersed the crowd, after compelling some of the more obstinate to take refuge in the river, from their pursuit, without any other detriment than a slight bruise, or a (lucking. The magistrates acted with much firmness, lenity, and propriety: and the volunteers, under the command of Robert Trotman, esq. , displayed great steadiness and good conduct. The people retired peaceably to their homes: and thus ended this memorable attack upon Rainbird's mill, without any bloodshed; when, through fear or rashness, many lives might have been lost

On the morning of April 12th, 1818, the neat stone bridge which connected Ipswich with the parish of Stoke, at the junction of the Orwell and the Gipping, was destroyed by a flood. From a heavy and incessant rain which fell the preceding afternoon and night, the Gipping overflowed its banks, and, by six o'clock in the morning, (Sunday) had flooded the whole of the marshes near Ipswich, to an extent scarcely remembered by the oldest persons in the neighbourhood. The flood continued to increase, and to roll down so impetuously, that, at about half past eight o'clock, two of the arches were carried away. Three men were standing upon the bridge at this awful moment, contemplating the swell and fury of the stream: they fell with the bridge: two of them were almost miraculously preserved, by means of a rope which was thrown to their assistance: the body of the third was cast ashore a few days afterwards, lower down the river.

In consequence of this accident, a temporary bridge of boats was speedily formed, under the superintendance of Mr. Cubitt, engineer: which admitted a free passage for carriages, without impeding the navigation.

The first stone of a new bridge was

laid on the 3rd of September, in the same year, by the bailiffs; who went in procession from the Town-hall, accompanied by the several members of the corporation. The inscription on the stone was— STOKE BRIDGE FOUNDATION STONE, Laid Sep. 3, 1818, hy

The expense of this bridge of cast-iron, described in our account of the Orwell, was £7,000.

In 1300, the twenty-ninth year of Edward I., Mr. Thos. Alvere, coroner, left, by his will, 30s. a year for the repair of Stoke bridge.

In the suburbs, beyond the river, stood the church of St. Austin, near St. Austin's Green. It is often called a chapel; but it had, in the Conqueror's time eleven acres of land, and procurations were paid for it by the prior of St. Peter's: so that it was parochial, and, as we suppose, impropriated to that priory. It was in use in 1482; bHt has been long since dilapidated. We suppose all the lands on the south side of the Orwell, now become part, of St. Peter's, to have been in St. Austin's parish.

Not far from this church, stood St. Leonard's lazarhouse, or hospital. It is now a farm-house belonging to Christ's Hospital.

On the premises occupied by Messrs. G. Bayley & Co., on the spot called St. Austin's Green, great numbers of human bones have been dug up, some feet below the surface of the soil; from which we might conclude that this was the burial-place belonging to St. Austin's church, and St. Leonard's lazar-house, whose dead were probably buried in St. Austin's churchyard: but then it seems that the bones, which are very numerous, are found crossed in various directions, immediately over each other, as if they had been promiscuously thrown and heaped together, into one vast receptacle for the dead. We have evidence from the court-books of the corporation, that the ravages of death in Ipswich, at the time of the Plague, were considerable: it is, therefore, probable that this was the general place of sepulture, on that awful visitation of Providence.

So long ago as the year 466, there was a desperate battle near Ipswich, between the Britons and Saxons; and there is a tradition that this spot was the battle-field.

Near this place, about a hundred and fifty years ago, was a spacious range of buildings called the King's. Cooperage.

Proceeding over Stoke bridge, the first turning on the left hand leads us up to the church of St. Mary Stoke, a neat little building; the porch, which is not inelegant, is of considerable antiquity: but nothing is known of the first erection of this edifice. The churchyard is an elevated spot, from which a greater part of the town can be seen. King Edgar gave Stoke a member of Ipswich, to Saint Ethelred; that is, to the prior and convent of Ely. This gift includes the hamlet—which takes in part of the parish of Sproughton—together with the advowson of the rectory, and the manor of Stoke Hall: by which word w e do not mean the modern house by the church, but what is called Stoke Park, where A. H. Steward, esq., has lately built his elegant residence. It is said, in Doomsday, to be of the yearly value of ten pounds; and had, in the Confessor's time, five caricutes of land, and nine villains for the manor; then fifteen borderers, one church of forty acres of freeland, one mill, twenty acres of meadow, and a mediety of a loch beyond the bridge, then of the value of one hundred shillings. King Edgar's grant was executed with great solemnity, as appears from the deed itself:— *Ego Eadgarus, SfC. Basileus non clam in angulo sed pedum, sub Dio subscripsi:* and it was attested by his queen, St. Dunstan, archbishop, and many of the first officers and nobility of the time. This was executed about the year 970. The living is in the gift of the dean and chapter of Ely: with whom this charter is deposited.

In this parish is the manor of Godlesford, now called Gusford Hall: which manor, with its appurtenances in Godlesford, Belstead Parva, and Wherstead, in Suffolk, were granted, as parcel of the possessions of the priory of Canons Leigh, in Devonshire, to Sir

John Rainesworth, knt. in the thirty-second year of Henry VIII. This house is described in the perambulation of the twenty-sixth of Edward III., by the name of Robert Andrews. It seems that that family inhabited there many years; for, in the thirteenth of Henry VIII., it is called the gate sometimes of old Robert Andrews, now of Sir Andrews Windsor: who was a considerable man, and took his christian name from the last-mentioned family of Andrews: he was afterwards Lord Windsor. Scarcely any part of the ancient edifice remains; for the house has been rebuilt and modernized by the present proprietor, Mr. Wasp; and is now a capital residence for a gentleman farmer.

Adjoining to the churchyard, is a handsome, spacious brick mansion, called Stoke Hall, built in the last century, by Thomas Cartwright, esq., wine-merchant. There are very extensive vaults upon the premises, extending even beneath the road; and, under these, is another tier of vaults calculated to contain, altogether, fifteen hundred pipes of wine. The house and offices ate very capacious and commodious; but there is not so much land attached as would be generally considered desirable for so handsome a residence. In a meadow, upon the high grounds between the house and the water's edge, is a reservoir or well, from which part of the town on the opposite side is supplied with water, by pipes carried under the bed of the river. This brings in a considerable revenue to the proprietor of Stoke Hall. The family of Turner resided here many years. It was afterwards purchased by the late Mr. Bleaden, formerly proprietor of the London Tavern, in Bishopgate-street: whose family sold it to J. B. Smyth, esq., the present occupier; who has greatly improved the place.

We now proceed to the spot which brings back to our recollection the halcyon days of childhood. For who that was a school-boy in Ipswich, thirty or forty years ago, has not passed some of the light-hearted hours of his existence upon Stoke Hills, occupied in climbing up the steep, rolling down the declivity, or, seated on the summit, counting the

twelve churches in the beautiful view of the town before him, free from the idea of interruption, or the fear of being considered an intruder.

"It may be lovely from the height
Of Skiddaw's summit, moss'd and gray
To feed the inexhausted sight,
On the magnificent array
Which such a prospect must display;
 On Keswick's lowly, peaceful vale;
 On Derwent Water's scatter'd isles;
 On torrents bright with morning smiles,
 Or mark'd by mist-wreaths pale.

"But not in the exultant bliss Of such a fascinating hour,
Hath scenery sublime as this,
 Where lakes expand, and mountains tower, Upon my heart so deep a power,
Or wakes in it such tender thrills,
 As when immers'd in busy thought,
 And reveries by memory brought,
I stand upon Stoke Hills."

But, alas! this haunt of our boyish days, where all could wander free and unconstrained, is now barricadoed and inclosed. It is with regret we observe that the spirit of encroachment, upon the privileges of the people, is become so prevalent as to leave little doubt, that, in a few years, most of the foot-paths in the vicinity of Ipswich, which were common right of passage, will be entirely done away with, and the public shut out for ever: and all this is suffered because no one has courage enough to protest against it, from the feeling, that, in what is everybody's business, no one likes to interfere.

Since writing the above, we learn, that, at the Quarter Sessions held in March, 1829, the Grand Jury has taken up this question, and presented these encroachments as a nuisance and injury to the inhabitants; and we hope that this evil will be redressed, and its future recurrence prevented.

On the 17th of April, 1801, the troops in garrison here, marched to Stoke Hills, with a train of artillery; the whole amounting to three or four thousand men: where they were drawn up in line, and the artillery fired a royal sulute of twenty-one guns, and a *feu dejoye* was fired three times by the troops; after which they gave three cheers, in honour of the victory obtained over the Danish fleet. This took place in the evening, after sunset; and had a sublime and animating effect.

Leaving Stoke Hills, we proceed between the two wind-mills, in the road which was formerly called Golden Rood Lane, from a miraculous rood which stood near the place; but is now called Golden Rood. Ascending the hill, about half a mile further, we have a beautiful view of the town, and the country about Bramford and Sproughton. There is no portion of the suburbs of Ipswich, that has so much improved, as where we now are;

M M and is, by far, the finest approach to the town. Some years ago, the late Mr. Joshua Head built a neat cottage, as a country retirement for his family; and it was, then, the only habitation near. It was, at his decease, purchased by Samuel Alexander, esq.: who has built a capital house, and planted and laid out the ground to such advantage, as to render it a residence worthy of t he spirit and opulence of the first banker in the county.

The first house we come to, after ascending the hill, on the left, is a neat building now occu;.od by Captain Steward.

A little further on is the residence of Mrs. Branigan. The house and grounds are fitted up with peculiar taste and elegance; and, from the front facing the sourh-east, it commands a most beautiful view of the river Orwell, over the lovely sylvan scene before you.

"Sweet stream! on whose banks in ray childhood residing, Untutor'd by life in the lessons of care;
In the heart-cheering whispers of hope still confiding,
Futurity's prospects seem'd smiling and fair.
"Dear river 1 how gaily the sunbeams are glancing
On thy murmuring waves, as they roll to the main!
While my tempest-tost bark, on life's ocean advancing,
Despairs of e'er finding a harbour again."

At a little distance, nearly opposite to this charming retirement, stands Birkfield Lodge, a splendid mansion, built by Count Linsingen: he had a commission in the German Legion, commanded by his father, when in garrison at Ipswich, during the last war. This noble German will be long remembered in this neighbourhood, where he ingeniously contrived to live for some years, in a style of princely splendour. The house and estate were purchased by a tradesman in London, and were afterwards sold to F. C. Campbell, esq.; who has much improved both the house and grounds: and it is now a magnificent abode.

On the left-hand side of the road, a little further on, are the grounds and elegant seat of A. H. Steward, esq., commanding a charming view of the river, built on the scite of the old house, called Stoke Park; which was long the residence, of an ancient family of the name of Clarke, originally from Bentley.

Abeut a mile further on the Belstead road, is situated, in a romantic little dale, the house lately belonging to the Pretyman family; now the residence of Mrs. Collins.

Having got nearly to the boundaries of the parish, we will make a retrograde movement, and, in coming back, enter through a white gate on the right, leading to the parsonage house, embosomed in a peaceful valley, sheltered on three sides by the well-wooded heights above it, with a lawn and garden before the house, sloping to the river, of which the prospect is soft, soothing, and delightful. We cannot turn away from this sweet seclusion, without exclaiming with the poet—
"Adieu, lovely Orwell! for ages still flowing,
On thy banks may the Graces and Virtues combine;
Long, long may thy beauties, fresh raptures bestowing,
Diffuse the sweet pleasure they've yielded to mine."

The late Dr. Baily Wallis resided here thirty-six years; during all which time he was rector of the parish. There is a handsome monument erected to the

memory of him and his wife, in the church of St. Mary Stoke. He died May 30th, 1820, aged sixty-three; and was succeeded by the Rev. Stephen Croft, A. M., the present resident and incumbent.

Close by Dr. WalhVs monument, is one to the memory of Thomas Reeve, A. M, twenty-six years rector of this church: he died in 1745, aged eighty-seven.

On the north wall, is a small oval tablet, to the memory of John Bleaden, esq., of Stoke Hall; who died September 1st, 1819, aged seventy-five.

Near the chancel door, in the churchyard, is a stone to the memory of Nathaniel Thurston; who died Sept. 19th, 1609, aged sixty-two.

In the churchyard, adjoining to the porch, is an elegant vaulted monument, inclosed with iron palisades, to the memory of Thomas Cartwright, esq., who died May 7th, 1754, and Dinarbas his wife.

On a tabular monument:—
"To the memory of JOHN Butleb, GENT.; whodiedDec. 10, 1696, aged S4. "

On the south side, near the foot path, is a stone to the memory of four maiden sisters of thc namc of Lockwood; who all lived to an advanced age: the last, Mary Lockwood, died Dec. 11th, 1816, aged a hundred and two years. This was a remarkably long-lived family; for, in the same vault, there are four other individuals buried, whose united ages amounted to 319.

In 1724, Captain Nathaniel Thurston left £100, the interest of which to be laid out in bread for the poor of the parish of St. Mary Sfoke, to be distributed weekly.

In 1734, Mr. Christopher Thorne, common-council-man, left the annual sum of £2: 10: 0, for fourteen penny loaves, weekly, to the poor of St. Mary Stoke and St. Peter's, alternately. There appear to be no other bequests.

In coming from the parsonage to the town, we pass over a piece of glebe land, from which, near the mill, is the finest panoramic view of Ipswich, anywhere to beseen; comprehending the whole of the town, the river, and sur-rounding country.

Before quitting this side of the water, we must notice the meeting-house be-longing to the church and congregation of the Baptist denomination, situated about half a mile from the bridge on the road leading to Manningtree, and gener-ally known by the name of Stoke Meet-ing. The church assembling here, orig-inally worshipped at Woolverstone, in this county: at which place the Rev. Sa-muel Sowden was their pastor. It ap-pears that a place wa« opened for public worship, on the scite of the present meeting-house, in 1774; but as it has, since that time, been three times en-larged, only a very small portion of the original building now remains. In 1775, the pastoral office was undertaken by the Rev. George Hall; who continued, for thirty-four years, to discharge its du-ties, in such a manner as to secure the veneration and respect, not merely of those in his more immediate connexion, but of the inhabitants of the town at large. On the east side of the pulpit, a neat marble tablet records the death of this excellent man, in the following in-scription:— In Memory of

GEORGE HALL,

thirty-four years Furor of thia church: his Ministerial office he discharged faithfully,
Affectionately, and Successfully.
In the firm helief of the doctrines he had preached, and in full assurance of Faith, he departed thia life 26th Feh. 1810,
Aged 64 Years,
Much lamented hy his church s and con-gregation,
and very generally
Respected.

Since that time, the ministerial office has been successively filled by the Revds. James White, James Payne, and James Sprigg, A. M. who now contin-ues to discharge its duties. — The meet-ing-house is an octangular building, about fifty feet by sixty, with a dome roof, and galleries on three sides; and is calculated to seat about nine hundred persons. Attached to it, is a cottage, large garden, and burying-ground. dur-ing his imprisonment, ho wrote a letter

addressed "To the Inhabitants of Ip-swich, both Teachers and People;" it be-gins with the following words:—"Oh! the pride, high-mindedness, and self-conceitedness which abounds in the town of Ipswich!" it is dated the first day of the ninth month, 1658: it is writ-ten with great fearlessness and spirit, and is to be found in Besse's Sufferings of the people called Quakers, vol. 1, p. 669, but is too long for insertion here. In the year 1660, no less than twenty-three persons were committed to Ipswich gaol, for congregating together, and for non-payment of tithes: and, for several years after, numbers of these people were fined, imprisoned, and otherwise persecuted, at Ipswich and many other places in the county of Suffolk. Amongst others who distinguished themselves, we notice Stephen Crisp, a highly-respectable and early member of the society; and who was convinced of Friends' principles, in 1655, by James Parnel, a youth who died a prisoner in Colchester Castle, under circumstances of peculiarly aggravated cruelty: Sewell, a Dutchman, the well-known historian of The Sufferings of Friends, has this remark respecting him:—" I visited S. Crisp, in prison, and found him in a cheerful condition, as well con-tented as if he had been at liberty; for he suffered for the ministry of the gospel, and continued to preach in prison, where his friends came to visit him;" and by which means the number of Friends was much increased. In 1655, George Fox, the founder of the society, visited Ipswich; and he says, " I had a little meeting, and very rude; but the Lord's power came over them. After the meeting, 1 said if any had a desire to hear further, they might come to the inn; and there came in a company of rude persons, who had abused friends, but they were restrained from doing any mischief:" and he also put forth a paper, warning the inhabitants of the day of the Lord, that they might repent of the evil they lived in, and turn unto Christ, iheir true teacher." John Crook, who was im-prisoned here, is mentioned by Gough, the author of another well-known histo-ry of Friends, not only as a man of lit-

erature, but of good estate and rank in life, and, previous to his convineement of Friends' principles, was in the com-mission of the peace.

We now, after recrossing Stoke bridge, take the first turning on the right, through College-street, till we come to St. Mary at the Key. This church was impropriated to the priory of St. Peter and St. Paul; and all the tithes belonging to it, were granted to Webb and Breton, in the seventh year of Edward VI. The church was new built. since the year 1448; for Richard Gowty, by his will that year made, ordered his body to be buried in the churchyard of St. Mary at the Key, in Ipswich, and gave Calyon stone for the whole church, which was to be built in the said church-yard. There was a stone for William Sabyn, esq., with his arms, — which are also on the glass in the church: he died in 1543, and is said to have built part of the south aisle. The present church is a neat building, the timber roof of which is beautiful: the steeple is of ex-cellent workmanship, of that species of flint which we may presume was called Calyon stone: it is surmounted by a small turret or cupola, upon which a large gilded key serves as a fane; and has a good effect. On the 11th of July, 1783, this cupola was set on fire by lightnmg, but it was soon extinguished.

In this church, Dowsing broke down six superstitious pictures, and many in-scriptions. There are several curious epitaphs, but there is only one upon brass now left; which is —

"Hen lieth the hody of Ar/GUSTIN Parker, 12th Mar. 1590, aged 60."

Amongst others, we observe the fol-lowing:—

"MARY CLEERE, wife of Thomas Cleere, gent. 1618.

"Cleere was my name, my life was also clear Like name like life, for I y« tight did love
Earst of this life I left this did appear
Even unto men as unto God ahove
Remit who did my aine my fears re-move
Ere y he call'd hy soul to Chriat my love.''

"FRAM: Crowe 1632. JOHN his 8on

1617. Retder

"If stones should speak if dead should rise
The living scarce would take advice
This stone might praise them that here lyes
But rather warn thee to he wise
Know Christ is gain in life and Death
All else is hat a puff of hreath."
"John Warner aged 92. 16"u.
"I Warner was once to myself, now Warner am to thee,
Both living, dying, dead 1 was. See thou immortal he."
"William Hasilwooi), a child of 2 years old of William Haulwood, Mariner.

"The Hasil nut oft Children Crops
God Hasil wood in Childhood lopps
Then parent yield God says he's mine
And took him home say not he's thine."
"John WING PI ELD, ESQ. son and heir apparent to the Rt. Worshipful Sir Anthony Wingtield, Knt. of the Garter, Captain of the Guard,
mid Vice-Chamherlain to the King, 1549."

Under a fair marble stone, from which the brass has been removed, is said to lie one Gosse, who was architect of the church.

In the middle aisle, opposite the pulpit, is a stone on which is —

"Robert STEVENSON, M. A. who was master of the Grammar School in this town four years, departed this life the 10th day of June, 1695, aged 61."

Upon the stone under which the remains of William Sahyn are said to have been deposited, brass plates were afterwards fastened, with this inscription:—

"Here lieth the hody of Christopher Merell
Whom God in his mercy hath taken from Peril
The third of Septemher this life ended he
One thousand five hundred fourscore and three
He married two Wives as time report can
The one named Ursla the other was Anne
By these his two wives which hence are now gone
He children in numher had twenty and one
Seven had he hy Ursla, and of all the other
Anne was the only, and also trae mother
A thousand five hundred forty and three
This Ursla her soul to God yielded she
This Anne of these two which last was his Wife
In faith and true hope here ended, her life
The fourth of Decemher as here you may see
A thousand five hundred fourscore and three.
"His love to Ood has zealous heen
His truth unstained to his Queen
His pity on the poor was great
As well hy money as hy meat
For whom this prayer they did make
Ood him reward for Jeans sake."

Last, though not least, we come to Tooley's monument; which is placed in the north aisle, with the following inscription; in which there is, doubtless, more truth than poetry:—

"Henriccs Toolyk ohiit «j Aug. Mil.
"Alicia Tool Ye ohiit s Feh. *bto.*
"Here Henry Toolie lies entomhde, that Man craonge the rest,
By Vertue, Wisdome, Welthe, and Worshippe names einonpst the hest,
A Merrhante welthye, whose Affayres God furthered with successe,
A Portman for his Wisdome choes and dyed whom God did hlesse
Withe vertoous Wyfe and Children three, a famous Matron sure
Whos Godlye lyfe Dame Fame preserves iri honour aye to endure
This man in Deathe, hy Will reportes whereto his lyfe was hent.
That Yearlie gave to WAY Es aud PORE his Lands, Tenements, and Annual Rents.
"In Ipswich aye to their Behoufe and his immortal fame
A Dlass to showe the use of Welthe; a Patteme how to frame
A Mortal Mynde; a Meane to move the Pore to extol the Name
Of God Almighty; hut Ipswich far unworthy two to keep
Of Vertuoue such, theere Bodies here, in Heaven their souls doth sleep."

In the year 1647, Mr. John Reynolds left, by his will, £100 to this parish: with which, and other money, was bought a parcel of land in Lindsey and Monks' Eleigh, in Suffolk, called Lustlands, that now lets for £30 per annum: which sum is distributed according to the will of Mr. Reynolds, every year, upon the first day of January, and upon St. John's day, in Christmas, for the relief and comfort of the best-governed poor people dwelling within the said parish, as the churchwardens and overseers shall think fit.

In 1708, John Reycroft, by will, gave £10 to buy land or other good estate: with which a house was bought in the Wash; which has been enlarged, and is now used for a workhouse: and from this gift, twelve pennyworth of bread is weekly delivered to the poor.

Directly opposite to the west entrance of St. Mary at the Key church, is the present Quakers' meeting-house: which was erected in the year 1796. It is a neat building, sixty feet long, by thirty-six feet wide, fitted up with the plain simplicity peculiar to this people, and is capable of holding about eight hundred persons. The earliest register of a marriage amongst them, in Ipswich, is dated the 11th day of eighth month, 1671. Earliest birth, 24th of tenth month, 1663. Earliest burial, 4th of seventh month, 1668.

In the year 1650, this mild and peaceable sect, were, in scorn and derision, first branded with the name of Quakers, though George Fox was imprisoned at Nottingham, as early as 1649: from which period, to the time of the Toleration Act, in 1689, they suffered grievous persecution, by fines and imprisonment; and the most aggravated acts of cruelty were exercised upon them, in the various modes of punishment to which they were barbarously subjected. Their tenets must have been propagated at Ipswich, at an early period; for on the 14th of August, 1655, Joseph Laurence was committed to the county gaol, at Ipswich, for promulgating his peculiar tenets: and in 1657, William Alexander, at Needham—from whom the present family of that name are descended—was imprisoned at Ipswich, on similar charges, till the sessions, then fined £5, and re-committed for refusing to pay it. In 1658, George Whitehead—who was a man of good birth, education, and circumstances — for exhorting Edward Wilson, the priest of Hoxne, " to fear God and cease from iniquity," was carried away, to Ipswich, on horseback, by night, and committed to prison; where he met with the aforesaid William Alexander,—whom he terms " an honest young man:' here he remained for sixteen weeks, till the death of Oliver Cromwell, when he was discharged;

N N

By this it will be seen, that this people, who were called seducers and deluders, and persecuted, wherever they went, as rogues, vagabonds, vagrants, and enemies to good government, had many men of talents and importance amongst them, even from the commencement of their career. From the memorable period of the Revolution, which placed William III. on the throne of these realms, they have been treated with great lenity and consideration. They are distinguished by a rigid correctness in their dealings, and a mild simplicity of manner; and, notwithstanding the singularity of their costume, and their determination to keep their heads covered in high places, no one can deny, that, as a body, they rank amongst the most respectable members of civil society; and, as such, they have long nourished at Ipswich.

Close by this church, at the bottom of Brook-street, is a handsome building fitted up by Messrs. Alexander & Co. for carrying on their extensive transactions as bankers. This establishment is generally called the Yellow Bank. It was originally commenced by the late Miles Wallis, esq. about a century ago. It has, now, branch houses at Needham, Hadleigh, Woodbridge, Manningtree, &c. and there are very few country hanks of higher repute.

The adjoining house is the residence of Henry Alexander, esq. one of the partners of this firm. He is a liberal benefactor to all institutions for promoting instruction and charity. "The Girls' Free School of Industy," consisting of a hundred children, without respect to religious denominations, educated and instructed for the purpose of fitting them for good and well-behaved servants, is carried on entirely at his individual expense; and the anxiety, kindness, and care, with which he has superintended this institution, exhibit his character in a very amiable point of view. His house and gardens are fitted up with costliness and taste; containing a choice assemblage of animals, birds, and fishes, in their appropriate departments: and his collection of new and old China, with rare ornamental articles of the like description, from all parts of the world, has been accumulated at the expense of thousands; and is well worth the attention of the curious.

At the corner of the Half Moon public-house, opposite the Bank, is one of those specimens of old carvings in wood with which this town formerly abounded: it is rudely executed, but has more meaning than these figures usually display; for a young rogue of a fox, seated on an eminence, seems to be holding forth to, and cajoling, the minor branches of the goose family, while Old Reynard is running away with the gander. This was a common satire on the Franciscan order of monks; who were a begging fraternity, that took care be paid for the blessings they bestowed. It is said to be the house that was left to the corporation, by the will of Richard Oake, May 26th, 1522, to the intent that all the profit and revenues, shall, for ever, discharge and acquit all the poor inhabitants of Ipswich, which hereafter shall happen to be taxed, or charged to pay the king's tax, as largely as the said profits and revenues will extend. Alas! we shall never live to see such a state of society, as when the rent of the Fox and Goose could exonerate the poor inhabitants of Ipswich, from the payment of their taxes.

Not far from this spot, in Foundation-street, was a house of black friars, Dominicans, called the Friars Preachers; who were settled here, in the latter end of the reign of Henry III. It was founded by Henry Mansby, Henry Redhead, and Henry de Loudham. In 1307, they had a patent from Edward II. to enlarge the precincts of their house. It is said, in Taylor's Index Monasticus, that it was founded by John Harys, Hares, or Haws. The following extract, from an old MS. may throw some light upon the subject:—" The Black Friars. Of this house I only find that one John Hares gave ground to build it larger. Those personages following, 1 find to have been registered in the Martirologe of this house: the Lord Roger Bigod, earl marshal, Sir John Sutton, knight, Lady Mary Plays, Sir Richard Plays, Sir Robert Ufford, earl of Suffolk." The scite of this establishment was of large extent; reaching from Star-lane, in this parish, to Dirtylane, in St. Margaret's. It was granted in the thirty-third year of Henry VIII. to William Sabyn; but, afterwards, purchased by the corporation, of Mr. Southwell, with the design of founding on it, an hospital for the relief and maintenance of aged persons and children, for the curing of the sick poor, and for the employment and correction of the vicious and idle; and it was confirmed to them, by a charter, in the fourteenth year of Queen Elizabeth, 1572: wherein she styles it "Christ's Hospital in our towne of Ipswich." It was at first supported by annual subscriptions; afterwards, the corporation made an order that every burgess, on being admitted to his freedom, should pay 3s. 4d. to this charity, out of the usual fee: but this benevolent regulation has been neglected for many years, and the hospital has received no benefit from these fees, though, at some general elections, perhaps, near one hundred freemen are admitted:—this ought to be better attended to. The corporation are not only trustees of this charity, but are entrusted in a great measure, with the care and application of it; they are to choose four governors, annually, and a treasurer; they are to make rules for the government of the hospital, and to appoint what officers and servants they think proper to act under the governors; and the four governors are to pass their accounts, annually, before the bailiffs, and the four new governors who succeed them. The former regulations for the government of this charity, have been simplified and condensed; and the following judicious new rules and orders, substituted in their place, were framed at a meeting of the bailiffs and governors of Christ's Hospital, September 20th, 1814:— *Rules and Orders at a meeting of the Bailiffs, and Governors of Christ's Hospital, held the* 26A *of September,* 18H.

That all rules, orders, and regulations, for the management of this Charity, be made by the Bailiffs and the Governors, or the major part of them, and be entered and signed by those present at the making thereof, in the books kept at the Hospital.

That the Treasurer do continue to enter in a book, his account of receipts and disbursements, and deliver over the same to his successor in office, at the audit at which his accounts shall be passed; and which shall be held before the next ensuing rent-day.

That the Guide do keep the boys daily employed in spinning; and when the work he sets them to do, is completed, do attend them to the School-house, where they are to be instructed in reading, writing, and arithmetic. That he do not suffer the boys to be employed by any person, without the consent of the Bailiffs and Governors, nor permit them to be about the streets at improper times, or their parents or friends to take them away without permission.

That the Schoolmaster do teach all the boys that are sent from the Hospital, in reading, writing, and arithmetic, at such hours and by such methods as the Bailiffs and the major part of the Governors for the time being shall direct: and that he continue to be paid at the rate of 6s. 3d. for each boy, per quarter, and be allowed the costs of the books and slates.

That no boy be admitted into this Charity, whose parents do not reside within the town; nor unless he appears to be in good hearth, and is above eight years of age; (such age to be proved by the Parish Register, or other sufficient proof) nor until the usual fee of four guineas shall have been paid for his admission. That no boy be permitted to remain upon the Charity after the age of fourteen years, nor be dismissed the same (except for misbehaviour) before that time: and that all boys which shall be expelled, be excluded the premium given with those who are bound apprentices.

August 27th, 1820, a meadow in the parish of St. Mary Stoke, in the occupation of John King, was purchased by the governors of Christ's Hospital, of the trustees of the late Mr. Robert Fulcher, for £250, and let to John King, at £10: 10:0 per annum, for the remainder of his lease; and is now merged in the adjoining farm, belonging to the Hospital, occupied by Mr. Thomas Betts.

Richard Phillips, of Ipswich, esq. by his will, dated Sep. 17th, 1719, gave £240, towards the support of this hospital. Dame Amy Kemp, his daughter, and relict of Sir Robert Kemp, bart., in 1745, gave £240: and the charity has been enriched by sundry other donations.

The following is a correct statement of the receipts for the year 1827:—

The number of boys is, at present, sixteen. They are clothed, boarded, lodged, and educated; and, at the age of fourteen, apprenticed to some trade, chiefly to the seaservice. Four guineas is paid at the entrance of each boy into the school; which sum is expended in defraying part of the expenses of binding him out, when arrived at a proper age. The expenses of the Bridewell are defrayed out of the funds. It is altogether an excellent institution; and, except in a few instances, has been managed with propriety: but there are some particulars which require to be looked into, by which the revenue of the Charity might be much improved.

A very considerable part of the ancient religious edifice is remaining: the cloisters are entire, and the portion set apart for the Hospital, and the Bridewell, is in good repair. Within these walls a room is fitted up very appropriately, with presses, for the reception of the books forming the town library. Mr. William Smart, by his will, dated January 8th, 1578, left his books and parchments', for the use of the town preacher; to which were added those purchased with the legacy ef £50, left by Mrs. Walters, to the bailiffs and corporation, in 1754: and, in 1612, the corporation fitted up a room under the Free Grammarschool for their reception; where they used to be kept till within these few years, when they were removed to their present situation. The library has been augmented by donations in money, and by the presentation of books from various persons; and according to the catalogue taken 1790, it then contained about seven hundred and fifty volumes; consisting chiefly of theology and antiquities, valuable as books of reference, but few of them either curious or scarce. The keys are kept by the bailiffs, and the master of the Grammar-school. Every freeman has a right to take any of the books, on his giving a proper receipt, but our worthy burgesses, we suppose, are more THE NEW YORK!

PUBLIC Libraryl" ASTOn, LENOX AND TILDEN FOUNDATIONS.

engaged in commerce than in literature; for the hooks are but little used or regarded.

Adjoining to the Hospital, is the Grammar-school, a lofty, and spacious room, about a hundred and twenty feet in length, and twenty-four feet wide. It was, formerly, the refectory of the convent: the walls of which are firm enough to endure for another century; though they are, now, probably, five hundred years old. The representation we have given of the interior, is from a drawing by Mr. Jabez Hare, of this town; whose mechanical genius is well known: and he has, in this instance, displayed, also, very considerable talent as an artist.

There appears to have been, formerly, a master's house and a school, on another side of the yard which is used as a play-ground; but the former was taken down, in 1712, and the materials employed in repairing the school and the walls of the school-yard: and, in 1763, the old school-room having fallen down or become ruinous, the school was removed to the room which is now used. The premises are kept in repair by the corporation.

The establishment of a grammar-school in this town, is of very ancient date; for, at a great court, held in the seventeenth year of Edward IV. 1477, it was ordered, "that the master of the Grammar-school shall have the government of all the scholars within the liberties of this o town, (excepting little onos called *Apes Eyes)* taking such salary as by the bishop of Norwich is appointed." What that salary was, or by whom it was pud, does not appear; but it seems as if it was not thought sufficient; for, in the twenty-second year of Edward IV. 1482, it was ordered that every burgess inhabitapt should pay to the master, for a boy, eight-pence per quarter, and no more. However, for the further encouragement of the said master, it was ordered at the same time, that he should celebrate o o the guild of Corpus Christi, during his life. In the same year, Richard Felaw, portman—who had been eight times bailiff, and twice member of parliament for this town— gave, by will, dated January the 2d, 1482, his house and lands in Whitton, for the sustenance of the master of the Grammar-school; and he says, "*Item I will that my Mees beyng agayne the Gate of the Fryers Preachers in Ipswich, be ordained to be forever a Common School House and Dwelling-place for a convenient Schoolmaster."* This is the old building opposite the Grammar-school-yard, still called *Felaw's house.* But, in 1524, Cardinal Wolsey having intimated to the University of Oxford, his design of founding a college there, now Christ's Church, he soon commenced that splendid work. Not long after, he founded his school and college at Ipswich, upon the scite of the priory of St. Peter and St. Paul; which was surrendered to him, on the 6th of March, 1527: and, at the request of the cardinal, Mr. Felaw's lands were alienated for that purpose, by the corporation, in the twentieth year of Henry VIII. 1528, as appears by a letter in the Exchequer Record Office, signed James Hill, Thomas Manser, bailiffs of Ipswich. Thus the old Grammarschool

was done away with, and merged in the cardinal's new school: which, for a short time, is said to have rivalled the establishments of Winchester and Eton; for he mixed ecclesiastical dignity with all his learned institutions. At the same time, he sent a circular address to the schoolmasters of England, recommending them to teach their youths the elements of elegant literature, and prescribed the use of Lily's Grammar, for his school at Ipswich; to which he himself wrote a preface. Dr. William Capon was the first and last dean; for this school was discontinued at the cardinal's fall. Although he was frustrated in the grandeur of his intentions, he may be considered as the cause of inducing the king, Henry VIII. to grant a new charter for the re-establishment of the Grammar-school: which charter was renewed, confirmed, and enlarged, by Queen Elizabeth, on the 18th of March, 1565: wherein she authorized the corporation to pay a handsome salary for that period, to the master and usher, out of the fee-farm rent; it was £24: 6: 8 to the master, and £14: 6: 8 to the usher: and the remaining £22: 6: 8 of the fee-farm rent was sold to the corporation, in the reign of Charles II.; and is now the property of the Rev. Thomas Hallum. In the reign of James I., James Leman having conducted himself improperly, as master, the corporation insisted upon his quitting the school; which he refusing to do, they set up another grammar-school, at the Hospital, in opposition to that appointed by charter: and, in the fifth year of James I. October 26th, the following appears, as an order of the great court, that "The treasurer of the Hospital, from time to time, shall receive the rents of Mr. Felaw's lands, and pay the same to *William Awder elected Schoolmaster,* by half years, without warrant from the bailiffs so that the Free Grammar-school was not kept in Christ's Hospital, till the fifth year of James I.

The master of the Grammar-school delivers a report of the free scholars under his care, annually, on the 29th of September, to the bailiff's; and they fill up all vacancies. The school is open to

the boys of the town, indiscriminately; but the preference is usually given to the sons of the burgesses: and the number, at present, is limited to thirty; each of whom receives forty shillings, annually, for the purchase of books, and is entitled to £5, on his being bound as an apprentice. Other day-scholars are taught, without limitation; and the master, having a good house and grounds, usually has many of the gentlemen's sons in the neighbourhood, as boarders: the number fluctuates, of course; but, at times, this school has vied, in importance, with the first public seminaries in the kingdom. There is no fixed age for the admission of pupils on the foundation, that being determined by the will of their parents. The Eton Latin and Greek grammars are used, and other books in rotation, dependent on the master's choice. The head master and usher are now consolidated. The master receives about £50 per annum, and a free house, with other privileges. The town preacher, or lecturer, at St. Mary at the Tower, is generally the master of the Grammar-school. They are both chosen by the majority of the burgesses, at a great court; and the master must be subject to the approval of the bishop of Norwich for the time being. This office was, formerly, made a matter of electioneering contest; but such contentions being deemed indelicate, and contrary to the interests of religion and literature, the master and the lecturer are now very properly left to enjoy their situations, unmolested by the numerous fluctuations of party by which our restless corporation is agitated.

The house appropriated for the master, is situated in Brook-street, with suitable offices and garden, and a considerable piece of land adjoining; from which there is an entrance into F ounda-tion-street, nearly opposite to the Grammar-school. This house was originally purchased in 1619, by the corporation, for the use of the *lecturer at the church of St. Mary at the Tower,* with the sum of £120, advanced by the corporation, and other sums contributed by individuals; but for a very long time past, the master of the Grammar-school has enjoyed the house as appurtenant to his of-fice: and, as the lecturer and the mas-ter of the Grammar-school are, usually, one and the same person, it prevents any dispute as to whose use the property ought to be appropriated. There is a sum of £6: 13:4 a year, mentioned in the re-port of Smart's Charity, as given by him to the master and usher of the Grammar-school; and it is a matter yet undecided, whether this sum is included in the £11 added to the master's salary, when the duties of the master and usher were con-solidated.

In the year 1820, after the successful election of Lennard and Haldimand, the apartments under the Grammarschool were, at a great expense, fitted up as kitchens, for the purpose of cooking a dinner for near three hundred and fifty persons; which was served up in the school-room above. The savoury fumes of good cheer once more ascended to the lofty roof of the ancient refectory; and the sounds of wassail, mirth, and revelry, were heard within its walls, much as in the olden time, when

"Merry in the hall, beards wagg'd all. "

The late worthy and venerable mas-ter, the Rev. John King, M. A., raised the reputation of this school to the high-est pitch, during the thirty-one years he presided over it, and died at the ad-vanced age of eighty-three, February 22nd, 1822. A tablet monument is erect-ed to his memory, in the church of St. Mary at the Tower, where he was town lecturer for twenty-three years, with an elegant Latin inscription, expressive of his talents and his worth; and, as one of his pupils, the writer retains the high-est respect for his memory. He resigned his situation, as master of the Grammar-school, in 1798; and the Rev. Rowland Ingram was elected in his room.

The present worthy master, the Rev. William Howorth, was elected to the of-fice, on the 13th of March, 1800. Among the many excellent scholars he has educated may be mentioned the learned Dr. William French, the present master of Jesus College, Cambridge, who ranks so high in reputation at the University.

A meeting of those persons who have been educated at this seminary, has tak-en place, annually, for several years past, at the Great White Horse, in Ip-swich; and there is, generally, a strong muster of the sons of the gentry, clergy, and yeomanry of the county, who dine together upon the occasion, mutually re-minding each other of their adventures at school: and we know of no more agreeable association than such an as-semblage of individuals, cemented by one common bond of union, calculated to keep alive the delightful recollection of boyish days, and to perpetuate the germs of friendship formed in youth, which frequently continue to the grave.

In the year 1558, Lawrence Mopted, B. D., some time master of Corpus Christi College, in Cambridge, gave £60 to Trinity Hall, for the founding of a scholarship. The scholar to be born in the diocese of Norwich, and brought up, for the space of two years, at least, in the common school at Ipswich or Bury.

On the 22nd of December, 1598, Mr. William Smart conveyed a farm called Diggers, in Wiverstone, in value £19 per annum, to the college of Pembroke Hall, in Cambridge, for the maintenance of one fellow and two scholars, to be called Smart's. These scholars were to be from Ipswich free-school, and of Mr. Smart's kindred, if any fit.

In 1601, Mr. Ralph Scrivener, who married Mr. Smart's widow, settled an annuity of £21 on the same college, for the erection of four new scholarships, to be filled out of the Grammar-school at Ipswich, to be called Scrivener's schol-ars.

Richard Martin, portman, by deed, the 18th February, 1621, in the nine-teenth year of James I. gave his farm in Westerfield, to the bailiffs and portmen of Ipswich, out of the rents of which was to be paid, yearly, £20 to two schol-ars of the University of Cambridge, who formerly were scholars in the free-school of Ipswich.

For these last thirty years, there have not been more than half a dozen exhi-bitions from the Grammar-school at Ip-swich, and, in general, no more paid than £6 per annum, at one time, and £14

at another. This very ill accords with the benevolent intentions of the donors: and we blush to see that the corporation, in former times, had more anxiety for the advancement of learning, than at the present more enlightened period; for in the twelfth year of Queen Elizabeth, the following entry appears in the court book of the borough:—" Robert Inglish, of Magdalen College, in respect of his poverty, and behig a toward young man, shall have a yearly exhibition of £2: 13:4 out of the' foundation:" and in the twentysecond year of the same reign, "James Erman had £5 granted, to pay his expenses at Cambridge, for his com-mencement, out of *Barnard's gift;"* and, soon after, an order for £14, yearly, for three years. We have never been able to discover what has become of this prop-erty called Barnard's gift. Frequently afterwards, orders for the payment of sums, for exhibitions, occur two or three times within the year. The neglect of these exhibitions cannot tend to raise the reputation of the school, upon which, formerly, so much patronage had been bestowed. Feeling for the hon-or of this excellent institution, we sin-cerely hope that some spirited individ-uals of the corporation, who have re-ceived their education there, will pro-ceed to investigate these claims, and rectify those abuses, that, from inadver-tency and the lapse of time, may have been allowed to continue; for if this were done, the reputation of the Free Grammar School of Ipswich would soon be restored to its pristine celebrity.

Another part of the ancient edifice is converted into dwelling-houses, for the persons receiving Tooley's and Smart's charities: and we cannot but observe the difference between the flimsy erections of modern date, and the durable buildin-gs of former times; for, after the lapse of three or four centuries, it appears, from the solidity of these walls, that they may yet continue for ages to come.

Mr. Henry Tooley, portman of Ip-swich, by his will, dated November 5th, 1550, left estates to the corporation, for the purpose of erecting alms-houses, for the maintenance of ten persons, which, at the time of their reception into the said house, shall be tried *unfeignedly lame, by occasion of the King's Wars, or otherwise; that cannot acquire or get their living, or the one half thereof* He likewise mentions other objects of charity, to which the overplus of the rents of these estates shall be applied, after these ten persons shall have been supplied with what was necessary, according to his instruction. He likewise left long and particular directions and regulations, for the management of the charity called " The House of the Poor of Mr. Tooley's Foundation." On the death of Mr. Tooley, some dispute arose between the bailiffs and his executors; when Sir Nicholas Bacon, the lord keeper, "took great pains and travail in devising rules, ordinances, and statutes, and compounding the controversies between the said Executors and the said Bailiffs:" and in consequence of his interference and exertions, Royal Letters Patent were obtained, bearing date November 30th, in the third and fourth year of Philip und Mary; in which the ambiguities in Mr. Tooley's will were obviated, and all disputes settled. It is declared that the bailiffs, burgesses, and commonalty of Ipswich, are trustees for the estates; that the bailiffs, portmen, and commoncouncil, are entrusted with the choice of wardens, and the passing of their accounts; and that the management and disposition of the profits of tin" estates devolved upon the wardens for the time being. What the annual value of Mr. Tooley's estates were, at the time of his decease, is uncertain: in 1556, they were supposed to be about one hundred marks: in 1747, the rent-roll amounted to £391: 6: 5: in 1827, the yearly rents paid were as follow:

Mr. Simon Jackaman 19 12 ©

Mr. Thoaias Kersey 135 0 0

Mr. Thomas Cooper, sen 150 0 0

Mr. Stephen Haward, 187 0 0

Sir William Middleton 8 0 0

Mr. James King 916 8

Mr. Edward Dove, Urverston Hall Farm, 400 0 0

Quit-rents of the Manors *oi* Ul version „ aud Saekvills, _.

£1005 18 8

In the year 1827, there were seventy-eight persons on the list'of pensioners, who were paid 2s. 6d. per week, and one person 3s. 6d. per week; making, altogether, for the year, £516:2:0.

The poor people on the Foundation, have, besides their pay, linen, &c. as follows: once in two years, each woman has 9s. 3d. allowed at some shop, for linen; each man has 12s. 6d.; man and wife, 21s. fid. Once in two years, each woman has a stuff gown j and each man, a coat. Such of the poor people as have rooms, are allowed, annually, one chaldron of coals and twelve faggots of wood; if husband and wife, or two in one room, one chaldron and a quarter, and eighteen faggots. Pn case of sickness, further assistance is rendered, at the discretion of the warden. A surgeon is appointed, at a salary of £50 per annum, to attend to the poor, in this and Smart's foundation.

p p

In the front of a house in Foundation-street, formerly part of this charity, the arms of Tooley are carved, with the following inscription:—

"In peaceful alienee let great TOOLKT rest;

Whoce charitahle deeds heapeak him hleat."

1 MI.

It is, certainly, not the fashion, at the present day, to bequeath money for charitable purposes. We are aware that such charities are, sometimes, perverted, and their funds abused; but, in this case, we have reason to believe that this institution is well managed, and the spirit of the donor's intentions strictly adhered to. Thousands have, already, partaken of its benefits; and thousands yet unborn, may have reason to bless the name of Henry Tooley.

Mr. William Smart, portman, by his will, dated January 8th, 1598, left several estates, in trust, to the bailiffs, burgesses, and commonalty of Ipswich, for the purpose of maintaining sundry poor persons, finding them with coals, clothing, &c. much after the manner of Mr. Tooley's bequest: and he likewise directed that the amount of the rents should be laid out, under the direction of the wardens of Tooley's foundation;

that they should receive and manage the revenues of this gift, and, every year, render an account of them. A portion of the same building is appropriated for the residence of those persons who are on this foundation; and they receive 2s. 6d. per week, in the like manner as Mr. Tooley's pensioners. The number of persons on the list of this charity, in 1827, was fifty-six; amounting, in the whole to £364: and the income, for the same year, was as under:—

James Tydeman's farm, at Creeting,.. 60 0 0

Simon Jackaman, part of farm, at Whitton 12 12 0

George Cook's farm, at Falkenham and

Kirton 5

In consequence of the intentions of Mr. Tooley and Mr. Smart, being so similar, respecting their bequests, and the direction of the latter, that the distribution of bis funds should be under the direction of the wardens of Mr. Tooley's foundation, these two charities have been, now, in a measure, blended together; and the following extract will afford a correct statement of the income and expenditure of both, for the year 1827:—

Weekly pay bill, amounting, annually, to 880 2 0

Coals and wood, for 53 rooms, to about. 140 0 0

Linen, to about 70 0 0

Surgeon 50 0 0

Minister of St. Mary at the Key,... 10 0 0

Clerk of St. Mary at the Key 3 0 0

Staff-bearer 300

Insurance, to about 16 0 0

Water-rent, 1 10 0

Treasurer of Christ's Hospital 2 2 0

Treasurer's salary 2 0 0

£1177 14 0

Income of Tooley's Charity, 1005 18 8

Income of Smart's Charity,. 482 12 0

1498 10 8

Disbursements, 1177 14 0

£310 16 8

Leaving a balance of £310: 16: 8, to be expended in repairs, &c. according to the respective wills of the donors:

but, in consequence of abatements in the rents of the farms, owing to the badness of the times, this apparent balance is materially diminished.

For a full account of the charters, wills, rules and regulations, &c. respecting Christ's Hospital, and of Tooley's and Smart's charities, we refer our readers to the excellent publication on the charities of Ipswich, as before-mentioned, edited by the Rev. William Edge, M. A., and published by Mr. Dorkin, in 1819.

The establishment of these several charities, on the same spot, has given the name to the street in which they are situated; which has been long called Foundationstreet.

The parliamentary commissioners seem to have found but little fault with the management of the several charities of Ipswich, except that of Crane's gift, and the Lending Cash Fund; the latter of which they were unable to go into, for want of the necessary accounts and documents: and they make the following remark:—" In the course of the preceding, and the next following reports of the corporation charities, we have pointed out what payments ought to be made by the corporation, as due, of right, to different branches or objects of these charitable trusts, and in what respect alterations in practical management, and a further degree of observance of the intention of the donors appear requisite. What we have suggested as proper to be done, may readily be effected by orders of the corporation; and we think that if these suggestions are complied with, the interference of a court of equity, as to the charities embraced in this report, will not be required."

We forgot to mention, that, within the walls we have just left, in the room appropriated for the reception of the books forming the town library, a society meets, that was, originally, formed by six or seven gentlemen, on the 30th of September, 1818, for the purpose of discussing literary subjects, and composing essays, intended for their own improvement in composition and oratory. After various fluctuations, it now consists of about twenty members— is

called the Philological Society, and is confined to the writing of essays upon subjects previously submitted to the members. Each writer reads his own production to the society, and a discussion arises Upon its merits; when the decision of the majority is entered in the minutes, which are recorded in the journals of the society, We have been fortunate enough to be present at some of the meetings, and were delighted with the talent displayed. Some of the essays that have been read, discover a great deal of research, erudition, and sound reasoning, combined with taste and elegance of composition; and if a selection of them were formed into a volume, they might vie with the transactions of the Manchester and Exeter societies, of the same description.—We are happy to observe, that one of the members of this society ranked amongst the *wramjlers* at Cambridge, last year.

We now turn to the Shire Hall, which stands before us, in an open, airy space of ground, called the Shire Hall Yard, and is a large and nearly square brick building, erected in 1699, by voluntary subscription. Sir Samuel Barnardiston, who was member for the borough at the time, contributed largely towards its erectiort. The ex terior is plain and un adorned, with little of elegance to recommend it. It is divided into two distinct courts, spacious, lofty, and commodiously fitted up for the purpose; having a good apartment adjoining, for" the use of the Grand Jury: and if a retiring-room for the Petty Jury were added, there would scarcely be a more commodious court of justice in the kingdom. It is the property of Christ's Hospital; and is let by the corporation, to the county magistrates, for the purpose of holding the quarter sessions for the hundreds of Hartesmere, Hoxne, Stow, Bosmere and Claydon, and Samford. The county magistrates have no jurisdiction within the liberties of the borough. The sessions for the town— which used to be held upon the Town Hall, on the Cornhill—are now held here, generally a short time previous to the assizes: the bailiffs and recorder preside, and their power is extensive; they

pass fines and recoveries, hear and determine causes, both criminal and civil, and even crown cases, preferably to any of His Majesty's courts at Westminster; but they seldom exercise their power to its fullest extent, prisoners for capital crimes being generally sent for trial to the assizes, held at Bury. We are not aware of any one suffering death by the sentence of the recorder, at the borough sessions.

On leaving the Shire Hall Yard, by a little gate at the south-east corner, we come into a narrow passage, called Pleasant Row, leading into Star Lane. In this row, is a malt-office, in the occupation of Mr. Harbur. This building is very little known, and has never been mentioned by any other writer: the walls are of stone, two feet thick, and about twenty feet high, with a tiled sloping roof,— the top of which is, perhaps, forty feet from the ground: the edifice is about seventy-five feet long, and twenty feet wide, within the interior. There are several projections from the wall, upon which appear to have been placed rafters of timber that supported the roof,— but these rafters seem to have been cut away, when the floor was inserted, at about twelve feet from the ground, for the purposes of malting. We know not how to describe, with technical precision, the construction of the roof; which is similar to what may be seen in St. Margaret's church, in this town, only there are large transverse beams inserted into the walls, upon which the roof rests,—but which would have been useless, had it been supported, as we think it originally was, on the rafters that formerly rested on the projecting buttresses below; therefore it is possible that these beams were inserted when the floor was made, or when the rafters were taken away. The whole roof, as well as the beams, are of thesnut, of capital workmanship, but very sparingly carved or ornamented. The lower portion or knee of each supporter of the roof, is a piece of timber, six or eight inches thick, grooved, but little carved, shaped by a segment of a circle intersecting two right angles; which pieces of timber project about three feet from the wall. In the space in the corner of each of these projections, is carved a plain shield, without any heraldic device; nor are there any armorial bearings to be seen, except a *mullet* on one of these shields, a St. Andrew's cross on another, and *two chevrons* upon another: but, upon the shields on both sides of two of these supporters, in about the centre of the building, is very neatly carved a pair of shears, precisely similar to those carved on the stone at the east end of St. Laurence' church, over the name of John Baldwyn, the *draper* who built the chancel; and these are all the ornaments, of any description, with which the building is decorated. The timber of the roof is perfect in every part; the proportions are just and symmetrical; it has a light and elegant appearance, and if the beams and the floor were taken away, it would be a very handsome apartment. It does not stand due east and west, but north and south; and could not, therefore, have been designed for a church or chapel. We are induced to believe that it was a hall for the public meetings of some one of the numerous guilds formerly in this place. Mr. Smart, in his will, dated 1598, left £10 each, to both Draper's Hall and Taylor's Hall; and, from the emblematical device of the shears, so exactly corresponding with the shears of John Baldwyn, the *draper,* it is probable thai this building was *Draper's Hall.* We are a ware that the shears had nothing to do with the armorial bearings of the Drapers' Company; but we are inclined to believe that they are used as the mark or insignia of the trade or manufacture in which the person who erected the building was engaged: and who was, probabiy, one of the society of Drapers. house in the town. Of this wo have given a wood-cut, executed from a spirited design by Mr. John Smart, jun. a native of Ipswich.

The design and execution of this structure is so simply elegant, and so unlike the confused and clumsy architecture usual in Elizabeth's time, that we should be puzzled to fix the era of its erection, unless the roof might have been brought from some other place—

perhaps from the chapel of Wolsey's college, or the priory of St. Peter, or old St. Peter's church—for it certainly surpasses, in elegance, any private edifice now remaining in Ipswich. It must have been built since the demolition of the convent; for it stands within the precincts of these friars' possessions, and was, probably, erected with the materials which formed the walls of part of that building: but we must leave the date of its erection, for the learned antiquarian to determine, satisfied with having attempted to bring its merits into notice. Some years since, it was in the possession of an old man, of this town, of the name of Bull: it now belongs to a person who is not able to afford to keep it in repair. We are sorry to see that, in consequence of this, the exterior roof is in such a dilapidated state, that the interior is liable to be injured by the weather. We, therefore, sincerely wish that some spirited lover of the arts would purchase the property, and rescue this really elegant structure from oblivion.

Nearly adjoining this building, at the corner of Lower Orwell-street, is a large house, of very ancient date, remaining, with its rude wooden front and open arched windows, without glass, in the same state as it must have been centuries ago; and is, probably, the oldest private

From thence we proceed a few yards further on, till we come to the Common Quay. Upon the crane, here, is the following inscription, in gold letters:—

"THIS CRANE WA8 ERECTED, AND WHARF RE BUILT, 17 27.
-JOHN CORNELIUS, ESfi.?BA1LIIT8."
"JOHN SPARBOWE, GENT. $

Here stands the Custom House: it is a low, ill-shaped, isolated building, supported, on the south, next the water, by a numerous range of pillars, reaching the whole length of the front, which is about a hundred and twenty feet, forming a colonnade, under which the masters of vessels and other seafaring people delight to perambulate, in preference to the most romantic and rural pedestrian excursion, as being, we suppose, more similar to the agreeably-varied amusement of walking the deck.

The Custom House must be one of the oldest houses m Ipswich: it is mentioned, in ancient writings, as the Town House; and, doubtless, the public business of the corporation was transacted there, previous to the erection of the Old Town Hall, on the scite of St. Mildred's church: it is constructed entirely of wood, and was, no doubt, erected before brick was in use here; and was, probably, an old building when the Town Hall was built: it has been standing, at least, between four and five hundred years: it has been patched up, in many parts, with brick, but it is, now, in a very crazy condition; however, the' chesnut beams in the interior, are, apparently, as sound as ever, and may hang together for many years to come. We may infer, from the size of the Custom House, that, in former times, the shipping trade of Ipswich was of much more importance than at the present day. An author who, himself, wrote a century back, has this remark:—" Ipswich, 'the Eye of the County:' it had, about an hundred years ago, a commodious haven, a great trade, and was very populous, having an abundance of rich merchants in it; but, at present, is much decayed in its trade and people, which hath caused a decrease of the shipping:" still it must be taken into consideration, that this was also the Town House, as well as the Custom House; and, therefore, but a part of the building would be appropriated to the business of the Customs, as is the case at present. — We believe there is a clause in some charter or act, in which it is said, that the Custom House must not be removed from its present scite; but as nothing terrestrial can last for ever, there must, one day, be an end of this wooden erection: and we hope that, in case of erecting a new Custom House, due care will be taken for accommodating the seamen with a covered promenade, or they will no longer consider Ipswich as a commodious port.

Amongst a quantity of lumber stowed away in an apartment little used, some years ago, that singular instrument of punishment, the *Ducking Stool,* was discovered; and, with the provident care for which our worthy magistrates have always been distinguished, it has been fresh painted, and made fit for use. It is in the form of a strong backed arm-chair, with a wrought-iron rod, about an inch in diameter, fastened to each arm, in front, meeting in a segment of a cir-cle, above: there is also another iron rod affixed to the back, which curves over the head of a person seated in the chair, and is connected with the others at the top; to the centre of which is fastened an iron ring, for the purpose of sling-ing the machine into the river. It is plain and substantial, and has mors the ap-pearance of solidity than antiquity, in its construe tion. It is thus spoken of, by a writer of some discernment: "In an unfrequented apartment in the Cus-tom House, is still preserved the duck-ing-stool, a venerable rehc of ancient customs. In the chamberlain's book are various entries of money paid to porters, for taking down the *Ducking Stole,* and assisting in the operation of cooling, by its means, the inflammable passions of some of the female inhabitants of Ip-swich." Entries for the payment of per-sons employed in taking down this in-strument, do certainly appear: and, in the year 1597, three unfortunate females underwent this opprobrious ceremony; but, from delicacy, we forbear to men-tion their names. The fee for inflicting this punishment, was 1 s. Od. and we blush to think it was ever necessary to enforce it. It is noticed, in Blackstone, that a common scold, who is a public nuisance to her neighbourhood, may be indicted; and, if convicted, shall be sen-tenced to be placed in a certain engine of correction, called the *trebucket, cas-tigatory* or *cucking-stool;* which, in the Saxon language, signifies the scolding-stool, though, now, it is corrupted into *ducking-stool,* because the residue of the judgment is, that, when she is so placed therein, she shall be plunged in the water for her punishment. We can-not, for a moment, suppose that such a punishment could be necessary in these times; but we have given a spirited sketch, from a design by Mr. G. Cam-pion, late of this town, of a scene ex-hibiting persons preparing to carry this ceremony into execution, as a salutary warning to those who may be apt to in-dulge too freely in licentious volubility of speech.

It has been asserted, that a malt-kiln, on the Quay, formerly known by the name of the Angel, was, in ancient times, a house of Cistertian monks. One writer observes, "From the remains, it appears to have been about eighty one feet by twenty-one:" but there is no ac-count to be found of such an establish-ment; and if ever there was a religious house on this spot, the building in ques-tion— which, certainly, is very old— could have been only a small part of such an institution, for the monks had, always, a considerable space of ground included in their possessions.

In ancient times, the banks on this side the river were inhabited by the principal people of the town: and it is certain that many of their houses have been converted into malt-offices; sever-al of which are still objects of curiosity, and their origin worthy of research. We can remember, in our time, when the most eminent merchants in the place oc-cupied the many capital mansions near this spot, which are now empty, and go-ing to decay; as it is, at present, the fash-ion for them to remove from the con-finement and bustle of business, to their elegant rural retreats in the suburbs: in consequence of which, the vicinity of Ipswich has been very much improved.

St. Clement's church was early and wholly impropriated to the priory of St. Peter, without any vicarage created: and its being thus impropriated, when the last valuation was made, it was not val-ued in the king's books. It was granted, in the seventh year of Edward VI. to Webb and Breton; but it afterwards came to Robert Broke and William Bloise; who presented a clerk to the rec-tory, in 1606, and thereby restored the rector to all his rights and dues. This church is now consolidated with St. He-len's. "King Richard gave Wykes, a member of Ipswich, to John Oxenford, bishop of Norwich; which shall answer to Ipswich for £10, and the bishop of Norwich holdeth it, but it is not known by what service." It appears, by Ipswich Doomsday, that, in the time of Richard

I., the town used to pay £10 per annum, to the bishop of Norwich,—to be de-ducted out of the fee-farm rent. The hamlet and manor of Wykes Bishop, was, afterwards, confirmed to John le Gray, bishop of Norwich, by King John; and it belonged to the bishops of Nor-wich, till it was given to King Henry VI-II., by act of parliament, in 1535; who granted it, 1545, to Sir John Jermie, knight. John Cobbold, esq., is, at pre-sent, lord of the manor. While the bish-ops of Norwich had it, they used, fre-quently, to reside at their house, situated near the south side of the road leading towards Nacton, from Bishops Hill; which is, now, a square field, that ap-pears to have been, formerly, moated round. Many institutions, &c. are said, in the books at Norwich, to have been granted at this place. The church of Wykes is sometimes mentioned in old writings; but it is not known where it stood, and, possibly, it might be no more than a chapel, for the use of the bishop and his family.

Within this parish lieth, also, part of the hamlet of Wykes Ufford, though the greater part of it is in the parishes of Rushmere and Westerfield: it was so called from the family of De Ufford, who were earls of Suffolk, to whom it was granted. In the tenth year of Ed-ward II. 1316, Robert de Ufford held, on the day of his death, a certain *soke,* in *fVyke juxta, Gippiwic,* with view of frank pledge, and other appurtenances, to the said *soke,* belonging of the King in Capite, by the service of one knight's fee, and £4:13:4 rent of the profits of the toll of the town of *Ipswich,* of the K. in C. by the service aforesaid, and a tenement called Kettleber-west-heath, in soccage, by the service of one pair of gilded spurs, annually; and, also, of the K. in C. the manor of *Ufford,* by the service of one knight's fee. The Wil-loughbys had it, afterwards, by descent, from Charles Brandon, duke of Suffolk; in Queen Elizabeth's time, Sir John Brewes; then Sir Edmund Witypoll, and it has gone with the Christ Church estate ever since; but the advowson is now vested in the Rev. J. T. Nottidge, A. M.

Beyond St. Clement's street, between

the two hamlets, stood St. James's Chapel; which probably belonged to St. James's Hospital, situated on a piece of ground abutting on the Rope-ground, about half an acre, more or less; which is glebe belonging to St. Helen's rectory. From hence, and from the fair which King John, in 1199, granted to the lepers of St. Mary Magdalene, in Ipswich, to be held on the morrow of St. James the Apostle, it may be inferred, that there was some connexion between St. James's Hospital and the leprous-house of St. Mary Magdalene; which stood somewhere near St. Helen's church.

It is not known at what period St. Clement's church was built, as it is not mentioned in Doomsday. It was, probably, erected instead of the dilapidated church of Osterbolt, which stood near where the stepples formerly were,at the Bull's Head corner, and took its name from the east-gate that was near this spot. The antiquated church of Osterbolt is mentioned in the twenty-first year of Edward III. 1348; therefore, the present church must have been built since that time, for it appears to be not very ancient.

The present church has three aisles; the middle one is narrow, but lofty, and lighted by twelve windows on each side; the north and south aisles are low, and the pews very irregular. The altar-piece is modern, handsomely panelled, with mouldings, in mahogany; in the centre, a circular glory is painted; on the north side is a painting of the *Salutation of the Virgin Mary,* and on the other side, the *Agony of Our Saviour,* very well executed, by Mr. J. Smart. The handsome brass chandelier was presented, as the inscription implies, by " Master Mileson Edgar, to St. Clement's Parish, Anno Domini, 1700."

In 1584, October 31st, the bailiffs, burgesses, and commonalty, granted a piece of land in St. Clement's, upon which five tenements have been built, for the poor of the said parish.

In 1680, Mrs. Elizabeth Robinson gave £100; the interest of which to be laid out in bread, for the poor of the parishes of St. Clement and St. Mary at the Tower.

In 1698, November 29th, Mary Wright, widow, conveyed, by deed, five messuages, to be converted into a work-house, for the poor of this parish.

In 1704, Captain Samuel Green, mariner, by his will, gave £50, to purchase a piece of land, the rent of which to be annually distributed to poor widows and children of seamen, of this parish, on the 29th of November; "he having, on that day, received a wonderful deliverance in a great storm at sea." The widow of the above Samuel Green, added £10; and land was bought at Westerfield, now producing £20 per annum.

In 1719, Captain Robert Cole, by will, gave £50, to purchase a piece of land, the rent of which to be laid out in bread. The money was used for repairing the church; but the bread is given away, every fortnight, at the expense of the parishioners.

Captain Edward Larke, by his will, left premises, the rent of which to be expended in bread; and ten shillings, yearly, for a sermon to be preached on the 22nd of October, "in remembrance of the mercies of God, in preserving him, on that day, when all his men and ship were lost at sea."

In 1727, Captain John Dorkin left, by will, £100; with which a piece of land abutting on the Woodbridge road, in St. Helen's parish, was purchased, now let for £15. This to go to pay ten shillings to the minister, for reading prayers on the 14th of September; as, on that day, in the year 1710, he was, " by the providence of Almighty God, remarkably delivered from shipwreck, and preserved in a storm at sea." The remainder of the money to be distributed among poor seamen, seamen's widows, and their children.

In 1810, Captain Robert Brown left £100, the interest of which to be distributed to the poor of this parish.

Id 1818, a subscription was raised in this town, for the widows and orphans of the crew of the " Endeavour," of Ipswich, lost off the coast of Scotland, January, 1818, and the " Unity," of Ipswich, lost off the Lincolnshire coast, April 23rd, together with the whole of the crew of each vessel; by which awful events, rive families, resident in this parish, and fifteen orphans, were deprived of support. The sum of about £200 was raised, and distributed to the widows, according to the number of their children.

Among the inscriptions, in the church and churchyard, we notice the following. The first in the church, is to the memory of Thomas Eldred, who accompanied Cavendish in his voyage round the world:—

"He that travela the world ahout, (teeth Gnd's winders, end God's works.

"Thomas Eldred travelled tile world about, and went out of Plinaouth ye 2d July, 1586, and arrived in PMinouth nain, the 9th of.Septemher, 15M."

And, in a house in St. Clement's, inhabited, some years ago, by Mr. Bransby, there is an old picture, representing a terrestrial globe, marked with the equinoctial tropics, Capricorn, Cancer—America, &c. with the following inscription, originally in black letter:—

"Thomas Eldred went out of Pliminouthe, I586, Jul) 2d, and ailed ahout the whole glohe, and arrived again in Pllmmonthe, the 9th of Septemher, 1388. What can seeme great to him that hath seen the whole world, and the wondrous works therein, save the Maker of it, and the world ahove?"

On the chancel floor, near the communion-table, on a common stone, inlaid with brass:—

"Here reatyth the Body of JOHN TvE, late a merchant, and one of thePortmen of Ipswich; who departed this life, July 18, 1583, aged.'8."

Near this, is another, somewhat similar,

"To William Cocke, 26 Decemher, 1607, aged 69."

There were, at one time, three families of this name living in Ipswich, which were thus distinguished: the one was plain Mr. Cocke; Mr. Cocke, of St. Matthew's, was called Mr. Portman Cocke; and this man, "Cocke with the golden spurs," because of his great property—but his' children soon shortened it.

Adjoining these, is a stone, with a Latin inscription, to George Taylor, rector of this church; who died 31st of May, 1699, aged forty-nine.

Directly under the front of the gallery:—

"Here resteth the hody of Mr. Benjamin Brunning, some time Lecturer of this Town; who departed thi lite, Novemher, 1688. Also his wife and daughter."

There is a newly-erected marble cenotaph, to the memory of the Rev. George Routh, A. M., rector of this parish; who died, aged eighty-one, January 26th, 1821.

Near the altar, is a marble monument, richly carved and ornamented, with an open circular-headed pediment, having a shield with the arms of Wright and Hill impaled:

"Here resteth the hody of JOHN WRIGHT, ESQ. senior Portman of the Corporation, who served five times Bailiff, and was freely chosen their Burgesae in four several Parliaments. He died in his Bailiffwick, 29 Nov. 1683, aged 68.

' To the memory of MRS. Judith, the loving (and as truly heloved wife) of John Wright, esq. the only child of Capt. William Hill, of

Ratcliffe. She was huried in Stepney church. She died 23d April,

1677, aged *49.*

A wife soe dear, a tender loving mother.

Ohliging all that had acquaintance with her,

Kind to the poor, great was the loss did fall

To Hushand, Children, Friends and Neighhours all."

R R

Near the gallery stairs:—

"To the memory of Thos. Cobbold, Common Brewer, who departed this life April 21, 1767, aged 39."

In the south aisle:—

"' To the memory of JOHN Forsett, Jl'N. (late Portman of this

Town) died May 10, 1818, aged 49."

Likewise several individuals of the Forsett family.

In the churchyard, by the west side of

the south porch:

"Here, without a name, for ever senseless dumh,

Dust, ashes, nought else lies within thia tomh.

Where 'twas I lived or died, it matters not,

To whom related, and of whom hegot.

I a'U, hut am not: ask no more of me;

'Tis all I am, and all that you shall he.

"D. P. May l5, 1726. Aged 33."

At the west end, on the north side of the church:— "Edmund West died Jan. 20, iro5.

"Al l mortal men that paseeth hy,

As you are now, so once was I;

Who in my youth hy death laid hy,

Between my first love and my wife I *lie.*
"

"' Mary West died Feh. j, iro.5.

All women that hehould me here,

Pray for your change do you prepare;

For in six weeks' time, as you may see,

I a maid, and wile, and widow, and huried he."

On the south side:— "Here lyith ye hody of Eliz. BENTLY; who died 3Oth July, 1706,

aged 29.

"O Earth of Earth, ohserve this well—

When Earth in Earth shall come to dwell,

Where Earth with Earth shall close remain,

'Till Earth from Earth shall rise again."

On the west side of the churchyard, is a handsome stone to the memory of Sir Thomas Slade, knt. Surveyor of His Majesty's Royal Navy. He died 1771.

On the south side, is a tomb—

"To the memory of Captain Margercm, and his wife: he died 1739. Also his son, John Margerum, several times hailiff of Ipswich: he died 1750, aged 49.

"Also Rev. Henry Close, whomarried the daughter of the ahove. Also his son, Rev. JOHN Margerum Close, who died 22nd Feh. 1791, aged 41."

At the south-east entrance, is a tomb, much decayed, to the memory of Edward Bowell, gent., portman, and twice bailiff of Ipswich: he died October 3rd, 1737, aged fifty-seven. He erected the

light at Foulness, in Norfolk, A. D. 1719.—The last of his family, Abigail Bowell, a very eccentric character, died in this town, a few years since, nearly a hundred years old.

On the south side, is a handsome tomb, railed in, to the memory of William Richards, esq. major in the Bengal Engineers: he died Oct. 17th, 1816, aged eighty-three.

Near this, is a stone to the memory of—

"J AS. BHOLSDOVE died 29th April, 1815.

"Death, like an overflowing stream, Sweeps ua away. Our life's, a dream— An evening talk—a morning flower Cut down and withered in an hour."

On a tombstone a few yards north of the steeple:—

"Here lyeth the hody of JOHN WOOLLWARD, the master of the wherry; who departed this life the 16th day of July, heing struck dead, in a moment, hy the lightning aud thunder, aged 36 years, 170s."

The following account of this thunder-storm, communicated by Orlando Bridgman, esq., is extracted from the Philosophical Transactions, and appeared in the Ipswich Magazine, edited by the ingenious Mr. J. Bransby, in the year 1799:—

"*Extract of a letter from Orlando Bridgman, esq.*— There happened, at Ipswich, July 16th, 1708, a most violent storm of thunder and lightning, the effects of which have been both wonderful and dismal. The passage-boat was, at the time, coming from Harwich, and just got to the town, or very near, when came a terrible flash, that killed the master, and three other persons who were on board. I saw one the next day: he had a wound in his thigh; his breast was lacerated, as if it had been whipped with wires, and his face and body as black as if he had been blown up with gunpowder, with thousands of black smull spots about him. The master of the vessel was not at all disfigured; but had one wound on his side, like a fresh burn, and no other murk about him, save the chain of his watch was melted, and no other harm nor burn could be perceived on his breeches or clothes. The third person, who was a servant, was very much torn and shattered about the head: the crown of his hat was taken clean out, as if it had been cut out, and several parcels of his hair driven into the surface of the hat. The fourth was very little disfigured, only a black spot on his side, and a small wound, as if made with a cauterizing iron. There were several others on board, wounded and stunned. One Artis, among the former, had his hair burnt close to his head behind, and his peruke untouched; he had a scratch on his arm, about four inches long, and a small hurt below the elbow: he fell, that night, into a violent fever, grew delirious, and, if not dead yet, is pronounced irrecoverable: no injury whatever was done to his clothes.

"Two of the persons killed, w ere on the outside, and the other on the tilt of the boat; and what is remarkable, the two that were within the tilt sat on each hand of a woman who received no damage. One person had the sole of his shoe ripped from the leather, and no other damage. There was another boat that followed, and received no injury, the master of which affirmed he saw the fire light on the bowsprit; where, meeting with a small resistance, it flew into small streams, like a rocket: which was, no doubt, the cause of the mischief being done in so many parts of the vessel. "

In our researches amongst these records of mortality, we observed that we could not pass over scarcely an inch of ground, without trampling upon a grave. So thickly are the dead stowed together in this churchyard, that it is, surely, desirable to obtain a new burial-place for this extensive and populous parish; and there is a piece of glebe land, but a short distance from the spot, that is well adapted for the purpose.

In the register-book, is an entry of the burial of Grace Pett, April 12th, 1744. This name suggests some serious reflection: poor Woodward and his companions were killed by lightning from heaven, but Grace Pett was consumed by internal fire. It is our duty to relate what borders upon the marvellous, as well as

more natural events. The manner in which this woman came by her death, is detailed in the Philosophical Transactions, in two different narratives; one by Mr. R. Lowe, and the other by the Rev. Mr. Notcutt, and agree in all the main points of the fact; which are as follow:—

On the 10th of April, 1744, Grace Pett, about sixty years of age, the wife of a fisherman, at Ipswich, was burnt, in a supernatural or miraculous manner, to ashes. When her husband was at sea, one of her daughters used to sleep with her: the mother had a custom, for several years, of going down stairs, every night, when half undrest; and, on the night preceding the above day, she went down, as usual, and her daughter fell asleep. When she awoke in the morning, finding her mother was not come to bed, she ran down in a fright, and found her burnt to death, before the fire-place, reduced to ashes, lying about half on the hearth and half on the deal floor: the floor was not injured by the fire, nor were her feet and ankles burnt; neither did they appear to be hurt by the five. Her daughter said she had no other apparel on her, beside her eap, shift, a cotton gown, an upper petticoat, stockings, and shoes; which, certainly, could not be thought sufficient fuel to reduce a human body to ashes, in a natural way. —Mrs. Pett had a daughter who came home from Gibraltar, on the preceding-day. They had been making merry on the occasion, drank plentifully of gin, and sat up late; which accounts for her daughter's sleepiness.—On the coroner's inquest, it appeared that the woman, though she had drunk plentifully of gin, the preceding night, was not addicted to that practice; that she was found lying on the brick hearth, in the kitchen, where no fire had been; and that the candlestick which she had carried down stairs, stood on the table, with the candle burned out.—There are several other persons, in different countries, who have met with a similar fate, and whose cases may be found in the Philosophical Transactions.

The death of Grace Pett occasioned a great sensation in the county; and per-

sons came from distant parts, to view the ashes of the deceased: and, as we wish to be as veracious as we can, we shall relate what follows, as narrated to us, by an individual who beheld these cinerous remains of Grace Pett, and was well acquainted with all the reports in circulation at the time. It is well known, to the immortal honour of this county, that the hatred to the abominable crime of witchcraft continued stronger and longer, here, than in any other part of England. That being the case, it is not to be wondered at, that this poor old woman had the reputation of being a witch, by the majority of her sapient neighbours. There was a Mr. Garnham, who lived at a place called *Purdis's Farm,* about two miles from Ipswich, who had lost many of his sheep, by some disease that occasioned them to whirl round, and cut sundry strange capers, previous to their death; and it was, at length, suggested that they were, undoubtedly, bewitched. Mrs. Garnham, with that provident sagacity which distinguishes a good housewife, advised her husband to consult the "cunning man," a Mr. Winter; who was then in high repute, at Ipswich: which town has always been noted for some individual who could read the stars, and dive into the secrets of futurity; but, thanks to the *march of intellect,* we believe that there is not, now, a single conjuror in the place; for the last of this race, the celebrated William Abinger, died only,six years ago, and is buried under a handsome coffinshaped tomb, in St. Clement's churchyard. On consulting Dr. Winter, as he was called, he told Mr. Garnham to take one of his diseased sheep, and burn it alive; and that, during the burning of the animal, the suspected witch would come to the spot, and make bitter lamentations; that no one concerned in this transaction must utter a word, or the charm would be dissolved; but, that, if silence was preserved, the guilty person would be consumed, even as the sheep was burnt away. It seems that a large fire was kindled in the backhouse, and the poor beast destined to the flames, made such violent efforts to escape, that it was thought proper to heat the oven, for the better fulfilling their intentions; and when this was accomplished, its four feet were tied together, and it was unmercifully thrust into the fiery furnace; where it was consumed to ashes, except the feet; which hung out of the oven, and, consequently, were not burned. It was said, and, we dare say, firmly believed, that the infernal Grace Pett was seen, in the darkness of midnight, galloping over Bishops' Hill, to Purdis's Farm, wringing her hands, in the bitterest agony, and intreating for mercy, whilst the sheep was suffering in the oven; that then she returned home, laid herself down upon her own hearth, and was supernaturally consumed, except her feet and hands; which, like the sheep's trotters, were left whole and entire. It is, however, well authenticated, that no more than sixty-four years ago, this barbarous sacrifice of the sheep was made, on the night previous to Grace Pett's extraordinary demise; and we leave our readers to draw their own conclusions.

We are sorry to say, that fires of a more destructive nature have frequently occurred in this county. In the month of March, 1821, the stacks and outhouses of Mr. Nathaniel Byles, of the Hill House, in this parish, fell a sacrifice to the flames. So secretly was this infernal system arranged, that no clue was ever found, that could lead to the discovery of the incendiaries.

In this parish is situated the Race-ground; where His Majesty's purse of a hundred guineas, the town purse of £50, and a subscription-purse of £50, are, annually, run for, the first Tuesday in July, and two following days. The royal purse was, originally, given by Charles II. and, in former times, these races were attended by all the nobility and gentry in the county, as well as by others, from a great distance, to the essential benefit of the town. In the time of Sir T. C. Bunbury, bart.—who was many years member for the county—he made a point of bringing horses himself, and inducing his friends to do the same: and the members, both of the county and the borough, thought it was a compliment due to their constituents, to be present at Ip-

swich races, each one vieing with the other, in the splendour of his equipage; it being not uncommon to see four or five carriages and six on the course. The town was crowded with company, the gentry having their houses full of visitors, and the trades-people letting their lodgings to great advantage. Amusements were encouraged, and public places were well filled; a great deal of money was circulated, and all classes of the inhabitants looked forward to the Races as a jubilee.

St. Helen.—Nothing appears to be known of the building of this church. It is not mentioned in Doomsday. There are no inscriptions left, of so early a date as are to be met with in any other church in the town: the oldest is no further back than 1627: there was one found by Tillotson, with the date 1594; and yet this building, particularly the steeple, bears marks of greater antiquity than any church now standing in Ipswich. Perhaps this is no proof of its early erection, but, rather, otherwise; as it implies that it has not been built long enough to need repairs, for it certainly seems to be in the same state as when originally erected, of flint, strongly cemented, but roughly put together, and very little mixed with any other material. It was, formerly, impropriated to the hospital of St. James, or St. Mary Magdalene; which stood somewhere nearly opposite this church: but the first mention of it is made in the ninth year of Henry VIII. when the leprous-house of St. Mary Magdalene, and the revenues of it, were annexed to the rectory of St. Helen, of Caldwell; and, with them, probably, thos"e of St. James8 Hospital: for, besides the piece of glebe before mentioned, in St. Clement's, the rector of St. Helen was entitled to some portion of the tithes, from lands in the hamlet of Wykes Bishop; for which a composition was constantly paid, by the rector of St. Clement's, before the consolidation of the two churches.

In a field almost opposite to Caldwell Hall, now called Cold Hall, on the south of the road leading to Kesgrave, stood the church of St. John Baptist, in Caldwell: of which no vestige remains;

though human bones, and fragments of a building, are frequently dug up. It was impropriated to Trinity Priory, and granted, with that, to Sir Thomas Pope.

The church of St. Helen enjoyeth, at this day, a piece of land within the Chauntry lands, in Sproughton and Stoke.

s s

In Rosemary-lane, which is in this parish, though situated in Brook-street, was, formerly, a chapel, dedicated to St. Edmund a Poutney, and impropriated to St. Peter's Priory; but, being, then, like St. Helen's, in the patronage of the bishop of Norwich, they were both given to the same incumbent, till they were united. This St. Edmund was archbishop of Canterbury; and, being weary of the Pope's exactions in England, became a voluntary exile; and, according to Matthew Paris, died in 1240, with the reputation of a saint, at Pontiniac, in France: from which place the addition to his name was a corrupt deviation.

The rector of St. Helen's is entitled to a portion of corn tithes, from certain lands in Hoxne; one field of which is called Pountney Close; and these tithes, probably, belonged to the chapel before mentioned.

In the church, near the vestry door, is a large stone, thus inscribed:—

"Here lleth Robert Dencon, Patron of this Church, and three time Bailiff of this Town, who died Oct. 19, 1670, aged 16 years, and Elizabeth his wife, who died Feh. 2l, 1661, aged 73."

On the partition wall, facing the communion-table, is a white marble tablet, to the memory of Aaron Tozer, who died July 11th, 1804, aged 72, and his wife and daughter.

On the north wall of the chancel, on a tablet, is an elegant sarcophagus of variegated marble:—

"Sacred to the memory of Robt. Parish, ESQ. died Dec. 4, 1774, aged 65, and his two wives and daughter."

On a black stone, near the vestry, is a Latin inscription to S. Bantoft, M. A. who died August 21, 1692, aged 73.

On the north side of the altar, on a common stone, is a long Latin inscription, to John Wallace, M. D. who died

February 5th, 1702, aged 52. Also to Job Wallace, A.M. Feb. 5th, 1 763, aged 83.

Near the chancel door, on a black slab:—

"ROBERT Hingeston, A.M. Rector of Groat Bealinga and Wet Creeting, 23 years Muter of the Grammar School in this town: he died April 9, 1766, aged 67."

Also others to several of the Hingeston family—one with a Greek inscription. On the north wall:—

"To the memory of Richard Burton Philipson, Esq. Lieut. General of His Majesty's Forces, of the 3d Regt. of Guards, and oue of the Representatives in Parliament for the Borough of Eye. Died lsth Aug. 1792, aged 66."

On the outside of the church, a small stone tablet is inserted in the wall facing the south— "To the memory of Ledea, daughter of Rohert Richmond, 1627."

And, close by this, is a vaulted tomb to the memory of Devereux Edgar, esq. who died July 7th, 1769. He was much connected with the corporation.

Against the wall of the arch, on the south side:—

"Near this place are interred the remains of RICHARD Canning, M. A. many years minister of the Parish of St. Laurence, in this'towu, a man of unhlemished honour and integrity, and of taste and erudition superior to most of his contemporaries. But ever considering all human knowledge and learning of no other use or service than as they might tend to advance the interests and promote the influence of Religion and Virtue. His preaching was recommended hy his practice, and the doctrines he delivered enforced hy *his* own example. How well and how successfully he imitated his divine Master, the several Charities instituted in this Town, which his indefatigahle zeal and industry placed, at last, on the most solid foundation, will ahundantly testify. Born Sep. 30, 170S—died Jan. 8, 177.5. This monument was erected hy his only surviving daughter, Cordelia Canning; who was cut off in the 36th year of her age, to the inexpressihle grief of all who knew her."

In addition to other charitable bequests, he left, by his will, £10,000 in the funds, for the benefit of The Society for promoting Christian Knowledge. On the south wall:—

"To Richard Canning, Esq. an active and experienced Commander in the Royal Navy; who, having served his Country with unexampled courage and conduct, during the wars of King William and Queen Anne, retired to this town, A. D. 17 12. He died a private Captain, 1726, aged 57."

Also his wife and daughter, and the aforesaid Cordelia Canning.

In the time of Charles I. Richard Rainsford was the minister, who married the daughter of Robert Cataline, minister of Whitsundine, in Rutlandshire, a grave, reverend man. The widow of Mr. Rainsford was married to Mr. Bacon, of Ipswich. Thomas Cave, who married another daughter of Mr. Cataline, succeeded Mr. Rainsford. The patron of the church, at that time, was

Cotton, gent. whose parents' monument is in Badingham church.

There are no charitable bequests to this parish.

On the high grounds adjoining to Caldwell Hall, near where the old VVoodbridge road used to pass through St. Helen's-street, then called Great Wash-lane, are several never-failing springs, belonging to the corporation, from which a great part of the town is supplied with water. The various streams are collected into about a dozen different brick buildings, most of them arched over; from whence they are carried into two main pipes,——one running on the left-hand side of Car-street, and another on the right-hand side of the same street. From these mains, quills, or smaller pipes, are laid on, branching off in all directions; and the water is carried to the intermediate parts of the town. The springs at the water-head rise from hills whose elevation is nearly sixty feet above the level of Major's Corner, near the Admiral's Head; and water could be conducted into the upper apartments of most of the houses in those streets which are supplied from these works. It has been suggested that it would be

more desirable that the streams should be all collected in one large basin or reservoir; but we are of opinion that the advantage would not be adequate to the expense, and that the purity of the water—which is as clear as crystal —is better preserved by the present method. From the variety of the level, in different parts of the town, some of the more elevated streets are not so well supplied us others which are not so high. In consequence of the increasing number of houses erected, and erecting, in Ipswich, the inhabitants cannot all be constantly accommodated, unless every landlord was under the necessity— as is the case in London—of erecting a cistern with a ball cock, as a necessary appendage to each house; because, from the present system, numbers of persons suffer the water to run waste, and the consumption of some individuals is so unnecessarily great, that the springs, at certuin periods, are not sufficient for the expenditure; and as the water cannot be turned on to all parts of the town at the same time, some persons must be, occasionally, inconvenienced: which inconvenience would be obviated by a cistern, and the water could then be turned on according to the supply at the springheads.

If a person was appointed to collect the water-rate, who was not liable to be discharged, except for misconduct; and if a fair and equitable assessment was adjusted, and no partiality shewn in the collection, the water-rate would become one of the best sources of wealth to the corporation—the town would be adequately supplied, and no rational person would grudge the increased emolument. The water-rate has amounted to £800 per annum; but, if properly assessed and collected, would reach to a much larger sum. The expense of management, and repairing the pipes, is, necessarily, very considerable.

There is a spring in Dairy-lane, belonging to the corporation, which supplies the upper part of Brook-street, as far as the White Horse. St. Clement's and the hamlets are chiefly supplied from a spring near the White Elm, and from another in a meadow on the south-west side of Bishop's Hill; both of which are private property. St. Matthew's is supplied, principally, from a spring in the Barrack-yard; from Mr. R. Alexander's reservoir, in the Globe-lane; and from one in Mr. Milbourn's garden; as well as from one on the Christ Church grounds, belonging to the Rev. C. VV. Fonnereau, LL.B. Stoke, and part of St. Peter's, receive a supply from Mr. Smyth's reservoir, near Stoke Hall. Thus, there is no part of this town without plenty of water; and that of so fine a quality, as to excite the admiration of every'person who tastes it.

At no great distance from, but opposite to, St. Helen's church, is the County Gaol: the first stone of which was laid by P. B. Broke, esq. of Nacton, September 22nd, 1786. In digging the foundation, a great number of human bones were discovered; and, also, many sepulchral urns —several of them quite perfect. This prison is remarkable for being one of the first erected in the kingdom, upon the plan of the late benevolent John Howard. The boundary wall encloses about an acre and half of ground, and is twenty feet high. In front is the turnkey's lodge; upon the top of which executions take place. From the lodge, an avenue, ninety-eight feet long, leads to the keeper's house, in the centre of the building; from which the several court yards are completely inspected. The prison consists of four wings; to which are attached spacious airy courts, about seventy-five feet by forty-five, and three smaller, about forty-four feet square; in one of which is the engine-house. The chapel is up one pair of stairs, in the gaoler's house, and is surmounted by a turret top, with an alarum-bell. The prisoners, both debtors and felons, are kept separate, according to their respective classes and sexes. The gaoler has a salary of £200 per annum, with coals and candles for his own use. There is a chaplain, who is paid £50 a year; and a surgeon is allowed £60 for his attendance.— The tread-mill, invented by Mr. William Cubitt, who then resided in this town, was introduced into this prison in the year 1821.

The House of Correction, which is very near this spot, stands in an airy situation, and is surrounded by a wall seventeen feet high. It contains three court yards, each fifty feet by thirty; and has a chapel in the keeper's house. This structure has lately been purchased by the corporation, and converted into the town and borough gaol.

In Rope-lane, near this spot, on the 18th of August, 1792, the foundation of a building was laid, for the purpose of a Jewish synagogue; and which has been, ever since, appropriated to that purpose. It was built by the late Mr. John Gooding, and is now the property of a branch of his family: to whom a yearly rent of from eight to ten pounds is paid. It is a small structure, not calculated to hold more than a hundred persons, and is not kept in very excellent repair.— The Jews are not numerous in Ipswich, and do not increase either in wealth or numbers, few or none of them having been engaged in the higher walks of mercantile transactions; and we believe that there are not more than fifty persons of that persuasion in the town. In the early part of the French Revolution, the Jews were unjustly suspected of being favourable to republican opinions; and, on the 14th of September, 1793, a tablet was put up in this chapel, exhibiting, in the Hebrew language, a form of prayer for the king and royal family, evincing their attachment to their sovereign, and their anxiety to be considered as peaceable and loyal subjects of the realm. But so strong was the prejudice against them, that they were frequently insulted and maltreated in their progress to and from their place of worship; and they, at this time applied to the magistrates for constables to protect them from the illiberal and disgraceful behaviour of the rabble.

In December, 1808, two couples were married in Ipswich, accordin to the Jewish ceremonies, in the presence of almost all the Jews in the town and neighbourhood, and many other of the inhabitants. The following is the manner in which it was performed:— the priest first gives a blessing, over a glass of wine, and reads the marriage ceremony; the bridegroom then puts a ring on the bride's finger, saying, in Hebrew, " Behold, with this ring I consecrate thee, according to the rites of Moses and of Israel;" the reader then reads over the certificate, and pronounces some prayers and benedictions: the bride-groom and bride drink part of the wine; after which, the bridegroom throws the glass on the ground, and stamps it to pieces After the ceremony, there was an elegant dinner provided, and a ball in the evening.

In this year, 1808, died, in this town, Sarah Lyons, a Jewess, in possession of all her faculties, at the advanced age of a hundred and five years. She had also a son and daughter, who both lived to be upwards of ninety years old: and all of them resided in St. Peter's parish.

During the last war, a large range of temporary barracks was erected, on an elevated situation, on both sides of the Woodbridge road, which was formerly called Rushmere-lane, at about a mile from the town, calculated to hold between seven and eight thousand men. They were built at the expense of £200,000. They were pulled down since the peace, and the materials sold by auction, on the spot, for less than £10,000; leaving no traces of their ever having been there, except a number of miserable huts: which have brought a great many residents who have become burthensome to the different parishes in which these tenements happened to be situated: but we learn that these are soon likely to disappear, to make way for better habitations.

Nearly adjoining to these cottages is a piece of ground, walled in, which was, some years ago, consecrated as a burial-ground for the soldiers dying in the barracks. From its locality, it will prevent a continuity of the buildings upon that spot; as it has become church property, and cannot be appropriated but to the original purpose for which it was intended.

On the right-hand side of the road, near this spot, is the Catholic chapel, a small unpretending building; which was opened for public worship, on the 1st of August, 1827, by the Right Rev. Dr. Walsh, bishop of Cambysopolis; who, in two sermons he preached on that day, endeavoured to combat some objections that have been made against certain tenets of the Roman Catholic faith, in a tone of great mildness and conciliation. This chapel —which is neatly fitted up, and calculated to hold between two and three hundred persons—has been erected almost entirely at the expense of the Rev. L'Abbe Louis Pierre Simon; who first came to this town, in February, 1793: since which time, he has, with the exception of a few years, exercised the functions of a Catholic priest, at Ipswich, without receiving any emolument for his labors; and, during a residence of thirty years, he has, by his unimpeachable conduct and integrity, exhibited a character that does honour to his profession. There are no Catholic families of any note in this town or neighbourhood: but, during the last war, Mons. Simon's exertions were extremely laborious; for he had not only to attend to his duties here, but to officiate at Woodbridge, Harwich, and other neighbouring places. Previous to the erection of the chapel, worship was performed in his own house, adjoining; and when he first came to the town, the Catholic residents were obliged to assemble together T T secretly, as much odium existed against them at that period—which has, now, happily subsided.

The buildings about this spot have rapidly increased, and are increasing. A number of elegant little villas have sprung up, within a short period; most of them commanding us beautiful views as are to be met with in any of the delightful suburbs of this town. We cannot help noticing a considerable space of ground late a barren hill, which has been planted and laid out, with a great deal of taste, by Mr. John King; and we know of no spot more eligible for building a handsome residence, wherein to enjoy *otium cum dignitate,* from the fatigues of business.

St. Margaret. — This church was impropriated to the priory of the Holy Trinity. Trinity church stood near St. Margaret's church: part of the steeple, and a considerable portion of this structure, were standing, in 1674; and the building is noted, in Ogilvie's Map, as Trinity chapel: remains of which now form part of the north wall of the churchyard. It is mentioned, in Doomsday, as being endowed, in the Conqueror's time, with twenty-six acres of land. Before the year 1177, a priory of Austin Black Canons, consisting of a prior and six or seven canons, was founded, or chiefly endowed, by *Norman Gastrode fil. Eadnothi Ernoldus et Fulco*—who were canons here— and *Simo?i fil. Osborni.* Not long after the founding of this monastery, the church and the offices being destroyed by fire, they were rebuilt by John de Oxenford, bishop of Norwich, before 1200. To this monastery were impropriated the advowsons, medieties or portions of the churches of St. Lawrence, St. Mary at the Tower, St. Mary at the Elms, St. Saviour, St John Baptist, St. Margaret, Trinity, and St. Michael, in Ipswich; Tuddenhara, Morningthorpe, Bentley, Higham, Foxhall, Willisham, Preston, Mendham, Uushmere, and Lecham; a mill in Hagenford, a fold course, and pasturage for four hundred sheep; free warren in eleven or more parishes; one hundred and forty acres of marsh, in Moulton and Rendham; and manors, lands, and rents, in many other parishes: all which are named and confirmed by a grant of King John, in the fifth year of his reign, dated the 11th of January, 1204. Thus, amply was this priory endowed, and thus anxious were the inmates of these establishments to increase their worldly possessions.

In this Protestant country, our prejudices are strong against these Catholic associations; which, like all human institutions, were doubtless, subject to abuse: but they were, originally, the abodes of piety and benevolence, and the only asylums for the poor. In the age of ignorance, they were the storehouses and seminaries of learning, and the heads of these houses almost the only patrons of literature, science, and the arts: and it is much to be regretted, that the bigotry of the Reformers should have led them to destroy so many beautiful specimens of art—so many of those sublime and elegant religious edifices, which ambition or enthusiasm, perhaps, induced the founders to erect—but which cannot be viewed without delight; some of those that remain, being, still, the pride of Gothic architecture, and the boast of even this Protestant country; and with which, except St. Paul's cathedral, we have nothing to come in competition.

Norman Gastrode, the founder of Trinity priory, and Langeline, his wife, were buried in the conventual church. King Richard I. in 1193, gave the patronage of this church to Bishop Lyhart, and his successors. The grant of the fair, was, afterwards, confirmed by King John; who also gave to the priory, all the lands and rents formerly belonging to the churches of St. Michael and St. Saviour, in Ipswich. From this expression, it seems that both those churches were, even then, dilapidated. This became a rich and powerful establishment, and was in a very flourishing condition at the dissolution. The arms of the priory were curious, and exhibited an ingenious definition of the Trinity.

At the suppression, the twenty-sixth of Henry VIII. the possessions of Trinity priory were valued at £88: 6: 9 per annum; and, in the thirty-sixth year of the same reign, they were granted to Sir Thomas Pope. The foundation of the steeple of Trinity church was, about half a century ago, blown up with gunpowder.

St. Margaret is not mentioned in Doomsday; but, as the church of the Holy Trinity was appropriated to the use of the convent, it is probable that St. Margaret's church was erected for the parishioners. The principal porch has two handsome carved niches in front. It is ornamented, on the west side, by the head of a monk, from the mouth of which the water-spout descends; and on the east side, that of a nun answers the same purpose. From the journal of William Dowsing, the principal of the parliamentary visitors—who were called the " window breaking visitors," and who acted in Suffolk, in the year 1648—it appears that they took down from this church, the Twelve Apostles in stone, and ordered between twenty and thirty pictures to be taken down.

St. Margaret's church being one of the largest, as well as the most convenient in the town, is generally used for performing the rite of Confirmation: and in May, 1820, the venerable bishop of Norwich confirmed two thousand three hundred young persons under its roof. The interior of this church appears to have undergone but few alterations: the beautiful timber roof remains in its original state, except having been indifferently painted over, in various colours; but this must have been done many years, as a number of figures and coats of arms are now defaced, and nearly obliterated. It has three spacious aisles, and is a regular-built, handsome structure. There is an ancient curiously-carved font, and several good monuments; amongst which we notice the following:— In the chancel is a handsome altar tomb, with this inscription—

"RDMUNDUS WITHIPOL, Ao. Din. 1574, sihi et posteritati posuit inortui sine hoste. E. W."

Sir Edmund Withipol was high sheriff of Norfolk and Suffolk, in 1571, and was knighted in 1601. He died November 25th, 1619.

Under a marhle lies MICHAEL GoODlEX, Portman of Ipswich, and Joan his wife, ifi2i."

On the wall:—

'" THOMAS REDRISH, (a minuter) 1628."

He had been a great benefactor to the town. Also—

"NICHOLAS STANTON, that had heen 8 years preacher here. 1649."

In the church is a handsome monument to the memory of

"JOHN Lany, of Cratfleld, fn Suffolk, Gent. a Counsellor at Law, and Recorder of Ipswich. He had heen 48 years Justice of the Peace, in Suffolk. Mar)' his wife, daughter of John Poley, of Bradley, Esqr. and of Anne, eldest daughter of Lord Thomas Wentworth, Baeon of Nettlestead. He died aged 81—she and he hoth in 1633. John, his eldest son, Counsellor at Law, who succeeded in his place, and Benjamin, his youngest son, Doctor in Divinity, aud Master of Pemhroke Hall, in

Camhridge, Mb only surviving children, set up this monument to his memory."

This Dr. Benjamin Lany was a man of great learning and piety: before the Troubles came on, he was prebendary of Westminster, and chaplain to the king. In 1643, he was ejected out of his mastership, and stripped of all his preferment. After which be suffered many persecutions and calamities, till the restoration of Charles II. when he was restored to his mastership of Pembroke Hall, and soon after made dean of Rochester, and successively bishop of Peterborough, Lincoln, and Ely: where he died, in 1674. He printed some sermons, and a small treatise against Hobbes.

In the middle aisle:—

"Here resteth the hody of NICHOLAS PHiliPS, Mercht. one of the Portinen of this Town who in his fifth Bailiffwicke carried the mace hefore King Chas. II. He died July 24, 1763, aged 74."

Against the wall of the north aisle is a very neat tablet:

"Near this place lies interred with military honours, the hody of Edmund Say Eh Poulter, (eldest Son of the Rev. Edmund Poulter, Prehendary of Westminster, and a native of Clare in this count)) an Ensign in the first Regiment of Foot Guards. Daring his short hut eventful career, he served his King and Country zealously and gallantly, in Sicily, Spain, and Holland. On his return from this last service, whilst engaged in the honourahle, voluntary, and truly Christian duty of attendiug to the sick, he was seized with the fever, fatal to himself and to so many of his comrades. Of which he died in this town, tinmaturely, Oct. 3, 1«09, aged 22."

On the north side of the gallery:— This tahlet was erected at the expence of St. Margaret's Parish, in memory of Benjamin Palmer Green, an inhahitant thereof, who died 26th of March, 1814, and is interred in the Churchyard. He hequeathed the sum of £.W0 to the Minister and Churchwa/dens, upon trust, to lay out the same in the puhlic funds, and to expend the interest thereof in Bread, to he distrihuted, weekly, among the

Poor and Needy helonging to this Parish.

"Whatsoever a man soweth, that shall he reap.

"Sacred to the memory of Jemima Green, niece of the ahove Mr. Green, who died Feh. II, 1831, aged 27.

"Look upon ine, gracious Lord, with an eye of mercy."

On the south side of the gallery is a very elegant monument:—

"Near this place lie interred the remains of RlCHD. PHILIPS, ESQ. who died 29th Fehruary, 1716, aged 77."

On the north wall of the chancel:—

"In his family vault, east of this monument, is deposited I he remains of the REVD. Wm. FONNEREAU, of Christ Church, in this Parish. Enjoying a constant flow of cheerfulness and good humour, with a hody and mind actively engaged in manly and rational pursuits, aud never allowing himself to view the crosses and disappointments of life through a discouraging medium, he calmly passed the last awful snd trying scene, Feh. 28, 1817, in the 85th year of his age, in a full confidence of the mercies of Uod towards his frail and degenerate creatures.

"Ps. 37, v. 36. Keep innocency, and takc heed unto the thing that » right, for that shall hring a man peace at the last."

In the north aisle is a tablet—

"Sacred to the memory of JOSEPH POOLBY, ESQUIRE, one of the Bailiffs of this Borough; who, to a zealous and active discharge of the Duties of the Magistrate, united the unshaken integrity of the Man, and the unaffected Piety of the Christian. Universally esteemed and regretted, he departed this Life, during his Bailiwick, on the 17th of April, 1828, in the 69th year of his age.

"And of Mary his Wife, the Daughter of Benjamin Garway, Gent. who died Dec. 18th, 1825, aged 71 years."

In the north side of the churchyard is a vaulted tomb to the memory of Rear Admiral Thomas Hallum; who died 23rd of March, 1804, aged 82. He was a portman, and had been four times bailiff of Ipswich.

In the north side of the churchyard:—

"To the memory of JON. QuiNTIN,

Bailiff and For tin an. 7 June, 17S3, aged 74."

In 1621, Richard Martin left, by will, forty shillings to be laid out, yearly, in apparel for the poor of this parish.

In 1628, the Rev. Thomas Rederieh, elk. gave a house now in the occupation of the Rev. Thomas Mason, in Car or Cross-Key-street, in this parish, at the yearly rent of £24. One half of which sum belongs to Jesus College, Oxford; and the other half to be distributed to the reli gious poor of this parish.

Mr. James Caston, April 23rd, 1660, gave to the bailiffs, £100, for them to buy eight pounds a year, to be bestowed 2s. a week, to the poor in St. Margaret's, and two dozen of bread, weekly, to the prisoners in the town or county gaols.

In 1688, three pieces of arable and meadow land were left, by a deed of trust, for the benefit of the parish, and the repairs of the church. They are now in the occupation of Mr. Ablitt, at the yearly rent of £28; also two tenements and cottages, with a piece of land adjoining the workhouse.

Thomas Bunning, gent. gave £25, and Mrs. Sarah Phillips £15; with which land was purchased at Copdock, now let for £9 per annum, to be distributed in bread. Mr. Richard Phillips gave £50, with which a piece of land was purchased, called Hungerford Dale; and Mr. John Phillips gave £60, with which another piece of land was purchased, in the road leading to Westerfield, containing about five acres of meadow ground: they are now let for £22:10: 0, and £15: 15: 0; which sums are laid out in bread, and distributed to the poor. Leicester Martin, esq. gave £50, with which a cottage was bought, producing £5 per annum. Mr. Benjamin Green's legacy of £500, as mentioned on his monument, has been vested in government securities, in the name of four trustees.

On the scite of the ancient priory, adjoining to the churchyard, is a spacious brick mansion, called Christ Church; which was erected and surrounded with a pale, by Sir Edmund Withipol, knt. in 1549, as appears by the following inscription over the porch of the entrance:— *Frugalitatem sic servos ut dissipationem non incurras,* 1549. This family came, originally, from Italy.

Sir Edmund Withipol married Frances, the daughter of Sir William Cornwallis, knt. and had a ton, W'illiam; whose daughter was married to Leicester Devereux Viscount Hereford. She died without issue: when his lordship married a second wife, Priscilla, daughter of John Catchpole, of this county; by whom he had a daughter, Anne, who became sole heir to Christ Church. She married Leicester Martin, esq. by whom she had an only daughter, Elizabeth; who married, in 1720, the Hon. Price Devereux, the only son of the then Lord Viscount Hereford; and dying without issue, August 16th, 1735, she was interred at Sudbourne, in this county. After her death, Lord Hereford sold this estate to Claude Fonnereau, esq. an eminent London merchant, whose family came originally from France; and it has descended eventually to its present possessor, the Rev. Charles William Fonnereau, LL.B.

The entrance-hall to Christ Church is very fine: it is overlooked by a gallery on two sides; is adorned with a great number of family portraits; and is fitted up in the old baronial style: and over a niche in the wall opposite the entrance is the following inscription: "*Res mihi non me rebus submitiere conor,* 1548." There are several suites of elegant apartments, of large dimensions and good proportion; containing many excellent portraits; two of which are beautifully painted, and are charming pictures: the artist's name, and the date of their execution, are unknown; but they bear the following inscription, in old-fashioned letters:—

"Chas. Be Yvery, Earl of Yvery, in Normandy, 1418.

"Mary of Montmorency, Wife of the Earl of Yvery, 1418."

On the lawn before the house are two well-executed figures of gladiators, as large as life, cast in lead; and are said to have been brought from Italy, by an ancestor of the present proprietor; who, with a praise-worthy liberality, allows, on certain days, free access to this park; which, for its dimensions, is one of the most pleasinglydiversified spots that can be imagined. It commands a fine view of the river, the town, and adjacent country. It contains some of the largest beech and Spanish chesnut trees in the kingdom; and is stocked with some peculiarly handsome deer, of a white colour, spotted with black. We have given a representation of an old beech tree, of extraordinary age, height, extent, and dimensions —its trunk measuring eighteen feet in circumference, breast-high from the ground. It is covered with initials, cut in the bark, some of them dated considerably more u u than a century back. One large arm has been shivered off, as it is supposed, by lightning; but what remains is in a healthy and flourishing condition: and, whilst towers, convents, and churches have mouldered into ruin, this venerable ornament of the grove has stood the shock of ages; and may, probably, still flourish and increase, for ages yet to come. The wood-cut is from a design by Mr. John Smart, jun. and we have been favored with the following stanzas, from the pen of Mr. J. T. Shewell, of this town:— 8TANZAS ADDRESSED TO THE AGED BEECH TREE IN THE PARK OF

CHRIST CHURCH, IPSWICH.

"Muse! hang my harp upon yon aged Beech,"
Once sang the bard of Nature and of Truth;
And surely these may here combine to teach
Reflection's lesson, both to Age and Youth.

For thy smooth rind, inscbribed in olden time,
The record bears of many a mouldering hand;
And thy young days/ perchance thy earlier prime,
Saw other Sceptres rule this sea-girt land.

Thou wert—when Tyranny our rights assailed—
When raged the despot's or the people's ire—
When moral darkness over light prevailed,
Or Discord raged, or Superstition dire.

And still thou stand'st, these happier days to see,

When Knowledge, Virtue, pure Religion, smile;

And, " reared by Freedom, sacred Polity"

Upholds, adorns, and guards our favored isle.

Reasoning from prohahilities, we may conclude that thw Beech Tree cannot he much lew than three hundred years old. When meek Philanthropy steps forth " to pour

"The fresh instruction," o'er th' unlettered mind;

Or seeks, by Gospel truths, from shore to shore

Diffused, to exalt and humanize Mankind.

Long may thy venerable form survive,

Long wave thy branches o'er their sylvan throne,

And round thee many a generation thrive,

Yet wiser, happier, better, than our own.

The park is altogether an enchanting spot, and a dehghtful promenade for all classes of the inhabitants; but, like many enjoyments that cost us nothing, it is not nearly so much appreciated as it ought to be. There is still to be seen, in the park, a large bowling-green; which was, formerly, considered as a necessary appendage to a gentleman's mansion: and it is somewhere recorded, that when the celebrated Lord Rochester was on a visit at this house, the park-keeper was driving two donkies attached to a large roller, for the purpose of keeping the turf smooth and level; and, that their hoofs might not penetrate the soil, he had contrived to put boots upon their feet; which induced the facetious earl to observe, " that Ipswich was a town without people, that there was a river without water, and that asses wore boots."

King John granted the prior and convent of the Holy Trinity, a fair, to be held the 25th of September, to continue for three days; and it was afterwards confirmed by Henry II. It is held in an open space of ground, adjoining to the churchyard, called St. Margaret's

Green. It was formerly a great mart for butter and cheese; and the extensive building occupied as out-houses for Christ Church, is said to have been erected for store-houses for the articles, during the time of the fair. Even in our own day, we can remember that the cheese and butter fair was a place of great resort for the neighbouring farmers; but, owing to the improvement in the internal trade and commerce of the country, this fair, like many others, has declined, and dwindled to nothing.

We cannot quit this subject without noticing how time changes men's opinions. Of this much traduced production, Suffolk cheese, Grose observes that it is, by some, represented as only fit for making wheels for wheelbarrows; and a story is told, that a parcel of Suffolk cheese being packed up in an iron chest, and put on board a ship bound to the East Indies, the rats, allured by the smell, ate through the chest, but could not penetrate the cheese. Bloomfield thus unmercifully turns it into ridicule:—

It, like the oaken shelf whereon 'tis laid,

Mocks the weak effort of the bending blade;

Or in the hog-trough rests in perfect spite,

Too big to swallow, and too hard to bite.

Of the very same thing, old John Speed has the following observation, in his *Theatre of the Empire of Great Britan,* printed in the year 1627: "Suffolk cheeses are traded not only throughout England, but into Germany, France, and Spaine; and are highly commended by Pantaleon, the physician, both for colour and taste."

Adjoining to the garden of Christ Church, at the S.W. corner, is Dairy-lane Meeting-house, commonly called "Bethesda." It was first used as a place of worship by the Independents, in the year 1792; but is now occupied by a congregation of Particular Baptists, who seceded from Stoke Meeting, about May, 1829. It is a small building, capable of holding between three and four hundred persons.

About a mile and a half from the

park, on the road to Westerfield, we come to the Red House, a spacious and handsome brick mansion, the residence of Mileson Edgar, esq. who will long be remembered in all the county meetings of Suffolk, where he has often distinguished himself. This house has the old-fashioned but venerable appendage of a fine avenue of trees, and has a pleasing and imposing appearance. It was built by the great-grandfather of the present possessor, a hundred and twenty years ago: and it is strange that, in no account of Ipswich, is there any notice taken of the Red House. The Edgar family has been, for many years, connected with the town of Ipswich: many of them are buried in the church of St. Mary at the Tower: they were settled in the county at a very early date—long before the Conquest. The manor and great tithes of Glemham Magna, or North Glemham, were granted to William Edgar, in the thirty-seventh year of Henry VIII. 1545: and from this branch is the present Mileson Edgar, esq. descended.

Adjoining to St. Margaret's parish, is Westerfield. Westerfield church is in the hamlet of Wykes Ufford. The patronage of this church, and Whitton, are said, in old writings, to belong to the bishop of Ely, in right of a manor he then had in Bramford. The manor of Westerfield, in 1596, belonged to John Dameron; w ho gave it, by will, to his grandson, Anthony Collett, esq. whose descendant, Cornelius Collett, and his wife, are buried beneath a vaulted tomb in the churchyard: and Mr. Plestow, who married the above-named gentleman's daughter, became lord of the manor. The church is very small, plain and unornamented; containing nothing worthy of note but an ancient font, of an octagon form, and grotesque workmanship: there is a neat marble monument co mmemorative of a melancholy accident that occurred in the neighbourhood of Ipswich; and some others, to the memory of several rectors of the parish, as follow:—

"In memory of MAJOR WmTEFOORD, late of the ieth Regt. of Hub Mrs, eldest eon of Sir John Whitefoonl, end hrother to the Rector of this perish: he m horn isth Aug. 1798,and died 15th Dee. 182. 1, of an accidental shot received from his friend's gun, while out shooting. A fond affectionate hrother, a hrave soldier, (severely wounded at the hattle of Waterloo) and a truly pious christian. Unmindful of his hodily sufferings, while life was ehhing fast, his only anxious wish was to offer up his prayers to his Creator: hut, alas! it was too late— he survived the fatal hlow only two hours; when he resigned his spirit to his Redeemer, with a calm, firm, and serene mind."

Near the communion-table, on the north side, is a stone with a Latin inscription, to the memory of the Reverend Joseph Raymond, thirty years rector of this parish; who died, 1741, aged seventy-three years.

On the south side of the communion-table is a tablet—

"Sacred to the memory of the Rev. Peter Lathbury, late Rector □f this parish; who died 16th April, 1768, aged 48."

In the aisle, in the front of the pulpit, is a monument—

"To the memory of the Rev. J As. Hitch, 34 years the highly respected rector of this parish; who died 17th Feh. 182S, aged 62."

In the churchyard is a vaulted tomb to the memory of Francis Brook, gent. 1757, aged 79. There are several other tombs to different branches of this family.

Bridget Collett, by will, 23rd September, 1662, devised a cottage and four acres of land, in Claydon, to the churchwardens, at Westerfield, in trust, to employ the rents for teaching and keeping at school poor children born in the parish. The premises are let to Joseph Cooper, as yearly tenant, for £10 per annum.

The sum of £300, bequeathed by James Brooks, in the year 1755, was laid out in the purchase of £323, Old South Sea Annuities, in May, 1761. One half of the dividends, £9: 13:8a year, to be applied to purchase clothes and religious books for poor children belonging to the parish, and the other half for buying coals for the industrious poor of

Westerfield not receiving parochial relief; but the greater part is usually laid out in coals.

What we, perhaps erroneously, consider the baneful spirit of enclosure has extended itself to this pleasant and sequestered village; for, in our memory, Westerfield Green, consisting of several acres, was the annual scene of rural festivity. Cricket-matches—foot-ball— donkeyraces, and other rustic amusements, took place upon this spot; which was a favourite resort of the population of Ipswich and the surrounding villages, We remember witii delight, these manly sports and pastimes of Westerfield races, and regret that the labouring classes are so much deprived of the power of enjoying them; for we believe that these occasional relaxations from labor, rendered the poor man more contented with his lot, and the Common, or the Village Green, contributed to the maintenance of his family, which now, alas! he is compelled to seek from the parish. The Swan public-house is no more, and the Green is enclosed.

"No peasant had pin'd at his lot, Tho' new fences the lone heath enclose;
For, alas I the blest days are forgot,
When the poor had their sheep and their cows.
Still had labour been blest with content,
Still competence happy had been,
Nor indigence utter'd a plaint,
Had avarice spar'd but the Green!"

By a short walk across the fields, we avoid the town, and arrive at the parish of Whitton. The church is generally called Whitton Chapel, but, improperly, as it has been instituted as a parochial church, upon the presentation of the bishop of Ely, ever since the year 1299, and probably long before. There has been no steeple standing, for many years; and there is not a single monumental inscription within the church; and, amongst the few in the churchyard, only the two following calculated to excite any interest—one of which is remarkable from its being a quotation from Shakspeare:—

"Sacred to the memory of CHA8. Kekne, und ELIZABETH his wife.
The evil that men do, lives after them—

The good is oft interred with their hones.'"

"T» the memory of Thos. Kemble Harvey, who was unfortutunately drowned, Dec. 28, 1819. Aged I5.

"Here lies our dearest, only hoy.
No douht hut he is gone to joy.
He was our dutiful, only son.
When he was lost, our grief hegun." s

The family of Sir John de Wayland were inhabitants of this parish, so far back as 129&; Sir James Tuddenham, in 1400; and Sir Thomas Bedingfield, in 1539.

John Reynolds, by will, dated March, 1647, gave twenty marks for a town stock; the profit thereof to be for the use of the town of Whitton, as the church-wardens and overseers should think fit. The land purchased for this purpose, in 1678, is in the occupation of Mr. Thomas Cook, at the yearly rent of £3: but the parishioners considering the rent inadequate, Mr. Cook has, in addition thereto, been accustomed, for many years past, to give'sixpence a-piece to each of the poorest families in the parish—the number of which is, at present, about forty. But the parliamentary commissioners say that "it appears, however, to us, that the rent should be advanced to the amount of the full annual value."

St. Botolph Whitton, and Thurlston, are both mentioned in Doomsday; and if any of the churches now in being, in the liberties of Ipswich, were built so far back as the Conquerors time, which may well be questioned, this is, most likely, one of them. At about half a mile distant, are the ruins of Thurlston church, now used as a barn, attached to the farm occupied by Mr. John Orford Flindel I. The manor of Thurlston, with the impropriation and advowson of the vicarage, belonged to St. Peter's priory. The manor and impropriation were granted to Cardinal Wolsey, in the nineteenth year of Henry VIII. and in the nineteenth year of Queen Elizabeth, to Thomas Seckford, esq. and descended to the heirs of Edmund Hammond, esq. The church was in use since the year 1500; but the vicarage being united to the rectory of Whitton, Thurlston is seldom mentioned; and many of the inhabitants of Ipswich never heard of such a place.

Whitton is a neat cheerful village: in which there is a handsome residence, within the bounds of the borough of Ipswich, now occupied by Mrs. Kerridge, daughter of the late respectable John Kerridge, esq. who was one of the original founders of the Blue Bank, as it is called, in Tavern-street, and eight times bailiffs of Ipswich: he died March 9th, 1807, aged seventy-two years; and is buried in the adjoining parish of Akenham. In this parish also is an old mansion, commonly called *The Sparrow's Nest,* but, formerly, Whitton Hall; and it is now in the possession of Mr. Samuel Gross.

St. Mary at the Tower.—Very little is known about the erection of this church; nor do we know what part of it has been rebuilt, since its first foundation; for it was given by Norman, the son of Eadnoth, to Trinity Priory: and this was afterwards confirmed by King John. It is one of the churches mentioned in Doomsday; and the walls which support the arches of the nave are very strong and massive, and have stood uninjured for many centuries; but the exterior walls are unquestionably of a more modern construction. The Holy Trinity Priory, founded by the aforesaid *Norman Gastrode Jil. Eadnothi,* was one of the oldest religious establishments in Ipswich; and as this church was given, by its founder, to the priory, we may infer that there was an intimate connection between them: and in the middle aisle of the church of St Mary at the Tower, there is an unusually large stone which appears to have been covered with many inscriptions on brass, now taken off, or worn away; but there is still left upon it, a whole length male figure, with its hands uplifted in an attitude of devotion, and likewise the arms of the priory of the Holy Trinity, with the words upon it, in Gothic letter; both the arms and the figure are exceedingly well executed, and remain, at present, perfect and complete; and we are astonished that this representation of the Trinity should have escaped the hands

of the spoiler Dowsing, who says he took up six brass inscriptions here: there is no name or date left to denote the period of sepulture, or the person interred; but we are led to suppose that it must be the family vault of some person who had been intimately connected with Holy Trinity convent.

About 1325, the confraternity of Corpus Christi guild was instituted. This brotherhood went every year in procession from this church, on the feast of the Holy Sacrament. They made their procession in the following order: 1. White Friars, Carmelites — 2. Grey Friars, Minors—3. Black Friars, Preachers — 4. Clerks in surplices— 5. The Tabernacle containing the Host — 6. Secular Priests—7. Canons of the Holy Trinity—8. Canons of St. Peter's—9. Bailives of Ipswich—10. Portmen — 11. Aldermen of the Guild, &c. Ac. Their tabernacle in which the Host was carried, their money, &c. &c. were kept in the church of St. Mary at the Tower: and Kirby observes, that, probably, that hollow place in the north wall of the vestry, guarded by an exceeding strong door, then very lately taken away, might be made for this purpose:—this shews the solidity of the walls, even five hundred years ago. It was a rule of this society that all the parish priests of Ipswich, on the death of any one of the fraternity, should say mass for his soul: and hence the present custom of tolling the bell of every church iu the town, on the death of a portman, probably took its rise.

In the chancel of this church there is a curious pictorial monument, with an acrostic in black letter, to the memory of William Smart, portman of Ipswich; who died in the year 1600. In several compartments at the bottom of this singular picture, is painted a view of the town of Ipswich, in tolerable perspective, in which the tower of St. Mary at the Tower church is surmounted by a handsome spire. On the 18th of February, 1661, this spire, by a dreadful hurricane of wind, was blown into the body of the church,-and did great damage, carrying away great part of the roof, injuring many pews, and t aking off part of the sounding-board of the

pulpit: it was called in the account given, " that most famous spire or pinnacle of the Tower Church:" the iron-work of the fane penetrated three yards deep into the ground, and broke through some of the grave-stones, which were shattered to pieces.

Mr. William Edgar, registrar of the archdeaconry of Suffolk—who lies buried uhder a handsome black marble tomb, at the entrance of the church—by his will, dated 31st August, 1716, gave an estate at Bently, " to be sold, and the money arising thereby to go towards the erecting or setting up a spire on the church of St. Mary at the Tower, in Ipswich, in the same form that it was before it fell down, if it may be; hoping that the governors of Ipswich, and other gentlemen, will make an addition thereto, for completing the same: and I do make and appoint my worthy friends Leicester Martin, Devereux Edgar, Orlando Bridgman, esqrs. Doctor Dade, and Mr. Thomas Day, and the bailiffs of the said town for the time being, trustees in this behalf, (if they please) and beg of them to concern themselves herein, it being so good a work.'' It seems, from the wording of this will, that Mr. Edgar had seen this spire. The estate sold for about £200; which was far short of the sum required to build such a spire as Mr. Edgar intended: and in consequence of some misunderstanding, the money was thrown into Chancery; but we have been able to trace the following particulars respecting it. At a general parish or vestry meeting, held by public notice, on the 12th of June, 1744, it was agreed that an application be made to the High Court of Chancery, in order to obtain the decree of the said court, that the sum of £196: 15: 11, given by the will of Mr. William Edgar, towards erecting a spire on jhe church of St. Mary at the Tower, might be applied in and towards repairing the organ, &c. belonging to the said church: but nothing was decided during an interval of twenty years; when we see that, on the 12th of Dec. 1764, a decree of Chancery was obtained in favour of the parish; and on it being referred to the Master of the Rolls, he ordered that the decree should be confirmed on paying the costs of the defendants, the heirs of Jane Edgar and John Nunn; which costs, after being taxed, amounted to £117: 16:2: and on March, 6th, 1767, there is a receipt for the balance, or nearly so,—being for the sum of £78:8:3;—which balance was to be laid out in new pewing the church, and making a new altar-piece therein. Thus, after forty years delay, the greatest part of this donation was swallowed up in that unsatiable gulf the Court of Chancery, and the testators' wishes frustrated. This receipt is signed by

"Thos. Bishop, Minister.

"Benjn Chenery, Ch. warden." Mr. Lott Knight—who was attorney for the parish—not charging for his expenses.

There is a handsome lofty stone porch at the entrance to this church, ornamented with battlements. On the top of this, in the centre, fronting the south, an elegant new clock has lately been put up. Directly over the outer door of this porch, on a space about eight feet square, is a well painted sun-dial: on which are represented the twelve signs of the zodiac, in their proper colours; and at the left-hand corner, below, is painted the figure of Atlas, with the terrestrial globe on his shoulders: on the right, the figure of Science regarding the celestial globe: on the left corner, above, Time with his scythe and hourglass; and on the right corner, Death: with an inscription over the whole, " The greater Light to Rule the Day." The exterior of the church and steeple has lately undergone a thorough repair; and it would have been much more pleasing to the eye, had a uniformity in colouring the stone-work been preserved. The interior is in excellent repair; but we regret that some of the paintings on the roof have been obliterated and whitewashed: however, those on the ceiling of the chancel, representing cherubs sporting in the clouds, still remain, as specimens of the good tuste of the artist by whom they were executed. The altarpiece is very tastefully fitted up with carved mahogany, and a well executed Glory in the centre. The pulpit — which is of oak — is large, lofty, and elegant:

it is ascended by a stair-case, the balustrades of which are richly carved. In the centre of the middle aisle, nearly opposite the pulpit, is a spacious elevated pew, commodiously fitted up, for the use of the bailiffs, portmen, town clerk, &c.: over this pew is a lofty square canopy, supported by four twisted pillars, in the front of which, upon the top, are placed the King's Arms, elegantly carved in oak,—as is all the rest of the pew: it is called the Bailiffs Seat; and whenever they attend officially, the two maces of the corporation, usually borne before them, are supported, in a reclining position, upon each of the two front pillars. Directly in front, not so much elevated, is a long pew appropriated to the use of the common-council; and is called the Four-and-twenty's Seat.— The town lecturer—who has been appointed by the bailiffs, burgesses, and commonalty, ever since the second year of Queen Elizabeth—preaches here once every Sunday. This has always been considered as the corporation church; and the town lecturer preaches before them, whenever the body corporate attend upon any particular occasion: and at these times it is the custom to announce the entrance of their worships into the church, by a grand burst of harmony from the organ; which has an imposing effect. This organ is a large and elegant structure; the exterior beautifully carved in oak, and the front richly gilt and ornamented: it is one of the richesttoned instruments in the kingdom; and the present organist, Mr. R. W. Foster, is competent to do ample justice to the extraordinary power and softness which this instrument is remarkable for combining.

The parish is a perpe.tual curacy, in the patronage of the parishioners. The present incumbent, the venerable Rev. Thomas Cobbold, has been their highly-respected minister upwards of fifty years.

This church abounds with monuments and inscriptions: among which are the following. On the east wall of the chancel is a fair monument to the memory of Mr. Matthew Lawrence, public preacher of the town nine years

and nine months: he died March 19th, 1H53, aged fifty-three.

On the north wall, over the vestry door, is a tablet containing the names of the town preachers which preceded him, from the second year of Queen Elizabeth, to the time of Mr. Ward:—

"DR. COLSE, 2d Eliz.

— NORTON, I8

MR. PEMBERTON, 24

— WRIGHT, 27

DR. BURGESS, 84

.,.— REKVES, 44 .MR. ASKEW, 2 Jacoh.

— WARD, 3."

Under a marble lies Samuel Ward, B.D. preacher of this town,—the year of his death about 1640. On the stone which was laid in his lifetime, in the middle aisle, are the following words:— n1,,.flT::'7q Vp::'".'! i: /»" —i 'i

"Watch Ward, yet a little while, and he that hall come, will eoine."

He was a native of Haverhill, in this county: he was born in 1577; educated at Sidney College, Cambridge—of which he became a Fellow; and was chosen town preacher at Ipswich, in 1604. In a poem called " The Worthies of Haverhill," he is thus spoken of, by the ingenious author, Mr. John Webb:—

"Yet let not science view this spot with scorn,

For here the learn'd th accomplish'd Ward was born!

A zealous minister, a pious man;

An humble persecuted puritan;

Who the mild fascinating art possess'd,

To soften and subdue the harden'd breast. i

Though vain philosophy such worth despise,

Yet he who ' winneth souls' is truly wise."

He was, says Fuller, an excellent artist, linguist, divine, and preacher; had a sanctified fancy; dextrous in designing expressive pictures, representing much matter in a little model; and possessed the singular art of attracting peoples' affections, as if he had learned from the loadstone (into whose magnetic virtue he was an inquisitive researcher) to draw iron hearts. But, excellent as he was, he found some foes as well as friends; who complaining of him to the High Commission Court, brought him into considerable trouble. He was at length silenced by an order from the Star-chamber. His talents were held in high estimation, both by the inhabitants and the corporation: he wrote in the quaint sententious style peculiar to the puritans; entitling one of his sermons, " A Coal from the Altar, to kindle the Holy fire of Zeal:" and he occasionally ornamented his productions with an emblematical frontispiece, engraved; one of which is prefixed to his " Woe to Drunkardswherein he contrasts " The times of ould" with "Thus now," by exhibiting a book between a leg in armour and an arm holding a lance; beneath which is shewn a pair of dice between a leg decorated with bows of ribbon, and an arm holding a drinking-cup and a tobacco-pipe. Mr. Raw, of Ipswich, has an original portrait of him, well executed. He is represented with an open book in his right hand, ruff, peaked beard, and mustachios: on one side is a coast beacon lighted, and inscribed Watche Ward. Jbtatm *Svjr* 43, 1620. Under a marble lies

"Robert Sparbowe, Portinan, 1594. Aged 94."

On a plain stone is inscribed

"gulielmos Smart, intergcren pietatis justitiaque senator defunctus est 23d Sep. 1599.

On the wall above it, is the painting before noticed, with the following acrostic to his memory:—

W hat can a dead man feed and clothe and holy precepts give?
11 cannot he, tueh tell not me, 1 know he Mill doth live

L ive thou sweet soul in ample ret, example to the hest

L ike thine his ground must low he laid that high will huild his nest

I ft" none think now of thanke, if out of sight he out of inind

A lthough 'tis wrong yet light's thy losse that heavenly thank doth find

H ay never yet fair Ipswich fry he foully so unkind

Schools, Churches, Orphanarey rooms shall keep thee still in sight

Men, women, children, old and young shall wail thee day and night

A las then not for thee we cry, hut for ourselves alas

R uing the want of such a wight as all thine age did passe

T hus Tie poor man one did mmirn thus grass hewayled grase."

This painting had been originally placed in a recess in the wall, and had been, for many years, plastered over, and entirely obscured. It was lately discovered on doing some repairs in the church: when it was placed in its present situation, and has been judiciously repaired.

There is a Latin inscription to Mileson Edgar, esq. who died November 8th, 1713, aged thirty-seven years.

'" Augustine Parker and Margaret his wire, they hoth died
May, 1629."

"Christopher Alugate, a Portman, I631. "

"William Tyler, Gent, one of Ihe Portinen, and twice Bailiff of this town, he died 1643."

"Elizabeth, Wife of Major Moll. I6M. "

"JOHN WRIGHT, GENT. 1623. He gave 40. yearly to the parish towards a Sermon to he pleached every Lord's day in the tfternoon, at this Church."

"Leonard Caston, who died 16l, and gave great gifts for the henefit of the Poor."

"Joseph Cutlove, an years minuter of this Parish, died Oct. It, 1707."

In the chancel, and near it:—
"John Chapman, Esq. died Oct. Is.'j7. "'

"CAPTN. Wm. Neave, Portman, thrice Bailiff, died Dec. 26, 1703, aged 77. Sarah his wife died Oct. 3, 1683."

"Tlios. Edgar, Esq. Recorder of Ipswich, died Ap. 12, 1692, aged 90."

Also his wife and children, with several others of the Edgar family.

Against the north wall is a splendid marble monument, to the memory of John Robinson, gent, and Elizabeth his wife. A male and female figure are represented kneeling on each side of an altar on which is laid an open book, and beneath are two male and two female

figures, weeping, the two last holding a skull in their laps. The inscription is as follows:—

"In this chancel, waiting for a hlessed resurrection, rest the hones of John Robinson, Gent, late Portman of this town, who deceased May the 9th, 1666, aged 69, and of ELIZABETH his wife, w ho deceased Feh. 3, 1694, aged.56. Besides four dying infants, they had issue, Thomas, John, Mary, and Elizaheth.

Y Y

"Meinoruud. The said John gave £ *io* to the Lihrary of tin town, and a fair common farm to the parish. The a.ud Elizaheth, July 1680, paid to the Bailiffs, Burgeaaea, aud Commonalty, £ 100 in trust, for the yearly payment forever of 52a. to thia parish, and 52s. to the parish of St. Clement's, to he diathhuted 12d. of hread every Sunday to 12 peraonaeuch: and Septr. 3, 1683, aha paid £100 to the Bailiffa, Ac. towarda the yearly maintenance forever of two wor king hoya in the Hoapital of this town.

"Rev. 14, v. *5.* They reat from their lahours, and their works do follow them."

In the south aisle, on a stone, are three figures in brass, with a scroll issuing from their mouth, with *ora pro nobis,* &c. and at their feet is the following inscription, in black letter, all in perfect preservation:—

"In your charity pray for the aoul of ALICE, late the Wife of Thoa. Baldry, Mercht. she died in Aug. 1506." err. ere.

This Thomas Baldry had been three times representative for the borough.

In the north aisle, behind the bailiffs seat, is a stone with three elegant figures in brass, at the bottom of which, on a shield, is the following mark:— and in the left-hand corner is a shield with the Ipswich arms. Several other shields are defaced. This was the vault of Thomas Drayle, portman; who died 1500.

Near this is a stone inscribed to Miles Wallis, gent. portmau; who died May 2nd, 1678, aged seventy. Also his wife Deborah; who died 1679, aged seventytwo.

Near this is a circular tablet on the wall:—

"This monument was erected hy Win, Wollaston, Esclr. Representative of Ipswich, to the memory of Miles Wallis, Esqr. Portman, who died Jan. 4, 1776, aged 15."

Another to

"Sarah, relict of Miles Wallis, and late wife of Emeeson Cornwall, Esqr. died Feh. 7, 1819, aged 78.

In the middle aisle:—

"Henry Capon, Portman, Jan. 3o, mo, aged 79."

"ANNE the wife of John Capon, i5 Sep. 1688."

Against the south wall, on an elegant blaek-and-white tablet monument, is the following inscripton:—

"As a puhlic testimony of respect for exalted talents and unwearied exertions in the cause of henevolence and charity, this monument is erected hy the general concurrence of an extensive circle of friends, to the memory of ELIZABETH COBBOLD, the heloved wife of John Cohhold, Esq. of Holy Wells. She died Oct. I7, 1824, aged 59."

Who can read these lines without feeling the truth of this elegant tribute to departed excellence; and who that has known the object of their praise can turn aside without dropping a tear of regret to her memory! Great indeed was her loss to the town of Ipswich! Our limits will not allow us to enter into a detail of her biography; and which is rendered unnecessary by the sketch of her life appended to the splendid edition of her works, edited with so much taste and feeling by Miss Letitia Jermyn. She was born in Watling-street, London, in 1767; and was the daughter of Mr. Robt. Knipe, of Liverpool. She was married to William Clark, esq. in 1790; and was a widow in six months. She shortly after married J. Cobbold, esq. who was a widower, with fourteen children.

Knowing her aR we did, and deeply fooling her loss, we will attempt to do justice to her character in a few words. Her genius, talents, and acquirements, were of a superior and varied description. As a poet, she was graceful, playful, or pathetic; and an easy elegance pervaded all the productions of her pen. She was eminently skilled in music,

drawing, botany, mineralogy, and conchology; well versed in the sciences, history, and antiquities; and had also an extraordinary talent of cutting portraits, landscapes, &c. in paper, with facility and correctness. She was possessed also of another rare accomplishment for a female,—she was a powerful and persuasive orator: which has been frequently evinced in the addresses she delivered at the various charitable institutions over which she presided, or of which she was the instigator, or the life and soul in this town. She was the friend and patroness of artists of every description; the promoter of all respectable public amusements, and the leader in every fashionable assembly; a liberal contributor to public establishments and private charities, and, blessed with a fortune to keep pace with her liberality, she was never weary of well doing. She died beloved and lamented by her numerous family and friends, and universally regretted as a public loss to society. The inhabitants of Ipswich, of every sect and denomination, high and low, rich and poor, felt that they had lost their best friend, patroness, and benefactor.

December 30th, 1617, Mr. Leonard Caston, portman, left, by will, £100, for the use of the bailiffs, &c. They to put forth and improve the said £100 as a stock; and out of the benefit and profit thereof, to pay £6: 12: 6 to be laid out in bread for thirty poor persons of the town, to be distributed every Sunday, at St. Mary at the Tower church; also twenty shillings to the minister of the said parish, to preach a sermon annually, on the day of his burial. And for the payment of the said £100, he tied the house he lived in, commonly called the Archdeacon's House, and the residue of the £6:12:6 towards the repairs of the said church, provided " the inhabitants of the said house shall enjoy the herbage of the north part of the churchyard, as it is now severed, and the benefit of the roses and plants there now growing, or hereafter to be growing therein." 1643. Mr. William Tyler, portman, gave forty shillings per year to the minister of this parish: which is paid out of lands lying in Southolt, in the county of Suffolk.

1664. Mr. John Parker gave forty shillings per annum —to be paid out of the Swan inn, in this parish—to buy coals for the poor. 1690. Mr William Neave, portman, gave the sum of £5 per annum, to be paid out of his dwelling-place, situate in the Butter-market, to buy coals for the use of the poor. Also Mr. John Rednall left the house now used as a workhouse, with several other tenements, to the parish.

In Tavern street, in this parish, in the house where one of the present proprietors resides, the Suffolk Chronicle was first printed and published, on Saturday, April 4th, 1801, by Mr. G. R. Clarke: but after carrying it on for two or three years, with every prospect of eventual success, he was obliged to relinquish it, for want of funds to proceed. The materials were purchased by two or three individuals, with a view of its continuance; but difference of opinion arising as to its management, it was for a time laid aside; when the idea of again commencing it revived on Mr. King's coming to reside at Ipswich. A fresh agreement was entered into; and after many fluctuations and reverses, it has, by extraordinary exertion and perseverance, been brought to its present perfection; for its reputation is unquestionable, and its circulation firmly established. The original projector—like many other sapient speculators — sowed the seed for others to reap the benefit of the harvest.

The spirit of improvement in building seems to have entered this parish in the year 1786, when the late C. A. Crickitt, esq. built the row of houses in Tavern-street, called the Bank Buildings; and, in conjunction with his excellent colleagues, J. Kerridge and William Truelove, esqrs. commenced the Blue Bank, as it is commonly called. Mr. Crickitt having secured his seat in parliament, remained at the head of the firm, from its first establishment, to the time of his death, in 1802, after having been eighteen years member of parliament for Ipswich. Robert A. Crickitt, esq.—son of the before-mentioned gentleman— succeeded his father in his banking concerns at Ipswich, Colchester, and Chelmsford: but in consequence of the panic, in 1826, and the run upon country banks in general, the bank at Chelmsford gave way, to the universal regret of every person who had ever known, or transacted buisiness with, Mr. R. A. Crickitt; for his honour and integrity were equal to his urbanity, and persons of all parties spoke of his losses with sorrow, and of his conduct with respect. The Ipswich Blue Bank stood firm, and has since gained an additional accession of strength: it is now carried on in the names of Bacon, Cobbold, Rodwell, Duningham, and Co. — R. A. Crickitt, esq. was representative for the borough for thirteen years, in several different parliaments, as mentioned in a former part of this work.

In the year 1789, in taking down an old house adjoining to the Bank Buildings, the workmen found secreted under one of the floors, a relic of the Romish church: it consisted of four figures, curiously cut in alabaster; in the centre is represented the head of the Deity; immediately

N THE NEW YORK PUBLIC LIBRARY ASTOB, LENOX AND I TILDEN FOUNDATIONS. under, a half length of the Pope; and on the left, that of St. Peter. The whole was fastened in a plain wainscot box of about a foot square, and was in fine preservation.

Great improvements have taken place within these few years, in this parish, in consequence of an act passed in the fifty-fifth year of George III. dated May 2nd, 1815, for amending and enlarging two other acts passed in the. thirty-third and thirty-seventh years of the same reign, for paving, lighting, cleansing, and improving the town of Ipswich. Accordingly, it was determined to widen the then narrow part of Tavern-street reaching from the Great White Horse to Tower-lane; and upwards of £5000 was paid as indemnification to the owners and occupiers of the houses fronting the street in that direction. The fronts of all the old houses were pulled down, and the street widened and improved, according to the plan of Mr. B. B. Catt, Mr. William Brown, and Mr. John Doughty. Amongst the houses taken down, we must mention the Old Coffee House, situated at the corner of Tower-lane, as it was ornamented with several strange and uncouth figures; and as they are curious relics of our forefathers' taste three or four centuries ago, we have given a representation of them, from the pencil of the late Mr. G. Frost. The old White Horse was almost entirely pulled down, and the present handsome and commodious building ereeted in its stead.

The houses in which the Rev. Thomas Cobbold, M.A. and William Hammond, esq. now reside, were formerly connected by an arched gateway, and formed a tavern of considerable importance called the Queen's Head.

In a court leading from Tavern-street into the churchyard of St. Mary at the Tower, called Hatton-court, formerly resided Sir Christopher Hatton; who *danced* himself into the good graces of Queen Elizabeth, and, in process of time, became Lord High Chancellor of England.

Adjoining the Great White Horse, in North gate-street, is an elegant suite of apartments called the New Assembly Rooms; comprising a supper and ball-room, card-rooms, news-room, &c. with all the requisite offices. They were built under the direction of Mr. George Mason. The front is handsome; and in the erecting and fitting up the premises, much taste has been displayed. They were undertaken by subscription, of shares of £50 each, in the year 1809; but owing to some unfortunate misunderstanding among the subscribers, the funds were not sufficient to defray the expenses incurred. There are six monthly balls during the winter: the subscription for the season is two guineas for gentlemen, and one guinea and a half for ladies, and there are about one hundred subscribers.

We have given a representation of a curious carving in wood, forming a corner of the Royal Oak inn, from a design by the late Mr. Frost. It exhibits the figure of a blacksmith working at an anvil.

In Upper Brook-street, in this parish, is the house formerly inhabited by the archdeacon of Suffolk, and sometimes called the Archdeacon's Place or Palace. The original edifice—of which the outer wall and gate now standing, seemed to have formed a part—was erected in 1471, by William Pykenham, then archdeacon of Suffolk. The lofty and spacious gate-way is in good repair, forming a more stately entrance than the gate to Wolsey's College; is one of the oldest brick buildings in the town, and the following sketch is a faithful representation of it, before it was so injudiciously disfigured by plaster and white-wash. The premises are now occupied by Dr. Beck.

The Tower Ditches, as well as the continuation of them called St, Margaret's Ditches, shew evident tokens that the *fosse* connected with the ancient ramparts, ran along the north side of the town in that direction.

SPROl GHTON.

According to our original plan, we are bound to give some account of the parishes immediately adjoining to the town; but we are so circumscribed in our limits, that we are compelled to be brief in the detail. We shall begin with Sproughton: part of which is within the liberties of the borough. The manor, the hall-house, the advowson of the rectory, &c. formerly was part of the Felton estate; which came into the possession of the Marquis of Bristol,— in whom it is now vested.

There is a fine seat in this parish, called the Chauntry, from its being erected on the land given by Mr. Edmund Daundy, portman of Ipswich, in the year 1514, for endowing a chauntry in the church of St. Lawrence. It is said by Kirby, that " the present house was built by the late Edward Ventris, esq. master of the Court of K. Bench but we suppose that he meant Peyton Ventris, esq. who was member for Ipswich, in 1688, when he was made a judge. It was purchased by Sir John Barker, bart. who enlarged the house; and it afterwards came into the possession of Metcalfe Russel, esq.; from whom it descended to Michael Collinson, esq. father of the present possessor, C. S. Collinson, esq. It is pleasantly situated on an eminence, and commands a fine view of the country surrounding.

There was formerly a seat, built by the late Sir Robert Harland, bart. which has lately been pulled down.

J. Josselyn, esq. has, here, a neat residence for a country gentleman.

This village is situated in the hundred of Samford, about two miles from Ipswich, and contains about four hundred inhabitants. The present venerable incumbent, the Rev. George Rogers—who is in his eighty-ninth year —has been rector here forty-five years. There is nothing z z remarkable in the church: the pillars that support the roof, have a light and airy appearance; and we notice the following inscriptions.

In the chancel is a curious old painted monument:— "Elizabeth Bull, wife of Anthony Bull, Reor. daughter of Thoa. Loinh, late of Trimley, E«Ir. Born 19th Feb. 1558: died Nov. i, 1636.

"In her alive «-w aeen what God requires of thee

To hiin in heart devout to men respectful he

To Poor he free in these a con«tant gmde was ahe

In her dead hehold what to thee must hefall

Who now does live in health has goods and friends withal!

The hody to corruption thy heauty perish ah«l l

And yet in her now dead behold there's comfort found

She rests in hopes expecting when the tnimp hall cound

To raise her corpec hy Chriat with glory to he crown "d."

Near the door in the north aisle, on a black marble slab:—

"In memory of PRrtiENCE Rowning (who waa compounded all of lovelinesa) the aweet and gloriotia wife of Henry Rowning of Brainford, Gent. (now with tfud) of aweet aorrowful memory. Who waa the youngeat daughter of Mr. Firmin of Woodhridge, Hercht. and Elizaheth his wife. Born 25th Jan. 1679, taken hence the 3 lst July, iro7. NonTua. Nec Mea. Sed Te.

As you enter the church by.the chancel door, is the following quaint inscription, on a small black stone:—

Maria J C -I 1 1681 et I P"''" An.

Doin. f George) Beeaton,.t«t. (,

Opposite the vestry door is a singular monument, the centre of which is black marble; upon which is traced, in white, a triple cross, with a waning moon,— the whole encircled by a cloud beneath: it is inscribed—

"Behold I come.
Rev. 16. 1.1."
then again is drawn an hour-glass with two wings expanded, resting on a Death's head:

"I. Waite."

Just below this is a stone inscribed as follows:

"JOSEPH Waite, M.A. after 15 years of conscientioiia and eminently faithful discharge of the miniatry in this place, departed this life June V9, and wa" here interred July I, 1670."

In the chancel there is a large and handsome white marble urn, on which are depicted the arms of Russel— the same as borne by the duke of Bedford— and beneath, on a tablet of the same material, is the following inscription:—
Metcalfe Russel of the Chauntry, Baur. Died the 14th day of Feh. 1785.
Aged 49 yeara.

If to have friends Constitute a good man

And to deserve no enemies Such was He

If Religion and henevolence Whoae remaina

Cha«tity of manners Now rest in the

Kindness to every dependent Vault heneath

With honour wholly unsullied This monument a a faithful memorial and a grateful

Trihute erected hy

Michael Collin Son, Er.

His natural and selected heir

Who loved him when living, and

Desires to sleep with nun in death.

In vain hlest shade with sighs and tears we turn

With deep regret to thy lamented urn,

In Tain inscrihe upon the vaulted stone,

In vain recite the virtues once thy own.

Thine is the glory far heyond the lays

Of grateful friendship or of human praise."

On a white marble monument, very

near the last:— ' This monument is erected

By Charles Streynsham Collin&on, E«Ir.

To the memory of his father,

Michael Collinson, EsIr.

late of the Chantry in this Parish, and also of Hendon in the County of Middlesex.

Who died the 21st Aug. 1795, Agrd r,r years,"

He was distinguished for his knowledge of natural history, and for the attention he gave to botanical subjects particularly: from his general well-informed mind and polished manners, his company was much esteemed by persons of the first eminence; and he endeared himself to his intimate connexions, by his benevolence and liberality. The enjoyment of the latter part of his life was greatly interrupted by a series of painful disorders; which he sustained with much exemplary resolution unci fortitude. Very near this spot is a stone

"To the memory of EdUMHt Bekston, M.A. rector of this church 1713. Alo hi M if mid wveral of hi children/'

Near the communion-table, on a black marble slab:—

Hie jacet Iunqiiid mortale eat ELIZARETH.fi l 'xoru rh«risiiiMP ei minquain atie dellendir Reverendi Viri GED-KGii Rogers, A. M. hujuwiue Kccleue Rectoria iaw ex hac vita migrant VIII. Id menis Martii Anno Christi M.D.CCC. XXVm. et iettie w LXXXIV. In memoha tain Cari Capitis hor poeuit marmor moTcne et nrhatus inariua.

The yearly sum of £1:6: 0 is paid as a rent.charge on a field in Whitton, belonging to Mrs. Hitch, for furnishing bread which is distributed monthly, at the church, among poor widows.

A double cottage in Sproughton is occupied, rent-free, by two poor widows, placed therein by the churchwardens, and is kept in repair at the expense of the parish. The cottage appears to have been settled for this purpose, by Elizabeth Bull, in 1618.

BRAMFORD.

Adjoining to Sproughton is Bramford; which is often mentioned in ancient records. The church was given to Battel

Abbey, by William Kufus; and that abbey retained the rectory and the patronage of the vicarage, until the thirty-third year of Henry VIII.; when it was granted to Christ Church, Canterbury, in exchange. In the twentysecond year of Edward I. it was the lordship and demesne of Robert do Tiptoth.

The family of Acton have long had their seat here, called Bramford Hall; which was, we believe, originally built by John Acton, esq. who was high sheriff for the county in the year 1631. William Acton, the father of this gentleman—who was a clothier at Ipswich, and who died in 1616—had three sons, for each of whom he purchased an estate, and the Bramford property was selected for John, who probably built the house. The present handsome mansion was, however, erected on the scite of the former building, by Nathaniel Acton, esq. in the year 1753. The manor has a peculiar tenure belonging to it, as the tenants hold their lease for twenty-one years, renewable from time to time, upon payment of a fine; and upon the death of a tenant, or an alienation, the new tenant is admitted to the remainder of the term unexpired.

There was another manor in Bramford, belonging to the bishop of Ely, as late as the year 1547; which was in the hands of Francis Colborne, in 1503.

Dowsing's Journal has the following notice: "Across to be taken off the steeple, we brake down eight hundred and forty-one superstitious pictures, gave orders to level the steps, and gave a fortnight's time: three inscriptions with *ora pro nobis.*" It must not be understood by the word *pictures,* that there were such an extraordinary number as eight hundred and forty-one paintings, but so many carved figures or images that were obnoxious to the feelings of these merciless marauders. On the battlements, on the top of the porch, and on the north side of the church, there are still left a number of rudely-carved figures of angels, sphinxes, griffins, and other uncouth objects; which we are astonished should have been allowed to remain. The church is large and handsome, with a steeple and lofty spire of

excellent workmanship: it has a good peal of six bells: the chancel is divided from the nave by a screen which is not inelegant; but the inside of the church by no means keep pace with the appearance of the exterior. We notice the following inscriptions:—

On the north side of the church, on a marble monument which has no appearance of antiquity, the inscription—which was to the memory of William Alston, barrister— has been nearly obliterated.

On a singularly-carved and painted monument is the following:—

"VITA.

PROCfcL L08A
In Adaino In Christu
inanto rare fataJU
morente natalia glorur
Kx una petpetuum ver
Quo Dens ne mora qudein ronjunxit
Beperit."
Beneath this monument, in the aisle, is a stone to the memory of the above-mentioned Thomas Dade; who died July 20th, 1688, aged seventy-four years.

In the middle aisle is a stone to the memory of Joseph Alston, esq. who died December 21st, 1643.

"Raphael Copinger, Gent. 1658."

"Here lieth the hody of TIIOS. 81CK-LEMORE, E«. one of the Portmen of Ipewich, was horne in An. 1540 and died the 2oihof Sep. 1619."

William Acton, by will, dated January 19th, 1703, gave to the poor of the parish of Bramford, £200, to be laid out in land, for the purpose of furnishing to such poor of the said parish as should most want the same, meat, bread, or other necessaries, as the overseers should think fit. Property was purchased.with this money, at Stowupland, consisting of a cottage and about fourteen acres of land; which are let to John Cobbold, at the annual rent of £20.

The sum of £5 a year, given by the will of Francis Brooke, for the poor, is charged on a field belonging *o* the Rev. Charles Brooke, of Ufiord, and is paid by the occupier.

Three tenements, under one roof, in Bramford, are occupied by poor widows, generally six in number, who are

placed therein by the parishioners; and the building is kept in repair at the expense of the parish.

This is an extensive parish, containing upwards of eight hundred inhabitants, and is situated in the hundred of Bosmere and Cfaydon. It is a vicarage—patrons, the dean and chapter of Canterbury—the present incumbent, the Rev. G. Naylor.

In June, 1809, a fire broke out in a cottage opposite the Angel inn, in this parish; by which ten or twelve houses were destroyed, and one poor woman of the name of Lee perished in the flames.

The following is a copy of an original letter, now extant, relative to the meetings of Quakers, in this parish, at the time of their persecution:—

"Suff. Whereas I am informed that a great number of persons called Quakers, are unlawfully assembled together at Bramford, to the great of his Majestie's subjects. These are in his Majestie's name to authorize you to disperse the *a* asscmblie and to attach such pvsons as you shall flnde to be heads or Ringleaders of the same. And such persons to carry before some Justice of the peace for this county to be dealt withall according to law. And hereof faile not. Given under my hand & seale the xith of March 1663.

"A. Jenney.

"To

Gilbert Lindfleld
& Mr. Robt. Clarke, or either of them." RUSHMKRl.

Rushmere is mentioned at a very early period, as a place where Ulfketel withstood the Danes, in 1010; and on the Heath, between this place and Nacton, are many hills which are said to have been the burial-places of the slain. Several of these mounds—which are some of them eighteen or twenty feet high—have been opened, and at the depth of two or' three feet, several layers of charcoal were discovered, spread over the different strata of earth; which confirms the supposition that these were the spots where the bodies of the dead were burned: no human bones have been found, but, in one of them, the entire skeleton of a horse was dug up.

In the time of King John, this was the lordship of William de Freney; who paid fines to Ipswich for himself and his villains in Rushmere and Brisete.

The church was impropriated to the prior and convent of Christ Church, Ipswich; and the impropriation and advowson of the vicarage were granted, in the thirtyseventh year of Henry VIII. to Austin Austins, M.D. and they were sold again by Dr. Austins, to Sir John Jeremy, knt. and Humphry Warren, gent. The following particulars are specified in the deed: "The parsonage barn, and the barn-yard, the little piece opposite to it, containing about three roods; also two pigl.tles, containing nine acres, lying in the parish of St. John Baptist, in Caldwell; and all other houses, &c. late in the occupation of Thomas Lord Went worth, and parcel of the possession of the said late priory:" but the right of patronage of the vicarage is not specified as sold with the rectory; which came into the possession of the Feltons, and through them is now vested in the Marquis of Bristol.

In the year 1521, Catharine Cadye, widow, left a considerable sum towards building a new steeple similar to that at Tuddenham; and the two steeples only differ in the form of the battlements.

"*Ex Testamento Katherince Cadye.* 29 *Mar.* 1521.—If the parishioners of Rushmere be disposed to make new their steeple in like fashion, bigness and workmanship as is the steeple of Tuddenham, *then I wUl* that my Executors in discharging fulfilling and perform, ing it, my husband William Cadye will bear all the cost of the masons' wages so that the said parishioners find stuff", meat, and drink for the said Masons. *Then I will* that Robert Cook of Rushmere that married my daughter Agnes pay or cause to be paid to my executors all such moneys as I lent him, and all that money that he owes me for Farm of all the houses and lands that he had of mine in farm and for farm of the houses and lands where he dwells. The reparations and rents issuing thence being allowed, the residue to be disposed towards making the said steeple."

"Test. Robt. Cook, 1523. I give to the building the steeple at Rushmere, Ten Pounds."

"Test. Wm. Byrde, 1538. To the Church of Rushmere and to the building the steeple I give Twenty Shillings."

In Dowsing's Journal it is said, "Jan. 27. We brake down the Pic. of the 7 deadly sins, the Holy Lamb with a cross about it, and 15 other superst. Pictures. Ap. 8. We brake down 9 superst. Pictures and gave orders to level the steps in 20 days, to make their windows, and we brake down a pot for holy water."

In the church are the following monuments:—

"Sacred to the memory of the REV. John EDGE, A. B. 33 yean Vicar of this Pariah, who died Oct. 16,1815, in the 59th year of hi age."

"S. M. of PETER Edge, A.M. a Prehend of the Epiecopal Church of Raffoe, and Rector of Drinholm in the Kingdom of Ireland. He lived respected and lamented died, on the 29th Decemher, 1782, in the 39th year of his age.

"S. M. of Mrs. Anm Edge, relict of the late Rev. P. Edge, who died on the 10th of August, 1793, in the 72nd year of her age."

"This humhle trihute of conjugal aud lilil affection is erected to the memory of the REV. PETER EDGE, LL.B. who died on the 26lh of August, 1 805, most universally respected, aged 56." AAA

"S. M. of MB. Wili.m. Tbuelovb, gent. a memher of the Common Council of the Borough of Ipswich. The office of a chief magistrate was couducted hy him with that vigilance and impaetiality, ae jus4ly procured him the general esteem of the pahlick. He died much lamented hy hie fdends and the pohlicfc, on the 25th August, 1798, aged 71."

As previously noticed, Mr. Truelove was buried in St. Lawrence' church, Ipswich: he was four times bailiff.

Rushmere is a vicarage—the present incumbent, the Rev. Charles Day, LL.B. —patron, the Marquis of Bristol. It is a small parish, with about five hundred inhabitants, and contains about twelve hundred acres of laud, chiefly belonging to the marquis. Every resident inhabi-

tant of the parish has the right of commonage on Rushmere Heath; and we wish it could be turned more to the advantage of the industrious cottager.

At a short distance from the church is a handsome and modern villa, called the Roundwood: which was built in 1700, and was purchased by Horatio Lord Viscount Nelson, in 1798, and was inhabited by Lady Nelson and his lordship's venerable father, the Rev. Mr. Nelson, from that time to 1800; when it was sold by his lordship, with fixtures and furniture, for £3300, to Mr. Robert Fuller, and it is now in the possession and occupation of W. F. Schreiber, esq.

Rushmere Heath was, for many years, the exercisingground for the troops in garrison at Ipswich and Woodbridge, during the last war: and, on several occasions, the present king and his royal brothers have been present at reviews which have taken place here, as mentioned in a former part of this work. On the 23rd of February, 18)9, a meeting was held at the Falcon inn, Rushmere, for the purpose of distributing the money received by the parish, for the rent paid by Government, for the use of the Heath as an exercising-ground for the garrison lately stationed in the neighbourhood. The sum amounted to £700, and was distributed amongst about seventy persons.

At about two miles' distance from Ipswich, a few yards on the right-hand side of the turnpike road, a gallows for the execution of criminals was erected; and those persons who were convicted of crimes, in the eastern district of the county, and condemned to death, were executed here, previous to 1786;' since which period these executions take place in the front of the county gaol. From the long catalogue of crimes committed by those who have suffered at Rushmere, we select the two following instances as the most remarkable. March 24th, 1763, at the assizes at Bury, Margaret Bedingneld, widow, and R. Ringe, husbandman, were found guilty of the murder of John Bedingneld, late of Sternfield: the woman was sentenced to be burnt, and the man to be hanged; and on the 8th of April, she was strangled and burnt, and he hanged, at Rushmere; and this woman was the last malefactor whose body has been burnt according to the sentence. April 21st, 1787, Richard Kedgson was hanged at Rushmere; when he made the extraordinary confession that he had enlisted forty-nine times, into different regiments in England, Scotland, and Ireland, and had obtained three hundred and ninety-seven guineas, as bounty-money, thereby.

We just pass the boundaries of this parish to notice a fine old building called Playford Hall; which was built in the sixteenth century, by Sir George Felbrig; from whom it came to the Feltons; and by the marriage of Elizabeth, daughter and sole heiress of Sir Thomas Felton, with John Earl of Bristol, in 1695, it came in succession to *lb '6* present Marquis of Bristol, together with the estate, consisting of nearly the whole of the parish of Playford, and the advowson of the living,—which is held in conjunction with Rushmere, by the Rev. Charles Day, LL.B. It is now become remarkable as the residence of Thomas Clarkson, esq.

A A A 2 THE ORWELL.

ONE of the pleasantest excursions a stranger can enjoy, is a voyage to Harwich, by the wherry or passage-boat which leaves the Quay, daily, so as to take advantage of the turn of the tide. Each individual pays one shilling for his conveyance; or a party may hire the wherry entirely for their own use, at a moderate expense. From the lack of wind, the passage may sometimes be tedious; but, generally there is plenty of time to dine and spend several hours at Harwich, or to go out some way to sea, and return home agreeably in the evening.

The Orwell is bordered the whole way, on both sides, by gently-rising hills, enriched with gentlemen's seats, villages, churches, woods, and parks stocked with deer, and abounding with all kinds of game; and lawns and lovely cultivated spots reach down to the water's edge, embracing every thing that can delightfully diversify a landscape: the stream being completely land-locked, has the appearance of a lake, and is, for its extent, one of the most beautiful salt rivers in the world. It is mentioned by Chaucer, in the prologue to his *Merchant's Tale,* and by Drayton, in his *Poly Olbion*; and has been the theme of many a modern poet's muse. We shall, therefore, enrich our pages with occasional poetical extracts, for the purpose of illustration, as well as to exhibit examples of the genius and talents of the poets connected with the town of Ipswich. The merit of the following sonnet, from the pen of the, author of *A Tribute to the Memory of William Cowper,* is sufficient apology for its insertion:—

Orwell, delightful stream, whose waters flow,

Fring'd with luxuriant beauty, to the main!

Amid thy woodlands taught, the Muse would fain

On thee her grateful eulogy bestow.

Smooth and majestic though thy current glide,

And bustling commerce plough thy liquid plain;

Tho' grac'd with loveliness thy verdant side,

While all around enchantment seems to reign:

These glories still, with filial love I taste,

And feel their praise;—yet thou hast one beside,

To me more sweet; for on thy banks reside

Friendship and truth combin'd; whose union chaste

Has sooth'd my soul;—and these shall bloom sublime,

When fade the fleeting charms of nature and of time.

We will first shew how the navigation has been improved, and cleared of many obstructions; and then, by beginning with the left side, where we embark, describe whatever may strike our attention as we glide along the bosom of the stream. In the year 1805, an act was obtained, " for improving and rendering more commodious the port of Ipswich;" and commissioners were appointed to carry it into effect, consisting of the bailiffs and the other members of the corporation for the time being, and Sir Robert Harland, bart. and his heirs, and Sir Philip Bowes Vere Broke, bart. and his heirs, with sixty-four other gentlemen, merchants, and tradesmen, particularly named; with power to raise and collect duties, to be employed towards the improvement of the river; £1500 to be laid out yearly, for that purpose, and the residue of the duties raised, to be vested in the funds, in the name of four commissioners, until £25.000, three per cent. consols shall be purchased, and shall remain funded for ever, and the dividends thereof to be applied to the purposes of the act. Much has been done towards widening and deepening the channel, by excavating and taking away many thousand tons of soil from the bed of the river; and the navigation is rendered much more commodious, and is annually improving, to the great benefit of the port. The money already vested in the funds by the commissioners, amounts nearly to the sum specified in the act, and the whole of the duties will be taken off in September, 1831, leaving the interest of the £25.000 for the annual improvement of the river.

We first pass the shipyard formerly in the possession of Mr. Barnard, whose descendants are now proprietors of the extensive establishment at Deptford known by the name of Barnard's Yard. It is now in the occupation of Mr. William Bayley.

The next object that strikes the eye, is a lofty pyramid of brick, one hundred and twenty-five feet high, rising from the Gas-w-orks; which were erected in consequence of an act of parliament passed the 28th of May, for lighting the town with gas, and empowering the subscribers to raise a capital or fund not exceeding £12.000, by shares of £10 each. This concern has been conducted with great propriety; the town is extremely well lighted, and it has proved a profitable speculation to the share-holders.

A little further on is a neat w hite house, built where the Fountain inn and the tea-garden formerly were.

Upon the elevated ground behind the *ci-devant* Fountain inn, is a handsome modern villa, built by John Cobbold, esq. formerly of the Cliff; which is called Holy Wells, and is now his place of residence. This gentleman has lived to the venerable age of a patriarch, and has had the felicity of seeing his very numerous offspring raised into wealth and opulence. — The church of Wykes Bishop—, which is sometimes mentioned in old records—is supposed to have been very near this spot; or perhaps it might have been only a ciiapel attached to the bishop's palace. There are some pure and limpid springs here, to which extraordinary virtues were attributed, by the priests of the establishment; and which are mentioned in Taylor's *Index Monasticus,* as being much resorted to in former times, by religious devotees, who had great faith in the efficacy of these waters: and from thence they obtained the name of Holy Wells. The late Mrs. Cobbold, in a legendary tale, has the following remark:—

"For know, if wounded christian lave
His gashes in the blessed wave,
They meet no ling'ring doubtful cure,—
His life is safe, his healing sure.

And she thus concludes this pleasing poem:—

"And shrine, and church, and holy ground,
A bishop's stately palace crown'd;
But time, with silent slow decay,
Sweeps earthly pride and pomp away,
Nor church, uor palace, now are known
By massy wall or mould'ring stone;
A moated square just marks the scite
Of mitred state and splendid rite:
Yet, pure and bright, the living rill
Rolls down the alder-skirted hill;
And fancy loves to linger here,
And paint the past in vision clear,
As, whisp'ring to the muse, she tells
The legend of the Holy Wells."

A strip of land on the ooze, extending from the Gasworks to the Cliff, has lately been purchased by John Cobbold, esq. jun. of the corporation, for £300, with a landing-place or right of boatway to be preserved for the burgesses and inhabitants of Ipswich.

We next come to the Cliff: this is a large pile of building, erected for the purpose of a brewery and maltingoffices, with granaries and warehouses, and a commodious wharf for the shipping of corn directly off the premises. In addition to the brewery, a most extensive business in the corn trade, &c. has been for many years carried on by the before-mentioned J. Cobbold, esq: it is now branched out into various parts of the county, and conducted by different members of this remarkably prolific and opulent family.

At a short distance from the Cliff, is the snug comfortable house belonging to Greenwich Farm. We have been told that it received its appellation in consequence of having formerly been the property of Greenwich Hospital.

We now reach a little neck of land, well planted with oak and other trees, denominated Hog Island. Tradition says that, ages ago, a merchant of Ipswich had speculated very largely in swine's flesh, and had imported a whole cargo of these animals from foreign parts, and, as a place of security, had turned them adrift on this spot—which was then an island, though it is not exactly so now— and that, in consequence of an extraordinary high tide, the water made violent irruption into the hogs habitation, and swept them all into the merciless waves; and it is well known that, from their inexpertness in the art of swimming, pigs commit suicide by cutting their own throats. There must have been, formerly, an extraordinary number of these animals in Ipswich; for, in various reigns, several orders were issued for the better regulation of this "swinish multitude," as far back as the fourth year of Edward IV. it is ordered by the bailiffs, that any person catching his neighbour's hog trespassing in his garden, may cause it to be sold, half for himself and half for the town.

We have now to refer to another calamity.which happened in this vicinity. Thomas Colson—better known by the name of Robinson Crusoe—resided many years in St. Clement's parish: he was originally a wool-comber, and had been, in his time, a man of many callings: he was fond of music, and, with the rudest materials, and simplest tools, actually made several violins, of a re-markably fine tone; some of which are yet in the possession of individuals in the town. But he relinquished all other pursuits, and became a fisherman on the Orwell: his little boat— every part of which was the work of his own hands— was a thing made up of shreds and patches, and was an extraordinary specimen of home-made naval architecture. By day and by night, in calm and in storm, he toiled for fish, upon the river. His mind was wavering and distempered: he was a believer in demonology and witchcraft, and fancied himself continually harrassed by the machinations of some evil spirit; against which he endeavoured to protect himself, by innumerable imaginary charms—from the renowned horse-shoe to the murderer's bones; which were fantastically strung about his body and his limbs. With these he felt himself secure, and, at times, apparently, happy; for, in pity to poor humanity, there is often

"A joy in madness madmen only know." He was unfortunately driven on the ooze, on the 3rd of October, 1811, although earnestly entreated by several persons who witnessed his perilous situation, to leave his crazy vessel; but persisting in the efficacy of his charms, he obstinately refused advice, and, at the ebb of the tide, in striving to get into deep water, his fragile bark, his amulets and spells, with poor Robinson Crusoe, all sunk to rise no more.

Here the river branches out into a beautiful expanded sheet of water, and becomes an estuary or arm of the sea. Those large vessels which we see, are lying at Downham Reach; where ships of almost any burthen can ride secure.

B B B

A vessel departed from this *spot,* with a very singular cargo, October 22nd, 1802. Twelve nuns of the English convent, who had, ever since the French Revolution, resided at Hengrave Hall, near Bury, arrived at the house of M. Simon, of this town, on Monday evening, and the following morning departed, in a wherry, from the Common Quay, and went on board a vessel at Downham Reach, which came into the river a few days before, for the purpose of conveying them to Bruges.

Near this spot is a farm-house called Pond Hall.

In that small inlet, close by, called John's Ness, or King's Ness—and thence King John's Ness—in the year 1741, the "Hampshire" frigate, of fifty guns, and in the year 1779, the " Champion" frigate, of twenty-four guns, were built, by Mr. Barnard; who died at an advanced age, and is buried in St. Clement's churchyard, in this town.

On the 5th of November, 1816, a dead whale was found, off the buoy of the Rough, near Harwich, and towed up the river, as high as Downham Reach: its length was from sixty-eight to seventy feet, and the diameter of its body about eighteen feet. Almost the whole population of Ipswich—men, women, and children—assembled on the shore, to see this huge monster of the ocean, in spite of the annoyance to their olfactory nerves;—

"For such the universal wish To see a sight so rare.
That thousands flock'd to see the fish,
    In spite of poison'd air.
"E'en female nicety stood by,
Though reeking perfumes rose,
Wisely resolv'd to please the eye,
    At peril of the nose."

On the 14th of August, 1828, another whale was towed ashore at Harwich, and brought up the river as far as Bourn Bridge, measuring thirty-six feet in length, and eighteen feet in circumference: the skeleton of which is preserved in the room of the Ipswich Mechanics' Institute.

Contiguous to John's Ness, was, formerly, a small priory of Augustine friars: on the scite of which is a farm-house belonging to Sir P. B. V. Broke, bart. and a barn occupies the place of the church or chapel. In 1452, it was united as a cell, to the priory at Woodbridge; and in the twentysecond year of Henry VIII. it was let by Thomas Cooke, prior of Woodbridge, to Thomas Alvarde, of Ipswich, by the title of *Manerium de Alnesborne et Ponds;* and in the description of some fields called Rysing's Pastures, they are described as in the hamlet of Alnesborne, in the parish of Hallowtree: and the farm-house now occupied by Mr. William Lambert, is still called Alnesborne Priory.

Within this district there appears, in ancient records, some account of three churches, besides the chapel of Alnesborne; viz. Hallowtree, St. Pentronille, and Bixley. Alnesborne and the church of St. Petronille, are both mentioned in Doomsday. In the year 1546, when the doctrines of the Reformation were making great progress, it is stated that the image of St. Christopher, near Sudbury, and the image of Petronille, near Ipswich, were demolished and destroyed. In this whole tract of land— which is extra parochial, and where three churches formerly stood—there are not now three houses remaining. There is a curious deed extant, of a grant from Charles II. to allow the corporation of Ipswich to shoot cormorants in the woods hereabouts: and so effectually has the breed of these birds been exterminated, that they are now rarely to be seen.

We now approach Nacton, the most picturesque and beautiful village in the county, and has been the favorite residence of more than one of our naval heroes. The first

B B B 2 seat is called Orwell Park, and was the residence of the celebrated Admiral Vernon. Edward Vernon was descended from a Staffordshire family, but born in Westminster, in 1684: he adopted the naval profession, in opposition to his father, who held the office of secretary of state to William III. He first went to sea with Admiral Hopson; and in 1704, he served under Sir George Rooke, at the battle of Malaga: he was also employed on many other occasions, and gradually arrived at the rank of viceadmiral. In 1739, when the treatment of the English traders, by the Spaniards, in America, had excited great indignation in this country, Admiral Vernon, who was a member of the House of Commons, spoke warmly against the indifference of the ministry to the complaints of the merchants, and pointed out the means of redressing the injuries which they had sustained. In consequence of these representations, he was sent with a squadron to the West Indies; where he took the town of Porto Bello, and destroyed the fortifications. In 1741, he was sent out against Carthagena; but the expedition proved unsuccessful. During the Rebellion, in the year 1745, he was employed in defending the coasts of Kent and Sussex; but, on account of his opposition to the ministry, he was subsequently superseded, and even struck off the list of admirals. He died October 29th, 1757, aged seventythree years. He was representative for the borough of Ipswich, in three successive parliaments—1741,1747, and 1754. He was a brave, virtuous, and honest man, and did high honour to the British flag. On his return to England, from Porto Bello, he was the adoration of all the kingdom; illuminations, in London and other places, took place, and he received the thanks of both houses of parliament, for his services. He was as remarkable for his humanity as his courage; and his name will be renowned over the ocean, as long as the ocean flows.

We have before us a production, in verse, called "A Voyage to 1 pswich, by Wm. Paget, Comedian. Ipswich: printed for the Author, 1747." From which we extract the following lines:—

"All this I said, and upward cast my eye,
Behold the dark'ning towers in the sky,
Faintly inform me wish'd-for Ipswich nigh.
Entering the town, a joyfnl crowd appears,
And cheerful peals of bells salute my ears:
Here, flames from burning piles ascend the sky;
There, grateful luminations glad the eye;
While glorious *Vernon* is the gen'ral cry."

In the year 1795, this house was occupied by the earl of Beverley; and in the month of July, in that year, the Right Honourable Lord St. Asaph, eldest son of Earl Ashburnham, was married there, to Lady Charlotte Percy, eldest daughter of the earl of Beverley.

The nephew of Admiral Vernon, to whom he left the mass of his property, rebuilt the house. He was elected member of parliament for Ipswich, in 1761; created a peer of Ireland, in 1762, under the title of Baron Orwell: in 1776, he was created Viscount Orwell; and, in the following year, earl of Shipbrook; but, dying without issue, in 1783, the title became extinct. The estate came into the possession of his nephew, John Vernon, esq. who was several years colonel of Colneis Hundred Loyal Volunteers, and, afterwards, of the Suffolk local militia: he is lately deceased, leaving an only sister, married to Sir Robert Harland, bart. the present possessor; who is high steward of the borough of Ipswich. This gentleman is the only son of the late Admiral Sir Robert Harland, bart. who resided at Sproughton, in a seat which has since been pulled down: he was a distinguished naval officer, and was created a baronet, for his services, in 1771; in the same year he sailed as commander-in-chief of His Majesty's fleet to the East Indies; in 1778, was second in command to Admiral Keppel; in 1782, he was appointed one of the lords of the admiralty, and died in 1784.

The next house—the approach to which is by a noble and wide-spreading avenue of lime trees—is the property and residence of Sir Philip Bowes Vere Broke, bart.; whose ancestors have long resided in this mansion. He is lineally descended from Gulielmus de Doyto del Brooke, the son of Adam, Lord of Leighton in Cheshire; who lived previously to the reign of Henry III. From him descended Sir Richard Broke, of London, knight, chief baron of the Exchequer, in the time of Henry VIII.; and who had, then, possessions at Nacton. Robert Broke, of Nacton, was created a baronet, in 1661; but the patent being made in the usual way, and he dying without issue male, his brother's son could not inherit the title: but he marrying his cousin, Sir Robert's daughter, he came into the estate; and the present Sir Philip—who was created a baronet, September 25th, 1813—is the eldest son of the late Philip Bowes Broke, esq. of Nacton. This gentleman was an able and upright magistrate, and of distinguished abilities as an orator: he generally presided at the county meetings, on public occasions; and was captain of the second troop of Suffolk Yeomanry Cavalry, in the year 1795: he married Miss Beaumont, of Ipswich: besides Sir Philip, he left two sons, now living, viz. Lieutenantcolonel Sir Charles Broke Vere, knt. and Horatio George Broke, a major in the army; both, by birth, free burgesses of the borough of Ipswich.

Sir Philip married the daughter of Sir William Middleton, bart. of Shrubland Hall, and has a daughter and two sons living. His memorable action with the American frigate, the "Chesapeake," must always be regarded as one of the most distinguished exploits in our naval annals; and occurring as it did, at the time when the Americans had more than once triumphed over our navy, it was hailed with enthusiastic rapture by the nation, and taught the enemy that our sailors were not to be conquered when they met upon any thing like equal terms: but the subject has been so thoroughly canvassed, and every particular of the transaction so minutely detailed, that no words of ours can add lustre to the glory of this gallant and brilliant achievement; but, as we are compelled to be brief, we must refer the reader to Sir Philip's own modest and sailor-like account which he wrote to Captain Capel, his senior officer, as soon as he was sufficiently recovered from the wound that he received in his head, after the " Chesapeake" had struck,—which will be found in a respectable periodical work called *The East Anglian,* published at Ipswich, in the year 1814, accompanied with Mr. Croker's gratifying official letter to Admiral Sir John Borlase Warren; and thus the text and the comment are properly recorded together. The first tribute to his merit was paid by the underwriters of Halifax; whose committee pre sented l.im with a piece of plate worth a hundred guineas. The Court of Common Council, in London, voted him their thanks, with the freedom of the city, and a sword of the value of a hundred guineas. And amongst the tokens of gratitude which were poured upon him, we must not forget to notice an elegant cup, presented to him by the hands of William Pearson, esq. of this town, with the following inscription:—" Presented by the members of the Free and Easy Club, at Ipswich, to their gallant countryman, Sir Philip Bowes Vere Broke, bart. commander of His Majesty's ship, the "Shannon," in commemoration of the skill and valour displayed in the capture of the American frigate, the "Chesapeake," off Boston lighthouse, on the 1st of June, 1813. " He was also presented with a magnificent piece of plate, from the gentlemen of the county of Suffolk, purchased by general subscription: it was a superb plateau, forty-four inches in diameter, splendidly engraved and ornamented; and was a noble tribute to his gallantry and merit: it was presented to him on the 7th of July, 1815, by Sir T. S. Gooch, bart. one of the members for the county, at a grand public dinner, at the Bear and Crown inn, Ipswich. On the 27th of Jan. 1814, he was presented with the thanks of the corporation of Ipswich: the freedom of which place he is entitled to, by birth. He was eulogised, both in prose and verse, from one end of the kingdom to the other: the following brief poetical effusion, from a Suffolk poet, aptly alludes to the little time wasted in the engagement; which lasted no more than a quarter of an hour:—

"Gallant Broke—men of Suffolk, your hero exalt in—
Has redeem'd Britain's falsely-defam'd naval glory;
For he fought, beat, and captur'd a rival insulting,
In less time than was needful to write the proud story."

Sir Philip has pretty well recovered from his wound; but it is to be feared that he will never be altogether free from its effects. We must now leave him to the enjoyment of his well-earned fame, with the sincere wish that he may live long in this peaceful retirement, as a blessing to his family and the neighbourhood of Nacton: it is certain that he will live, for ages, in the hearts of his countrymen.

At a short distance from the coast, is the House of Industry, for the incorporated hundreds of Carlford and Colneis, erected in 1757, at an expense of £4,800, and was first inhabited in the following year. The poor are employed in spinning wool and making sacks, and there is no fault to be found with its management; but it is somewhat problematical whether, in such an establishment, the evil arising from the demoralization of the poor thus congregated together, is not greater than the benefit accruing to society.

In the year 1765, the hatred of the lower orders, towards these establishments, led them to proceed to mad and unjustifiable outrage. On the 8th of August, that year, several hundreds of people assembled on the heath near Nacton, with the intention of pulling down the House of Industry. The magistrates having had intimation of the design, were on the spot, assisted by a party of dragoons, and used every means to persuade them to disperse, without avail. The Riot Act was read, but had no effect. The mob furiously attacked the soldiers, with forks, hooks, and various offensive weapons; but, in five minutes, they were dispersed, and seven persons taken into custody.

In April, 1804, an act was passed for enclosing part of the parishes of Nacton, Kirton, and Trimley, by which much waste land was brought into cultivation.

We now come to Levington Creek. In the parish of Levington is an almshouse, for six poor persons of this parish and Nacton, built and endowed by Sir Robert Hitcham, who was a native of this place. The steeple of this church was also built by him, as appears by the arms and date upon it. Dowsing observes that, here, he took off" three popish inscriptions in brass, and brake down ten superstitious pictures and gave orders to level the steps in twenty days.

A very handsome mansion was lately erected in this parish, for Major Charles Walker, on an elevated spot cf ground, commanding a most beautiful view of Landguard Fort, Harwich, and the German Ocean. It does credit to the builder, Mr. Harvey, of Ipswich, though its effect would have been greatly increased if it bad been a loftier structure.

c c c

At a short distance are the ruins of Stratton church or chapel, now overgrown with weeds and bushes, in what is still called the chapel field. Here was formerly a lazarhouse, endowed with the moiety of the tithes of Stratton: it is extra-parochial, and nothing is left standing but the hall, now a farm house.

In Levington, the first crag or shell that was used for manure, in the improvement of land, in the county of Suffolk, was dug up in a farmer's *yard,* and brought into notice by one Edwards, in 1718, by his accidentally spreading some upon the soil, which proved unusually productive. This crag is frequently found on various parts of this coast, in masses from fifteen to twenty feet deep. It is said that shells found in the crag are turned the different way from those of the present time; and it has been argued that they must have been there since the Deluge: but this we believe is an erroneous opinion, for there is only one shell found amongst them, the *Murex Contrarius,* which opens the reverse way of shells in general, and is similar to those commonly called *yrilkes,* but is, in all cases, differently striped. We must, however, leave these matters to the learned in antediluvian conchology.

Almost every spot on the banks of the Orwell has been consecrated as classic ground, by the muse both of ancient and modern poets. Probably, one of the earliest efforts in verse, relative to this neighbourhood, is the following fragment:—

"Come, row the boat, row, to Levington Crick,
The boat full of Roses as e'er it can stick.
Row the boat, row, Yoho! yoho!
For the pride of the castle, fair Ellen, we go."

We find that, in 1540, Thomas Clarke possessed the manor of Chases, in Levington—which he bought of the first Lord Wentworth—and his nephew William Clarke sold it to William Cavendish. In the fragment before referred to, are the following lines:—

"Down came Mr. Clarke, in his morning gown—
'You shall not have my daughter for ten thousand pound;'
Down came Mrs. Clarke, in her white hood—
'You shall not have my daughter if you're ever so good.'" therefore, if the heroine of this ballad was the heiress to the then lofd of the manor, this composition is, probably, three hundred years old. On mentioning this ballad to a gentleman in Scotland, who is one of the most learned antiquarians of this day, he said he made no doubt but it was of northern extraction; as he remembered hearing something very similar to it, once, when he was gliding over the surface of the Baltic, in an ice-boat, near the Isle of Rugen; and he has introduced it into a quarto volume, entitled "Northern Illustrations," published by him, in conjunction with Sir Walter Scott, as one of the many instances in which our legendary tales assimilate closely with the effusions of the ancient Scandinavian bards. Now if any of our fair readers, or others, versed in legendary lore, could furnish the sequel to this old ballad, it would be entitled to a place in the second edition of the *Suffolk Garland,* which was first published in Ipswich, by Mr. Raw, in 1818: it contains many curious and agreeable poetical effusions, relative to the county; and the valuable and entertaining preface and notes do great credit to the editor.

Adjoining to Nacton is Trimley St. Martin. The manor of Grimston, with Morston, and a good estate besides, came into the possession of the late George Nassau, esq. half brother to the present Earl of Rochford, by the will of the late Sir John Barker, bart. who, on making his last testament, was at a loss to whom to bequeath his property; c c c 2 when his professional adviser, the late Samuel Kilderbee, esq. of Ipswich, recommended the aforesaid Mr. Nassau, as a gentleman of ancient family and small fortune, and he succeeded accordingly.

Grimston Hall, in this parish—which is, now, a farmhouse, occupied by Mr. Last—was, formerly, the seat of Thomas Cavendish, esq. the second Englishman that sailed round the world:

he was born here; and there is an ilex still standing, said to have been planted with his own hand. This gallant seaman fitted out three ships, at his own expense;—the " Desire," of one hundred and twenty tons; the "Content," of sixty tons; and the "High Gallant," a bark of forty tons: on board of which he had no more than one hundred and twenty-three hands, men and boys. He sailed from Plymouth, in July, 1586; passed through the straits of Magellan, and entered the South Sea; then returned home, by way of the Cape of Good Hope, and reached Plymouth, September 9th, 1588, after an absence of two years and fifty days. He met with strange and wonderful adventures, and captured many rich prizes. He had no historian to relate his exploits; but the best account of his expedition will be found in n letter of his to Lord Hunsdon, at that time lord chamberlain to Queen Elizabeth—but it is too long for our narrative. — The success of his first voyage encouraged the hero of Trimley to make a second attempt, with a larger force: he departed from Plymouth, with five ships, on the 26th of August, 1591; but after passing the straits of Magellan a second time, on the 20th of May, 1592, he was separated from his fleet, in the night, and never after heard of. We regret that our limits will not allow us to insert the whole of a poem upon the exploits and probable fate of Cavendish, written by Bernard Barton, but we give the concluding stanza:—

"Whate'er the fate of that, or thee, No stone records thy name;
Let ocean thy mausoleum be!
   Thy epitaph, thy fame!"

The churches of Trimley St. Martin and Trimley St. Mary are contiguous to each other, and stand in the same churchyard, though it has not yet been determined in the neighbourhood, whether it be possible for *two* churches to be in *one churchyard*. The steeple of St. Mary's church is in ruins, and being overshadowed by some lofty trees, is a charmingly picturesque subject for the pencil of an artist. The eye of the common observer will, perhaps, be better pleased with the steeple of St. Martin,

as it has been very neatly rebuilt. Dowsing's Journal states, "August 21st, 1644. There was a friar with a shaven crown, praying to God in these words, *miserere meiDeus,* which we brake down, and 28 cherubims in the church, which we gave orders to take down." The church of St. Mary is said to have been built by Thomas de Brotherton, son of Edward I. and his arms are still to be seen over the front entrance-door, at the west end of the church; the arch of which door, as well as that of a window in the ruins of the steeple, is very light and elegant. The advowson of St. Martin is vested in the right honourable the earl of Rochford, and that of St. Mary, in the Crown.

April the 19th, 1765, the body of a Portuguese Jew, decently dressed, was cast upon the Salts, at Trimley. In his pocket was found a prayer-book, in the Hebrew language, and about his arms were fastened, by a leathern cord, phylacteries composed of texts of scripture, written in different slips of parchment, curiously concealed in pieces of leather. These were worn by the Jews, in our Saviour's time, on their foreheads or palms of their hands, to denote their respect for the old Law.

We now come to Landgnard Fort; from whence we have a grand expansive view of the German Ocean bursting on our sight: and who but must recollect the extraordinary sensation experienced on first beholding the sea! This sensation is finely expressed, and the mighty wonders of the deep admirably depicted, in the following extract from a poem called *Dumcich, or the Splendid City,* by Mr. James Bird; who passed several years in Ipswich. The work displays poetical beauties of the first order.
"Beats there a heart which hath not felt its core
Ache with a wild delight, when first the roar
Of Ocean's spirit met the startled ear
Beats there a heart so languid and so drear,
That hath not felt the lightning of the blood
Flash vivid joy, when first the rolling flood

Met the charm'd eye, with all its restless strife.
At once the wonder and the type of life!
Thou trackless, dark, and fathomless and wide
Eternal world of waters! ceaseless tide
Of power magnificent! unmeasured space
Where storm and tempest claim their dwelling-place.
Thy depths are limitless! thy billows' sound
Is nature's giant voice—thy gulph profound
Her shrine of mystery, wherein she keeps
Her hidden treasures—in thy cavern'd deeps
Is stor'd the wealth of nations, and thy waves
Have been—are now—and will bo dreary graves
For countless millions! Oh, thou art alone
The costliest footstool of God's awful throne.
The mighty tablet upon which we see
The haud of power—the sign of Deity!"
Landguard Fort stands upon the point of land which forms the south-east corner of the county, at the mouth of the Orwell, and has the appearance of an island, at high water. Camden notices a ridge called Langer Stone, which runs two miles out into the sea, to the danger of mariners; but is of use for the fishermen drying their nets, and serves as a fence to the harbour of Orwell. The first fort was built at the commencement of the reign of Charles I. for its chapel was consecrated by the bishop of Norwich, Sept. 7th, 1628. Lady Betty Thicknesse— the second wife of the eccentric lieutenant-governor, Philip Thicknesse—is buried in the chapel. This lady was the mother of the late Lord Audley. The governor's third wife was Miss Anne Ford—to whom he was married at the fort, October 1 st, 1762: he was a volunteer in Sir Armine Wodehouse's battallion of the Norfolk militia, and was married in the uniform of a private of that corps, receiving the hand of his fair bride from his colonel. He was convicted at Bury assizes, August the 5th,

1763, of writing and publishing a false and scandalous libel, reflecting on the character of Lord Orwell, and was committed to die King's Bench prison, from which he escaped, but was afterwards retaken, and sentenced to be imprisoned three months, to pay a fine of £100, and find sureties for his good behaviour for seven years. He was the author of the life of Thomas Gainsborough, R. A. and was his first patron.

The old fort had four bastions, with fifteen large guns on each, and stood a little to the north of the present erection, on the spot which is now the burial-place for the garrison.

Xear this spot, the Dutch, in the year 1667, landed three thousand men; and, marching under cover of some sandhills, lodged themselves within musketshot, on two sides of the fort. After an hour's incessant firing with their small arms, they were put to flight by the discharge of two or three guns from a small galliot which fired upon the shingle, and scattered the pebbles so destructively, that they threw die Dutch army into complete confusion.

The old fort was demolished, and the present erected in its stead, in 1718: but the soil being very unfavourable, the foundations were not laid without great labour and expense. It completely commands the entrance into the harbour; which—though between two and three miles over, at high water—is too shallow to admit ships of any great burthen, except by a narrow and deep channel on the Suffolk side. The entrance to the fort is by a drawbridge. Over the gateway is the chapel. On the right are apartments for the governor and lieutenant-governor; and, facing the gate, are the barracks for the soldiers,— which generally consist of a detachment of two companies. The governor has a salary of £365 per annum; and the lieutenant-governor, who constantly resides on the spot, £182:10:0.

According to tradition, the opening of the two rivers, Orwell and Stour, was, anciently, on the north side of Landguard Fort, through Walton marshes; and it is likely—from the soil and situation of Langer common and Langer marshes—that they may have been covered by the ocean: but, if so, it must have been at a very remote period, for frequent mention is made, in the court rolls, of the manor of Walton, of Langer common in Felixstow, upwards of two hundred years before any fort was built there. From the corruption of the word, *Langer* has been changed into *Landgard* Fort, which it is now called.

We must speak of Walton and Felixstow together. They are now distinct parishes; but, till of late days, Felixstow was always reckoned as a part of, and to be in Walton: and so late as Henry VIII. Cardinal Wolsey was said to have had an annual income from the church of Felixstow, in Walton. Thus largely taken, it was, anciently, a place of great consequence, and continued so till long after the Norman Conquest. There is no doubt of its having been a Roman station, from the variety of Roman urns, coins, rings, &c. that have been found there. It is thought to have been established in the time of Constantine the Great, when he withdrew his legions from the frontier towns in the east of Britain, and built forts or castles to supply their place. The coins that have been dug up are of the Vespasian and Antonine families, of Severus, and his successors, to Gordian the Third; and from Gallienus to Arcadius and Honorius. Several dies for coining money have likewise been found. Governor Thick nesse placed an effigy of the person whose grave had been disturbed, against the minister's door, with a label attached to the mouth, with these words— "Give me back my gravestone, or you shall never rest in peace:" which stratagem induced the reverend livine to restore the gravestone to its proper place.

The following is a list of coins—principally silver— found at Walton and Felixstow, in good preservation, in the possession of a lady at Ipswich:—

The Rev. William Myers, vicar of Walton, collected a vast number of coins—principally Roman—in 1743-4-5, which were bequeathed to his nephew, the Rev. Mr. Brown, of jjaxmundham; on whose death, they were disposed of, by auction, January 26th, 1827. He was also a poet, and exercised his muse in a poem called "The Humours of Landguard Fort," written in doggerel verse. This Mr. Myers—who lived in the house now Miss Deck's boarding-school—with a wanton disregard to all right feeling, took up a gravestone, from the churchyard, and laid it down as a step to the entrance of his house; when

D D D

The following description appears in the minutes of the Antiquarian Society, in 1772:—" Some distance east of Walton, are the ruins of a Roman wall, situate on the ridge of a cliff next the sea, between Landguard Fort and the Woodbridge river, or Bawdsey haven: it is one hundred yards long, five feet high above ground, twelve broad at each end, turned with an angle; it is composed of pebbles and Roman brick, in three courses; all round footsteps of buildings, and several large pieces of wall east down upon the strand by the sea undermining the cliff—all which have Roman brick. At low water mark, very much of the like is visible at some distance in the sea. There are two entire pillars with balls. The cliff is one hundred feet high."

Such are the encroachments which the sea has made upon this coast, within the last fifty years, that no remnants of this wall remain, except a few fragments, which may occasionally be seen at low water, above the waves: and, what is more extraordinary, it is confidently asserted that, some miles out at sea, at a place well known to mariners by the name of the West Rocks, fragments of those rocks w hich have been occasionally broken off, are formed of materials for building, cemented together, and hardened by the water, so as to have become something like petrified wall. It is, therefore, supposed that Felixstow has, in former times, been a place of greater extent than we have any positive evidence to prove; and that the sea has encroached for many miles upon the shore 11 is stated in the eleventh volume of the *A rchceologia*— but upon what authority we know not—that " there was formerly a town called Orwell, which extended into the sea, to the place now called the West Rocks.'

Felixstow was, most likely, one of the very first places in this part of England, in which Christianity reared its head: and it derived its name from Felix the Good, the first bishop of Dunwich; of whom we have the following account. Felix, the pious Burgundian, was invited by King Sigibert, into his kingdom, to promote the conversion of his subjects to Christianity. He was consecrated first bishop of East Anglia, by Honorius, archbishop of Canterbury, in the year 036. Many famous men resorted to him, to be his coadjutors in promoting this grand design; which, by his sincerity, charity, and indefatigable preaching, he effected. The sable clouds of paganism being dissipated by the glorious rays of the gospel, and to establish this great and noble work at Dunwich, Felixstow, and other places, were erected schools; which were seminaries of sound literature and ingenious education, and tended greatly to the promotion of piety and religion. Felix governed his see seventeen years; died in 647, and was buried at Dunwich. The memory of the bishop will be perpetuated here, from his having bestowed his name on this place; where he founded a religious house, called the Priory of St. Felix: and all that remains to note the scite of this very ancient establishment, is a piece of land still called "the old abbey close," and a fenny close called "the old abbey pond." A great quantity of a peculiar herb is found in these pastures, which, at a certain time of the year, taints the cream and butter made from the milk of the cows which have fed upon it, with the flavor of onions: it is extremely difficult to eradicate, and is held

D D D 2 in great detestation by the peasantry; who know it by no other name than "monk's grass."

In Doomsday, Felixstow is written Fylchestowe, Fylstow, and Walton St. Felix. Robert Bigod, first earl of Norfolk, had given to him, at the Conquest, one hundred and seventy-six manors in Norfolk, and one hundred and seventeen lordships in Suffolk. Upon one of

these he founded his priory of Benedictine monks, and endowed it with the manor of the ancient priory of Felixstow, with the churches of Walton and Felixstow, and with the tithes and other appurtenances in Walton. About the year 1105, the earl gave it as a cell to the monastery of St. Andrew, at Rochester. This gift was confirmed byKing William; and the monks here, were, ever after, called " the monks of Rochester."

The scite of this priory, with the great tithes of Walton and Felixstow, were given to Cardinal Wolsey, in the twenty-sixth year of Henry VIII.: but, long after his fall, in the nineteenth year of Queen Elizabeth, they were granted to Thomas Seckford, her master of Requests; who built the celebrated almshouses at Woodbridge.

Lord Rochford is the present lord of the manor of Walton with Trimley, and the small manor of the old priory at Felixstow.

The church of Felixstow must be a very ancient edifice: we have no account of the date of its erection: it is in a very dilapidated state: the steeple is nearly in ruins: it is a vicarage, dedicated to St. Peter and St. Paul, and with Walton, was in the patronage of G. Thompson, esq. in 1780; but it has since passed through so many hands, and has become so intricate and involved, that it is matter of dispute who has the next right of presentation.

In the year 1173, the earl of Leicester landed on this coast, with his Flemings, and was well received by Hugh Bigod, earl of Norfolk, lord of the manor, and of the ancient castle of Walton—which was then standing. In consequence of several of the barons having, at this time, taken part with the sons of Henry 11. in their unnatural contest with their father, this monarch, in 1176, caused all the castles whose owners had acted against him in this rebellion, to be razed to the ground: amongst the rest, those at Walton and Ipswich were included; and so effectually was the demolition of this castle completed, that the stones were carried into all parts of Felixstow, Walton, and Trimley, and foot-paths raised with them, on both sides of the road—

fragments of which are yet to be met with. A view of this castle is published in the fifth volume of " Grose's Antiquities.''

Soon after the destruction of the castle, the priory was removed to a spot abutting on Walton church; where some remnants of it are yet to be seen. The steeple of this church is entirely in ruins; but the remainder of it has been repaired, and is neutly fitted up for religious worship.

About a quarter of a mile north of Felixstow Highstreet, and about the same distance, east, from the bounds of Walton, are some remains of an ancient building of considerable extent, known by the name of *Old Hall;* and was, most likely, erected for a manor-house, soon after the castle was destroyed. It was here where Edward III. passed some time at his manor, of Walton, before his expedition to France, when he gained the memorable victory over the French, at Cressy, in the year 1338: and here, among other regal acts, he confirmed the charters of Ipswich. — There is still a portion of this structure remaining, composed entirely of flint-stones, in their original state, strongly cemented together. The foundation of the exterior walls now to be seen above the earth, occupies a space of ground, of an irregular form, about one hundred and sixty feet long, and one hundred and twenty feet wide. We are told that the pick-axe and the spade have been continually making encroachments, and that it was, formerly, of much greater extent. Nearly in the centre of this area, stands a wall about two feet thick, thirty feet high, and rather wider at the base, but not near so wide towards the top—in which is a round arched aperture for a window, not above five or six feet high, and about half the breadth. The building stands east and w est; but the window is so small, that we cannot think it ever formed part of a chapel or place of worship, but, probably, lighted the east end of the great baronial hall of the manor-house. The outline of the wall, as well as that of the window, is so dilapidated and undefined, that it is impossible to say what style of architecture was used in this erection. The entire space of the enclosure is overgrown with grass, weeds, and underwood; the wall is partly covered with ivy; and, though exhibiting no features or outline of beauty, is an interesting relic of what was, nearly two hundred years ago, the seat of regal splendour—the scite of which is, now, only the occasional residence of the pheasant or the hare!

Roger Bigod had the grant of a market at Walton, in the seventeenth year of Edward I.; and it is not a great many years since the market-cross was standing.

Orwell harbour has, in some old court rolls, been frequently denominated Wadgate haven, from the hamlet of Wadgate, in Walton—in which there is, now, only one solitary building to be seen: it is a farm-house, called Wadgate, belonging to Charles Collett, esq. of Walton.

In the year 1802, a Baptist meeting-house was erected at Walton, upon a small scale; but the congregation increasing.it was rebuilt, in 1812; and is, now, calculated to hold about five humlred persons. It was originally undertaken by Mr. A. K. Cowell, of Ipswich; who has always officiated as minister. He is, now, retired from Ipswich, and lives in a delightful situation very near the spot.

There are a number of martello towers all along this coast; which were erected in the reign of George III. at an enormous expense.

Bones of a prodigious size have, it is said, been frequently met with in this vicinity; and it is puzzling to naturalists to account for their being there. A petrified elephant's tooth, dug out of the cliff, here, is now in the possession of Roger Pettiward, esq. of Finborough Hall: and we give the following veracious extract from Lambert, with full permission to our readers to believe as much of it as they please: " Since the beginning of the reign of Queen Elizabeth, there were found in Suffolk, over against Harwich in Essex, by a gentleman called Candish, that is, our celebrated circumnavigator, the bones of a man; whereof the skull was able to contain five pecks, and one of his teeth is as big us a man's fist, and weigheth ten ounces. These bones had sometimes bodies not of beasts but men, for the difference is manifest!!!" Alas! what a pitiful race of pigmies we are become, in comparison with the former men of Suffolk.

From the records of antiquity, and the region of fiction, let us descend to the situation of things as they really are. Walton is a neat and remarkably pleasant village, containing many good houses; several of which are most desirable places of residence, enjoying beautiful prospects of the surrounding country, with an extensive view of the German Ocean. Amongst these we may enumerate those of the late Mr. Collet!—now occupied by Mr. Boby— Charles Collett, esq. the Rev. Samuel Reeve, Richard Dykes Alexander, esq. and Mr. Fulcher.

The Rev. John Edgar has a beautiful marine retreat at Felixstow; and Mr. Quilter has a handsome house: but the one most worthy of particular remark, is Langer Lodge, or Felixstow Cottage, situated under the shelter of the eastern cliff. This was, originally, a fisherman's hut; but, by the taste of the celebrated Philip Thicknesse, it was converted into a charming residence. Mrs. Thicknesse was a lady of great talents and accomplishments, and took much delight in adorning this spot. She has described it at length, in her entertaining memoirs, referring particularly to an arch formed of huge stones, in the front of the cottage; which has been removed, in order to obtain a more extensive prospect from the terrace that winds round the edge of the cliff". Her husband, the lieutenant-governor, on relinquishing his command at Landguard Fort, sold this cottage to the dowager Lady Bateman. It is now the favourite summer residence of Sir Samuel Brudenell Fludyer, bart. whose mother purchased it for £2000. The present proprietor has materially added to the former embellishments of this beautiful, but heretofore neglected spot. Bernard Barton thus speaks of it, and its benevolent possessor:—

"Enchanting Elysium! long, long may'st thou flourish,
To gladden the eye with thy verdure and flowers;
And may each future year which rolls over thee, nourish
Thine exquisite beauties with sunshine and showers.
And O may the taste which has planned and perfected
This fairy abode, its full recompense reap;
And, surrounded by sweets which itself hath collected,
Long enjoy the bright Eden that blooms by the deep."

But it is with regret we notice that the ruthless waves have washed away great part of the garden and plantations; and it is much to be feared that, ere long, they will sweep away the whole; for it is doubtful whether any human precautions can avail against their force.

For some years, a number of workmen have been employed, under the direction of Mr. Wyatt, in splitting the rocks—being composed of a stone called *septaria*—visible here at low water; and we have seen a fleet of thirty or forty sail of small vessels collecting these stones together, to carry them to Harwich; from whence they are shipped for London, for the purpose of manufacturing them into what is called Parker's Roman cement. There is a manufactory of this kind, at Harwich, under the direction of the Ordnance Office; and there are, generally, between two and three hundred boats employed in this trade. This article is sent to all parts of the world; for, by exposure to the air, it becomes nearly as durable as stone itself. It was sent out as ballast, to the East Indies, and was used in the erection of the new Mint lately built at Calcutta.

When tired of contemplating the world of waters.' and gazing on the surface of the mighty deep, the naturalist may find much amusement in tracing the texture and color of the sea-weeds and other marine productions to be met with here, in great variety: amongst many others, we notice the following:—

Besides a variety of corallines and shells are also found agate, cornelian, jet, jasper, and amber: a most splendid piece of the latter, weighin twenty-seven ounces, is in the collection of a lady at Ipswich. About thirty or forty varieties of shells are found in the cliffs; amongst which is the *murex contrarius.* The water on this and the opposite coast seems to have more than the usual power of producing petrifaction; for vast quantities of petrified substances are found, which will receive a most beautiful polish, and are manufactured into a variety of articles, at Harwich.

During the last war, when the Durham militia were quartered in the fort, the men amused themselves in excavating the sand from an elevated cliff at Felixstow, so as to form a cavern; into which you enter by two arched apertures, one to the right, and the other to the left: these wind round a shaft some yards thick, and terminate in a circular room, large enough to hold twenty people, and is about seven feet high.

The whole extent of the beach, here, is particularly pleasant and agreeable, and the sand so firm and delightful to walk upon, thai numbers of persons have, of late years, resorted to this spot, for the enjoyment of seabathing; and such is the mutability of things in this fluctuating world, that this may, soon, again, become a place of bustle and importance, and a new town of Felixstow arise from the mouldering ruins of the old: for a very large and commodious house has recently been erected by Mr. Porter, in a charming elevated situation, a little distance from the shore, affording every convenience that can be afforded by the best regulated hotel. A handsome row of houses, called St. George's Terrace, has also been built by Mr. Meadows, of Ipswich, expressly for lodginghouses; others have been fitted up by Mr. Quilter; Mr. John Cobbold, of Ipswich, has lately purchased some land here, and has erected a handsome house near the beach; and other persons will, doubtless, follow this example. Many strangers, as well as a great number of the families from Ipswich, Woodbridge, and the neighbourhood, frequently make excursions to this delightful spot, to enjoy the sea-breezes. If sufficient

houses were built, baths erected, a reading-room established, and some amusements introduced, so as to induce an adequate number of residents to congregate together, as would render it worth while to establish an easy communication and daily conveyance to the great road by Ipswich, Felixstow would soon become a delightful place of resort, as well as a fashionable watering-place: and as the walks and rides upon the beach, here, are equal, if not superior, to any other bathing place in the kingdom, we have little doubt that, in a few years, this will actually be accomplished.

The view from Felixstow beach is admirably calculated to excite the feelings so poetically depicted in the following stanzas, by Bernard Barton:—

"Beautiful, sublime, and glorious-,
Mild, majestic, foaming, free;—
Over time itself victorious,
  Image of eternity.
  Epithet-exhausting Ocean!
'Twere as easy to control
In the storm thy billowy motion,
As thy wonders to unrol.

  Sun, and moon, and stars shine o'er
thee, See thy surface ebb, and flow
Yet attempt not to explore thee
  In thy soundless depths below.
E E E 2
  Whether morning's splendours steep
the
With the rainbow's glowing grace;
  Tempests rouse, or navies sweep
thee,
Tis but for a moment's space.
  Earth—her valleys, and her mountains,
'Mortal man's behests obey;
Thy unfathomable fountains
  Scoff his search, and scorn his sway.
  Such art thou, stupendous Ocean But
if overwhelni'd by thee,
Can we think, without emotion,
  What must thy Creator be?"

Having now completed our survey on the left side of the iiver, we will stretch out a little, as far as the Rolling Ground, in order to e,ijoy the delightful influence of a sea-breeze; but as all pleafcures may border on pain, when carried beyond the bounds of prudence, let us beware of proceeding too far; for

the indication of seasickness is, certainly, very remote from u pleasurable sensation; so we will now tack about, in our way home, and take a view of Harwich—where we may land, or not, as time and inclination suit. Our limits will not allow us to say any more of this place, than that you can be comfortably accommodated at the principal inns; and that the Government Packet to and from Helvoetsluys and Gottenburgh, sail Wednesdays and Saturdays with the greatest punctuality.

Near Harwich cliff, about the year 1790, a book or tablet of brass was found, composed of four leaves or plates folding upon each other after the manner of a screen, and connected by hinges. Each leaf is divided into four compartments; representing« some incident in our Saviour's life; with characters on the top, conjectured to be a mixture of the old Greek and Russian letters; and which, if deciphered, are, no doubt, explanatory of the subject represented. The figures are all raised, as if embossed or stampt, executed with great delicacy of finish, and are in excellent preservation; for the leaves fall into grooves so nicely and closely together, as to prevent the interior from bein injured, either by air or water. The following subjects are supposed to be represented:— FIRST LEAF.

Luke 1st Chap. 26th , . ,, , ., ,, and iollow.ng veraes. Luke. 2nd Cliap. aliW and Wowing verses. *J 2.* On the upper port of the square, are the AnMaWhew. Chap. 2nd,V gels appearing to the Shepherd.-; and on the 1st and foilowin;% lower part, the Wise Men fining unto Jesus.

verses. *J 3.* Not sufficiently intel'igihle, without a translation of th« character on ihe lop, to warrant a conjecture as to the suhject designed to he represented.
Luke 2nd Chap. 1st , l.
and following verses.
6EC0ND LEAF.

Luke. Chap. 2nd, 24th.., andfollowingveesea.r-Smteon and Anna's prophecy concerning Jesus.

Matt. Chap. 3rd, I3ih? _,,. _....
and following verses. *S '" '"*
Matt. Chap. 17th, lst. _, _ and follow-

ingver«». ». '"-Transngurat.on. Matt. Chap. 21st, let!

and following verses. »" "' "" «als THIRD LEAC".

Matt. Chap. 12th, 10th _,....

end following verses, $ TM-

Luke. Chap.2lh,.lotH _

and followingver.es. J' The Ascension. Matt. Chap. 10th, lst3. Christ's charge to his Apostles on sending them and following veres. $ forth to preach the gospel.

Luke. Chap. 7th, I2th. ",. ,.

,. ,, . 4. Christ raising the widow's son. and following verses. J FOURTH LEAF.

This is divided into four coin part men ts, the same as the others; hut no con- jecture can he formed as to the suhjects represented. Besides thee,

on the top of each leaf, which i of a Gothic form, six inches and a half hy four wide, there are four other designs; hut of which, except the flrst—-which, evidently, represents the Crucifixion— we are left in the same uncertainty, for want of a translation. On the outside is a kind of frontispiece or title-page, with a numher of characters interspersed.

This singular tablet has been inspect- ed by the most learned linguists in the kingdom, and has been submitted to the Antiquarian Society; but no person has yet been found competent to translate the incriptions. It is now in the posses- sion of Mr. F. J. Hooker, chemist, Ip- swich; who would feel pleasure in shewing it to any one inclined to inspect it.

The next thing to be observed, is the junction of the Stour or Manningtree river, with the Orwell, which is thus de- scribed by Drayton:—

"For *Orwell* coming in from *Ipswich* thinkes that shee

Should stand it for the *Stour,* and lastly they agree,

That since the Britons hence their first discoveries made,

And that into the East they first were taught to trade;

Besides of all the Roads and Havens of the East,

This Harbour where they meet is reck- oned for the best."

The view here is very fine and impos-

ing. Harwich church and town on one side, with Landguard fort and Felixtow cliffs on the other, and the two noble streams stretching into a beautifully en- closed country before us. On the point of land at their junction, on the Suffolk coast, stands Erwarton hall. Neither the house nor the offices are remarkable for the antiquity of their appearance; yet the gate of this mansion has attracted con- siderable notice. From the whimsical taste of its construction, it is urged that it must have been built in the time of El- izabeth, or James I.; for it is a discor- dant jumble of different styles of archi- tecture—and, upon the whole, has not a disagreeable appearance. It was built by Sir Henry Parker, knight, about the year 1575.—The lordship of this place formerly belonged to the family of the D'Avilers. It afterwards came to the Ba- cons. Sir Robert Bacon married Isabel, daughter of Bartholomew D'Avilers, about the year 1330. In 1345, this fam- ily procured the grant of a market and fair here. In the forty-ninth year of Ed- ward III. Robert Bacon, knt. held, by the courtesy of England, the manor of Everlwaton, with the advowson of the church of the said parish, *in capite,* by the service of leading one hundred foot- men from Newmarket to Wales. It after- wards came into the hands of Sir Philip Parker, bart.—whose family had their residence here, for many years—and it now belongs to Charles Berners, esq.

Erwarton church is a beautiful little building; in which there are two very handsome monuments—one to the aforesaid Sir Bartholomew D'Avilers, and the other to his grandson, a Sir Bartholomew D'Avilers likewise.

Near this place is Shotley. Here was, anciently, a hamlet called Kirketon. A market and fair were granted to William Visdelieu—who was lord of the manor, in the thirty-first year of Edward I. It now belongs to the marquis of Bristol.

The ancientiamily of the Tilneys for- merly had their seat in this parish. Hackliut tells as that Sir Frederic Tilney was, for his valour, knighted at the siege of Acre, in the Holy Land, by Richard I. and that he was a man of great stature and strength of body. Sixteen knights, in

a direct line, succeeded him; and when their heir general married the duke of Norfolk, there was a male branch living in this village. Philip Tilney, esq. of this place, was highsheriff for the county, in the thirtieth year of Elizabeth.

In this village is Shot ley-gate or fer- ry. The direct road from Ipswich to Har- wich, by land, is to Shotley—where per- sons are ferried over the Stour, to the Essex coast.

Nearly opposite to Shotley church, there is a small branch from the river, called Crane's Creek.

The first object we meet with, is a solitary residence, by the water's edge, called Burrel's House.

We now pass a little inlet or creek, leading to a few straggling huts and cot- tages, called Pin Mill—where the weather-beaten fisherman and daring smuggler meet in friendly intercourse, to relate their hair-breadth escapes and wonderful adventures, over a pipe and a jug, at the Butt and Oyster public-house.

As we proceed, we next come to a view of the elegant mansion of Charles Bcrners, esq. at Wolverston. The house is built of Woolpit brick; the centre of the principal front is adorned with a pediment, supported by four Ionic pil- lars, and is connected, by the wings on each side, by an elegant colonnade; the bow front, next the river, commands most beautiful views on the water and the opposite shore. The interior of this edifice corresponds with the elegance of its exterior: the apartments are fitted up with great taste—they contain some good pictures, and the ceilings are beau- tifully painted. The stables are very or- namental—standing I'etachcd from the house, on the spot where the old man- sion formerly stood. The present hall was erected in 1 776, by the late Wil- liam Berners, esq. proprietor of Bern- ers-street, in London.

At some distance from the house, nearer the river, we may see an inter- esting object of filial affection: ii is a square obelisk of free-stone, ninety-six feet high, with an ascent, in the interior, to the top—which is surmounted by a g'lobe, encircled with rays. The base is encompassed with iron palisades. On one side of it is this inscription:—

In Mcinoriam
Qi/UELMi Berners, Ariiiig.
Pdtri optimi et
hene inerenti hunr ohelicuin extnixit fil-
ius
Carolus Berners,
I793.

On the contrary side, next the river, is the following:— Gitlielmus Berners
Natna
Jul. 10, A.D. ir09,
Denetus
Sep is, I7U.

The park contains about five hundred acres, well planted, and most agreeably diversified. It is plentifullystocked with beautifully spotted deer, and abounds with game of every kind—which may be seen playing their gambols, down to the very edge of the water: and in Gough's edition of Camden, it is observed that this park may be justly said to be the finest spot in the eastern part of England.

The estate, early in the last century, belonged to John Tysson, esq.—who became a bankrupt, in 1720; when the notorious John Ward, of Hackney, claimed it, in right of a mortgage which he had upon it. The matter was brought into Chancery; and the editor of the Suffolk Traveller makes this observation: "It has this surprising circumstance attending it, that the cause doth not appear to be nearer a conclusion now than it was at first." This cause remained undecided for upwards of half a century: at length, about the year 1773, the property was ordered to be sold; and was purchased by the father of Charles Bern erg, esq. the present possessor.

On a gently-rising eminence, on the margin of the river, stands a picturesque building, commonly called the Cat House, the property of Charles Berners, esq.

Freston Tower, about a mile further on, has an imposing appearance; and we are, at first, led to suppose that it is some precious relic of ancient architecture. It is a strong quadrangular building, about ten feet by twelve feet, with a polygonal turret at each angle. It is six stories high, and contains as many

rooms, one above another, communicating with a winding staircase—which, on the exterior, forms the principal face of the edifice, having three sides, and numerous windows. The best apartment seems to have been on the fifth story: it is higher than any of the others; and was, probably, hung with tapestry, as the small nails yet left in the wood seem to indicate. The top is formed by a number of open arches, and each of the small turrets at the angles terminates in a pinnacle. The windows are square, and, except in the principal apartment, very small. In the building there is but one fire-place—which is on the ground floor—and even that seems to be of recent construction, and has no chimney; therefore, could not be designed as a permanent habitation. Excepting a farm-house, at a few yards' distance, there is no trace of any building near the spot. It is not easy to say for what purpose, nor is it certainly known at what period this tower was built. But in the records of the manor-house, and all the out-buildings and offices belonging to it in the time of Henry VII. there is no mention made of the tower, from which we may conclude it was not then erected. The hall, manor, and advowson of this church were anciently vested in a family who took their name from this place. Philip de Freston, was admitted a freeburgess of Ipswich, as early as the 18th of Henry III. The estate continued in his family for many years, when it came to the Latymer's in the time of Henry VIII. They continued here till about 1590—when the Goodings, of Ipswich, had the estate. It is therefore conjectured that the tower was built by one of the Latymer's a short time previous to the year 1655, as an occasional pleasant retreat, or gazebo for a better view of the river; or, probably, it constituted part of an intended house— which may be inferred from a note in some MS. collections for Suffolk, dated 1655, where it is said, "Here is part of a house lately built, not farre from the channel, commonly known by the name of Freston Tower." For whatever purposes intended, it is a very pleasing object on the banks of the Orwell. The beautiful little

sketch we have inserted is from the pencil of Mr. George Campion; and we have been favoured with the following lines by a gentleman residing in Ipswich, on viewing this engraving:—

Who can o'er thy summer tide,
Winding Orwell, ever glide;
Nor with raptur'd eye coufes
Many scenes of loveliness,
Spreading fair thy banks along,
Subjects meet for poet's song?
But the scene I love the best,
Here is faithfully express'd,
By the artist's skilful hand—
Mightier than wizard's wand.
Yes! old Freston, stern and gray,
Looking o'er the watery way,
Hath, to me, more charms than all—
Wooded park, or lordly hall.
O! methinks 'twere sweet to lie,
When the sun is riding high,
'Neath the shadow of these trees,
On the daisied turf, at ease.
Listening to the sheep-bells round,
Tinkling with a silvery sound;
Or, adown the vista bright,
Watch the bark so trim and light:
Or, upon those turrets high,
Turn a fixed and musing eye,
Till the visions of the past,
O'er the mind come crowding fast;
And, by fancy touch'd, ideal
Things become as true as real.
And unto the mind supply
Pages lost to history.
Here, perhaps, when winds were loud,
And the seaman's guiding star,
Hid her face behind a cloud—
Weeping o'er the drowning tar—
Sat some young and lovely dame.
Feeding well the beacon-flame,
F F F 2

Striving vainly to discover,
Through the gloom, her ocean rover.
Or, perchance, some hoary sage,
Dread and wonder of the age,
Here, at midnight, calm, profound,
Watch'd the planets in their round.
Or, the zealous devotee,
Here might bend repentant knee;
Deeming fleshly penance can
Cleanse the soul—mistaken man!
Or, the merry hunter, here,
Spent the night with hearty cheer;
Till the cry of hound and horn,

Woke the chace, at peep of morn.
Thoughts like these my mind engage,
Poring o'er this pictur'd page;
Pen of mine may not reveal,
What the exile lone shall feel,
When, beneath far distant skies,
Freston Tower shall greet his eyes-
He will own, with swelling heart,
The power—the magic power of ART.

In the year 1595, Mr. Thomas Goodwin, portman, of Ipswich, left to the poor of the parish of Freston, a yearly rent charge of £1: 6: 8, and 20s. a year for the preaching of four sermons in the parish church here.

The next parish is Wherstead, spelt in Doomsday, Querstede, Wervestede, &c. In an old deed without date, to which Gerard, prior of Ipswich, is one of the witnesses, is mention of the priory of Wervestede, perhaps some small foundation of short continuance united to the priory of St. Peter and St. Paul, in Ipswich, to which belonged the church and manor and several lands in this village. Gilbert de Reymes had this lordship in King John's time, he was admitted a free-burgess of Ipswich, and compounded for an exemption from toll, custom, &c. for his villains in Wherstead; and Hugh de Reymes did the same, in the fifth year of Edward I. In the first year of Edward IV. Sir John Howard had a grant of the manors of Layham and Wherstead, in Suffolk, which were in the crown by the attainder of John, earl of Wiltshire. It afterwards came to the famous Lord Chief Justice Coke, who resided here some time. The rectory is held by lease from the dean and chapter of Ely, but the advowson is in the Crown.

Wherstead Lodge, the property of Sir Robert Harlatid, bart. is a handsome modern building, delightfully situated. It was lately occupied by Lord Viscount Granville; but is at present the residence of John Fitzgerald, esq. M. P. It was rebuilt in 1794, and contains several handsome rooms fitted up with great taste, and a very noble staircase. There is also a splendid collection of pictures, by the first masters; amongst which is a Venus, by Titian. The park is finely wooded, and commands some beautiful views on the river, and the town of Ipswich.

Wherstead Church stands surrounded by wood, on the brow of the hill. On the top of the tower, from its elevated situation, a mark has been placed as a beacon for navigating the river.

We now come to Bourn Bridge, built over a small branch of the Orwell, on the road to Manningtree. It is probable that the Orwell formerly ran further inland here than it does at present, and that the bridge is of very ancient construction; for in the nineteenth year of Queen Elizabeth, we find an order of the great court for a large sum to be expended in repairing of Bourn Bridge: and it is mentioned in the perambulation of Ipswich, made in 1351, in the twentieth year of Edward III.

Within a few yards of this bridge is a neat little publichouse, called the Ostrich; in the garden belonging to which there is a most beautiful view of the town and the river that takes a fine sweeping curve about this spot—which is admirably depicted in our frontispiece, by Mr. Henry Davy.

It has been frequently observed, that no place is better fitted for the Greenland trade than Ipswich, as the same wind that bears the vessels out of port will convey them to Greenland: and an attempt of this kind was made by some merchants here," Messrs. Cornwell, Mangles, and others, in December 1786; when two ships named the "Ipswich" and "Orwell," were employed, and it was carried on for two or three years; but, from the badness of the seasons, it did not turn out a profitable speculation, and was relinquished. Some of the buildings erected for the purpose of cutting up the whale and extracting the oil are still standing; and it is probable that another attempt would be more successful.

As we proceed homewards, we pass two dock-yards, called Halifax and Nova Scotia. In the ship-yard at Halifax, lately occupied by Mr. Bayley, several large East Indiamen have been built, as w ell as some smaller vessels for the navy, particularly the "Cruiser" gunbrig, about the year 1 787; but the vessel of most importance was the "Orwell" East Indiaman, which was launched here, August the 28th, 1817: a humourous poetical account of which was published at the time, containing some curious and valuable notes. The contract for building this fine and commodious vessel—which is one of the largest of her class—was made by Mr. Jabez Bayley, with Captain M. Isacke, of Greenwich, in May, 1816. Her keel was laid in the beginning of the same month, so that little more than fifteen months were employed in building her; during which period she furnished employment, directly and indirectly, to some hundreds of individuals. Her admeasurement was one thousand three hundred and fifty tons, and the length of her keel one hundred and fifty-three feet. In her construction, upwards of two thousand loads of select oak timber, chiefly grown in the county, one hundred tons of unwrought iron, and thirty tons of copper, were used.

The "Transit" yacht, of two hundred and thirty tons, was launched from this yard, Sept. 7th, 1819. This vessel was built under the special direction of Capt. Gower. The "Transit" is intended for quick sailing, and is built peculiarly sharp, both fore and aft. The rigging, when complete, with sails bent,&c. assimilates very nearly to a Danish ketch. She has three masts, the principal or mainmast the foremost. The lower sails or courses are lore and aft gaff-sails, which will enable her to lie closer to the wind than vessels in general. The "Transit" was fitted up in the most elegant style of accommodation for the Hon. G. Vernon, son of the Archbishop of York, who has since made a trip in her to the islands of the Archipelago.

From the time that Mr. Jabez Bayley commenced business, till the launch of the Orwell, he had built eightytwo vessels of various descriptions; comprising five thousand eight hundred and seventy-three tons, of which, six were ships, ten brigs, nine sloops, ten smacks and cutters, three schooners and three packets, all for the merchants' service: and for government, eighteen brigs and sloops of war, two corvettes, one transport, one advice boat, two sailing lighters, and eleven gun-boats. In addition to these, two more East Indiamen, and several fine vessels have since been launched; and it is a remarkable fact, in the history of naval architecture, that not one of the ships built of Suffolk oak, have been affected by the dry rot. This is an example of the great exertions of one individual, and we heartily wish success to similar undertakings.

Nova Scotia is a station on the western bank of the river Orwell, about a mile and a half below Ipswich; and was, for ages, a scene of busy commerce. Previous to deepening the river, in 1S04, it possessed an excellent ship-yard and launch-way; also extensive wharfs and warehouses. January the 30th, 1763, the " Speaker" East-India-man, of seven hundred and two tons burthen, was launched from this yard; also two lire-ships, the "Spitfire" and another, in 1783. These unsightly buildings were taken down, in the year 1820; and the shore, for the most part, now assumes the more pleasing appearance of lawn and plantation, laid out with much judgment and taste

This estate is now the property and residence of Mr. R. H. Gower, a gentleman who was in the sea-service of the East-India Company, and is the author of a well-known work on seamanship, and several publications relative to marine affairs and inventions—particularly that of a vessel which differed, in a material degree, from the usual form, both in the shape of the hull and rigging; and in the author's supplement to *Seamanship,* is this account: "It appears that she was built at Itchenor, near Chichester, during the last war; and, what is unusual, principally by house-carpenters, under the superintendance of the inventor, as master-builder. Her burthen was two hundred tons; she was named the "Transit," and was launched on the 10th of May, 1800, being afterwards commanded by the inventor. She was rigged with four light masts, and, by the narrative of her performance under canvass, in a sea-way, opposed to the fast frigates of His Majesty's navy, her good qualities were highly conspicuous. She sailed

with much celerity; but, as she possessed great weatherly powers, she appeared to the greatest advantage upon a wind, and is shewn to have performed that most desirable object in the art of sailing—viz. *the making a passage across the open ocean, against a strong dead wind and high sea.* The sailing of the "Transit" was, at all times, effected with a degree of dryness, and quietude of motion unknown on board vessels of the usual form. These valuable qualities gave much sea-comfort to all on board, and it is to be regretted that an invention possessed of the advantages we have stated, did not meet the encouragement that was needed to keep the plan alive to public view. As it appears that all vessels can make their passage if the wind continue fair, but that none can perform it if the wind blow strong in a foul direction, surely to construct such a vessel as will make a passage with contrary winds is a fit subject of enquiry for the philosophical mind, and worthy the patronage of a great maritime nation; and we sincerely hope, that the ingenious inventor may yet receive the reward of his labours.

Mr. George Tovell has erected buildings for the manufacture of Roman cement, and from the convenience with which he will be enabled to execute and ship off the articles manufactured by this business, it may be carried on to any extent.

The first patent slip for hauling up vessels to repair, was introduced into Ipswich, by Messrs. G. Bayley & Co. in the spring of 1826, and is worthy of description. This invention is beautiful for its simplicity: it consists of three parallel railways of great strength, each about eighty yards long, which are fixed, upon a solid and substantial foundation, capable of carrying any necessary weight. The carriage or cradle upon which the vessel is placed is of course very strong, and yet simple in its construction. It can be taken to pieces and removed from under one vessel if required for the purpose of hauling another o o o up before the first is launched. The cradle has a great number of small iron-flanched wheels, which travel upon

the railways—thus reducing the friction at five-sixths of that which had to be overcome in the old mode of hauling up. At the upper ends of the railways stands a powerful train of wheel work, to which a chain of similar construction to that of a watch is attached: this chain is connected at the other end to the cradle, and by this contrivance, they are able to haul a vessel up along the railway at the rate of from two and a half to five feet per minute. The advantages of this plan of repairing vessels are so obvious, that at the present time, there is scarcely a vessel which is repaired in any other way at this place. We cannot but regret, that the ingenious patentee, who was a shipbuilder at Leith, had to see half the terra of his patent expire before the advantages of the plan began to be appreciated.

It is obvious from these details, that the port of Ipswich is admirably calculated for the purpose of ship-building, for from the improvements that have taken place in the river in consequence of the late act, ships of almost any burthen might be launched here, and we should not be surprised to see in a few years, quays, wharfs, and warehouses erected along the banks on this side of the river all the way to Bourn Bridge.

In 1821, by the spirited exertions of our townsman, Admiral Page, a subscription was set on foot to build a life-boat from a design and under the superintendance of Capt. Gower, to be stationed at Landguard Fort. She was launched from Mr. Bayley's yard near Stoke Bridge, on the 4th of April, and a number of experiments afterwards made of her powers and capability in the presence of an immense multitude of spectators, and appeared to answer every purpose for which the Ipswich Life Boat was intended. An advertisement expressing public thanks to Admiral Page and Captain Gower was inserted in the papers, and must have been exceedingly gratifying to their feelings.

The scene now closes with a view of the town, appearing to great advantage, accommodating itself in a sort of half-moon to the winding of the river, and terminated by the cast-iron bridge at Stoke, with a single elliptic arch sixty feet in the span and rising ten feet. Thus terminates our voyage! and fastidious indeed must the passenger be who is not pleased with an excursion along the Orwell to and from Harwich.

A plan of this river, neatly executed, was published by Mr. John Bransby, in 1814, in which the boundaries of the jurisdiction of the corporation are correctly defined: and we conclude our remarks by the following poem; for which we are indebted to the pen of a gentleman who has before contributed to these pages:—

Let mountain spirits fix their airy throne
"By the blue rushings of the arrowy *Rhone,"*
Or trace its devious course through Gallia's soil,
Where generous wine rewards the peasants' toil;
Let placid *Seine* in sinuous channels glide,
Whilst verdant islands its broad streams divide;
Or swains, reclin'd in rustic ease, require
Or pipe or dance beside "the murmuring *Loire:"*
Thro' rich Champagne, with purple clusters gay,
"Let *Marne's* slow waters weave their mazy way,"
Or glassy *Mease,* in soft succession, show
Its beauteous banks, reflected clear below.
Where snows eternal circle freedom's home,
Let the broad cataract, cream'd with whitening foam,
Or castles crowning wildest crags, combine,
With vine clad hills, t'embellish "lovely *Rhine;"*
Let *Anio* boast " of art, the priucely shrine."
Replete with wonders scarce miscall'd—"divine;"
o e e 2
O'er rugged rocks, *Ticino* "madly stray;"
Or *Dora* "swift, thro' flowery rallies

play:"
Let "Rome's vast ruins darken Tyber's wave,"
Where weeping history, shews a " nation's grave."
'Neath *Vesta'* hallowed fane and classic shade
Resistless Anio urge his bold cascade;
Round Capua's ancient walls, Voi.turnus flow,
And "trees weep amber, on the banks of Po."
Let busy *Thamet* with swelling sails, impart
The world's rich stores to London's crowded mart,
Or, thence, meandering 'midst patrician bowers,
Groves evergreen, or meads begemm'd with flowers,
Reflect proud Richmond's heights, or Windsor's regal towers
Let fair *Sabrina,* seek the " western springs,"
With health and plenty on her breezy wings;
Let *Cam* and *his,* rival tributes bear
From cloistered courts where science' sons repair;
Romantic *Wye* survey with tearful smile
His time-worn Tintern's venerable pile;
Or *Avon,* murmur, where his favorite child
"Warbled," at will, "his native woodnotes wild."
Let these,—'midst *rude or gentle* scenery plac'd, With proud or classic recollections grac'd. Awhile detain th' admiring eye, and claim A passing tribute to each honoured name: The *patriot spirit,* and the *generous mind,* Affections only, lastingly can bind; And these, howe'er for health or taste we roam, Concentrate round that spot we call our home. With these—ev'n desert wastes have power to bless Without them—Eden were a wilderness. Let then these prouder streams resplendent shine And art with Nature's softer charms combine, Tho' Mincius live in Maro's deathless song, Or tuneful Horace, Tyber's praise prolong, By "

Ouse's tide" chaste Cowper's genius smile, Or Burns, "by banks of Ayr," and his " sweet Ballochmyle" Give me, fair Orwell! thy bright, beauteous shore, With virtuous friendships grac'd—I ask no more. O, lov'd in youth! nor less as steals that day That strews my temples with time's silvery gray,
Admir'd—thy wood-crown'd heights, thy vallies green,
With sloping lawns and Tillas fair between,
Skreeu'd by rich clumps of venerable trees,
Where gay Hygeia sports on every breeze;
Thy wide-spread waters, hastening to the sea,
While o'er them *Summer* suns smile pleasantly,
Or *Sprint/'* fresh tints, or *Autumn's* changeful hues,
Thy banks adorn, and tempt the vagrant Muse,
And o'er thy bosom glides the frequent sail,
Plies the smooth oar, or sweeps the freshening gale,
May well, with many a far-fam'd stream compare
Nor Fancy's self depict a scene more fair.
Here, tho' some change the nerveless frame require
Here, let me learn to limit vain desire,
And taste the blessings Providence has sent,
With christian confidence and calm content;
Where duty's voice pervades the social camp,
And pure religion holds her hallowed lamp,
That marks the peaceful road, to souls perplext
By doubts and fears, from this world to the next;
And leads the widowed heart, by sorrow riven,
To fix sublime, its holiest hopes on heaven.
Or should disease or pain, that frame invade,
May resignation lend her potent aid
That shafts invenemom'd, faith my

shield and guide,

May fall innocuous, from the guarded side;

And when this mingled scene of time is o'er,

Its conflicts clos'd, and gain'd th' immortal shore,

Hence, let my loosened spirit soar away,

Thro' death's dark portals, to Heaven's brighter day,

Where He, " who died below and reigns above,"

Inspires the song of gratitude and love.

We shall endeavour to give a brief summary of the present state of this ancient town. Ipswich is the county town of Suffolk, and the election for the representatives for the county takes place here. The town itself sends two members to parliament; it is a borough, market town, and port; it gives the title of Viscount to the Duke of Grafton; it is locally situated in the hundred of Bosmere and Claydon, for Bosmere hundred before the conquest was called the hundred of Gepes; it is in the diocese of Norwich, within the jurisdiction of the archdeacon of Suffolk; is twenty-six miles from Bury St. Edmund's, and sixty-nine miles east from London, on the direct road to Yarmouth, which is distant fifty-four miles.

The spot upon which Ipswich stands has so many advantages that it could not fail of attracting settlers at a very early period: in approaching it by the London road it seems to stand low, but viewing it from Wherstead hill, or from the new road entering by IStoke, it rises into more importance, being situated on the side of a hill with a south aspect, declining by a gradual descent to. the quay, where the foot of it is washed by the Orwell. The soil is sand, crag, or gravel. The hills which rise above it to the north and east contribute greatly to its health and convenience, sheltering it from bleak and inclement winds, and furnishing abundant springs of pure and excellent water, with which the town is so well sup

plied, that it has suffered less from the ravages of fire than perhaps any place of similar extent and population. It possesses another advantage not common in large towns, there are few houses of any importance but what have gardens attached to them, even in the heart of the town; the place is much resorted to as an eligible residence for invalids, as the walks and rides in the neighbourhood are of the most picturesque and delightful description. And it is with much pleasure we are able to state that Mr. Shaw hus recently erected on the premises lately occupied by Messrs. Smart and Buchanan, opposite the church of St. Mary at the Key, a most convenient range of baths, which comprise vapour and medicated baths; hot air, and medicated air, or fumigating baths; salt or fresh water warm baths; hot and cold show er baths, &c. and we sincerely hope that this gentleman will meet with support and encouragement adequate to his exertions. This is a further inducement for us again to endeavour to impress upon our readers the importance of bringing our *Mineral Waters* into repute, for the use of the waters and the baths together, could not fail of bringing an influx of visitors to the town. The streets are irregular, and strangers passing through, are not aware of the number of handsome streets and excellent houses to be met with in different parts of the town. We have given an engraving of the Cornhill and Tavein-street, in which may be seen the present Townball, Corn Exchange, &c.

Several of the streets have been M'Adamised, and answer exceedingly well, particularly St. Matthew's, from the entrance of the town to the Suffolk Hotel, and we wish that the same system had been extended across the Cornhill, along Tavern-street, through Car-street, iBto the Woodbridge road, for if this were done, travellers in the way from London to Yarmouth would not have the inducement which they now have to avoid the town, in order to escape the inconvenience of passing over the stones. When any of the streets are re-paved, care should be taken to bring

the kennel on each side of the street as near to the kerb stone as possible, by which means a better and wider carriage way would be obtained; but we do hope, shortly, to see the whole of the principal streets M'Adamised. It is much to be regretted, that when the paving act was obtained, it did not empower the commissioners to cause common sewers to be erected; by which all the waste water could be carried under ground into the river. We are persuaded that this might be easily done even now, for no town can possibly be better situated for the purpose, as almost every part of it stands upon a declivity, and water could be readily conveyed into the drains, whenever it became necessary to cleanse them. It would add greatly to the neatness and cleanliness of the town, and materially encrease the health and comfort of the inhabitants.

We trust that the plan for carrying the street or road opposite the New Assembly-rooms into the Woodbridge road, at the Post Chaise inn, will be accomplished. Or if this cannot be effected the road might be carried on through Car-street, by making an entrance into the present turnpike road, through Mr. Bond's or Mr. Wright's premises. If either of these roads cannot be completed at the public expense, it would surely be worth while to effect it by the joint subscription of those proprietors whose property would be so much improved in value by the alteration. It has also been suggested, that what is called Water Lane, might be widened and levelled, at a very trifling expense, and would form an excellent communication from the Woodbridge road into St. Helen's; unci it is evident, that the more entrances there are made into the town, the more convenient it will be both for travellers and the inhabitants.

The trade of this place formerly consisted in the manufacture of broad cloth and other woollen goods, and was doubtless carried on with all quarters of the globe. All the towns and villages for many miles round were employed in it, and many of the best estates in the county were raised from its profits. On Feb. the 3rd, 1783, in commemoration of peace with America, a procession of the wool-combers guild or fraternity took place here, in which Bishop Blaise appeared in his full canonicals, attended by shepherds and shepherdesses in appropriate costume, with a large train of followers employed in the various branches of the trade. Even then in every cottage in the vicinity women and children were employed in earning a portion of their maintenance, by preparing the wool for the manufacturer, but the busy hum of the spinning wheel is no longer to be heard, and the cottagers occupation is ended. We are led also to believe that the shipping trade is much decreased, particularly with regard to those huge colliers, called Ipswich cats; but we question whether the aggregate number of vessels employed was greater than at the present moment. These cats were of large tonnage, standing very high above the water; we remember to have seen one or two of them in our early days, they were wider in proportion than other vessels of similar burthen; their hulls were painted black, and with their dingy crew and gigantic bulk, they had a gloomy and terrific appearance. It is still a common expression among the old seamen, in reference to the form of a vessel, to say that she is *catbuilt.* The shipping belonging to this port now, amounts to one hundred and forty-seven vessels of various sizes

H H H and denominations; the total amount of tonnage, eight thousand five hundred and thirty-eight tons, which affords employment to between four and five hundred persons. Ships of any burthen can come up as far as Downham Reach, but none of more than two hundred tons can approach the quay. The navigation of the river is intricate, but safe; for from the nature and extent of the ooze, if a vessel should be driven ashore in a gale of wind, she would probably get afloat again the next flowing of the tide. Our shipping is principally confined to the coasting trade, and to the metropolis; there are some vessels that carry corn and flour directly to Liverpool, and bring back chiefly salt in return, there are also several vessels

to the Baltic for timber, and likewise some communication with Holland and Hamburgh, and occasionally to America. A vast deal of business is done in the corn and coal trade; forty thousand chaldrons of coals are annually imported, and sent through the medium of the Stowmarket navigation into all parts of the interior of the county; vast quantities of grain and flour are forwarded to the London market. Our corn market is the best in the county. Ipswich, Yarmouth, and Lynn, export the most corn coastways of any ports in England. Ipswich sends annually to London alone, from sixty to eighty thousand quarters of malt. Several shipping companies have been formed, and have well answered the purposes intended. On the 1st of January, 1825, a number of merchants and tradesmen became subscribers under a trust deed, to raise the sum of £20,000 by shares of £100 each, and agreed to form themselves into a society or partnership, to be called the "Ipswich Steam Navigation Company," for the conveyance of goods and passengers to London. Vessels were built as steam packets, to sail to and fro, between this port and the metropolis, and met with considerable encouragement; but owing to a variety of unfortunate circumstances, the intention was unhappily frustrated, and this useful speculation failed. These steamers were not long since both sold for £ 1800, being about a seventh part of their original cost. Notwithstanding the failure of this plan, we are of opinion, that a steamer built upon a proper construction for the navigation of our river would still answer the purpose of the proprietor, and be of public advantage. Since writing the above we have seen one of these vessels in Messrs. G. Bayley and Co's. yard, which has been re-constructed, and improved so much, that she will draw not more than four feet and a half of water; her decks have been taken up and altered in a manner well adapted for the conveyance of both passengers and goods, and she is now a large, commodious, and beautiful vessel, capable of accommodating two hundred passengers. She will be ready for sailing in

the month of May, and if well managed, we are firmly persuaded she will produce profit to her proprietors, and benefit to the town; and that many of the citizens of London, who are annually in the habit of making an excursion to the sea side, will prefer the novelty of exploring the picturesque and beautiful banks of the Orwell, to the constant never varying voyage to Margate and Ramsgate; for in a voyage to Ipswich, there is every thing to gratify the wishes of a visitor.

In the time of Elizabeth, a great number of orders and regulations appear in the books of the corporation, respecting the preservation of the oyster beds in the river, and various other fish then brought to the market. A regular fish market was then held opposite to St. Lawrence' church, in what is now called St. Lawrence'-street. It is strange how these desirable articles of consumption have

H H H 2 been so much neglected, for the fishermen from Wivenhoe and other places have been allowed to take the spat from the oyster beds with impunity, which is greatly to be lamented, for our river oysters, if they were properly fed, would bo equal to any in the kingdom. The Orwell and waters adjoining are well stored in their seasons with various sorts of fish; which seldom, except by accident, find the way to our market. Our soles are well known to be of the finest quality; and mullets, turbots, smelts, skate, whitings, haddocks, and lobsters, might be caught in abundance; salmon was formerly plentiful, and shoals of the grey mullet, of a large size and delicious flavour, are frequently to be seen beyond Stoke bridge, and there is only one old man in the town who ever attempts to take them, when if a net was properly secured across the arch of the bridge, not one of them could escape. Surely it would not exceed the powers of the "commissioners for the improvement of the river" to set aside a portion of their fund for the encouragement and improvement of our fisheries, it would give employment to a valuable and industrious class of men upon the river, be of great benefit to the town, and would be money advantageously laid out. We respectfully submit this to consideration, and hope to see the Ipswich fish market once again revived; or if it be out of the jurisdiction of the commissioners, why do not the corporation take it in hand *l* for a herring fishery might be carried on in our port as well as at Yarmouth and Lowestoft, and with much greater safety to the vessels employed. There was some idea of carrying this. into execution, in the year 1812; and a building was about to be constructed for curing the fish, on the south side of the river, but it never was completed. As it is difficult for persons who now have capital to employ it to advantage, why not form a "herring fishing company," by shares and subscriptions; and by offering premiums to those fishermen who distinguished themselves, the object might be accomplished for a third part of the sum necessary for forming a shipping company; it would be the means of subsistence to hundreds of poor families, not like a manufactory depending on the caprice of fashion or the versatility of public opinion, but deriving its wealth from the exhaustless storehouses of the deep.

In consequence of the introduction of a great many troops during the late war, the place being considered as a garrison town, it was roused from its apathy and dulness, and quickly became the scene of bustle, business, and importance; lodgings and houses w ere let at high prices to the officers and their families, and many new houses were erected. The agriculturists received enormous prices for their productions, and spent their money with liberal profusion; the weekly circulation of thousands gave a stimulus to exertion; trade of every description flourished in Ipswich, and many handsome fortunes were made. Acts of parliament were procured to pave and light the town, to widen and improve the streets; obstructions were removed, old buildings pulled down, new and elegant houses and shops were erected: the place assumed altogether an altered appearance, and it has been improving ever sjnce; new erections are in progress and it will soon be justly considered a handsome and well-built town. From the circumstances of the times, this influx of wealth has subsided; but the stimulus has been given; the spirit of improvement is aroused; there is still a great deal of business carried on, and Ipswich has suffered less from the pressure of events than most places in the kingdom. From 1811 to 1821, the population of the place encreased, from thirteen thousand six hundred and seventy to more than eighteen thousand, and is now about twenty thousand. There are some manufactories of note; the spacious and commodious buildings erected in St. Clement's, by Mr. Ranson, in which the whole, process of manufacturing tobacco and snuff, as well as that of paper is accomplished by steam, aud is well worthy of observation. The iron-foundry established many years since, by Mr. Robert Ransome, is an extensive concern, and is now carried on by James and Robert Ransome, his sons: these gentlemen have obtained patents for sundry progressive improvements on ploughs—which are in general use. There is also another concern of general iron-works in the town, carried on by Mr. Jacob Garrett, to a considerable extent. The brewery and establishment of Mr. John Cobbold, at the Cliff, is of vast importance, and is more particularly described in our account of the Orwell. Mr. Richard Gooding has a pottery of considerable consequence. There is also a manufactory of Roman cement, by Mr. Tovell, on the south bank of the river; and the beautiful Suffolk bricks, both red and white, are made in great quantities in the vicinity of the town. There is a manufactory for stays, by Messrs. Edwards, which is deserving of every encouragement, as upwards of seven hundred women and girls are engaged; thus affording employment and maintenance to numbers of the industrious inhabitants.

In the forty-seventh of George III. an act was passed, constituting the members of parliament for the borough, the corporation for the time being, and fifty-six merchants and tradesmen particularly named, as commissioners, to form a court of justice for the recovery of debts under £5. to be called "The Court of Requests, for the town and borough of Ipswich, and the liberties thereof in the county of Suffolk;" which is held every Tuesday, usually in the Town-hall. The qualification of a commissioner who is not of the corporation, is a real estate of £40. per annum, or personal estate of the value of £800. There is a table of fees hung up in the court. Its powers require to be executed with delicacy and discretion, as.they are peremptory and extensive, for ho action commenced in this court can be removed to any superior court except by the plaintiff, when the defendant shall have removed himself and his effects out of the jurisdiction of this court.

The more opulent inhabitants of Ipswich have not been unmindful of the wants of their poorer neighbours, for the public charities and benevolent institutions are unusually numerous, and do honour to the town. A full and detailed account of them is to be found in the last edition of" The Ipswich Gifts and Legacies," &c. edited by the Rev. William Edge, and published by Mr. Dorkin in 1819, forming a volume of three hundred pages. We must therefore content ourselves with a brief enumeration. The first, in point of date and importance, is the charity school of grey-coat boys and blue-coat girls, instituted in the year 1709. This charity is supported by annual subscriptions, and every subscriber of one guinea per annum, is entitled to the recommendation of a child. Many very important donations have been given, and legacies be-queathed, and the amount has, from time to time, been vested in land and funded property; and from Michaelmas 1828, to Michaelmas 1829,

The receipts were 968 0 0

The disbursement 646 3 1

Leaving a balance in favour of the Charity of £322 17 2

No child can be admitted unless the parents are members of the church of England. Eight pounds are allowed with every boy bound out as an apprentice, and two pounds to purchase clothes and linen, if going to service for a year at least; the girls are allowed forty shillings for clothes and linen upon their going into reputable services, besides their own earnings from sewing and knitting. The nnmber of children now in the school is seventy boys and fifty girls; since the first institution near fifteen hundred children have been admitted. It is an admirable charity, and many individuals who have received their education in this school have risen into wealth and importance, and become leading men in their native town; and we cannot refrain from mentioning the following instance of gratitude and right feeling. On March the 1st, 1830, Mr. Thomas Read of Mile-end, Old-town, departed this life, aged 61. He had realised a competency, as commander of a vessel trading between Hull and Petersburgh, and he bequeathed the sum of £500 as a legacy to this school, wherein he received his education.

The Red-sleeve school was reestablished in 1752. The master, according to the rules of the school, must be a member of the church of England, and attend at St. Lawrence' church, every Sunday with his scholars. The number of boys who are clothed and educated is thirty-six. It is supported by subscription and some legacies of considerable importance.

The Green-sleeve school, instituted in 1736. This establishment is entirely supported by voluntary contributions; there are ten boys and eight girls, who attend every sabbath at the meeting-house, Tacket-street.

The Ipswich Education Society, instituted 1811, on the plan of the British and Foreign School Society, in which about two hundred boys are educated.

The Ipswich Female Charity School, instituted 1811, with a view of qualifying the girls for useful servants, in which about eighty girls receive their education.

Ipswich Centre 1 Schools, of the Suffolk Society, for the education of the poor, in the principles of the established church, instituted 1812, about three hundred boys and girls are taught upon Dr. Bell's system; and there are upwards of a thousand children educated at the various Sunday-schools.

The charity for the relief of poor widows and orphans of clergyman of Suffolk. Mr. John Pemberton, portman, of Ipswich, by his will dated the 23rd of March, 1718, gave his rectories of Pettistree, Wickham, and Bing, to trustees which he named, that they should yearly raise and pay to the widows and orphans of church of England clergymen, truly so in doctrine and discipline, inhabiting within fifteen miles of Ipswich, viz. to such widows and orphans only as are indigent and necessitous, £25 per annum, to be paid half yearly by the said trustees. The funds of this excellent charity have been greatly augmented by liberal donations, annual subscriptions, and legacies. The sum usually given to the widow that applies, is from twenty-eight to thirty pounds according to the age, and the orphan obtains an annuity in proportion to the widow; respect being had to infirmity and age. Thus the name of Pemberton will be handed down to posterity as the author of this noble institution, which in hundreds of instances has been a blessing to the orphan, and caused the widow's heart to leap for joy.

The next charity is of a similar nature, called the Suffolk Benevolent Society, for the relief of necessitous widows and orphans of protestant dissenting ministers, also of such ministers as through age or infirmities may be incapacitated for public service, in the county of Suffolk, instituted 1790. The fund has been greatly augmented by annual contributions and donations.

Ipswich Public Dispensary, for the relief of the indigent sick, instituted 1797.

Ipswich Humane Society, for the recovery of persons apparently dead from drowning, &c. instituted 1801. A medal was presented by this society to Master Acton, then only thirteen years old, who had, at the risk of his own life, saved a boy of eight years of age from drowning, on the 1st of October, 1818.

Ipswich Bible Society; Ipswich and Suffolk Church Missionary Association; Suffolk Society m aid of Missions; Baptists' Missionary Auxiliary Society; Wesleyan Missionary Association; Association for promoting Christianity amongst the Jews; Society for superseding the necessity of climbing-boys; in sweeping cbimnies; a society for clothing the infant poor; two lying-in charities; three friendly and benevolent societies, for visiting and relieving the sick and indigent; two savingbanks; one female and thirty-one male benefit societies; and a penny-club, to assist the poor in the purchase of clothes for their children.

In the year 1823, a number of individuals agreed to enter into an annual subscription towards forming an Anti-Slavery Society. A committee was chosen to act as an auxiliary to the London committee, whose object is "to ameliorate the condition of the slaves in the British colonies, and gradually to abolish slavery." There has hitherto been little opportunity of bringmg the exertions of this committee before the public, but they are quietly doing their duty. Richard D. Alexander, esq. is treasurer, and the Rev. J. Charlesworth, secretary; and when it is considered that the great champion of the slaves, Thomas Clarkson, is their coadjutor, there will be no lack of *perseverance* to obtain the humane object of their desire. There is also a committee of ladies formed for the same benevolent purpose: and it is worthy of remark, " that there is no town in the kingdom where political animosity has been carried higher than at Ipswich; yet this has never been allowed to prejudice the cause of the poor slaves; for of whatever party the bailiffs were who were in power, the town-hall has never been refused from the year 1788 to the present time, to those who solicited for petitioning either for the abolition of the slave trade, or the abolition of colonial slavery.

The Seamen's Shipwreck Benevolent Society, for the purpose of relievin spipwrecked seamen, and preventing imposition by persons pretending to be sailors, is supported by a subscription of eighteen-pence per quarter, by each member; who, on being brought to distress by shipwreck, is entitled to a certain sum. This society is governed by a set of excellent rules and orders; which are enrolled according to act of parliament, and were revised and altered, and confirmed by the magistrates, on the 12th of July, 1826.

A Mendicity Society has been, for some time past, in operation; and it has lately been reorganised, upon a plan that is calculated, in a great measure, to abolish vagrancy.

In a former part of this work we gave the history of the corporation, and of the formation of its municipal establishment—we shall now briefly state their oflices and powers. The office of high steward is an honorary appointment, generally presented to some nobleman in the neighbourhood, or some person who has distinguished himself eminently, as a statesman or as a commander of our fleets and armies; and the only instance known of its being put to the vote was when our present high steward, Sir Robert Harland, bart. had a majority in his favour in opposition to the duke of Wellington. The two bailiffs, whose power is equal, are the chief magistrates. Clerks of the market and conservators of the river, who are chosen

I 1 1 2 annually, by the majority of the freemen, on the 8th of September, at a great court. There are twelve portmen, who whenever a vacancy occurs have the power of filling up their own body by a majority of their whole number; which power they have lost, by suffering their number to fall lower than seven At present there are only five portmen living. The bailiffs choose annually four of the portmen to act as assistant justices. The twenty-four common-council-men are chosen by the majority of their own body, in the same way as the portmen: twelve of them are headboroughs or chief constables. The bailiffs, portmen, and common-councilmen form the *assembly;* any number of whom are sufficient to transact business: this is the *deliberative body* of the corporation, to agree upon the terms of leases, &c. &c. The town clerk is chosen annually, at a great court, and is generally an attorney, who is a freeburgess; but there have been two or

three exceptions. Two chamberlains, who attend at the sessions and receive fines. Four clavigers, who keep the keys of the records of the corporation; which are deposited in the Moot-hall of the borough, principally in a strong oaken chest, curiously carved, and of great antiquity—of which the following is an accurate representation.

Town treasurer, who receives the rents. Clerk of the market, who collects the dues at St. George's fair, and should account to the bailiffs. Water bailiff, common crier, bridewell keeper, gaoler, four Serjeants at arms, two beadles, and five musicians.

The bailiffs, portmen, common-council-men, and an indefinite number of free-burgesses constitute a *great court:* forty burgesses at least are usually present. The charter days for holding great courts are the eighth and the twenty-ninth of September: the bailiffs may call a great court any day they please, by giving forty-eight hours' notice to the portmen. No person can legally be admitted to the freedom of the borough, unless two of the portmen are present at the great court: the freedom of the borough is obtained by patrimony, or by apprenticeship for seven years, to a free-burgess, residing either in or out of the borough. Some persons have, at different periods, been presented with their freedom, or become, as they are called, honorary freemen: this has been resorted to by both sides, to serve the purposes of party: it has never been a popular measure, but a constant cause of dispute and litigation. The two representatives in parliament are chosen by a majority of the free burgesses, in great court assembled; and the total number that voted at the last general election, in 1826, was nine hundred and eighty-four. The great court is summoned by the crier blowing an ancient brass horn; which is said to have been presented by King John. The regalia of the corporation consists of two maces, a silver oar, and a silver cup.

On the 7th of September, 1829, a great court was held, for the purpose of submitting a petition to the consideration of the free-burgesses, to be present-

ed to His Majesty, for the purpose of obtaining a renewal of the charter granted to the borough the 11th of February, in the seventeenth year of Charles II. which confirmed all the charters that, at various times, had been granted to the corporation. After the usual preamble, the petition stated —

"And your petitioners most humbly beg further to represent that divers differences having of late time arisen within the said town and borough, informations in nature of 7110 *warranto* have been prosecuted in your Majesty's Court of King's Bench, and judgments of *ouster* obtained against the bailiffs and several other members of the said corporation or corporate body, and that there now exist only five portmei) of the said town and borough, and that such five portmen being fewer in number than a majority of the integral number of twelve, no further election of portmen can be had; and that iu consequence thereof, the said corporation is now not only incapable of enjoying and exercising all its liberties and franchises, but is in danger of being altogether and entirely dissolved and annihilated.

"Your petitioners therefore most humbly supplicate and pray your Majesty will be graciously pleased to grant to the burgesses and commonalty of the town and borough of Ipswich, your Majesty's royal charter or letters patent, to remedy the defects herein-beforementioned, and provide for the due administration of justice within the said town and borough, and in other respects enable your Majesty's subjects, the said burgesses and commonalty, to exercise and enjoy all their accustomed liberties and franchises fully, and without delay.

"And your Majesty's grateful petitioners, as in duty bound, shall ever pray," &c.

This petition was proposed by the Blue Interest, and objected to by the opposite party, upon the grounds that there was no necessity for a new charter, as the decision of the Court of King's Bench, that the present number of portmen were unable to fill up their own body, was contrary to law and common sense, and that it was brought forward for the purpose of introducing some of the common council into the body of portmen, which was contrary to the present charter. A poll thereupon was demanded, and the numbers, at its close, were—

For the petition, 265

Agnint it, I 30

Migorit) in favour of tht petition, 131

The petition was presented, and the parties for and against it have been heard before the attorney-general; but as they could not agree about the manner of filling up the body of portmen, matters still remain in the same unsettled state: and we sincerely wish that whenever the new charter is granted, it will put an end to the disputes and litigation by which the corporation has been, for so many years, distracted.

We shall conclude our remarks upon matters connected with the corporation, with a list of the representatives of the borough, the high stewards, the bailiffs, the recorders, and the town clerks.

REPRESENTATIVES IN PARLIAMENT. 26th Henry VI. 1447. John Smith and William Ridout, burgesses resident. 26th Henry VI. 1448. John Smith and William Wetherold, at Ave marks each. 27th Henry VI. 1449-John Andrews and Richard Felaw. 28th Henry VI. 1450. John Smith and Thomas Dunron. 29th Henry VI. 1451. Gilbert Debenham and J. Smith. 31st Henry VI. 1463. John Smith and Edmund Winter: the last without fee.—This we think was the first bribe. 33rd Henry VI. 1455. John Timperley and Gilbert Deben ham, jun. esq. 39th Henry VI. 1460. William Worsop and John River, at 13d. per day each. 1st Edward IV. 1461. Richard Felaw and Win. Baldree.

William Worsop and John Lopham. Worsop to have 20d. a day at York; at any nearer place 16d. and at London 12d. Lopham 12d. a day every where.

John Lopham and Wm. Worsop.

John Wallworth and Wm. Ridout.

John Wymondham and J. Hobart.

John Timperley, jun. and John Alfray of Hendley. Timperley at 8d. per day; Alfray serveth in consideration of his admission to be a free-bnrgess. Wm. Worsop and John Wallworth. Worsop

at Ss. per week, and if the parliament be adjourned, to have Is. per day; Wallworth 3s. 4d. per week.

James Hobart and John Timperley, at 26s. 8d. each, or two marks.

John Timperley and Roger Wentworth.

Thomas Baldry and John Wallworth. Baldry at 2s. per day; Wallworth at Is.

Benet Caldwell and Thos. Baldrey.

Thomas Samson and Wm. Wimbell.

Thomas Fastolf and John Wallworth, at 12d. per day each.

John Yaxley and Thomas Baldrey. Their wages to be at the order of the great court.

John Fastolf and Edmund Booking; at£l: 6: 8 each, if at Westminster; if further off, to be ordered by great court.

N. B. The great court ordered £4. more to Fastolf, and to Bocking, £3. 21st Henry VIII. 1529. 31st Henry VIII. 1539. 33rd Henry VIII. 1541. 1st Edward VI. 1547. 6th Edward VI. 1553. 1st Mary. 1553. 1554. 1st Philip & Mary. 1554. 2nd and 3rd ditto. 1555. 4th and 5th ditto. 1557. 1st Elizabeth. 1559. 5th Elizabeth. 15G3. 13th Elizabeth. 1571. 14th Elizabeth. 1572.

Thomas Alvard and Richd. Bailey.

Thomas Baldrey and Thos. Alvard. To serve without wages, not otherwise.

William Spencer and Thomas Hall. Spencer to have 40s.

N. B. He had 6s. 8d. more.

Thomas Baldry and Edmund Daundy. The same.

Humphry Wingfield and Thos. Rush; and they came into court, and took their oaths of freemen. T. Rush and T. Howard. Win. Sabyn and Edmund Daundy. Ralfe Gooding and John Sparrowe. John Gosnold and John Smith, alias

Dyer.

John Smith, alias Dyer, and Richard Bird.

John Gosnold, esq. and John Sulyard, esq.

Clement Higham, esq. privy counsellor, and Thomas Pooley, esq.

Ralfe Gooding and John Smith, alias Dyer.

J. Sulyard, esq. and Richard Smart, esq.

Wm. Whecroft and Philip Williams. The said Williams remitted to the town half his burgess fee.

ThomasSeckford, jun. esq. and Robert Barker. Barker had £31:4:0.

Thomas Seckford, esq. master of requests, and Edwd. Grimeston, esq.

Edward Grimeston, esq. and John Moor, gent.

Thomas Seckford, esq. jun. and Edwd.

Griniestone, esq. K K K

Sir John Higham, and John Barker' esq. provided Sir John Higham shall take the freeman's oath

John Lany esq. recorder, and J. Barker, porfhian

J. Barker, esq. and Win, Smart, gent.

Robert Barker and Zachariah Lock, esq. Lock £5.

Michael Stanhope and P. Bacon, esq. The same.

Sir Henry Glemham and Sir F. Bacon.

Sir Francis Bacon, R. Snelling; and afterwards W. Cage in the place of Sir Frain is, who was elected by the university of Cambridge.

Robert Snelling and William Cage, gent. Snelling £50.—Cage £50.

Robert Snelling and Wm. Cage, esq. The same.

Robert Snelling and Sir Wm. Younge.

Wm. Cage, esq. and E. Day, gent.

William Cage and John Gurdon, esq. of Great Wenham. J. Gurdon had 104 votes, Edmund Day, 95.

John Gurdon and William Cage, esq. and in the place of Cage, deceased, Francis Bacon, esq.

N. B. 18th Charles I. Cage had £100, and December the 5th, 1643, John Gurdon had £100, and Cage £60. more, besides the C100. formerly granted.

Nathaniel Bacon and F. Bacon, esqrs. The same.

The same.

Sir Frederick Cornwallis, in the place of Nathaniel Bacon, deceased.

John Sicklemore and Wm. Bloise, esqrs. and John Wright in the room of Sicklemore.

Gilbert Lindfield and J. Wright.

John Wright and Gilbert Lindfield.

£60. was ordered for Mr. Wright and £20. for Lindfield. The same.

John Wright and Sir J. Barker, bart.

Sir John Barker, Peyton Ventris; and in the place of Ventris (made a judge) Sir Charles Bloise.

Sir John Barker and Sir C. Bloise.

Sir John Barker and Chas. Whitaker.

S. Barnardiston and Richard Phillips.

J. Martin, esq. and Sir C. Duncomb.

Charles Whitaker and Richard Phillips.

Charles Whitaker and J. Bence.

Henry Pooley and John Bence; and in the place of Pooley, William Churchill, esq.

J. Bence and William Churchill.

Wm. Churchill, and Sir Wm. Barker.

Wm. Churchill aud Sir Wm. Barker.

Wm. Churchill and Wm. Thompson. Returned, but set aside on petition, and Richard Richardson, Serjeant at law, and Orlando Bridgman, esq. the petitioners declared duly elected.

Sir Wm. Thompson and F. Negus, esq.

Sir William Thompson and Francis Negus. In the place of Sir Win. (made a judge) P. Broke in the place of Negus, dead, William Wollaston.

William Wollaston and Samuel Kent.

Samuel Kent and Edward Vernon.

The same.

The same. In the place of Vernon, Thomas Staunton; in the place Kent, Gi'orgf Monlgomerie.

K K K 2

George III. 1761. Thomas Staunton and Francis Vernon, (afterwards Lord Orwell.) 1768. Thomas Staunton and Wm. Wollaston.

1747. Thomas Staunton and Wm. Wollaston. 1790. The same..1794. William Middleton and John Cator.

Mr. Cator's election was declared void, and C. Alexander Crickitt was elected in his room.

1790. Sir John Hadley D'Oyley and Charles Alexander Crickitt. 1796. Charles Alexander Crickitt and Sir Andrew Snape Hamond. 1902. The same. In place of Mr. Crickitt, deceased, Wm. Middleton. 1806. Hon. Robert Stopford and Richard

Wilson.

180T. Sir Home Popham and Robert Alexander Crickitt.

1912. R. A. Crickitt and John Round, jun.

1919. R. A. Crickitt and William Newton. 1920. Thomas Barrett Lennard and William Haldimand.

1926. W. Haldimand and Robert Torrens, both ousted by 1927. Charles Mackinnon and Robert Adam Dundas.

HIGH STEWARDS.

The first High Steward was William Cordell, (afterwards Sir William) who was master of the Rolls, in the third and fourth years of Philip and Mary, 1557, with an annual allowance of £4. payable half yearly.

2nd Elizabeth. 1581. Sir Thomas Walsingham. 1590. Lord Hunsdon. 1596. The Earl of Essex. The patent of these three were to hold during the pleasure of the corporation, at the yearly fee of £4,0.

In 1601, the Earl of Essex being accused of High Treason was discharged, and the patent declared void.

Thomas Lord Buckhurst, afterwards Earl of Dorset, was elected in his room. Mr. Walton the then town-clerk, having been removed from his office, he petitioned the High Steward, who was then also Lord High Treasurer of England, who directed all the particulars respecting the business to be laid before him; but it does not appear that he had any power to interfere, nor are the duties of the High Steward any where set forth at the time the office was originally created.

James I. 1600. The Earl of Salisbury was chosen, but did not accept the office, when the Earl of Suffolk was elected, and 40s. given to his Lordship's secretary for his pains. 1st Charles I. 1627. Theophilus, Earl of Suffolk, then Lord Lieutenant of the county was chosen 13th Charles II. 1663. John, Earl of Suffolk, then Lord Lieutenant, succeeded. William III. 1692. Charles, Lord Cornwallis.

1703. The Earl of Dysart. 1729. Lionel, Earl of Dysart. 40th George III. 1800.

Horatio, Lord Nelson. 1806. Wilbraham, Earl of Dysart 2nd George IV. 1821. Sir Robert Harland, bart. 17th Elizabeth. 18th Charles I. 12th Charles II. 12th William III. 7th Anne. 13th George II. 2nd George III. RECORDERS. 1561. John Clenche. 1579. John Laney. 1639. Nicholas Bacon. 1679. John Sick lemur. 1700. Charles Whitaker. 1704. Leicester Martin. 1707. William Thompson. 1739. Richard Lloyd. 1761. Charles Gray. 1776. Humphrey Rant. 1779. William Mayhew. 1787. Charles Alexander Crickitt. 1803. Robert Alderson. "Whereas Mr. (and elect) Aldus heing sent for to come and take his oath of Bailiff of this town, he not heing well, ent word he could not come up, whereupon the romt doth order that Mr. Aldus hali take his oath at the next petty court," hut we Mipptw 1m di.l not recover, for his name doc." not appear afterwarda, and Mr. Lura-Jours-crved thwhole year alone. t Richard Phillipe, e«j. was elected, hut paid £loo. u a line, for not erving the office. On the death of Pooley, Seekainp disdaiined, and was re-elected with Charles Hammond, for the remainder of that year. BIOGRAPHICAL CATALOGUE OF DISTINGUISHED PERSONAGES CONNECTED WITH THE TOWN OF IPSWICH.

If this part of the volume were to be executed with the talent necessary for a complete biographer, it would, doubtless, be the most interesting portion of the history of Ipswich; but it must, for several reasons, be little more than a catalogue *raisonnie*. or a brief abstract and chronicle of names, with a short memorial of each individual character; and it is probable that some have been omitted who were worthy of insertion. Wherever we have found a monument erected to the memory of a person in any way distinguished, or could note the place of sepulture, we have inserted our notice of such individual, with a view of varying the necessary dulness of parochial history. This is also the case when the persons mentioned were immediately connected with any particular parish or place, whether they had died there or not. Whenever this has been previously done, we have merely inserted the name in the Index, with reference to the page of the book where such sketch is to be found.

To do full justice to the character of the numerous distinguished individuals who have been, and still are, connected with this town, we could swell our materials into ponderous volumes; but, in order to keep faith, as near as we can, with our subscribers, we must compress our matter into a much smaller compass, having, now, been compelled to trespass upon their indulgence, for extending our publication somewhat beyond the bounds originally proposed.

Acton, Eliza, a native of Ipswich, is author of a volume of poems which display much feeling and taste, and have been so well received, that a second edition was printed at Ipswich, by R. Deck, 1827.

Albemarle, George Monk, duke of, the restorer of Charles II. to his crown, was presented with the freedom of the borough—was born December 6th, 1608, and died 1670. This extraordinary man was an author; for, after his death, the following treatise was published by authority, which he composed while a prisoner in the Tower: it is called "Observations upon Military and Political Affairs, written by the honourable George, duke of Albemarle, &c." London, 1671, small folio. He was also the writer of several other tracts. Cromwell had strong suspicions of his intentions; for, a little time before his death, he wrote to him a letter, with the following curious postscript: "There be that tell me, that there is a certain cunning fellow in Scotland, called George Monk, who is said to lie in wait there, to introduce Charles Stuart; I pray you use your diligence to apprehend him and send him up to me."

Anolesey, marquis of. This distinguished nobleman is collaterally descended from Sir William Paget, Knight of the Garter; who was elevated to the peerage, in the third year of King Edward VI. in 1549. The late earl of Uxbridge was summoned, by writ, to parliament, in 1770, and in 1784, was created earl of Uxbridge; who was succeeded by his son Henry-William, created marquis of Anglesey for his ser-

vices in the late war—in which he greatly distinguished himself as a general of cavalry. He is a general in the army, and colonel of the 7th Hussars; who were several years in garrison at Ipswich; where his lordship resided for a considerable time, and was conspicuous for his munificence and liberality. He was with the duke of Wellington in many of his campaigns, and displayed great bravery and skill as a cavalry officer—particularly at the battle of Waterloo; where his leg was carried off by a shot, and buried at Hougomont, and where a somewhat singular monument is erected to *its* memory: which circumstance produced the following *jeu (T sprit;* and, from its whimsicality and humour, we have been induced to insert it here:—

"Here lies—and let no saucy knave
Presume to sneer and laugh,
To learn, that, mouldering in this grave,
   Is laid—a British calf.
"For he who writes these lines, is sure
That those who read the whole,
Will find such laugh were premature,
   For here, too, lies—a sole.
"And here five little ones repose—
Twin-born with other five—
Unheeded by their brother toes,
   Who all are now alive.
"A leg and foot—to speak more plain— Rest here, of one commanding;
Who, though his wits he might retain.
   Lost half his understanding.
"Who—when the guns, with murder fraught, Poured bullets thick as hail—
Could only in this way be brought
   To give the foe leg bail.
"Who, now, in England, just as gay
As in the battle brave,
Goes to the rout, review, or play.
   With one foot in the grave.
"Fortune in vain here shewed her spite, For he will still be found.
Should England's sons engage in fight,
   Resolv'd to stand her ground.
"But Fortune's pardon I must beg—
She wished not to disarm;
And when she lopped the hero's leg,
   She did not seek his h—arm:
"And but indulged a harmless whim,
Since he could walk with one,
She thought two legs were lost on him
   Who never deigned to run."

Avlmer, John, bishop of London, was born at Akenham Hall, near Ipswich, in the year 1521, and became tutor to Lady Jane Grey—who spoke of him in the most affectionate and friendly terms. He was very rigid against both the papists and puritans, and was a warm-tempered, irritable man. He was rather a man of business than a theologian, and died very rich, at Fulham, 1594.

Bacon, Francis, was born the 22nd of January, 1561. He was several times member of parliament for Ipswich, previous to the year 1614, when he left that borough on being elected for the university of Cambridge. It would be idle to attempt here, the history of the great Lord Chancellor Bacon, the father of experimental philosophy, whose wonderful talents and extraordinary fall from greatness are known to all the civilized world, and whose littleness of conduct, contrasted with the magnitude of his mental capacity, induces us to exclaim, alas! poor frail humanity. In the affairs of common life, the most enlightened philosophers are no more than common men.

The best editions of Lord Bacon's works are in five volumes, quarto, and ten volumes, octavo;'they have been repeatedly re printed on thc continent, in Latin. He died in April, 1G26; and, notwithstandin his delinquency, will live for ever in the recollection of every lover of science.

Bacon, Nathaniel, was third son of Edward Bacon of Shrubland Hall, who was the third son of Sir Nicholas Bacon, the lord keeper. Nathaniel was a bencher of Gray's Inn, and sometime recorder of Bury St. Edmund's; he was member for Ipswich during three or four successive parliaments, in the period from 1654 to 16G0, in which year he died. He finished his "Annals of Ipswich" previously mentioned, during the time that he was member and recorder for the borough; and he concludes the volume with pathetically lamenting the death of the unfortunate monarch Charles 1. He never accepted of any political power under the Protector, but he was frequently consulted by Cromwell, who had a high opinion of his talents and integrity.

Bacon, Sir Nicholas, lord keeper of the Great Seal, in the reign of Queen Elizabeth, was born at Chislehurst", in Kent, 1510, and died February the 20th, 1579. Camden describes him as " a man of gross body, but most quick wit, singular prudence, supreme eloquence, happy memory, and for judgment, the other pillar of the state." He interested himself much in favour of the charities of Ipswich.

Baldry, Joshua Kirby, is a native of this town, the son of Mr. Baldry, a painter, who long resided at Ipswich. He was apprenticed to an engraver, and exhibited considerable talents in his art. He undertook a representation of the magnificent east window of the chapel of King's College, Cambridge; which was drawn, engraved, coloured, and published by him, in the year 1809. It is accurately delineated, and the brilliancy of the colour exceedingly well preserved. It is a work of great labour and perseverance; and he was eleven years in completing the copies necessary for the subscribers. He died at Cambridge, in the year 1829.

Barton, Bernard, the celebrated Quaker Poet, as he is usually called, was educated at Ipswich, and was under the tuition of Mr. William Candler, from 1790 to 1798. He was born in the neighbourhood of London, on the 31st of January, 1784; and is now residing at Woodbridge, in Suffolk. The following is a list of the publications of which he is the author: "Poems," fourth edition, foolscap 8vo. 7s. 6d.; "Minor Poems," including "Napoleon," second edition, 7s.; "Poetic Vigils," foolscap 8vo. 8s. ; "A Missionary's Memorial," 8vo. Is. 6d.; "Devotional Verses," 12mo. 6s. 6d. ; "A Widow's Tale, and other Poems," 12mo. 5s. 6d.; "A New Year's Eve, and other Poems," 8vo. 9s.; two anonymous volumes, and " Metrical Effusions and Poems, by an Amateur;" besides contributing to a number of Annuals and other periodical w orks From his residence in Ipswich at that period of life when the mind is likely to receive strong and lasting impressions, many effusions of his muse are to be found

scattered through his works, in which he displays his early predeliction in favour of the picturesque beauties of nature so conspicuous in the vicinity of Ipswich. His fame, as a poet, is so well established, that it is almost superfluous for us to attempt to add our feeble tribute of admiration;

M M M but we may be permitted to say, that there is an harmonious flow of versification in his poems, combined with an easy elegance of diction that cannot fail to please. Manly and liberal sentiments, blended with a truly christian feeling in the cause of piety and virtue, are conspicuous in all his productions; and, though he has written much, it may, with propriety, be said of him, that he has not written a line—

"Which, Jiving, he could wish to blot. "

Bennett, John—who has resided in Ipswich for some years—is the author of " Short-hand Explained," and a volume of " Poems"—the second edition of which w as printed in Ipswich, by S. Cowell, 1830—"An English translation of ' Cilery's Captivity of Louis XVI. King of France;"" "An Expeditious Method of Writing in Common Character," &c. &c.

Bird, James, was born at Deerbolts Hall, in the parish of Earl Stonham, November 10th, 1789. He resided some time at Ipswich; and is now settled at Yoxford, in this county, as a bookseller. He is author of the following works: "The Vale of Slaughden, a poem, in five cantos;" "Machin; or, the Discovery of Madeira, four cantos;" "Cosmo, Duke of Tuscany, a tragedy, in five acts;" "Poetical Memoirs, in two cantos;" "The Exile, a tale;" "Dunwich, a Tale of the Splendid City." We have already given an opinion of this gentleman's powers, as a poet; and the more we see of his works, the more are we convinced of their excellence.

Bransby, John—who has long resided at Ipswich, as a bookseller and land-surveyor—is author of " The Use of the Globes; containing an Introduction to Astronomy and Geography; a Description of Globes and Maps, and a variety of Problems performed by the

Globes, and by Calculations; with copious and suitable Examples:" printed at Ipswich, by J. Bush, 1791. A second edition appeared in 1808; and several pieces on geometry and navigation, in "Leyburn's Mathematical Repository." Also a very neat map of the liberties of Ipswich; and has issued proposals for publishing a complete map of the town, from actual survey.

In 1805, Mr. Bransby invented a very ingenious and useful astronomical instrument, to which he gave the name of *astromenuma,* or star-pointer. This is, in many respects, similar to an equatorial; but has some moveable, and many graduated circles. A small telescope is attached to it, which may be, at any time, directed to any star or other object above the horizon. By it the hour of day by the sun, or of night by any known star, may be readily obtained, and the time of the sun's rising and setting. The declination and right ascension of a star, planet, or comet may be accurately determined; also its altitude and azimuth. Many other useful problems may be performed, without any other instrument, or the least calculation. All this may be done at any place, let its latitude be what it will.

Brett, Sir Piercy, knt. Admiral of the Blue, an elder brother of the Trinity House, and one of the directors of Greenwich Hospital, was born in 1 709, and died October 12th, 1781. He was a distinguished naval officer; and his biographer remarks that, " whether living or dead, the voice of slander and malevolence was abashed at his manifold virtues." The freedom of the borough was presented to him for his services.

Broke, Sir Robert, a great lawyer, and Lord Chief Justice of the Common Pleas, in the reign of Queen Mary.

M M M 2

He wrote an excellent abridgment of the Law. This gentleman resided at Nacton, in this county; and from him the present Sir P. B. V. Broke, bart. is descended: and one of his descendants, Sir Robert Broke, hart. was appointed recorder and portman of Ipswich, under the charter granted July 8th, 1685.

BrowNrioo, Ralph, D. D. was son of a merchant in Ipswich. At the early age of fourteen years, he entered Pembroke Hall, Cambridge; where he became a fellow. He took his degree of M. A. in 1617; B. D. in 1621, and D. D. in 1626. He held the mastership of Catherine Hall for several years, and served the office of vice-chancellor; and was consecrated bishop of Exeter, in June, 1642. He was a man of extensive acquirements, and exemplary virtue. He died in 1659, aged sixty-seven, and was buried in the Temple Church—where there is an epitaph to his memory. A volume, in folio, of his sermons, was printed after his death; and reprinted in 1674, with an additional volume.

Bunbury, Sir Thomas Charles, bart. was descended from Thomas Bunbury, esq. who was created a baronet, in 1681. He married Sarah, daughter of Charles, second duke of Richmond; for whom his late Majesty, George III. had formed an early attachment. She was distinguished for elegance and beauty; but the marriage was dissolved by act of parliament, in 1776.

Sir Charles—as he was usually called—was, for many years, representative for the county of Suffolk; and was devoted to the pleasures of the turf. He was a great promoter of the races at Ipswich; which he always attended, as well as his colleague in parliament, the late earl of Stradbroke, then Sir John Rous. Through their influence, our racecourse became, annually, a scene of fashionable resort. The baronet, in early life, was remarkable for the elegance of his person and address; but, latterly, became slovenly in his dress, and eccentric in his habits and opinions; and had so great an apprhension of the instability of the Bank of England, that, it is said, he had the sum of one hundred thousand guineas, in gold, in his possession, at the time of his decease. He died without issue, and was succeeded, in his title and estates, by the present Sir Henry-Edward, son to Sir Charles's brother, Henry-William, the celebrated amateur artist and caricaturist.

Butler, William, M. D.—one of the greatest physicians and most capricious humourist of his time—was born at Ipswich, about 1535. He died January 29th, 1618, aged eighty-two years, and is buried in St. Mary's Church, at Cambridge. Many droll stories have been narrated of his bluntness and eccentricies, and some extraordinary cures as strangely performed.

Chambers, James, the wandering poet, died January 4th, 1827, aged seventy-eight; he was a native of Soham, in Cambridgeshire, and died at Stradbroke, in Suffolk. He left his home in early life, and continued a strolling mendicant all his days, procuring a miserable subsistence from the effusions of his muse, and living by choice in a barn or out-house covered with rags and dirt, in preference to a bed with cleanliness and comfort, which would have been to him restraint. A few years back, several ladies in Ipswich raised a subscription sufficient to clothe him decently, and maintain him in a comfortable cottage for some time; but confinement to one spot became misery to him, who had been accustomed to range the world at large, and he resumed his wanderings, and died at last in a shed. He was an honest and inoffensive creature, not altogether in possession of sanity of mind, yet could not be said to be deranged; for some of his poetical effusions which have been printed are not destitute of merit, discover no disarrangement of ideas, but contain occasionally very judicious and moral reflections. He is thus spoken of by the ingenious Mr. John Webb, of Haverhill:—

"An hapless outcast, on whose natal day,
No star propitious beam'd a kindly ray,
By some malignant influence doom'd to roam
The world's wide dreary waste, and knew no home;
Yet heav'n, to cheer him as he pass'd along,
Infus'd in life's sour cup the sweets of song.
Upon his couch of straw, or bed of hay,
The *poetaster* tun'd the *acrostic lay;*
On him an humble muse her favours shed,
And nightly musings earn'd his daily bread.
Meek, unassaming, modest shade, forgive
This frail attempt to make thy memory live."

Clamp, Robert, a native of Ipswich, he died in 1808, aged thirty-nine. He was articled to Joshua Kirby Baldry, of Cambridge, who also was a native of Ipswich; after which he practised as a portrait engraver in London, and many of his productions are to be seen in a work called "Harding's Biographical Mirror," three volumes, quarto.

Clarke, Robert, served the office of town-clerk, except in the short interval when the charter was surrendered to Charles II. from 1661 to 1697. In the charter of the seventeenth Charles II. 1685, he is expressly declared to be common town-clerk for the borough, to be continued in the said office during his natural life, unless by misbehaviour in his office or any other *reasonable* cause. He was a man of great weight and importance in the town; his daughter was married to Mr. Robert Sparrow, who was for many years of great note in the corporation; and at that period, whenever the finances of the corporation were at a low ebb, they borrowed money of Mr. Robert Sparrow and the town-clerk.

Clarke, Stephen, was born at Ipswich, in the house where the "Suffolk Chronicle" is at present printed; was educated at the Grammar-school, and now resides in London. He commenced his career as an author, by publishing "An Ode on the Death of Lord Nelson," printed in 4to. at Ipswich, by his brother, G. R. Clarke. He is author of a comedy called " The Kiss;" which was performed with applause, at the Lyceum theatre, in the Strand, when under the management of Mr. Arnold. He is also author of " The British Botanist, or an Introduction to the Study of Botany," 1 vol. 12mo.; "Hortus Anglicus, or a description of the Plants, &c. usually cultivated in an English Garden," 2 vols. 12mo.; "Conversations on History, being a History of England, more particularly of the disputable parts of English History," 2 vols. 8vo.; " Geographical Dictionary of Yorkshire," in 1 vol. large 8vo. designed as an accompaniment to a splendid map of Yorkshire; also " Geograhical Dictionary of Lancashire," 8vo. designed also to accompany a map of Lancashire. This gentleman's works discover taste and ability, and have been well received by the public.

Clench, John, was the first mentioned recorder of Ipswich, in the sixteenth year of Elizabeth. He was afterwards made a judge. He died in 1607, and is buried in Holbrook church, where a monument is erected to his memory. There is a fine portrait of him, the only one said to be extant, in the possession of Mr. Sparrow, the present town-clerk.

Cobbold, Rev. Richard, A. M. son of Mr. John Cobbold, of Holy Wells, by his second wife, the late lamented Mrs. Cobbold. He was born at Ipswich, and educated at Caius college, Cambridge. He officiated as curate for his uncle, the Rev. T. Cobbold, at St. Mary Tower church for several years. On his leaving this town to reside upon his living at Wortham, near Diss, his parishioners presented him with an elegant piece of plate, as a testimony of their regard and esteem, for the admirable and truly christian-Iike manner in which he executed the duties of a preacher of peace and good-will tow ards man. He possesses much of the taste, talents, and amiable qualities of his mother, and is author of a volume of poetry on the subjects of "Truth, Love, and Virtue," illustrated with etchings, drawn and executed by his own hand: it was published at Ipswich, by E. Shalders, in 1827.

Coke, Sir Edward, one of the most eminent of English lawyers, was born in 1550, and resided sometime at Wherstead, near Ipswich; and in 1558 was representative in parliament for Aldborough, in this county. He rose through various degrees of his profession, to be Chief Justice of the King's Bench; and though in some cases, particularly against Sir Walter Raleigh and Lord Bacon, he exhibited much arrogance and severity, he made a bold stand for the privileges of the Commons and the

rights of the people; and he proposed and framed the celebrated " Petition of Rights," the most explicit declaration of English liberty, which had then appeared. In mere forensic learning, he has perhaps never been exceeded, but he was a lawyer only, not a statesman; and the haughty arrogant judge submitted as meekly as a lamb to the sound of his wife's voice. His numerous treatises on the law are valuable treasures of legal information, and his famous commentary on Lyttleton's "Treatise on Tenures," has acquired universal celebrity. He died in September, 1034, in the eighty-fifth year of his age, a shining ornament to his profession.

Collier, Jeremiah, an eminent nonjuring divine, was born in 1650; he was sometime master of the Grammar School, at Ipswich; he was admitted a poor scholar of Caius college, Cambridge, and in 1679 was instituted in the rectory of Ampton, in Suffolk; in 1683 he refused to take the oaths of the new government, and became a zealous partizan in favour of the dethroned monarch, for which he was imprisoned, but afterwards discharged without being brought to trial. He pertinaciously persisted in the publication of his tenets, and courted imprisonment and persecution; in 1666 he, in company w ith two other nonjuring clergymen, attended the execution of Sir John Friend and Sir William Perkins, who had been condemned for engaging in the assassination plot, to publicly absolve them by imposition of hands; this conduct the bishops declared to be insolent and inconsistent with the constitution of the church. Collier, as usual, published a reply and vindication, for which he was outlawed, but suffered to remain unmolested, and he w as quiet till 1697, when he published three volumes of " Essays on several moral Subjects," octavo; the following year appeared the work by which he is now most remembered, entitled " A Short View of the Immorality and Profaneness of the Stage," together with " The sense of Antiquity on this Argument," octavo. In 1721, he published a translation and enlargement of "Moreris's Dictionary," in four vol-

umes, folio. In the reign of Queen Anne he refused all preferment in the church, which was liberally offered him, but he honourably maintained his principles, employing himself on his "Ecclesiastical History of Great Britain," the second volume of which appeared in 1711, about which time he

N N N was privately consecrated a nonjuring bishop; and this intrepid writer fell a victim to the stone in 1726, in the seventy-fifth year of his age. The learning, spirit, and ability he exhibited, and the integrity and constancy with which he maintained his opinions entitle him to the highest degree of respect and admiration.

Colson,Thomas, son of Thomas Colson, alias Robinson Crusoe, whose premature death we have noticed, was apprenticed to Mr. Raymond, shipbuilder, in Ipswich; from which situation he went to London, and is now engineer and superintendent of the woi'ks on the Croydon canal. He gave in a plan for the new London bridge, which was considered the next in point of excellence to that which was accepted; but being without interest or friends, he received no recompense, and what was a singular coincidence, there was scarcely any difference between his plan and the one adopted, except in the character of the centre arch; there is, however, no doubt but his strong natural genius will eventually surmount all difficulties, and he will become an eminent man.

Condeh, James, was the youngest son of the Rev. John Conder, D. D. He died March the 22nd, 1823, aged sixty-one, and was buried in the cemetery of the meetinghouse, in Tacket-street, Ipswich. He was much attached to the study of antiquities, and had an extensive numismatic collection; he was author of a work called "An arrangement of Provincial Coins, Tokens, and Medalets, issued in Great Britain, Ireland, and the Colonics, within the last twenty years, from the Farthing to the Penny size," 1799, octavo, and two volumes small quarto; besides being a frequent contributor to many periodical and other publications.

Cordinoley, John, (a native of the

town) is author of a volume of " Poems," printed at Ipswich, by R. Deck, in 1827. In the preface he thus speaks of his own producductions: "Should they fail in the accuracy of the scholar, it will, it is hoped, be a sufficient palliative to recollect that their author has received but a very limited commercial education.'" It is but justice to say that there is a great deal of merit in these pleasing unpretending effusions.

Crickmore, Thomas, came from Beccles to Ipswich, in 1809, and died the 6th of January, J 822, about forty years of age. On his first arrival in this town he was a performer in the band of the Suffolk militia, and at the peace he married and settled here as an optician, and had he lived, would probably have risen to eminence in that occupation; for though he was self-taught, his knowledge and excellence of execution was known and appreciated by many men of science. In a letter addressed to him from Capel Lofft, esq. dated 19th March, 1818, is the following remark:—

"Dear Sir,—I am perfectly satisfied and surprised by your improvements in my two reflectors, the largest of them small enough to admit so much power of light," and he concludes with his professions of friendship and esteem.

This singular man was endowed with a variety of talent, was possessed with a vein of wit, combined with a humourous eccentricity of character, which rendered him so entertaining a companion that he was much esteemed, and his loss regretted by all his friends and associates.

Cubitt, William, civil engineer, was several years a resident in this town; during which time, he was the means of establishing a company for lighting the town with gas; and was employed as engineer in the erection of the elegant cast-iron bridge over the Orwell—which was built by Messrs. J. and R. Ransome—as well m in various public and private undertakings. The patent N N N 2 sails for windmills, so universally adopted, and the treadmill, were invented by him; and he received a medal from the Society of Arts, for an

instrument called the *elipsograph*. He is now engaged in one of the most important works ever undertaken in this part of the country—that of opening a communication between Norwich and the sea at Lowestoft.

Dannelly, J. F. professorof music, resided some years in Ipswich; where he practised professionally. He is author of " An Encyclopedia or Dictionary of Music, with upwards of two hundred engraved examples:" printed at Ipswich, by S. Piper, 1825.

Davy, Henry, is a native of Beccles, and has resided some time at Ipswich, following his profession as an artist. He is the author of " Suffolk Antiquities," in folio, containing seventy plates, the drawings and etching for which were executed by himself; also "Suffolk Views," in quarto; and he has published several beautiful views of Southwold.

Duck, Arthur, was born in 1680. He was author of a volume of poems called "The Thresher's Miscellany," 1730. In some account given of his life, he says, " Gentle reader, the good town of Ipswich now boasts the honour of my birth, as it formerly did that of the great Cardinal Wolsey. I was conceived in sin, and brought forth in iniquity, Anno, 1680."

Dysart, Lionel Tollemache, earl of—who was chosen high steward of the borough, in 1703—was descended from one of the most ancient families in the kingdom, and has flourished, with the greatest honour, in an uninterrupted male succession, till the demise of the late earl, in the year 1821, in the county of Suffolk, since the first arrival of the Saxons in England—a period of more than thirteen centuries.

In 1561, Queen Elizabeth visited Helmingham; where she remained, from the 14th to the 18th of August, and was hospitably and sumptuously entertained.

Dysart, Wilbraham, the last earl of, was chosen high steward of the borough, in 1806. He died the 30th of March, 1821; but being without issue, he was succeeded by his sister, the present countess of Dysart. He was a man of the most humane and benevolent dis-

position; and his loss was severely felt in the neighbourhood of Ipswich.

Euston, George-Henry Fitzroy, earl of—member of parliament for Bury St. Edmund's—was born in the year 1790. As colonel of the West Suffolk Militia, he was stationed, for some time, at Ipswich; and was universally esteemed for the urbanity of his manners, and the benevolence of his disposition.

Fastolf, John, knt. and Knight Banneret, a valiant and renowned general under Henry IV. V. and VI. Knight of the Garter, &c. &c. He was member of parliament for Ipswich, in 1494. He died ut the age of eighty years. His mansion and estate were at Caistor, near Great Yarmouth; and he possessed lands in Suffolk and various other parts of the kingdom.

Firmin, Thomas, was born at Ipswich, 1632. He was apprenticed to a linen-draper, in London; where he carried on the same business, and amassed a large fortune. He was an eminent philanthropist; for his charity extended to all sects and parties, and particularly to the French protestants, who were expatriated by the revocation of the edict of Nantes; he gave large sums in relieving the poor during the plague, and expended for many years the sum of five thousand pounds in acts of benevolence. He was a Socinian, professing anti-trinitarian doctrines, yet he numbered several eminent prelates of the church amongst his friends. John Wesley, in describing his character, though he blames him for his errors, makes the following remarkable confession:—" I dare not say Mr. Firmin was not a good man, for he imitated the example of Him who went about doing good." He was a liberal benefactor to Guy's, St. Thomas's, and Christ's hospitals, in the latter of which is a marble monument to perpetuate his memory, by which it appears this amiable and beneficent man died in the year, 1697.

Flowerdew, A. published a volume of " Poems on Moral and Religious Subjects," to which are prefixed, "Introductory Remarks on a course of Female Education." This pleasing publication has received the meed of public approbation, so far as to occasion a demand for a third edition, printed in 1811.

French, William, D. D. was born at Eye in this county, March 26th, 1789. He received his education at the Grammar-school here, and was admitted a member of Caius college, Cambridge, 1807; proceeded to the degree of B. A. in January, 1811; was second wrangler that year, and was declared equal to the senior wrangler in the examination of Dr. Smith's prizes; appointed master of Jesus college in 1820, and was elected vice-chancellor in November, 1821. His learning, talents, and character, are held in high estimation at the university.

Frost, George, was born at Barrow, in this county, and died at Ipswich, June the 28th, 1821, in the seventyeighth year of his age; he was for many years in a confidential situation in the Old Blue coach-office; where, by his care and industry he realised a comfortable competency for himself and his wife in their latter days. He was shy and reserved to strangers, honourable and upright in all his dealings, and was a truly independent man, enthusiastically devoted to the study of his art, which he followed at his leisure hours, from a very early period of his life. It is evident ttiut Gainsborough was his model, but he studied nature with the closest attention, and many of his productions, particularly his drawings, were of distinguished excellence; his efforts were unaided by instruction, but he became a delightful artist by the power of his native talents alone, and in many instances displayed touches of genius worthy of a master's hand, and there are few of the picturesque beauties in the vicinity of this town but what have been sketched in a bold and masterly manner by his pencil.

"His genius lov'd his County's native views,

Its taper spires, green lawns, and shelter'd farms;

He touch'd each scene with nature's genuine hues,

And gave the Suffolk landscape all its charms."

He possessed a small collection of paintings, and many valuable drawings of his favourite Gainsborough; some of whose pictures he had so correctly copied, that it is said in one instance, that Gainsborough himself would not distinguish his own productions. He lived respected and esteemed, and died universally lamented; and he will be long remembered as an artist, who was an honour to the town of Ipswich.

Ford, Rev. James, B. D. fellow of Trinity college, Oxford. He is author of "The Devout Communicant," "Century of Prayer," " Life of Thomas Green, esq. ;" he is also a valuable contributor to " The Gentleman's Magazine." He was elected to the curacy of St. Lawrence, Ipswich, in the year 1808, which situation he now holds.

Gainsborouoh, Thomas, the celebrated English landscape painter, was born at Sudbury, in Suffolk, 1737. He used to amuse himself by rambling in the woods, and employing himself in sketching the scenery around; but attracting some attention, he was sent to London for improvement, where he married a woman of some little property, and removed to settle at Ipswich, where he resided some years, and Governor Thicknesse was greatly instrumental in bringing him into notice, for having mistaken for reality the figure of a man which appeared to be looking over the garden wall of Mr. Creighton, the printer, with whom the governor was walking, he immediately felt an interest for the artist, and he employed Gainsborough, by whom it was painted, to execute a view of Landguard Fort, which was unfortunately destroyed. He was of an irritable disposition, and was not so grateful to his patron as could have been wished; he rose into high reputation, and his landscapes are distinguished for a portrait-like representation of nature; many of his early productions are scattered over the county, several of which were lately sold at the sale of the Rev. Dr. Kilderbee's effects. He died of a cancer in his neck, August the 2nd, 1788, and is buried at Kew.

Garrick, David, was born at Lichfield, February, 1716, and died January the 20th, 1779. It was on the Ipswich boards he commenced his career as an actor, in 1709, in the company then under the direction of Messrs. Giffard and Dunstall, in the character of *Aboan,* in the play of *Oroonoko.* Some affirm that it was *Dick,* in the *Lying Valet;* but it is probable that he played both the same evening.

Gloucester, William Frederic, duke of—cousin to his present Majesty, was born the 15th January, 1776. He was, during the last war, commander-in-chief of the eastern district, and remained some time in Ipswich, where he rendered himself extremely popular by the affability of his demeanour, visiting in a friendly manner several of the families, in this town and neighbourhood.

Grey, Lady Jane, probably resided, at some period of her life at Ipswich; for her father came into the property of Sir Anthony Wingfield, and mention is made in a former part of this work of the Lady Grey's chapel, which was probably situated in Tacket-street. The fate of this accomplished and unfortunate female is so interwoven with the history of England, that it is unnecessary to detail it here; she was born about the year, 1537, and was beheaded on Tower Hill, February the 12th, 1554; her husband, Lord Guildford Dudley, to whom she was fondly attached, havin previously suffered the same day.

Green, Thomas, was born in 1722. He resided some years in Ipswich, and was a gentleman of considerable literary attainments,, and in 1769 published a periodical work in folio, entitled "Euphrasy," which was extended to twelve numbers. It was written after the general election in 1768, at which time the Dissenting interest at Ipswich gained a complete ascendency, and this work is chiefly intended to shew the danger likely to arise to the church and state from this circumstance. It displayed much warmth and sarcastic severity, but he lived long enough to acknowledge that "he saw *good reasons* for altering his opinion." He was author also of " A Prospect of the consequences of the present conduct of Great Britain towards America:" London: octavo, 1776. "A Discourse on the Impressing of Mariners:" London: octavo, 1777; and several other pamphlets. He died at his residence at Ipswich, October the 6th, 1794, and was buried in the family vault, at Wilby, in this county.

Green, Thomas, the only son of the before-mentioned Thomas Green, was born on the 12th of September, 1769; was educated at the grammar school, at Ipswich, and admitted of Caius college, in 1786, but on the day previous to his setting out for Cambridge he was attacked with illness, which then prevented this design, and it was never resumed; but he was admitted a member of the Inner o o o

Temple in 1791, and was in due course called to the bar. His extreme diffidence however prevented him from rising as a barrister, and he relinquished his profession for the ease and pleasures of a literary life, and fixed his residence at Ipswich, where he remained till his decease, the 6th of January, 1825, in the fifty-sixth year of bis age, and was buried in the family vault, at Wilby, Suffolk. He was possessed of various and extensive attainments as a man of literature and taste; he was passionately devoted to music as a science, and was a liberal admirer and patron of the fine arts; he had the best collection of pictures of the great masters of any person in Ipswich, which still remain entire, at the house where he lately resided, in Brook-street; having provided in his will that they should be so preserved till his only son, to whom they were left, should come of age. He commenced author at the early age of fourteen, and in 1788 published a volume called " Micthodion, or a Poetical Olio, by a young Gentleman." In 1789 he published ' A Vindication of the Shop Tax, addressed to the Landholders of England," which was considered to contain extraordinary force of argument for a youth of eighteen. In 1791, " Slight Observations upon Paine's Pamphlet;" "Political Speculations, occasioned by the progress of a democratic party in England;" "A short Address to the Protestant Clergy of every denomination, on the fundamental corruption of Christianity;" "The Social Compact, and the Natural Rights of

Man examined and confuted." In 1794 he edited "Critical Observations on the sixth book of the jEnied," which had been published anonymously by Gibbon, in 1770. In 1798, "An Examination of the Leading Principles of the New System of Morals, as stated and applied in Mr. Godwin's Political Justice." In 1810 he published his largest and principal work, "Extracts from the Diary of a Lover of Literature," quarto, printed at Ipswich, by J. Raw. It has been well observed by his biographer, that " a spirit of the gentleman, the scholar, and the man of extensive reading, pervades the whole of this interesting and entertaining publication." In 1819 was published a fourth edition of "Prayers for Families," by the late Edwd. Pearson, D. D. to which Mr. Green prefixed a biographical memoir of the editor, which was an elegant and interesting tribute of affection to the memory of his intimate friend. He was the author also of several detached pieces of poetry which appeared in various publications, and a contributor to the European and Gentleman's Magazines. His merits were known and appreciated by many of the most eminent literary characters of his time. Dr. Parr makes this remark when speaking of Mr. Green, of Ipswich, "whose penetration, whose taste, whose large views in philosophy, and whose great talents for composition entitle him to my respects;" and the learned historian, Sharon Turner, had so high an opinion of his talents and taste, that, in his work on modern poetry, there is a portion of the volume thus entitled: "Prolusions on Modern Poets and Poetry, addressed to Thomas Green, esq. by the author, in May, 1819." We have been induced to conclude our brief memoir of this amiable and excellent individual, with the following beautiful eulogy to his memory, by, we believe, Mr. Mathias:—

"Farewell! thou lov'd and gentle one, farewell!
Thou hast not liv'd in vain, or died for nought!
Oft of thy worth survivors' tongues shall tell,
And thy long cherish'd memory shall be

fraught
With many a theme of fond and tender thought,
That shall preserve it sacred, what could years
Or silver'd locks, of added good have brought
Unto a name like thine? even the tears
Thy early death has raus'd, thy early worth endears."
o o o 2

And we cannot refrain from inserting, also, the concluding stanza of "A tribute to the Memory of Thomas Green," by the elegant muse of Mrs. Biddell, of Playford.

"Bct vainly I attempt that mind to paint.
In thine own page superior traits are seen;
Nor deem this sketch, imperfect all and faint,
A tribute worthy of the name of Green."

We are proud to acknowledge that we have drawn our materials of this sketch from a memoir written with great feeling, judgment, and taste, by the Rev. J. Ford; which was printed in qnarto, at Ipswich, by J. Raw, in 1825, for private circulation only. And as an excuse for the length of this article, we can only say that the subject of it was universally beloved and respected by all who knew him, and that he was a man of whom Ipswich has reason to be proud.

Gwynn, Dr. resided many years in the large house opposite the theatre, where he died Jan. 20th, 1798, in the eighty-eighth year of his age. He studied physic under the great Boerhave, at Leyden, where he resided several years: he was well skilled in botany, and was a man of literature and taste; his manners, figure, and dress, formed a complete model of a gentlemen of the old school. The late Mrs. Cobbold presented him with a copy of verses in his eighty-seventh year, which concludes with the following lines:—

"Long may that elevated mind
Thro' learnings walks range unconfin'd;
That converse gay, that look serene
Breathe rapture o'er the social scene:
Long round the heart-strings friend-

ship twine,

And ever be that friendship mine."

Hamilton, Robert, M. D. of Scotch extraction, was born at Colerain, in Ireland, in 1748; he was educated for the medical profession at the university of Edinburgh. He entered into the army as a regimental surgeon in 1780, and came to settle at Ipswich, as a physician, in 1784, where he practised with much reputation and success till March the 31st, 1795, when he became totally blind, having been for some time afflicted with a disease of the optic nerve, from a rheumatic affection; he has resided in Ipswich ever since, and has never recovered his sight. He is the author of " The Duties of a Regimental Surgeon," two volumes, octavo; "A Treatise on Hydrophobia,' two volumes, octavo, with several other medical tracts. He was a man of an active and benevolent mind, and was a strenuous advocate for the abolition of the slave trade. He issued proposals for publishing by subscription a work called " An History of Health, Longevity, and Population, with the duration and value of Life, in the county of Suffolk," but this was never carried into execution.

Hamond, Sir Andrew Snape, bart. died Sept. the 19th, 1828, aged ninety. He was member of parliament for Ipswich from 1796 to 1802; he was captain in the royal navy, an elder brother of the Trinity-house, and comptroller of the navy during the most arduous part of the late war, and he executed the duties with punctuality and correctness.

Hardino, Samuel, son of Robert Harding, of Ipswich, A. B. of Oxford, 1658; author of " Sicily and Naples; or the Fatal Union," a tragedy.

Hartn All, Rev. John, for several years minister of Salem chapel, Ipswich, was an extraordinary instance of successful study, unassisted by early education. He was the author of a sermon on the death of George III. and also one on the death of Queen Caroline, both printed by S. Piper. Some idea of the estimation in which his character and talents were held, may be inferred from the circumstance of £500. having been raised by voluntary subscriptions, from persons of various denominations, for his orphan children. He died May 11th, 1625, aged forty years. He has left many valuable MSS. from which some may be selected for publication at some future period.

Hatton, Sir Christopher, resided at Ipswich, and from whom Hatton-court takes its name. On his appearing at a masque at court, Queen Elizabeth was astonished by the elegance of his person and his graceful dancing, and he rose to the situation of Lord Chancellor in 1587, when he was also created Knight of the Garter. He was a liberal patron of learning, eminent for his piety, charity, and integrity. He died, 1588

Hatlky, John, resided some years in Ipswich. He was first lieutenant of the St. George, ninety-eight guns, one of Lord St. Vincent's fleet; he was appointed master and commander in August, 1797, in consequence of his suppressing, in conjunction with his captain, a most dangerous mutiny of the crew: and of so much importance did the admiral consider this act, that in his public thanks to him, he said it was of more importance than capturing an enemy's ship of equal force. This gentleman sailed round the world with Captain Cook, and was well known in this town by the familiar appellation of Jack Hatley.

Hitcham, Sir Robert, knt. Serjeant at law. In 1639, he bought the house occupied by Wm. Rodwell, esq. and resided there some years. He purchased the manor of Framlingham, of the earl of Suffolk, where he erected and endowed extensive alms houses, and likewise in the parish of Levington, where he was born. He left a large estate to pious uses, principally to Pembroke Hall, Cambridge. He died August the 15th, 1636.

Howard, John, the celebrated philanthropist, is no otherwise connected with Ipswich, than having, on his tour through the country, visited our county gaol; which was one of the first built after the plan which he suggested. He was born about the year 1727, and died at Cherson, a Russian settlement on the Black Sea, of a malignant fever which he caught in exercising his humanity, January 20th, 1790. The Russian authorities paid every respect to his memory. His death was announced in the London Gazette; and a cenotaph is erected to his memory, in St. Paul's cathedral.

Kemp, Sir Robert, bart. died in 1735, aged sixty-eight, son of Sir Rohert Kemp, bart. of Ubbeston, whose father, Sir Robert Kemp, of Gissing, was privy counsellor to King Charles I. and, for his loyalty, was created a baronet without any tines for passing his patent. Our Sir Robert was a great benefactor to the town, and died member for the county, when Sir Cordel Firebrace was elected in his room.

Kirby, John, was a schoolmaster at Orford, and then occupied a mill at Wickham-market. He took an actual survey of the whole county, in the years 1732, 1733, and 1734, and in 1735, published his "Suffolk Traveller" at Ipswich, which was a small volume 12mo. ; and an enlarged edition in one volume, octavo, by the Rev. Richard Canning, was published at Ipswich in 1764.

Kirby, Joshua, eldest son of John Kirby, author of the "Suffolk Traveller," was born at Parham, near Wickhammarket, in 176G, and settled at Ipswich in 1728, as a house-painter. He published twelve prints of castles, ancient churches, and monuments in Suffolk, with a small descriptive pamphlet; but the work which brought him most into notice was " Dr. Brook Taylor's Method of Perspective," with a curious frontispiece designed by Hogarth. He was made clerk of the works at Kew. Under his Majesty's patronage, who defrayed the expense of the plates, he published, in 1761, his very splendid work, "The Perspective of Architecture," two volumes, folio. He died June the 20th, 1774, and was buried, by his express desire, by the side of his friend, Gainsborough, at Kew. He left two children, William, a promising artist, who died in 1771, and Sarah, afterwards Mrs. Trimmer. He likewise, in conjunction with his brother William, published a new and enlarged edition of his father's map of Suffolk, with twelve views, and the arms of the different families in the county: published at Ipawich, by J. Shave, 1766.

Lee, Thomas, D. D. president of Trinity college, Oxford, died June the 5th, 1824. He was a native of Warwickshire $ was admitted a commoner of Trinity college in 1777, chosen a scholar of the society, and in 1781, he obtained the degree of B. A. and in 1794 was elected a fellow; and in November, the same year, he took the degree of M. A.; and on the 20th of September, 1790, he was licensed to the perpetual curacy of St. Lawrence, in the town of Ipswich, on the nomination of the parishioners, where he remained till he was elected president of his college, in 1808; and on the 7th of April following, he proceeded to the degree of D. D.; in 1812 he was appointed a delegate of estates and a commissioner of the market, and in the year following a delegate of accounts; in 1814, he was appointed vice-chancellor of the university, in which distinguished situation he continued until October, 1818. His remains were deposited in the anti-chapel of the college, and the pall was supported by the fellows, and followed by all the resident members of the society, by whom he was sincerely and affectionately beloved and lamented.

Lofft, Capel, esq. was born at Bury St. Edmund's, November the 14th, 1751, and died in 1825. He was educated at Eton, from whence he went to Peter House, Cambridge, where he studied the law and was afterwards called to the bar. He is the author of numerous publications, on various subjects; the first of which was "The Praise of Poetry," a poem, 1775, and, amongst others, "Eudosia, or a Poem on the Universe," printed at Ipswich, 1781, besides a number of Essays, Letters, &c. in various periodical works. He was in the habit of attending as counsel upon this circuit, and was a man of great learning and research, and his patronage of "Bloomfield's Farmer's Boy" will always redound to his honour.

Lanoston, Rev. John, minister of Tacket-street chapel, 1686. He was a man of great learning, and author of

"Lusus Poeticus Latinae Anglicanus in usum Scholarum," "Poeseos Grecae Medulla," and a Vindication of himself.

Londonderry, Charles Wm. Vane Stewart, marquis of—a lieutenant-general in the army, and colonel of the 10th regiment of dragoons. He distinguished himself greatly for his bravery, as a cavalry officer in the Peninsula, and was a long time stationed at Ipswich. He is author of " The History of the Peninsula War," quarto.

Marlborouoh, John, duke of, was entertained with a dinner by the corporation of Ipswich, the 21st of Nov. 1719, when he was presented with the freedom of the borough. A memoir of this great soldier and statesman would include the political history of England for half a century: he was born in 1650, and was undoubtedly the greatest general this country ever produced till our own times, for there is a wonderful similarity of character between Marlborough and the present premier.

Milton, Christopher, knt. was appointed deputy recorder in the charter granted July the 8th, 1685, and is buried in St. Nicholas'church. He was brother of the great poet. He was trained to the practice of the common law, and in the great rebellion adhered to the royal cause. In the reign of James II. he was made judge of the Common Pleas, and he died not long after the revolution.

Miollis, John Charles, was born at Rome, in 1790, and came to Ipswich in 1827, where he has since resided as teacher of the French, Italian, and Spanish languages; and some years ago he had the honour of giving lessons to his royal highness the late Duke of York, and has had many of the nobility of this country as his pupils. He held a captain's commission in the sixth Polish lancers, under Buonaparte, and was afterwards captain in the guard of honour to Pope Pius VI. and on Napoleon's return from Elba he again entered his service. He is the author of the following works: "The African Slave," "The True Friend," "The Advice of a Mother to her Children," all in Italian, "L'Enfant de Famille" in French; he has also in the press, "The Imperial Dictionary," in

English, French, Italian, and Spanish, in four volumes, quarto, and is about to publish by subscription, "Les Aventures de l'Exile," in two volumes, octavo, which will include the extraordinary adventures of his eventful life. He had just been liberated from a Spanish prison and driven as an exile from France, when he first came to Ipswich; where he was received with so much hospitality by some of the inhabitants, particularly by the society of Friends, that he was induced to fix his residence amongst them, and now carries on his profession here.

Mole, John, the self-taught algebraist, was born at Nacton, where he resided many years, and died in Sept. 1827, aged eighty-five years. He was the author of "Elements of Algebra," octavo, 1788, and "A Treatise on Algebra," 12-mo. printed at Ipswich, by J. Bransby, 1809.

Moor, Edward, esq. F.R.S. F.S.A. author of " Suffolk Words and Phrases; or, an attempt to collect the Lingual Localisms of that County:" printed at Woodbridge, by J. Loder, 1823. This gentleman was educated at Ipswich. He went to India at an early age; where he obtained the rank of major in the army; and has, for some time, resided at Bealings, near this town.

Nassau, George, esq. of Trimley, was born the 5th of September, 1756, and died the 12th of August, 1823. He was high sheriff for the county in 1805, was a great promoter of the fine arts, and his collection of manuscripts, &c. relative to the history and antiquities of the county of Suffolk, were of the most rare and valuable desciiption. He presented to the corporation of Ipswich, Ogilby's map of the town, Kirby's "Suffolk Traveller," inlaid in two quarto volumes, splendidly bound, and illustrated with very fine portraits and views, and two volumes of very rare tracts relating to this borough and the county of Suffolk, for which he received a letter of thanks.

Neous, the Hon. Francis, departed this life in Sept. 1732; his death was much lamented by the inhabitants of Ipswich, to which town he was a great friend and benefactor. A long poem on his death inserted in the Ipswich Gazette, commences with the following lines:—

"Is Negus gone? ah, IPSWICH, weep and mourn.

His t'un'ral rites with briny tears adorn; His death demands this tribute now from you,

Who best his worth and excellency knew."

Nelson, Horatio Lord Viscount— who was for several years high steward of the borough—was born at Burnham Thorpe, Norfolk, September the 29th, 1758, and died p p p 2 gloriously, in the hour of victory, at the decisive battle of Trafalgar, October the 21st, 1805. No words can do justice to his merit—suffice it to say that he was one of the bravest and most successful commanders, and the greatest naval hero the world ever produced.

Ooilby, John, published a nine-sheet map of Ipswich, the title of which is as follows: "The Borough or Corporation of Ipswich, in Com. Sun", actually surveyed and delineated, an. 1674. By John Ogilby, esq. his Ma"cosmographer, and exactly engraved by Thomas Steward, *an"*. 1698, and are to be had at his house in Brook Street, Ipswich." On the borders of this map are engraved representations of the twelve churches, Christ church, and Squire Gawdy's house.

Page, Admiral Benjamin William, was born at Ipswich in 1765, and commenced his naval career in 1778, on board the Superbe, of seventy-four guns, bearing the flag of Sir Edward Hughes; he shared with him in all his hard-fought battles, and was twice wounded in that ship, and made a lieutenant in 1784. In January, 1794, he was appointed first lieutenant of the Suffolk, of 74 guns, Capt. Rainier, and served in the fleet under Lord Howe till 1794, when Capt. Rainier was appointed to the East India command with the rank of commodore, and he accompanied him to that station, and although they had forty-four ships under their convoy, they sailed from Spithead to Madras without dropping an anchor: on this occasion the commodore had no captain under him to assist in the duties of the

ship, and Mr. Page was allowed the batta or pay of a commander, at the commodore's request, till a captain was appointed. In September, 1795, Lieutenant Page was promoted to the rank of commander, and appointed to the Hobart sloop of war, of eighteen guns and on the 1st of October, with a detachment of troops under colonel Monson, took possession of tie Dutch factory of Molletive, and the eastern parts of Ceylon In January, 1796, he sailed with the admiral on an expedition against the Molacca Islands; but previous to their capture he was sent to Madras with important despatches, and by that means was deprived of the prize money. In December, 1796, he convoyed a valuable fleet of China traders from Prince of Wales's Island to Bombay; for which he received tho thanks of both government and the merchants, and a present from the latter of five hundred guineas, and was appointed a post captain in the Orpheus, of thirty-two guns. On account of ill health, he was obliged to return to England, 1798; but on his restoration in January, 1800, he was appointed to the Inflexible, of sixty-four guns. He sailed under sealed orders with fourteen other ships, having altogether five thousand troops on board, to Minorca; where he joined Lord Keith, and afterwards proceeded to the blockade of Genoa, but being sent to Leghorn the day before its surrender, he was again deprived of his share of the profits arising from the capture, but assisted in removing the French troops from Genoa to France. On his return he was ordered to England with a convoy, and on arriving at home with them, he was again ordered to the Mediterranean, and conveyed part of the 42nd regiment, which he landed in Egypt, March 8th, 1801, and was then employed in the blockade of Alexandria; on the surrender of Cairo he was ordered to convey the French troops to Marseilles, but was not allowed to share in the spoils of the Egyptian campaign, not being able to return previous to its close, but brought home General Coote, the second in command, and the remaining part of the third Guards. He returned to England, and was paid off in

1802. Lord St. Vincent soon afterwards appointed him to the Caroline, of thirty-six guns, on the Irish station, where he remained till May, 1803, when he suddenly received orders to sail to the East Indies, and in one hour afterwards he left the Cove of Cork, and reached his destination in one hundred and three days: in his passage he captured some French ships and detained two Dutch ships, one of greet value, which wore made droits of admiralty, and the Caroline's crew only received part of their value as prize money. In the bay of Bengal he captured two French privateers from France,before they had made any captures; for which the merchants of Calcutta and Madras sent from each settlement their public thanks and a present of five hundred guineas. He was then ordered by Admiral Rainier to take under his command the Grampus, of fifty guns, the Dedaigneuse, of thirty-eight guns, and Dasher sloop of eighteen guns, and protect a valuable convoy to and from China. In January, 1805, Captain Page returned with his convoy to Prince of Wales's Island, and in March was promoted by Admiral Rainier to his flag ship, the Trident, of sixty-four guns, when he returned to England with forty-four ships, and having on board the present Duke of Wellington. On the Trident being paid off, the court of the East India Directory presented him their thanks and a present of five hundred guineas, and Lord Mulgrave appointed him to the Sea Fencibles on the coast of Essex, till they were disbanded. On the 12th of August, 1812, Lord Melville appointed him to the command of the Puissant, of seventy-four guns, stationed at Spithead. Captain Page repeatedly solicited to be appointed to a sea-going ship, but in vain. In 1819, he was made a rear-admiral, and now resides in his native town.

Pearson, Rev. Edward, D. D. (brother of Mr. Wm. Pearson of this town) was some time resident here: he was born at Norwich, October the 25th, 1756; in 1778 he was entered at Sidney college, Cambridge; he was elected master of his college in 1808, on which occasion he received by royal mandate the degree of

D. D., and in the same year was chosen vice-chancellor; in 1810 he was elected by the university to the office of Christian advocate; and he died August the 11th, 1811. His talents and his virtues will be long remembered by many of the inhabitants of Ipswich, and his character has been faithfully delineated by his friend, the late Thomas Green, esq. in a brief memoir printed for private circulation, in 1819. He was author of the following works: "Remarks on the Theory of Morals," octavo, "Annotations on Paley's Philosophy," octavo, "Sermons at Warburton's Lecture," 1811, octavo

Penninoton, Joseph, published a map of Ipswich from actual survey, in the year 1778, which is considered to be executed with an extraordinary degree of correctness. At his suggestion, the names of the streets of Ipswich were first affixed. This gentleman i still living, and is upwards of eighty years of age.

Popham, Sir Home Riggs, who represented the borough from 1807 to 1812, was knight commander of the Bath, was born in Ireland in 17C2, and rose to the rank of lieutenant in the American war; and during the peace he discovered a passage for navigation at Palo Penang in the East Indies; he returned to the service in 1794, and was of considerable service to the Duke of York in Holland, when he was appointed post captain; he was next employed in the Baltic, and in 1800 appointed to a command in the East Indies; in 1806 he entered the Red Sea and settled advantageous terms of commerce for the English merchants, but was violently accused of interested views; he was afterwards engaged in an expedition against Buenos Ayres, as stated, without adequate authority, and being brought to a court martial was sentenced to be reprimanded. He finally obtained the command on the Jamaica station, and had just returned to England, when he died at Cheltenham, Sept. the 13th, 1820. He was a brave and enterprising officer, and possessed considerable powers as a writer and speaker, for he defended himself both in and out of the house with much spirit and ability.

Porter, Sir Robert Ker, knt. who was quartered here with his regiment, the Royal Westminster Militia, about the year 1803, when he painted the picture in ot. Lawrence' church, alluded to p. 206. He early discovered talents as an artist, and entered as a student at the royal academy in 1790; he was only twenty-two when he commenced his large panoramic picture of the storming of Seringapatam, and though there were nearly seven hundred figures as large as life, he finished it in less than ten week8: this was succeeded by the siege of Acre and the battle of Agincourt, which last he presented to the city of London. He had an early predilection for military pursuits, and he entered as a captain into the Westminster militia; he was however invited to Russia, and was made historical painter to the emperor—here he gained the affections of Princess Scherbatoff, but was obliged to quit Petersburgh on account of the rupture between the two countries, but he afterwards returned to Russia and married the princess. He passed into Sweden with a view of joining the forces under Sir J. Moore, and was knighted by the king of Sweden. He served with Sir J. Moore in the Peninsula, and has since travelled into Persia and other parts of the globe. He has published many volumes of his travels, ornamented with plates from his own designs; and he is now appointed consul-general to the Ciiraccas.

Prince, John, lieutenant-general. This gentleman was formerly of the 1st Dragoon Guards, and Enniskillen Dragoons. In his younger days he was remarkable for the manly symmetry of his person; and, in consequence of his forming a matrimonial connexion with a lady of considerable fortune, he rose from the ranks to the situation of a lieutenant-general in the army. He resided for many years at Ipswich, and died on the 11th of September, 1824, aged seventy-four years, universally esteemed and respected.

Reeve, Clara, born January the 16th, 1728, and died December the 3rd, 1803, aged seventy-eight years. She was the daughter of Wm. Reeve, A. M. Rector of Freston and Kirton, and perpetual curate of St. Nicholas; her mother's maiden name was Smithies—whose father was jeweller to George I. She was the author of " The Old English Baron;" "The Exiles;" "Widow's Vows;" "Love's Pilgrimage," and several other productions: but she must rest her fame upon the first of these works— written in contradistinction to Horace Walpole's romance, "The Castle of Otranto," with a view to prove that more interest may be created by natural means than by supernatural agency. Her work was extremely popular at the time of its publication, and has gone through many editions. The favourite opera of "The Haunted Tower," was founded on the story. She was a woman of very considerable literary attainments; and though the events of her career—passed in comparative retirement, principally at Ipswich—furnish but few incidents of interest, yet her life has been written in a spirited biographical sketch, by Sir Walter Scott. She is buried in St. Stephen's church, without any inscription to her memory; but we are glad to learn, that a monument is about to be erected by the family, worthy of her talents and her virtues.

Reevr, Vice Admiral Samuel, was a native of Ipswich, and was the eldest son of the Rev. William Reeve, thirty years the respected minister of St. Nicholas' parish; and his family had, for a long series of years, been free burgesses of this corporation. He was born February 9th, 1732; and entered into the royal navy at the early age of twelve years, under the immediate patronage of the celebrated Admiral Vernon, then member of parliament for Ipswich. After having honourably distinguished himself, during a long period of active service, he was accidentally killed, in the seventy-first year of his age. This gentleman was for a long time an active officer. He was promoted to the rank of captain, 1778; rear admiral, 1795; and vice admiral of the white, 1799. He was much respected in the service.

Rutland, duke of, (John Henry Manners) Knight of the illustrious order of the Garter, lord lieutenant of the county of Leicester, and recorder of Cambridge and Scarborough; who, as colonel of the Leicestershire militia, was stationed, for some time, at Ipswich, and resided, with the duchess, in a house in St. Stephen's lane.

Salisbury, marquis of, (James Gascoigne Cecil) knight of the Garter, and lord chamberlain from the year 1789 to 1806. Ho was colonel of the Hertfordshire militia, and resided here during the time they were stationed in this garrison. He occupied a marine pavillion at Aldborough, for several years; and was the means of bringing that spot into fashion as a watering-place.

Say, Rev. Samuel, dissenting minister at Lowestoft and Ipswich, author of " Poems on several occasions," in 4t6. 1735, and several detached pieces from 1736 to 1740. His works are still held in considerable repute.

Smart, Mr. John, was born at Ufford in this county, in 1752. He went to London in 1782; and, in the following year, he presented a drawing to the inspection of Sir Joshua Reynolds, who ordered it to be admitted into the Royal Academy, without any further recommendation, and he became a student in the academy in April, in the same year. He immediately turned his attention to portrait painting—in which he excelled. He settled at Ipswich about the year 1787, and has painted the likenesses of a great number of persons in this town and neighbourhood, several scripture subjects as altar-pieces for churches, and a variety of landscapes and other pieces, and is still residing at Ipswich.

Thicknesse, Philip, many years governor of Landguard Fort, was born 1720. He was married to Miss La Nouve, a French lady; with whom he expected a fortune of £40,000. but received only £5000. He afterwards married Lady Elizabeth Touchet, daughter of the earl of Castlehaven; by whom he had one son, who succeeded to the title of Lord Audley. He afterwards married Miss Ford; who was a lady of great beauty and accomplishments. He was remarkable for a fine person and address, and distinguished for his accomplishments, as well as for his courage,

eccentricity, and humour. On retiring from his native country—where he had supposed himself illused—he travelled through great part of France, in a cabriolet; on which was painted the word Cosmopolite, and on a conspicuous part was a representation of Belisarius, with the motto—*Voila son recompense.* He was dressed in the English fashion, and drove the vehicle himself; a monkey, equipped in the French style, with jack boots, and a red jacket laced with silver, acted the part of postillion, and an English dog was seated behind the carriage as a footman. He was author of a life of Gainsborough, and was one of the earliest patrons of that celebrated artist.

Q a Q 2

Thicknessk, Mrs. the third wife of the governor, wan born the 22nd of February, 1727; she was a lady of great attainments, and before her marriage had greatly attracted the notice of the fashionable world, and being strongly pressed by her father to choose a husband from the numerous suitors by which she was assailed, she withdrew herself from his parental authority, and formed the resolution of singing in public. She hired the Italian Opera-house for three nights; and though her father took extraordinary pains to prevent her appearance, she was supported by Prince Edward and a great many of the nobility, and actually cleared £1500. by her exhibition. After the death of her husband, she published a work called "The School for Fathers," 2 vols, which is written with great spirit and humour, as well as with delicacy and good feeling, but exhibits the characters of many well known individuals of that time, in a striking point of view, and abounds with many curious anecdotes of her eccentric husband. She lived to a very advanced age, for, we believe, she died at Bath, in the year 1823.

Torrens, Lieutenant-colonel R. was born in Ireland, in 1783. In March, 1811, he distinguished himself greatly in the defeat of the Danes, on the island of Anholt, and was rewarded with the rank of major of marines, in which corps he had entered at an early age. He next served in the Peninsula, where he

was appointed colonel of a Spanish legion. He is author of several works on the corn trade, cash payments, catholic emancipation, &c. He sat as representative for the borough a short time, in the present parliament, but was ousted by the present members.

Trimmer, Mrs. Sarah, who w as daughter of Mr. Joshua Kirby, was born at Ipswich, in the house where the Suffolk Chronicle is now printed, in the year 1741. She married to Mr. Trimmer in 17G2, by whom she had twelve children. She was distinguished through life as an aclive and benevolent instructress of youth, for whom she produced a great variety of ingenious publications, the first of which we believe, was " An Elementary Introduction to the Knowledge of Nature." She lived to a very advanced age, and died without a struggle, in her easy chair, whilst reading a letter from a friend, in the winter of 1810.

Tusseh, Thomas, styled the British Varro, was born at Rivenhall, near Witham, Essex, 1515. Receiving a college education, and holding some situation at court, after ten years' attendance upon his patron, Lord Wm. Paget, he settled as a farmer, at Cattawade, encountering a more diversified life than generally falls to the lot of a poet, and died in London, 1580. He was the author of the celebrated book "The five hundred Points in Husbandry," which was extremely popular in its day, and has passed through many editions, the last was edited by Dr. Mavor, and published in 1812. In a poetical life of this author, written by himself, he thus speaks of Ipswich:—

When wife could not, through sickness got,
More toil abide, so nigh sea side,
Then thought I best, from toil to rest,
And Ipswich try.

A town of price, like Paradise,
For quiet then, and honest men,
There was I glad, much friendship had,
A time to lie.

There left good wife, this present life,
And there left I, house charges lie,
For glad was he, might send for me,
Good luck so stood.

In Suffolk there, where every where,

Ever of the best, besides the rest,
That never did, their friendship hide
To do me good.

Uvedale, Admiral Samuel, son of the Rev. Samuel Uvedale and Sophia his wife, was born at Barking in the county of Suffolk, June 7th, 1729; of which parish his father was rector. He entered the royal navy at the early age of twelve years; and, by the interest of the earl of Ashburnham, he was made lieutenant, master, and commander, and was also promoted to the rank of post captain into the Boreas frigate, at the age of twenty-five years. January 16th, 1760, this hero distinguished himself as a brave officer, in the victory off Cape St. Vincent, obtained over the Spanish squadron under Admiral Don Langara: in which gallant action, under Sir George Brydges Rodney, Captain Samuel Uvedale commanded the Ajax, of sixty-four guns, and gallantly engaged three of the enemy's ships at the same time; one of which, the St. Domingo, up in the action. Captain Uvedale was wounded, and was obliged, in consequence, to leave his station; and was appointed by Sir George Rodney, to convey his dispatches to the admiralty:—for more minute report of which, see the public journals for January, 1780. Not being successful in his application, on his recovery, for further employment—which his services well merited— he retired to Bosmere House, the mansion built by him, in the parish of Creeting-all-Saints, Suffolk: but increased age and infirmities rendering a town residence more desirable, he disposed of his property, and purchased a house in Ipswich; in which he departed this life, on the 10th of December, 1809, and was interred within the church of Creeting-all-Saints.

The family of Uvedale reckons among the most ancient in the county of Suffolk; being, on record, lineally descended from Nicholas Uvedale, lord of the manor of Wickham, in Hampshire; who patronised William of Wickham, bishop of Winchester; and, after being at the expense of his education, sent him to college, at his own expense. In the chancel of the church of Wickham is a very ancient chapel, built by the U W dales, as it was then spelt, in which are two very large monumental tombs: the one bears the date of 1564, and the other 1615.

Wakefield, Priscilla, was born at Tottenham, January 31st, 1751. This lady, who has written so much and so well for the instruction of young people, had not, originally, the advantages of education, but accomplished all that she has performed by dint of unwearied application. From the extensive catalogue of her works, we may notice the " Introduction to Botany," "Leisure Hours," and "Mental Improvement," as some of her most popular productions. She was married to Mr. Edward Wakefield of London, January 3rd, 1771; who resided in this town for some years, and died here a short time ago. She is aunt to the celebrated Mrs Fry, and mother to Mrs. Head of this town, with whom she now resides; and, though nearly fourscore years old, is still remarkably calm and cheerful.

Wellinoton, duke of, (Arthur Wellesley) was presented with the freedom of this borough, on the town-hall, on Sunday, January 7th, 1821; when his grace accompanied the bailiffs, &c. to St. Mary Tower church. Upon the death of the late Earl Dysart, his grace was put in nomination for high steward of the borough, in opposition to Sir Robert Harland, bart. It would be folly to say any thing here of this illustrious character.

Wentworih, Sir Thomas, of Nettlestead, was created Baron Wentworth, by King Henry VIII. He presided, with great aversion, at the execution of the protestants who were burnt at Ipswich, in the year 1546. He afterwards fell into disgrace for the loss of Calais; for which he was condemned for high treason, during his absence: but, Queen Mary dying soon after, he was tried and acquitted by his peers, in the reign of Queen Elizabeth. He died at an advanced age, in 1590.

Williams, William-Henry, M. D. took up his residence in this town, as a physician, in 1801. He is a Fellow of the Royal College of Physicians, of the London Medical Society, and of the Linnean Society, and one of the senior members of Gonville and Caius college, Cambridge—in which university he first took the degree of bachelor in medicine, and, five years subsequently, the degree of doctor in that faculty. He received part of his professional education at the Bristol Infirmary, one of the largest country hospitals, and in the London hospitals—more especially those of St. Thomas and Guy'; in which having completed his studies, and passed the several necessary examinations, he entered into the army, during one of the most eventful periods in the history of this country, as surgeon to the eastern regiment of Norfolk militia, varying in numbers, from five hundred to a thousand men, besides women and children; of whom, whether in camp, in garrison, or in quarters, there were seldom less than one, two, or three hundred; forming, altogether, from the sick soldier, his wife and children, a medical and surgical school for practical experience of an extensive and efficient kind.

In 1795, when the East Norfolk regiment was encamped near Deal castle, he was appointed senior of twenty English surgeons; to whom was given, at different times, the charge of several hundred sick Russian sailors, labouring under malignant fever and dysentery: three Such was the opinion of the late celebrated John Hunter, then surgeon-general of the army; by whom the subject of this memoir was introduced to the present Lord Wodehouse, at that time colonel of the East Norfolk Militia. hundred of whom were, in the first instance, brought on shore in boats, from the Russian men-of-war and frigates then stationed in the Downs, and placed in tents formed chiefly of the sails belonging to the English ships of war, each tent accommodating one hundred men.

In 1798," Williams' Field Tourniquet," so denominated by the Army Medical Board, in their printed directions respecting the use of it, was ordered by field-marshall the commander-in-chief, his late royal highness the Duke of York, to be employed in every regiment in the King's service, both at home and abroad; and the non-commissioned officers, drummers, and musicians, to be instructed in the use of it, agreeably to the plan suggested by the inventor: so that, in a regiment of one thousand men, not less than one hundred and twenty individuals would be enabled to apply this tourniquet, in cases of loss of blood by the sword, by the bayonet, or gun-shot wounds.

Previously to the adoption of this instrument, no regiment, however numerous, had more than two or four tourniquets; and, with the exception of the surgeon and assistant surgeons, no individuals in the regiment were competent to apply it.

" *To Sir John Wodehouse, Bart., Colonel of the East Norfolk Regiment.*
Dear Sir,

I waited till we had seen Mr. Williams, surgeon of the East Norfolk Regiment of Militia, before I acknowledged the honour of your letter. He appeared at our board yesterday. We were much pleased with the simplicity and good construction of the Tourniquet; and after having thanked him for the communication, we desired him to leave the Instrument with the Surgeon General of the Army, and assured him he should hear from the Board again.

I have the honour to be, &c. &c.

L. Pepys, Physician General."

"April 16th, 1797."

R R R

The expense of the Field Tourniquet is a mere trifle, not exceeding sixpence; the screw or common tourniquet usually supplied by government, costs from seven to twelve shillings; the former, in case of accident or loss, is easily repaired or renewed; the latter is soon rendered unfit for use, and in a regiment on a foreign station can scarcely be repaired or replaced. The Field Tourniquet enables the wounded soldier, without risk or pain, when the bones of the arm, thigh, or foot have not been fractured, or the muscles much injured, to continue his duty in the hour of battle, as if no injury had been sustained— the Screw Tourniquet is destitute of these advantages.

In 1810, He had the honour of being appointed by the Physician-General of the army, to be Physician to the South Military Hospital; which, and the North Military Hospital, and most of the cavalry and infantry barracks then situated on each side of the Woodbridge road, near this town, were filled with the British sick soldiers just returned from Walcheren; of whom some hundreds suffering from obstinate fever, ague, and dysentery, were received here, as well as in the military hospitals and barracks at Colchester and Harwich. He continued in this appointment till the soldiers who survived were sent to join their respective corps, when he received a flattering letter from the Army Medical Board.

In 1824, having filled the office of Physician to the Public Dispensary for a period of twenty-one years, he resigned.

His first work, published in 1798, " On the Ventilation of Army Hospitals, and on Regimental Practice," together At Walcheren alone, 10,000 out of 15,000 of our brave but unfortunate countrymen were reported " Sick in Hospital," Sept. 14, 1809, a few weeks after they took possesion of that pestilential island, and from twenty-five to thirty deaths took place daily.
with his persevering and successful endeavours to introduce his Field Tourniquet into the army, procured for him distinguished marks of approbation from his Royal Highness the Duke of York. His publications are—, 1. On the Ventilation of Army Hospitals, 1798, 8vo. 2. A concise Treatise on the Progress of Medicine since the year 1573, 1804, 8vo. 3. Animadversions on certain Cases of Consumption and Dropsy, treated by the Foxglove, 1807, 8vo. 4. General Directions for the recovery of Persons apparently Dead from Drowning, &c. 1808, 12mo. :. Pharmacopoeia Valetudinarii Gippovicensis, edendam euraverunt G. H. Williams, M. D. et A. Bartlett, Chir: 1814, 12mo. ti. Observations on Dr. Wilson's Tincture, the Eau Medicinale, and other pretended Specifics for Gout, 1818, 4to. 7. On the Discovery and Efficacy of the Seeds of the Colchicum Autumnale, in Rheumatism and other painful Disorders, published in the London Medical Repository, vols. XIV. XV. and XVI. 1820, 1821, four essays. 8. A concise View of the History, Literature, &c. of Gonville and Caius College, Cambridge, with a View of the College, on a royal sheet, 1823.

Dr. Williams is Brother to Charles-Frederick Williams, esq. Barrister-at-law, and a King's Counsellor, one of the Benchers of Lincoln's Inn, and Recorder of Bridport.

Wolsey, Thomas, is the greatest name we have to record; but his character and actions are so interwoven with the times in which he flourished, that they cannot be unknown to every reader of the history of England; we shall, therefore, chiefly confine ourselves to his domestic life, and to those points most immediately referring

R R R 2 to the place of his nativity. Thomas Wolsey was the son of Thomas and Joan Wolsey, and was born at Ipswich, in August, 1471. His life has been written by several historians, and there has been much controversy respecting the occupation of his father. Bishop Godwin notices the cardinal as the son of a poor man; or, "as I have heard, a butcher." Skelton, the poet laureate of Wolsey's time, sarcastically calls him " the butcher's dog;" and Luther speaks of him by the same coarse appellation. The nobles of his day contemptuously reiterated this degrading cognomen; and, as there is no proof to the contrary, we are inclined to believe that the common report is correct: and there are some further remarks on the same subject, in our account of the house wherein he was born; and it is probable that his father was a butcher and grazier of some wealth and importance.

It is traditionally stated, that, in the ancient shambles or butchery which formerly stood upon the Cornhill, in Ipswich, there was a stand or stall over which were carved the initials, or some other marks or insignia, denoting that it belonged to, or was occupied by, Thomas Wolsey the elder, for the purpose of carrying on his trade as a butcher. However this might be, the father certainly prospered in his calling, and became a man of property; for his will is preserved in " Fiddes's Life of Wolsey," wherein it appears that he left his lands at the disposal of his wife Joan, and the rest of his worldly wealth to his son Thomas, his wife, and another person; and he also left money for religious purposes, as previously noticed in the history of the parish of St. Nicholas.

Wolsey was sent to Magdalen college, Oxford; where he was admitted as a bachelor of arts, at the early age of fifteen: from which circumstance, according to his own account, he was generally called the boy bachelor. His talents soon attracted the notice of that discerning monarch, Henry VII. who promoted him to the situation of domestic chaplain. We shall forbear to follow him through his splendid political career, during the reign of Henry VIII., but refer our readers to the pages of English history.

It is not only as a churchman and politician that he was conspicuous, but as a promoter of literature and science. No one but himself could have been able to procure the dissolution of forty-one monasteries, in order to raise a fund for the erection of new seminaries for learning; for in 1524, he obtained this object of his desire—but not without much murmuring against such obnoxious and daring innovations. He had already secured students in progress, for his projected college at Oxford, in his native town at Ipswich; where, two years before, he had erected a school: for which he himself drew up rules and regulations, and wrote a preface to the grammar intended for its use. He was afterwards able to add the revenue of twenty-four more small monasteries to the means already stated, and the first stone of his college at Ipswich was laid 1528, as previously related in pages 27 and 251; where a full account is to be found of this munificent establishment—of which only one solitary gateway now remains, fast falling to decay. This college—the remembrance of which the pen of Shakspeare has immortalised —was scarcely completed when its founder fell under the king's displeasure, and his implacable enemies assiduously hastened his ruin. He was deprived of nearly all his wealth and possessions, and soon after arrested for high treason, at his palace of Cawood, about seven miles from York; whither he had retreated to spend the remainder of his days in the duties of his diocese: but his ill treatment and disgrace so preyed upon his mind, that his constitution gave way under the shock. On his journey to London, to take his trial, he departed this life at Leicester abbey, where he had halted, and his body was interred in the abbey church of that town; and all that remained of the man w ho had lately been the arbiter of the fate of Europe, the corpse of Thomas Wolsey, was there deposited in the grave, by torch-light, between four and five o'clock in the morning of St. Andrew's day, November 30th, 1530, without the slightest memorial to mark the spot where his bones are laid—and there is now scarcely one stone left upon another, to indentify he scite where the abbey stood. His life has been written by so many able hands, and his character so well represented and defined, that it would be folly to attempt it here. The frailties of human nature inherent in his composition, were, however, thrown into the shade by the vastness of his conceptions, and the skill and celerity with which he carried them into execution. His cupidity and his personal ambition seldom led him to compromise the dignity of his king and country; for England, under his administration, held a high degree of importance in the scale of European policy: and never was there a subject of these realms, who, from so lowly an origin, raised himself to so high a pitch of power, both in church and state, as did Thomas Wolsey. His munificent intentions towards his native town ought never to be forgotten; and as his name is for ever immortalised in the pages of Shakspeare, so will the name of Ipswich be handed down to remotest posterity, as having been the birth-place of Cardinal Wolsey.

ADDENDA.

As we promised our readers the result of the chemical analysis which had been undertaken by Mr. John T. Barry, we submit the followin report of his examination of the water from a well, situated on premises belonging to Dykes Alexander, esq. Ipswich.

"This is a chalybeate water, holding proto-carbonate of iron in solution, the proportion being rather more than *half a grain of prot-oxide of iron in the pint.* As the specific gravity of the water ia only 1.00082, it contains but little saline matter; one part only remains on evaporating 1200. to dryness.

"There are some circumstances regarding this water, which render it a little remarkable. The first is, that when pumped from the well, it contains a minute quantity of black powder, which is found to be *sulphuret of iron.* This, possibly, arises from decomposition, *within the well,* of a portion of the carbonate of iron previously held in solution; and which may happen by the influx of other water containing sulphuretted hydrogen, or by the proximity of decomposing pyrites, evolving that gas. In consequence of this precipitation of sulphuret of iron taking place, as well as from the slow access of atmospheric air to the well, the proportion of chalybeate matter in the water, must be supposed to vary a little at different periods.

"Aiiot her remarkable circumstance is that the well water holds some *bituminous* matter in solution. To this must be attributed its peculiar smell,—which is not, as has been supposed, owing to the presence of sulphur; for the sulphuretted hydrogen presumed to have entered the well, must have been entirely decomposed by the excess of dissolved carbonate of iron, aided by the earthy carbonates, and, in fact, none of this gas is found remaining in the water.

"A third point deserving notice, is the absence of sulphates, a description of salts usually present in springwater. The other substances found in solution, are not materially different from those met with in our common wells. They consist, principally, of the bases — lime, magnesia, and soda — in combination with the carbonic and muriatic acids, together with a little silica."

This analysis only refers to one particular spring, but there are several others whose waters have various powers and properties, and from the opinions we have obtained from several eminent medical practitioners, we have no doubt but that they might be rendered serviceable, and by a little perseverance and exertion brought into general use.

We cannot close our labors better than by giving the following account of the town, in the words of a highly popular writer who has visited Ipswich since the commencement of this work: "I know of no town to be compared with Ipswich except it be Nottingham, and there is this difference in the two, Nottingham stands high, and on one side looks over a very fine country, whereas Ipswich is in a dell, meadows running up above it, and a beautiful arm of the sea below it. The town itself is substantially built, well paved, every thing good and solid, and no wretched dwellings to be seen on its outskirts. From the town itself you can see nothing; but you can in no direction go from it a quarter of a mile without finding views that a painter might crave."

Acton, William, 196; his family, 356.
Addresses, 56, 95, 102, 112, il3, 130, 136, 137, 111.
Alexanders' Bunk, 151, 257.
Alderson, Rohert, recorder, 2 16.
Alfred, 3.
Alneshorn priory, 37I.
Anuuls of Ipswich, hy Bacon, 7.
Anti-slavery Society, 136.
Archdeacon's gate, 352.
Assemhly of the corporation, 42.
Assemhly-rooms, 163, 352, 4 16.
Assizes, 66, 7l, 74, 133.
Austin, St. 261, 262.
Bacon, Francis, 23S.
Bacon, Nathnuiel, 7.
Baeual, John, 215.
Bailiff, 6, 10, 17, 46, 65, 97, 117, 155, 156, 164, 341, 342; list of, 143.
Baldwyn, John, 200.
Barnard's gift, 287.
Barnardiston, Sir Samuel, 293.
Barracks, Horse, 192.
Barracks in the Woorfhridgc road, 320.
Baring, Heury, HI, 142.

Barton, Beromd, Poem on T-nkurd Room, 226.
Butley, William, 7, 259.
Bayley, George & Co. 259, 409.
Bayley, Jahex, 406.
Beech tree in the Park, 329; stanzas on it, 326.
Bihle soeietie-, 426.
Biographical cataloging, 441.
Bi'd, Juines, his poem ou Wolsey's gate, 253; extiucl from, 382.
Bixley, 371.
Blaise, Bishop, procession in houour of, 417.
Botlold, John, 200.
Bourn hridge, 405.
Blake, tow n clerk, curried away the records, 12.
Bray, Rohert, a-sists in Ipswich Doomsday, 19.
Brandon, Charles, duke of Suffolk, 220, 221, 222.
Bridewell, 2s0.
Bridgmau, Orlando, 307.
Bristol, .Marquis of, 353, 360, 363.
Broke, Sir Philip B. V., hurl., 3(15, 374.
Broke' Hall, 183.
Brunton, manager, 228.
Brunton, Miss, 22k.
Burgesses, A, II, 11, 109, 159 T.S. s s s
Caldwell, St. John Bautls) nt, SIS.
Caldwell, or Cold Hull, SIS.
Camhridge, duKe of, 134.
Cnnal lo Slowmurket, 184, 185.
Canning, Rev. Richnrd, pdilor of the Suffolk Traveller, 7, 205, 315.
Capon, William, his letter oo Wolsey's college, 2S to 32.
Caroline, Queen, in.
Chapels. Snlem, 195; Wesleyan. 217; Tncket-steel, 230; St. Nicholas' street and Unitarian, 22; Sioke, 269; Quakers', 273; Jews' Synagogue, 319; emholic-Chapel, 321; Beihesda, *Hi.*
Chantry Id St. Lawrence, 201; house so called, 353.
Charities, 423.
Charles I., curious painting of, 207.
Chnrles II., 46, 47, 50, 51, 54, 812, 2 IS, 2S3.
Charters, 9, 12, 13, 14, 15, IS, 17, 25, 36, 43. 58, 59, 430.
Cuedworth, Lord, monument and nc-

couutof, 179.
Christ Church, description of, 328.
Christ's Hospital, account of, 277.
Chronological account of kings, poetical, 22.
Churches, 4, 169. St. Matthew, 169; St. Mary at Elms, 195; St. Lawrence, 200;
St. Stephen, 217; St. Nicholas, 231; St. Peter, 249; St. Mary at Sioke, 262;
St. Mary nt the Key, 270; St. Clement, Son; Si. Helen, 32; St. Margaret, 322; St. Mary ai the Tower, 337; Westerfteld, 333; Whitton, 345; ThurU-ton, 336; Sproughlon, 353; H ram ford, 356.
Clarence, duke of, IS5.
Clnviger, 11, 86.
Cliff descrihed, 367.
Cohhold, Klizuholh, 229; her monument awl character, 317, 349.
Coins, Saxon and Norman, 3; Roman, found ut Walton and Felixstow, 385, 415.
College, Wolsey's, 27, 250.
Colsoo, Thomns, *alias* Rohinson Crusoe, 368, 369.
Common-council, 12, 55, 65, 97, 342.
Common Quay, 297.
Convents and Religious Houses. St. Mary's Chapel, 178; Carmelites, or Wi-iilc
Friars, 199; Franciscan Grey Friars Minors, 241; St. Peter and St. Paul, 250; St. Leonard's Lazunr House, 261; Friars Preachers, or house of HI i k
Friars Dominicans, 277; St. James's Hospital, 302; Leprous House of Si. Mary Magdalen, 302; Trinity Priory of Austin Black Canons, 322; Alneshoru Priory, 371; Priory at Felixstow, 388.
Corn Exchange, 176.
Cornhillos it was, I7 I, 173, 174; as it is, 4!5.
Corn, scarcity of, 4 4, 100, 103, 107, 109, 124, 127, 257.
Corporate hody, 49, 139; poem on ditto, 139, 140; 158.
Corporation surrender their charter, 57; charter restored to, CO; privileges, 62;
hints for improvement, 61; disputes of, 72; feuds of, 75; power of, 78;
further disputes, SO; with Mr. Cooper Grnvenor, 86; examine into the chari-

ties, 95; into the accounts, l2; description of 423.

Cranes Gifts, 292.

Crickitt, C. A., Ill, 350.

Cromwell, 45.

Cuhitt, William. Stoke hridge,260; tread-mill, 319.

Curxon, Lord, 25; his house, 241.

Cuslom-house, account of, 297.

Danes, invasions of the, 3; destroyed the ramparts, 167.

Dauudy, Edmund, erected the Market Cross, 173; Alms-houses, I7S; represented the horough, 201; founded a chantry, 201; died, 201.

Dedham, Jacob, strange account of, 197

Doomsday Book, nine churches,4.

Doomsday Rook, Ipswich descrihed, 19.

Downhnm Reach, 369.

Dowsing, William, destroyed images, 201,256.

Draper's Hull, in Star Lane, 291.

Ducking Slool, 298.

Duncan, Lord, visits Ipswieb, 127.

Dundns, R. A. entry with his colleague, 160.

Dunkon, Rohert, his Letter in favour of the Quakers, 51; his tumh, 31 1.

Dysart, Earl of, 106, 148.

Edgar, King, 262.

Edgar, Mileson, account of the family, 33S.

Edgar, Master Mileson, St. Clement's, 302.

Edgar, William, steeple nt St. Mary Tower, 339.

Edmund, St. a Pountney, 314.

Edward I. seized the horough, 12; renewed the charter, 12.

Edward II. granted a charter, 13.

Edward III. confirmed the charters at Walton, I t.

Edward IV. guaranteed former charters, 36.

F, iward VI. confirmed former charters, 36.

Elections, the first contested, 61; violent contest, a man killed, 91; a mun lost his life, 91; remarkahle contest, 101; hrihery suspected, 110; for the county, lid; for the horough, 116; for officers of the horough, 118; contest lor two days, 132; for six days,!11; again, for six dny, I48.

Elephant aud Castle, 67, 310.

Ely, Dean and Ch 'pter of, Patrons of Stoke, 263.

Elizabeth, confirms nil the charters, 37; visits the town, 37; hill of her expeuces, 38; proclaoiation, 38; act lor paving the town, 40; horses sent to Tilhury Fort, 42; Ipswich vessels serving against the Armada; grants a charter to Christ's Hospital, 277.

Erwarton Hull nod Gate, 39S.

Fairs, for lamhs, 184; St. Margaret's fair, 331; St. George's, May 4, for toys, dec.

Felaw, Richard, 282.

Felixtow and Walton, 384; Names in Doomsday, 388; Old Hall, 389; Edward III. passed some time there, 389, confirmed the charters of Ipswich theie, 389; Wadgate Haven, 390; Baptist Meeting-house, 391; Mnrtello Towers, 391; Prodigious Bones, 391; Good Houses, 391; Felixstow Cottage, 392; Marina Productions, 393; Bathing Place, 395; Verses hy Bernard Barton, 396.

Felix, the pious liurgundian, 3S7.

Fire-works, ilie first in Ipswich, 93.

Fishery and FUh Market, 419.

Fludyer, Sir S. B. hart., residence at Felixstow, 392.

Fonnereau, Rev. Charles William, owner of Christ-church, 329.

Freston Tower, account of, 401; Sketch of it, 403; Original Poem on seemg the Sketch, 404.

Fuller, his account o(Wolsey's College, 262; Description of Rev. S. Ward, 343.

Gaol, county, description of, 318.

Garrett, Jacoh, his cnsl-iron manulactory, 432.

Gurrick, David, his first uppearance on the stage, 22.

Gus Works, 366.

George II. visits Ipswich, 92.

George III. Address on his accession, 102; Ou his escape, 112; Poetical Address, 113; On his recovery, 114.

George IV. Accession celehrated, 142; His ooronntion, 149.

George's St. Chapel, 170.

Gipping, the river, 257.

Gloucester, Prince William, of, resides at Ipswich, 125.

Goward Miss, 161; Her history, 228.

Gower, K. H., his residence and puhlications, 403.

Grammar-school, account of, 281.

Granville, Lord, resided at Wherstead Lodge, 405.

Great court, the first, 9; or er of, 49; respecting the Plague, 50; respecting the head-horoughs, 83; for preserving the churters, 85; respecting the water, 85; restrictions on trade, 89; how constituted, ifec. 429.

Green, Benjamin Palmer, leaves £500. to St. Margaret's parish, 32b.

Greenland trade at Ipswich, 406.

S S S 2

Green Mm inn, a mao killed there, 109.

Greenwich farm, 368.

Grey's, Lady, chapel, 821.

Grey, Lady Jane, £20.

Guild-holders and Guild wardens, 15.

Gasford Mull descrihed, 202.

Haldimand, W., s,leudid procession at his chairing with T. B. Leonard, 114.

Half Moon puhlic-house descrihed, 276.

Hallowirca, 371.

Handford hridge descrihed, 184.

Handtord hall, mortgnged, 55; again, 74; again, 76; in danger of heing lost, 85; description of it, 183.

Harlan.I, Sir Rohert, hurl., elected high steward, 150; commissioner of the river, 365; his residence at Nacton, 373; some account of his father, 373.

Harrison, Susanna, her tomh, J33; her works, 234.

Hurwich, encampment m, 121; short account of, 396; curious missal found near, 397.

Hat ton, Sir Christopher, resided at Ipswich, 351.

Head-horoughs, exceed their authority, 84.

Henry, son of Henry II., landed at Ipswich, 12.

Henry VI. grants a heneficial charter, 15.

Henry VII. confirms former charters, IS.

Henry VIII. grants a charter and defines the liherties, 25; appoint-a suffrn-8an hishop, 241; his arms on Wolsey's gate, 251; grants a new charter for the rammar-school, 283.

High stewards, list of, 427.

Hilt"ham, Sir Rohert; his alms-houses at Levington, 377.

Hog Island, 368.

Holy Trinity priory, 171.

Honorary freemen, 151,152, 153, 155.

Horticultural Society, 185.

House of Correction, 319.

Howorlh, Rev. William, master of the Grammar-school, 285.

Humane Society, 426.

Ipswioh, names and derivation, 2; paring and lighting, 121; Ipswich regiment, 123; improving the port, 129; Ipswich Journal, 214; Ipswich Mercury, 215; Ipswich Gazette, 215; Ipswich New Fly Coach, 216; finest view of the town, 268; Ipswich spa waters; present state describhed, 414,415.

Isahel, queen of Edward II., lauded, 13.

James I. confirms all former charters, 43; present of a horse to the king of Denmark,43.

James 11, visited the town, 46; receives the charter into his own hands, 58; grants another, 59; annuls this last, 59.

Jews' Synagogue, 319.

Jews' weddmg, 320.

John grants I he first charter, 9; ramparts repaired, 167; confirms the fair to Trinity priory, 323.

John's Ness, 370.

Jury, exemption from set aside, 17.

Justices, os-istunt, the first, 14.

Kemp, Dame Amy,297.

King, Rev. John, master of the Grammar-school, 2M.

King's Head, 32.

Kirhy's Suffolk Traveller, 6.

Lamh-fair, 184.

Laudguard Fort describhed, 382.

Lnny, John, recorder, his monument, 325; John Lnny, his son, ditto, 325; Benjamin Lany, also his son, Bishop of Ely, 325, 326.

Lawrence, Rev. Matthew, town lecturer, 342.

I.eman, Roheri, and his wife, singular monument, 218.

Lennurd, T. B., petitions against R. A. Crickitt, 1U; extraordinary procession his chairing, 144.

Lending Cash Fund, 292.

Letes or words, stated in Doomsday, 168.

Levinglon, description of, S77.

Liherties of the horough, 26, 27; hy water, 161.

Life-hoat, 410.

Linen manufactory, 65.

Linsineen, Count,entertains the Prince Regent, 140; huilds Birkfield Lodge, 266.

Louis XVIII. arrives at Ipswich, 133. — Lutestring-manufactory, 68.

M'c Adam's mode of paving recommended, 416.

Mackinnon, Chns., with his colleague, R. A. Dundas, make their triumphal entry, 160.

Man-of-war, suhscription for, III.

Market, regulations of, 7O; new market describhed, 213.

Market-cross, history of, 173, 174.

Marshalsea-rate, 61.

Martin's gift, 287.

Mary's, St. chapel, 178.

Matthew's, St. gate, account of, 193; street M'c Adamised, 11S.

Mechanics' Institution, 207.

Medical and Vapour Baths, 4I5.

Mendicity Society, 427.

Mildred's, St. church, part of the old town-hall, I7O.

Milton, Christopher, deputy-recorder, 59; his chupel, 226.

Mineral springs, account of, l«7; spa water, 2I6.

Mint, King John, 3; Stephen and Henry II., 4.

Missal, curious, in the possession of Mr. Hooker, 397.

Missionary societies, 426.

Mortality amongst the cuttle, 108.

Nelson, Lord, 126; chosen hi«hstewnrd, 127; sorrow for his death, I30.

New Place, or New Palace of Queen Edith, 5.

Norman, sun of Kadnoth, 199.

Norwich, Bishop of, preached at the church of St. Mary at the Tower, 138.

Norn Scotia ship yard, 106.

'Odd family, in the reign of King William, 69.

Old chest on the Town-hall, 428.

Old house in Lower Orwell-street, 296.

Orange, Princess of, and Hereditary Prince of, 124.

Org m, magnificent, at thechurch of St. Mary at the Tower, 342.

Orwell, the river. Derivation, 2; high tide, 163: ground sinks nenr it, 103; lines on its heauties, 266; description of it and its hanks, 364; sonnet to the, 365; act for improving it, 365; a town so called, 387; junction with the Slour, 398; verses hy Drayton, 398; poem in praise of it, 411.

Orwell, Lord Viscount, 37S.

Osterhald church, 302.

Ostrich puhlic-house, view from the garden, 406.

Our Lady of Ipswich,chapel and image, 178.

Paget, William, his poem on Admiral Vernon, 373.

Parishes. St. Matthew's, description of, 169; St. Mary nt Elms, 195; St. Lawrence', 199; St. Stephen's,217; St. Nicholas',238; St. Peter's, 249; St. Mary at Stoke, 262; St. Mary nt the Key, 276; St. Clement's, fOO; St. Helen's, 312; St. Margare's, 322; Weslerfield, 333; Whilton, 335; St. Mary at the Tower,S37; Sproughton,353; Brumford, 356; Rushmere,360; Playford, 363.

Parker, Sir Henry, huilt Erwarion Hall, 398.

Pemherton, John, bis tomh, 202; his charily for widows, 425.

Pelronille, St. Image at, destroyed, 371.

Pelf, Grace, her extrnordinnry death, 309.

Pelt, Sir Phineas, extract from his journal, S3.

Peyvale, Riohnii', author of Ipswich Doomsday, 19.

Phillips, Richard, his legacy to Christ's

Hospital, 279.

Philological Society, 293.

Pin Mill, 399.

Piper, Sic.ihfn, curious picture of Charles I. Id his possession, 207.

Pitt cluh dinner, 152.

Plague raged at Ipswich In the year 1666, 5fl.

Pleas, Court of Small, CO.

Poleshead, extent of the liherties hy water, 26.

Pond Hall, S7n.

Pooley, Joseph, died in his hailiwick, 163; his monument, 327.

Pope, Sir Thomas, owner of Christ Church, 324.

Popululion, 69,128, 148.

Porter, Sir Rohert Ker, his picture in St. Lowrenco' church, 206.

Portmen, the first, 10; several discharged, ten of them discharged, and others elected, 99; two of them ohliged to disclaim,) 55.

Present state of the town, 414.

Press-gang, a m"n killed in u scuffle wilh the, 10.

Prince Regent, at a hall at the Assemhly-rooms, 135; slopped two or three days at Ipswich, 136; receives an address at Sudhourn, 140.

Printing in St. Nicholas' parish, 39.

Protestants hurnt, 33; imprisoned and persecuted, 36.

Puhlic Dispensary, 426.

Quakers persecuted and imprisoned, 51; Rohert Dunkon's letter in their favour, 51; meeting-house descrihed, 273; first received their nume273; account of them, 273; persecuted at Hnimfor.l, 359.

Queen's Head tavern, Mr. Hammond's house,35l.

Races, 107, 129, 3G2.

Rainhird's mill, account of riot there, 257.

Rampurls, fragments of, remaining, 167.

Hanson's, R. G., paper and tohacco manufactory, 422.

Ransome's, James and Rohert, ironfouddry, 422.

Raw, Johu, hos a curious portrait of the Rev. S. Ward, 314.

Read, Thomas, left £500. to the Hlnecoat School, 424.

Recorders. Judge Clenoh the first, 41; list of, 437.

Red House descrihed, 333.

Regalia of the corporation, I":".

Representatives, the first, 15; first contested election, 64; how chosen, 129; list of, from 1447 to 1827,436.

Requests, Court of, 422.

Richard I. fined the town, 9.

Richard II., reference to charter of, 14.

Richard III. confirmed former charters, 17.

River-commissioners, 366.

Rochester, Earl of, his description of the town, 331.

Rotunda descrihed, 176.

Royal Oak,carved corner at the,352.

Russel, Metcalfe, cured hy the medical waters, l TO; his tomh, 351.

Sailors riotous on the Quay, 121.

Schools, 423.

Seamen's Shipwreck Society, 427.

Sessions for the horough, 294; for the county, 293.

Shamhles, description and representation of, 173.

Sharford, Judge, offended wilh some sailors, 14.

Shire"hall,.suhscriptiou for huilding it, 71; account of it, 293.

Shipping employed against the Spanish Armuda, and against Cadiz, 42; the Ips wich 7n gun ship, 13; account of, 417.

Small-pox rages, 107; means lo prevent contagioo, US.

Smart, Willinm, founder of Ihe Town Lihrary, 2so; leaves two exhihitions from the Grammar-school, 2S6; his alms-houses descrihed,290; incorporated with Tuoley's charity, 291; his pictorinl monunuint, 339; ncrostlo to his memory,

Smith, Mrs. Ann, her alms houses, 197.

Sorrel, Andrew, died in his hailiwick, 1675, 53.

Sorrel, Sir Al miel, his tnmh and nccount of, 255.

Sparrow, the family vault of, culled Avrfwit Vusscntm, 203.

Sparrow's N'est, house so called, at

Thurston, 337.

Sparrow, John liddowes, his house in the Old Butter-market described,211.

Sparrow, Rohert, huilt the house in the Butier-market 211.

Slur-lane, curious old huilding there, 294.

Steam Nuvient km Company, 418.

Steam vessel used at an election, 159; the Suffolk steamer hrings n cargo of free hurgesses, 162; new steam vessel, 419.

Stoke hridge destroyed iiy a flood, 260; first stone of the new hridge laid, 261; new hridge descrihed, 411.

Stoke hills, verses on, hy Bernard Barton, 261; descrihed, 265,

Stoke park descrihed, 267.

Suffolk Benevolent Society, 425.

Suffolk cheese, 332.

Suffolk Chronicle first printed, 319.

Suffolk G irlund, printed hy J. Raw, 379.

Tankard, curious room at the, descrihed, 222.

Tavern-street, widened uml improved, 351.

Theatre, plays performed hy ihb military, 122; performance hy amateurs, 163; history of the, 226.

Thunder-slorm, several persons killcd, 307.

Tiptoth, Lord, account of his family, 212.

Tooley, Henry, his epitaph, 272; description of his alms-houses and charity, 288 incorporateit with Smart's charily, 291.

Torrens, Colonel, 157

Town-clerks. John Blake eloped with the records, 12; non-freemen declared incompetent to serve, 163; how elected, 12s; list of, from 1700 to 1S29, 443.

Town-hall. Old one pulled down; first stone of the new one laid, 171.

Town-lecturer, the first, 41; list of them, 242.

Town Lihrary, in Christ's Hospital. 281.

Tower Ditches, the ancient fosse, 352.

Tovell,George, manufactory of Rom,in cement, 409.

Trade of the Town, 4 IS

Transit Yacht, huilt under the direction of Mr. Gower, 407.

Trimley, St. Martin, and Trimley, St. Mary, descrihed, 379.

Trinity Chureh, stood near St. Margaret's, 322.

Turkish Amhassador, 127.

Cvtrecht, Joanna, Baptute, M. I), his tomh, 203.

Vaux, George, his house where Wolsey was horn, 239.

Ventri, Sir Peyton, his tomh, 237; huilt the Chantry, 353.

Vernon, Admiral, instructions to, 101; died, 101; his life and character, 372, 373; poem on him, hy Willinm Paget, 373.

Volunteers, n corps of, formed, 123; Ipswich Volunteers offer to march, 12S.

Waggon, Betls's, caught fire, 146.

Walton and Felix-tow descrihed, 3S4; u Roman station, 388; Flemings landed, 389; castle eazed, 389; view of the castle in Grose's Antiquities, 28S.

Ward, Rev. Samuel, town-lecturer, 343; his tomh, and some account of him, 344.

Water, supply of, to the town, 316.

Wehh, James, distrihuted upwnrds of £400. in the town, 136.

Wellington, Duke of, his thanks for a suhscription for the wounded, 137; visits Ipswich, 142; took up his freedom on the Town-hall, 117; proposed as high steward, ISO.

Wentworih, Lord, presides at the hurning of the protestants. 33 , presented wilh a hutt of sack, 41; resided at Settlestead Hall, 213; his daughter, the Lily of Nettleeteiid, 842.

Westerfield descrihed, 333.

Whales hrought up the Orwell, 371.

Wherstead descrihed, 404.

Whitton descrihed, 335.

Whitaker, t'has., Recorder, 236.

William III., Lord Damhartoo's regiment revolt against, 64; visits the town, atid is entertained hy the corporation, tis.

Wilson, Thomas, huilt the new chapel in St. Nicholas'street, 249.

Windsor, Sir Andrew, afterwards Lord Windsor, resided at Gusford Hall, 262.

Wingfield, Sir Anthony, his house descrihed, 220, 221,

Withipol, Sir Edmund, his tomh, 325; huilt Christ Church, 328.

Woodhridge, half-market of 32.

Wool-trade flourished, 212; procession of woolcomhers, 417.

Wolsey encourages literature, 35; his ancestors, 236; house where he was horn, 239; account of his college, 250; his own description of it, 251; Wolsey's Unte, 25l; poem on the gate, hy James Bird, 253; takes the Grammar-school under his protection, S2; writes a preface to Lily's Grammar, 282.

Woolrerstone, described, 400.

Woolward, John, killed hy lightning, 307,

Wykes Bishop, 301; Wyke Uflbrd, 301.

York, Duke of, arrives in Ipswich, 128; slept at Lord Paget's, 130; reviewed the troops, 131; wilh the Dukes of f umherlnud Hnd Cnmhridge, reviews the troops, 132; address of condolence on his death, 159.

Lightning Source UK Ltd.
Milton Keynes UK
UKOW06f0050190914

238863UK00008B/219/P